T3-BSJ-927

Political Communication Yearbook
Edited by Keith R. Sanders,
Lynda Lee Kaid, and Dan Nimmo

Also in this series

Political Communication Yearbook 1984

New Perspectives on Political Advertising

Edited by

Lynda Lee Kaid
Dan Nimmo
Keith R. Sanders

Southern Illinois University Press
Carbondale and Edwardsville

Printed in the United States of America
Edited by Sally Master
Designed by Dan Gunter
ISSN 8755-0210
ISBN 0-8093-1264-6
89 88 87 86 4 3 2 1

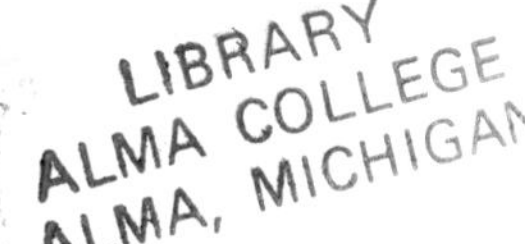

Contents

Tables

Figures

Introduction

Lynda Lee Kaid, Dan D. Nimmo,
and Keith R. Sanders

This volume is part of a series of anthologies which cover various topics in the study, teaching, and practice of political communication. The purpose of the series is to make available to researchers, teachers, students, and other specialists, findings, analyses, and commentaries which are representative of current scholarship in the rapidly evolving field of political communication. The focus of this volume—political advertising, its history, forms, styles, settings, uses, and effects—seems appropriate because there are few, if any, forms of political communication which are more prevalent, more expensive, more highly developed, and which have been the object of more controversy and less serious scholarship than political advertising, especially the political commercial made for television.

It is no longer possible for a candidate to run for a major regional, state, or national office (see chapter 2) in the United States without feeling it necessary to spend substantial portions of his or her campaign budget on television and radio advertising. And as chapters 12 and 13 indicate, the same situation is beginning to develop in Great Britain and Australia.

Studies of political advertising have presented a variety of sometimes contradictory findings. Some have concluded that most voters get most of what they know about candidates and issues during election campaigns from the televised spot commercial and that these commercials influence the outcome of elections by increasing interest, making the candidates better known, persuading the uninformed, influencing the "late decider," reinforcing the "early decider," modifying candidate images, and helping raise money. Yet, others argue that without complementary reinforcement from other forms of communication, such as the television newscast or newspaper editorial, televised political commercials have little impact, or, at least, that effects are nearly impossible to identify given the cacophony of messages which assault the voter during campaigns, especially during presidential campaigns.

On other fronts, it has been contended that the televised political commercial should be taken off the air, or, if aired, should be no less than five minutes in length, prohibited from doing anything other than showing the candidate speaking to an issue, and otherwise changed to bring it more into conformity with a classical democratic theory approach to political communication. Most of these reforms have been rejected partly on First Amendment grounds and partly because the "lobby" for the political commercial is strong among political decisionmakers. Candidates become office holders and office holders feel that they should be denied no form of communication with the electorate, especially one thought to be as effective as political commercials. Moreover, from the point of view of mass media decisionmakers, the brief political commercial produces vast new reviews each campaign year and fits neatly into on-air slots ordinarily reserved for product commercials. For these, and other reasons, Australia is the only democrary to pass legislation aimed directly at the content of political advertising.

In any event, we feel it appropriate that a volume on political advertising presenting some of the latest thinking on the topic should appear in early 1986 in the midst of the "off-year" election campaigns. We trust that every reader of this volume will find himself or herself in a better position to assess the role, propriety, and contribution of political advertising, that a few questions will be answered, and, more importantly, that productive new questions will be raised in the minds of scholars and practitioners. To facilitate this process, we offer below a synopsis of each chapter.

The volume begins with a chapter by Jamieson in which she traces the "Evolution of Presidential Advertising in America." Food, drink, and torchlight parades were among the earliest forms of presidential campaign advertising. As a candidate for the House of Burgesses in

Virginia, George Washington attracted the attention of voters by offering rum, punch, wine, cider, and beer; history does not record which was the most popular enticement.

As the nature of campaigning changed so did campaign advertising. By the mid-nineteenth century, the song took its place among soft drinks, hard drinks, speeches, and torchlight parades as modes of political advertising. Songs and chants had the advantage of reaching the literate as well as the illiterate, of whom there were many prior to the advent of compulsory schooling. The most famous of all campaign songs and chants was perhaps the one produced after Grover Cleveland admitted that he may have fathered an illegitimate child. His opponents took up the chant "Ma, Ma, where's my pa? Gone to the White House. Ha! Ha! Ha!"

Jamieson makes the provocative point that those who pine for presidential campaigns as they were in Jefferson, Jackson, or Lincoln's time and who see the nation's political decline and fall mirrored in the rise of political spot advertising on television remember a day which never was. The banners, songs, cartoons, and strongly partisan newspapers of early campaigns telegraphed conclusions without evidence. Their messages were often more brief, more extreme, and less substantative than those of today's sixty second spot advertisements.

In "An Analysis of Presidential Television Commercials," Devlin reports that 70 percent of the money Ronald Reagan spent on advertising in his 1980 campaign was spent on television advertising; that, in 1976, Jimmy Carter spent 74 percent of his advertising budget on television; and that an even larger percentage of Eisenhower's 1952 campaign budget may have been devoted to television. Apparently, well-financed presidential campaigns have, since television became available, spent a major portion of their budget on television advertising. According to Devlin, televised political advertising can serve many functions, including making a candidate better known, influencing late-deciding or disinterested votes, reinforcing supporters and partisans, attacking the opposition, developing and explaining issues, softening or redefining an image, targeting certain demographic groups, and raising money. However, the author concedes that it is difficult to judge the effectiveness of political commercials because, even though they are neatly packaged, they occur at a time when candidates are receiving unplanned media attention and exposure through other nonmedia campaign projects.

In chapter 3, "Fighting Back: American Political Parties Take to the Air Waves," Kolar contends that although the aim of American political parties remains the same—the acquisition of political power—their methods have changed because of the growth of the mass media. Parties, he says, are not declining but are changing ". . . their role and function in the electoral process to remain a primary source of information and influence to voters" (see page 57). In support of his position, Kolar describes in some detail the work of the National Republican Campaign Committee and the Democratic National Committee from 1976 through 1984 as they produced television and radio advertisements and provided facilities and advice on campaign communication for presidential, senatorial, and congressional candidates. The reader will notice that the quite different approaches taken by the two major parties to these tasks reflect great differences in their attitudes about candidates, campaigns, the media, and the political audience.

Nevertheless, both the Republican and Democratic National Committees believe that television advertising is successful and can help political institutions, the parties, and the candidates. Indeed, the Republican Campaign Committee argues that its group of experts can produce better commercials cheaper than the ad agencies, that candidates strapped for money can better use the party, and that such candidates can use the party early in the campaign prior to major fundraising activities.

After the Three Mile Island Crisis in 1979, the nuclear power industry decided that it was necessary to influence public opinion in its direction. Chapter 4, by Dionisopoulos, is an analysis of how the industry used newspaper advertising toward this end.

The nuclear power industry argued through its newspaper advertising that nuclear power is safe and that it is the one best answer to the country's need for energy. These positions were designed to define the issues in a fashion favorable to the industry and, therefore, to construct a positive image while putting public fears to rest. Dionisopoulos observes that industry advertising enhanced the industry's public image and, at the same time, offered an unflattering portrait of the anti-nuclear movement as "a conglomeration of movie stars, aspiring politicians, and leftover radicals" (see page 103). The industry's newspaper ad campaign had a lot to do, says the author, with keeping nuclear energy from being a major campaign issue in the 1980 presidential election.

Shyles, in chapter 5, "The Television Political Spot Advertisement: Its Structure, Content, and Role in the Political System," reports research which analyzed the content of thirty and sixty second televised advertisements used during the 1980 presidential primaries. The focus of the study was on the images, issues, and methods of presentation evidenced in the commercials. A detailed descriptive analysis is presented along these three lines, with the audio as well as the visual features of the commercials being taken into account. The most salient images were found to be those associated with experience and competence. The study's most interesting findings came from the examination of presentational styles. Shyles concluded that "issue spots tend to use relatively straightforward formats featuring formally dressed candidates talking directly to the camera, while image spots tend to use more slickly packaged formats featuring still pictures of candidates in rapid succession with announcer voice-overs, testimonials by citizens, famous persons, and stirring music. In other words, there are unique image and issue codes operating in political advertising" (see page 127).

"Political Advertising and the Meaning of Elections," by Joslyn, is a successful effort to examine political commercials in the broad context of the modern American election campaign. One can, says Joslyn, take one of four different theoretical perspectives when trying to understand the role of elections in the United States: the prospective policy choice approach, the retrospective policy satisfaction approach, the benevolent leader approach, and the ritual approach. Having assessed the extent to which these four approaches are consistent with televised political advertising, he concludes: "The world of televised campaign commercials is much more likely to delimit citizen understanding to perceptions of candidate personas and the recognition of cultural icons and values than to an appreciation of policy alternatives; much more likely to restrict elections to choices between competing images of candidate personalities, unbalanced perceptions of incumbent and challenger records, or a choice between participation or non-participation than to a choice between competing programs of governmental action or political belief; and much more likely to reveal a truncated message as sent by the electorate than a message rich with preference or guidance for a future course of governmental action" (see page 183).

The study reported in chapter 7, "Elements of Videostyle: Candidate Presentation through Television Advertising," by Kaid and Davidson is "the first attempt to describe systematically the style of political commercials" (see page 186). Video style combines verbal content, nonverbal content, and production techniques. Fifty-five commercials from three United States Senate races in 1982 were coded in an attempt to capture their style. "These preliminary findings clearly validate the hypothesis that videostyles among candidates differ. In fact, the very similarity of the appeals that candidates made in terms, of image, issue, party, or ideology suggest that they are all saying essentially the same thing to voters. The differences lie in how they say it, how they present themselves" (see page 198). The videostyles of the commercials of incumbents and challengers were clearly different.

Supplementing their quantitative findings, Kaid and Davidson, interviewed five of the producers of the commercials which they had analyzed. Two themes emerged from those conversations: "producers, both for challengers and incumbents, are preoccupied with reaching the voter/viewer emotionally. Their aim was to make the constituency *feel* something—'comfortable,' 'confident,' 'an emotional connection' " (see page 208). Also, the producer's felt a strong need to consider the environment in which they were working. "Each state possesses its own unique political heritage" which must be taken into account when making commercials (see page 208).

Evidence illuminating the effects of the televised political commercials is not strong, and is of dubious scientific validity, according to Cundy, the author of chapter 8, "Political Commercials and Candidate Image: The Effect Can Be Substantial." However, the evidence is affirmative and suggests that televised political spots can have some influence on the image of political candidates.

Cundy reports a quasi-experimental study using commercials about a fictitious United States Representative. The outcome of the study was positive, leading the author to conclude that "paid political ads are apt to be most effective early on in the game when the candidate is little known, in primaries where the convenient cue of the party identification is absent, in lower level races where the candidates are not heavily covered by the media, and hence are likely to have little other information to go on" (see page 233).

Chapter 9, "Candidate Image Formation: The Role of Information Processing," by Garramone, describes an experimental study which investigated the interrelationships among audience motivation, commercial type, information processing, and candidate image formation. The study failed to produce the hypothesized direct effects of audience motivation and commercial type on image formation, leading the author to suggest that the information processing variables might, in the future, best be studied as contingent variables.

One interesting outcome: "exposure to issue commercials results in a more positive candidate image than does exposure to image commercials, but only when the individual engages in a high degree of inference or a high degree of image information processing" (see page 247).

As Nimmo and Felsberg indicate in chapter 10, "Hidden Myths in Television Political Advertising: An Illustration," there has been a general tendency for scholars to examine political advertising within the context of the campaigns for which the commercials were produced. Most researchers would agree with the producers interviewed by Kaid and Davidson: context is important, perhaps essential, to any understanding of the commercials, their uses, and potential effects. Nimmo and Felsberg challenge this notion. They contend that there is much to be learned from viewing political advertising as representative of commercial advertising in general "especially in the way that such advertising reflects transcendent human aspirations and anxieties" (see page 249). The purpose of the study reported in this chapter was "to suggest one method for exploring the hidden myths of political advertising and to illustrate that method through a comparison of competing ads in a single campaign" (see page 249). Applying methods developed by Leymore (1975), the authors probe the "deep structure" of advertising from a 1978 gubernatorial race conducted in a southeastern state. First impressions of the ads made for the Democrat led the authors to surmise that they were observing a log cabin campaign, much like what we have witnessed in this country since 1840. However, closer analysis revealed that the ads claimed that the candidate could lead the state out of its current primitive condition toward a new tomorrow. Three myths, summarized by Jocques Ellul (1958), were found embedded in the Democrat's televised political advertising, "the myths of Work, Progress, Happiness. Work is redeeming. Progress is inevitable through work. And, thereby, happiness is assured" (see page 260).

The Republican candidate took a quite different approach. "Its defining characteristic was dirt. The world had become a dirty, filthy, grimy place" (see page 262). The Democratic incumbent had, according to the ads, used his pardoning power too freely, was a "wheeler dealer" who had hired too many patronage employees, used a Lear jet, and paid too much attention to special interests. "But the root of the dirt, and ultimately of the form of evil that constitutes the Republican's advertised vision of the current state of the state, is money . . . money equals dirt" (see page 263). Cleanliness is, therefore, transcending.

Nimmo and Felsberg acknowledge that the kind of criticism and analysis which they illustrate in chapter 10 could construct systems of sign relationships which are simply not present but are created in whole or part by the researchers. "What is perhaps more to the point is whether or not viewers who are the targets of televised political advertising consciously or unconsciously perceive the unifying by hidden myths that inform such efforts at political persuasion" (see page 267). In order to get at this issue, researchers would, according to the authors, have to turn their attention more seriously to the manifest and latent content of ads and would have to abandon conventional research, asking "whether the overall impact of televised political advertising is to reinforce and enhance an entire sociopolitical structure that undergirds a political regime and/or system" (see page 267). "Is it possible," they ask, "that videopolitics contain not only hidden myths but hidden, not overtly, readily measurable effects as well?" (see page 267).

Mansfield and Hale, authors of chapter 11, "Uses and Perceptions of Political Television: An Application of Q Technique" state that while they do not view image formation as a direct effect of the motivation for viewing a commercial, they are curious about "whether persons who view political advertisements for certain reasons might differ from persons viewing for other reasons in the way they attend to the ads and in the information they take in into account when they construct images of the candidate" (see page 268). Thus motivated by curiosity, the authors apply Q-methodology to the quasi-experimental study of audience motivations. Factor analysis of their pretest data indicated that there were two distictive motivational patterns among the forty-two undergraduate subjects in the study. Twenty-five subjects said they watched political commercials for "entertainment/social/nonpolitical" reasons while seventeen watched for "surveilance/vote guidance" reasons. After the pretest, subjects watched a videotape containing commercials from a congressional campaign, followed by a measuring of their perceptions of the commercials. In this study, audience motivation did not substantially effect audience perceptions.

In 1967, Epstein contended that with the growth of modern communications technology, the functions of political parties would change and that various of their traditional tasks would be taken over by mass media. Epstein (1967) saw evidence of this trend in the United States and thought this "contagion from the Right" was spreading to Europe. Johnson and Elebash, authors of chapter 12, "The Contagion form the Right: The Americanization of British Political Advertising" report a study which "examines one particular European nation, Great Britain, for possible evidence supporting the contagion from the right thesis. The study traces the evolution of political advertising in Great Britain, and presents a detailed quantitative and qualitative content analysis of the use of political advertising by the Conservative, Labour, and Social Democrat/Liberal Alliance parties during the 1983 general election" (see pages 294–295). The authors report a recent trend in Great Britain which is similar to the one Jamieson found in the United States and reported in chapter 1 of this volume. Jamieson found that a more independent reporting and editorial style emerged in newspapers in the United States as newspapers began to shed their overt partisian or candidate-oriented biases. Johnson and Elebash report that in Great Britain "when the national newspapers were no longer owned by political parties, a shift in journalistic behavior was observable. Journalists have changed from the party/parliamentary model of quoting party line . . . to an independent/journalistic model of actively attacking and debating party lines. No longer do parties define the agenda of a political campaign. Rather, it is the newspapers and the broadcast media that define the political agenda" (see page 296).

In 1983, campaign advertising involved much more issue discussion than image discussion, but the accusation that American-style campaigning was gathering momentum in the 1979 and 1983 campaigns contained more than a few elements of truth. "However reluctant the British might be to admit it, their tradition of 'standing' for office rapidly appears to be giving way to 'running' for office" (see page 313). May we soon expect the British political parties to react to this trend in much the same way that parties in the United States are reacting: by, in effect, becoming their own ad agencies (see chapter 3)?

In a second interesting, comparative analysis, O'Neil and Mills, in "Political Advertising in Australia: A Dynamic Force Meets a Resilient Object," observe that there is much in political advertising in Australia that is like political advertising in the United States, but that there are also important differences. Their chapter "seeks to identify where and why local factors—institutional and attitudinal differences—have created an identifiable Australian advertising campaign. [Their] framework casts the growth of political advertising in Australia as a struggle between a dynamic technology and a resilient set of public institutions and beliefs" (see page 315).

Their paper outlines the history of Australian electoral advertising, describes its elements of style and tactics, and discusses the "Australian institutions and attitudes which have acted to modify, and which have also been modified by, political advertising" (see page 315).

The three principal aspects of Australian political life which have influenced political advertising are: the parliamentary system of government, the dominant role of party structures, widespread cynicism about advertising, and a tradition of parliamentary and judicial rule making. After controversial campaigns in 1980, parliament began a sweeping renovation of election laws. A Commission of Parliament recommended that it should be an offense to print, publish, or distribute a political advertisement that was untrue or was likely to be misleading. "Parliament accepted the recommendation, and so Australia became the only democracy to make an offense of deceptive election advertising" (see page 328).

The authors conclude that while there are a number of similarities between Australian and American political advertising, there are many differences as well. For example, "Australian ads deal less with identification and more with arguing and attacking. Visionary ads do not occur as the quiet finale to a campaign but increasingly provide a theme for the entire strategy" (see page 336). These differences are due to a parliamentary context in which "rivals for the prime ministership rarely need to be introduced to an electorate already familiar with them as party leaders" (see page 336). However, the authors conclude "As in other countries, there is no definitive proof about the ability of advertising to swing votes" (see page 337).

It is fitting that this volume conclude with comparative analyses and that it include other unusual approaches such as the search for hidden myths in political advertising. One of the expectations of any anthology of original essays and reports is that it uses its freedom to call forth studies which are typically not found in other sources and which might otherwise not have been conducted. We have attempted to meet this expectation while working to achieve the other purposes to which the volume is dedicated.

Acknowledgments

The editors are grateful for the support of several individuals for their efforts with the preparation of this manuscript. The help and general coordination assistance of Anne Wadsworth was essential to the project at every stage. Jeannine Freeman was invaluable in performing typing and word processing tasks, but her contributions far exceed those routine responsibilities. Jeannine, along with Finessa Ferrell, executed the tedious and meticulous process by which the bibliography was compiled and checked.

Notes on Contributors

Donald T. Cundy is Associate Professor of Communication and Political Science at Utah State University. His research interests include public opinion, political advertising and propaganda, electoral behavior, mathematical modeling, and social learning models. His articles appear in the *Journal of Politics, Political Methodoloy, Social Science Journal, American Journal of Political Science,* and *Political Behavior.* He teaches courses in the presidency, state and local govenment, political campaigns and the mass media, political psychology/political socialization, and others.

Dorothy K. Davidson is a senior research associate in the Center for Governmental Studies, Social Science Research Institute at Northern Illinois University. She is currently working on an interdisciplinary team conducting the annual "Illinois Policy Survey." Her research focuses on the role of candidate image in vote decisions, the process by which candidate images are formed, and the impact of image manipulation on voter decision-making capabilities.

L. Patrick Devlin is Professor of Speech Communication at the University of Rhode Island. He is an archivist and analyst of presidential campaign television commercials, the author of numerous articles in political communication, an activist who has worked in presidential campaigns, and the author of the books *Contemporary Political Speaking* and *Political Persuasion in Presidential Campaigns.*

George N. Dionisopoulos is Assistant Professor in the Department of Speech Communication at San Diego State University. He received his

Ph.D. from Purdue University in 1984. His research interests include corporate advocacy and political communication.

Camille Elebash is Associate Professor of Advertising, University of Alabama, Tuscaloosa. Her research in political communications included a sabbatical in London (summer and fall 1983) during which she taped thirty-eight interviews with people directly involved with recent British general elections. Her work in political communications has been published in *Journalism Quarterly* and *Journal of Advertising.* Her current research involves campaign techniques of Alabama governor and presidential candidate George Wallace.

Arthur C. (Jay) Felsberg is a graduate assistant in the Department of Political Science at the University of Tennessee. He held an internship with the American Enterprise Institute for Public Policy in 1981 and has conducted research in the fields of management, political communication, international relations, and military policy. Felsberg assisted in the editing of the *A. E. I. Foreign Policy and Defense Review.*

Gina M. Garramone is Assistant Professor in the Department of Advertising at Michigan State University. Her research interests include information processing, uses and effects of the media, and political communication. She has published in *Public Opinion Quarterly,* the *Journal of Broadcasting and Electronic Media,* and *Communication Yearbook.*

Katherine Hale is Assistant Professor in the Center for the Study of Political Communication, University of Oklahoma. Her teaching and research interests include mass and political communication. Her work in political communication has been published in *Journalism Quarterly,* and she has presented papers on political and mass communication at national and international communication and political science conferences.

Kathleen M. Hall Jamieson is Professor of Speech Communication at the University of Texas, Austin. Her research interests include rhetoric, political communication, and aging. She is the author of *Packaging the Presidency,* and the coauthor of *The Interplay of Influence.* She has written numerous articles for scholarly journals such as *Presidential Studies Quarterly, Quarterly Journal of Speech, Central States Speech Journal, Communication Education,* and *Speech Monographs.*

Karen S. Johnson is Assistant Professor of Broadcast and Film Communication at the University of Alabama. Johnson teaches courses in broadcast news, mass media and society, international communication, and political communication. Her research interests include: presidential impression management, news analysis, and cross-national media studies.

Richard Joslyn is Associate Professor of Political Science at Temple University where he teaches courses in public opinion, the mass media and politics, elections and voting behavior, and research methods. He is the author of *Mass Media and Elections,* coauthor of *Campaign '80: The Public and the Presidential Selection Process,* and the author of numerous articles on political socialization, public opinion, and campaign communication. He is currently conducting research on political commercials, based on his personal collection of televised spot ads and his observation of the work of media consultants during the 1984 election.

Lynda Lee Kaid is Professor of Communication and Director of the Center for the Study of Political Communication at the University of Oklahoma. She is editor of *Political Communication Review* and coauthor of *Political Campaign Communication,* and her articles appear in *Journalism Quarterly, Journal of Broadcasting, Communication Research, Social Science Quarterly, Communication Yearbook,* and *Handbook of Political Communication.*

Barry Kolar is vice-president of Onion Creek Publishing and managing editor of the Onion Creek Free Press newspaper in Buda, Texas. He formerly served as television production coordinator with the National Republican Congressional Committee. He holds a Master of Arts degree from the University of Tennessee-Knoxville and a Bachelor of Arts degree from Baylor University.

Michael W. Mansfield is Associate Professor of Political Science at Baylor University. He is coeditor of *Drama in Life: The Uses of Communication in Society* and *Government and the News Media: Comparative Dimensions* and contributes regularly to books and journals concerning communication and methodology.

Stephen Mills recently completed a two-year Harkness Fellowship in which he studied journalism and campaign technologies in the U.S.

presidential election campaign. He completed a Master of Public Administration degree at the Kennedy School of Government at Harvard. He is a political reporter with *The Age* newspaper of Melbourne.

Dan Nimmo is Professor of Communication at the University of Oklahoma. Among his books in political communication are *Newsgathering in Washington, The Political Persuaders, Popular Images of Politics, Political Communication and Public Opinion in America, Subliminal Politics, Government and the News Media: Cross-National Perspectives,* and *Handbook of Political Communication.* He was editor of *Communication Yearbook* 3 and 4.

Helen O'Neil is a senior political reporter with the Australian Broadcasting Corporation, and has covered several State and Federal election campaigns for radio and television. She recently completed a Master of Public Administration degree at the Kennedy School of Government, Harvard, where she was selected as a Littauer Fellow. Her research interests include media-government relations and economic studies.

Keith R. Sanders is Professor of Speech Communication and Dean of the College of Communication and Fine Arts at Southern Illinois University at Carbondale. He was founding chairperson of the Political Communication Division of the International Communication Association and the founding editor of *Political Communication Review.* He coauthored *Political Campaign Communication* and coedited the *Handbook of Political Communication.* His articles and reviews on the role of interpersonal and mass communication in political decision-making have appeared in such publications as *Journalism Quarterly, Journal of the American Forensic Association, Central States Speech Journal, Journal of Broadcasting, Communication Research, Quarterly Journal of Speech,* and *Communication Yearbook* 1 and 2.

Leonard C. Shyles (Ph.D. Ohio State University, 1981) teaches at the University of Maryland, College Park, in the department of Communication Arts and Theatre. His current research involves the analysis of the structure and content of televised political advertising. Some of his research has been published in the *Journal of Broadcasting, Video Systems, The Journal of Applied Communication Research,* and *Political Behavior.*

New Perspectives on Political Advertising

• 1 •

The Evolution of Political Advertising in America

Kathleen Hall Jamieson

BEFORE THE ADVENT of the mass media made it possible to situate political advertising between the comics and the obituaries, between Fibber McGee and Molly, between the trenches of "Winds of War" and the clenches of "Dallas," those aspiring to public office were faced with the need either to make multiple copies of their message to transmit to individual voters or to assemble voters in order to deliver the campaign's appeals to them. Accordingly "treats" and torchparades drew voters to political messages; partisan newspapers and pamphlets infiltrated voters' homes; banners, broadsides, and billboards insinuated their messages into the public forum; buttons, badges, kerchiefs, and bandannas transformed the supporter into an advertisement; and existing channels such as postcards and envelopes were suborned for political purposes.

Although we tend to recast our forebearers as dour, starched, otherworldly Puritans motivated to civic involvement by an oppressive sense of obligation, from our earliest elections, food and fun were used to motivate political participation. So, for example, as a candidate for the House of Burgesses in Virginia, George Washington "treated" the electors in his district to rum, punch, wine, cider, and beer (Chambers,

1963, p. 4). Many long-lived political traditions have their roots in forms of colonial treating. The bull-roasts that characterize Maryland politics, for instance, are throwbacks to the Federalist candidates' oxroasts.

While roasts and treatings enticed voters with the promise of food and drink, torchparades lured them into groups with promise of entertainment. The first president systematically to carry his message to voters in televised commercials recalled in his memoirs that he entered politics in 1896, when, as a boy in Abilene, he helped campaign "by marching in a nighttime parade with a flaming torch made of a rag soaked in coal oil" (Eisenhower, 1963, p. 47).

From the inception of the republic to the childhood of Dwight David Eisenhower, political parades were a major means of public concelebration. Parades were not simply a means of election but also a means of heralding successes. Huge parades in Boston, Baltimore, and Philadelphia commemorated the Constitution's ratification; similarly, Harry Truman reminisced about his father, mounted on a grey horse, carrying a torch in a parade marking Cleveland's victory over Benjamin Harrison in 1892 (Miller, 1973, p. 166).

The explicitly partisan parade matured as a political form in the campaign of 1840 when, as an observer recalled, "Great processions showed the barrel of cider, the coonskin, and the log cabin with the latchstring hanging out, which typified Harrison's democracy, while in a carriage rode an image of the aristocratic Van Buren, seated on English cushions and holding the golden teaspoons which he had purchased for the White House. . . . Long banners declared that the Whigs would 'teach the palace slave to respect the log cabin' " (Hone, 1969, p. 493). In 1860, with the rise of Lincoln's "Wide Awakes" and other marching groups, the torchlight parade, complete with cannons and fireworks, became a fixture of the political campaign. Campaign banners and flags, transparencies and torches were carried through the streets by marching enthusiasts—some professional paid marchers, some volunteers—often dressed in patriotic uniform. As they marched they shouted campaign slogans or sang campaign songs. A writer for Harper's Weekly explained that "All men cannot be orators, or editors, or ward bosses, or even patient listeners," and further that "any man with arms and legs can carry a Kerosene torch around the streets, and come reasonably near keeping step with a band. The theory is that the fidelity of the voter who undertakes such simple political labor is clinched, and that his example has an effect besides on the unorganized multitude" (1892, p. 971).

As the notion that the office sought the "man" gradually gave way to the belief that the "man" could actively seek the office, presidential candidates participated in the parades. So in the later quarter of the nineteenth century a presidential candidate occasionally was seen marching with the torch, banner, and transparency carriers; and if the situation called for it, he also might deliver "a brief felicitous response" to a speech of welcome by a local notable (*Harper's Weekly*, 1884, p. 669).

A parade for Grover Cleveland in Buffalo in 1884 lasted two hours and included at least 18,000 persons. After Cleveland's "brief felicitous response," the procession counter marched for another two hours as Cleveland watched from a balcony. Not until 2 A.M. did what *Harper's Weekly* (1884) called "the largest and most significant [demonstration] . . . ever witnessed in Buffalo" end.

Producing these extravaganzas was expensive. A reporter for *Leslie's Weekly* (1904, p. 342) estimated that in the presidential campaign of 1904 several million dollars were spent for "flags, banners, uniforms, torches, buttons, canvas, and muslin and paint, in crude creations that are ruined by the rains, ripped by the winds, and utterly useless after election day."

During night parades, the crowd's attention was riveted by Kerosene torches mounted within a frame to illuminate the cloth's message. These transparencies were to the nineteenth-century voter what political spots are to the voter in 1984. Called transparencies because they were constructed of partially transparent cheesecloth or cotton, these were messages wrapped around either wooden or steel frames and affixed to a pole. In the late 1880s, a transparency complete with portraits of the candidate sold for $1.50. In 1887 The Folding Transparency Company of New York replaced the transparency's support, a bulky, cumbersome, difficult to store, wooden box, with four rotating steel wires that could be locked into place before affixing the cloth, but that could be folded to save space in storage. "Sixty of them occupy no more space than one of the old-style wood frame transparencies" boasted the company's ads. The making of transparencies had become big business with innovations of its own.

The transparencies carried both messages of support and of attack. "The jokes of Mr. Lincoln were a favorite subject for the legends upon the transparencies" noted *The Illustrated London News* (15 October 1864), "the rather grim one of 'Coal, 14 dols. per ton' being greeted by the populace with groans as it swayed past." "The mottoes [on the transparencies] were various," noted *Harper's Weekly* on 11 October 1884, "but the majority referred in some way to the admitted honesty of Governor Cleveland and the bad reputation of Mr. Blaine."

Political speeches, chants, and songs fleshed out the skeletal claims of the transparencies and banners. Although political songs were both sung and chanted in the torchlight parades of the second half of the ninteenth century, their use antedates the republic. In 1734 "A Song Made upon the Election of New Magistrates for This City" was composed to memorialize the victory of some of Governor Cosby's opponents in the New York City elections. The song praised "you good lads that dare oppose all lawless power and might." In response, Cosby had the hangman burn a copy of the song in front of City Hall (Silber, 1971, p. 17).

Campaign songs came into their own in the country's first contested election. Adams supporters sang "Adams and Liberty" while Jefferson's followers sang of Jefferson, "honored son of liberty." Songs were also a medium of attack. To the tune of "Yankee Doodle," Jeffersonians chorused their conviction that Adams coveted a crown "like Georgy, great."

Published in 1840, the first campaign lyric-book parented decades of heirs. From 1840 to 1916 the publication of a campaign songster was as much a part of every national campaign as the publication of a campaign biography. The lyrics, set to familiar music of the day as well as to old battle standards such as "Battle Hymn of the Republic" and "Yankee Doodle," were sold at newsstands and distributed by party organizations. As advertising, songs had a major advantage over the printed banners and broadsides, for they reached the illiterate as well as the literate, an important advantage before compulsory schooling increased literacy.

So pervasive was song as a mode of campaign communication in the 1840 campaign that a Democratic editor was moved to write, "Some of the songs I shall never forget. They rang in my ears wherever I went, morning, noon and night. . . . If a Democrat tried to speak, argue, or answer anything that was said or done, he was only saluted with a fresh deluge of music" (Silber, 1971, p. 41).

The expectation that the lyrics would rhyme evoked a level of literary license that often sanctioned ingenious compromises with syllables and sense. The candidacy of vice-presidential nominee Frelinghuysen, whose name was often misspelled in his own advertising, taxed the creativity of the lyricist who wrote: "Hurrah! hurrah! the country's risin', / For Harry Clay and Frelinghuysen!" The dictate that songs rhyme also produced some sublimely silly lyrics, as for example, "Let us sail on the raft, crowded down fore and aft, For our good Bill Taft." Since good Bill Taft weighed 326 pounds, one would hope that those sailing on his raft were accomplished swimmers. Occasionally rhyme maliciously underscored attack, as when Clay supporters sang in 1842 "Do you know a traitor viler, viler, viler / Than Tyler?"

In addition to an occasional forced rhyme, the songs personalized the candidates. Henry Clay became Harry Clay. One of Coolidge's campaign songs urged that voters "Keep cool with Cal." And William Howard Taft became: "B-I-Double L-Bill!" The song concluded with the reminder "Taft's no counterfeit Bill."

Like the broadcast commercials they prefigure, the campaign songs tended to ally their candidates with revered predecessors, creating in the process the sense that Washington had fathered not only the country but also endless generations of candidates, some legitimate, some bastards. In 1864 voters sang, "We'll have another Washington—McClellan is the man!"; in 1916 voters chorused, "I think we've got another Washington (and Wilson is his name)" In 1920 Democrats assured the country that Cox was like Washington: "The man we have has oft been tried, / Like Washington, he's never lied."

Just as the broadcast ads of the twentieth century condense the central claims of the campaign, so too do the songs and chants of the ninteenth century. In a campaign in which Cleveland admitted that he may have fathered an illegitimate child, his opponents took up the chant "Ma, Ma, where's my Pa? / Gone to the White House, Ha Ha Ha." That refrain found its way into the chorus of a campaign song as well.

Use of attack songs survived into the twentieth century. A song titled "Elliot, I Wanna Be a Cap'n Too!" implied that Elliot Roosevelt obtained his commission by act of nepotism. In 1964 the Chad Mitchell trio released a barbed song sung to a soft shoe that chided Goldwater' candidacy by proclaiming: "We're the nice young men who wanna go back to 1910, We're Barry's boys."

Songs survived in political commercials as a means of building name recognition. "Adlai, Adlie" sang one commercial in 1952 "don't care how you note it. Just go out and vote it." In 1960, a song-as-commercial also served to build name recognition, to increase audience comfort with the candidate, and to impart the illusion that the momentum of the campaign was irresistible. In one of the television ads created for Kennedy in 1960, for example, Kennedy placards, posters, pictures, and buttons flashed across the screen as a full chorus sang Kennedy's virtues.

Just as political songs have survived into the last fifth of the twentieth century so too chants akin to "Ma, Ma, where's my Pa" survive today not as means of mass participation in torch parades but as greetings to candidates entering a rally (recall the omnipresence of "Four More Years" during the 1972 Nixon campaign) and as expressions of hostility ("Hey Hey LBJ: How Many Kids Did You Kill Today").

Often a campaign's songs and chants simply amplified the themes of its banners. If a banner's message was to be deciphered while being carried along a parade route, its message had to be short and clear. Headaches comparable to those the ticking clock induces in the producer of the thirty second ad were created for the nineteenth-century advertiser by the small amount of square footage available on a banner.

The need for brevity favored the flag banners that asserted the patriotism of the candidate by insetting his portrait into the flag's stars and overlaying his slogan or symbol on the bars. Flag banners were popular as early as 1840 and prevalent until 1905 when Congress prohibited compromising portraits or marks on a flag.

The banners rarely noted either the candidate's party or the year of the election. Instead, a portrait or symbol (e.g. rails for Lincoln) identified the candidate. Other revered symbols such as the eagle or the flag also appeared on banners, occasionally accompanied by a brief slogan.

Those who painted portraits for the banners aspired to producing recognizable likenesses of the candidates. Rembrandt's reputation is unmenaced by the results. In the portraits on the banners of 1904 Teddy Roosevelt is often recognizable only by his eye glasses and the ever present chord hanging from them. "In some of them the President seems in great suffering; in others he appears to be filled with an awful fear; in others he is in a towering rage; but most of them suggest a mortal offense to his olfactory nerves," wrote a reporter for *Leslie's Weekly* (1904, p. 342). Still, in the reporter's judgment, the visual indignities inflicted on Teddy Roosevelt pale in comparisons to those visited on the Democratic candidate, Judge Parker, whose stiff necked portrait "seems to have been made after the subject's death." As the campaign progressed and the business of political portraiture quickened, the quality of the portraits declined, occasionally approaching the "grotesque" (*Leslie's Weekly*, 1904, p. 342).

Generally the slogans accompanying the banners' portraits consisted of little more than an innocuous pledge of affirmation. "Blaine. Logan. The Nation's Choice," "Our Candidate. William H. Taft," "Harrison and Reform," or "Benjamin Harrison. Whitelaw Reid. Protection and Reciprocity." Others simply carried a brief identification—"William Henry Harrison. The Farmer of North Bend" or "Gen Harrison. The Hero of Tippecanoe"—or a single assertion "Harrison and a

National Bank" or "Clay, Frelinghuysen, and Protective Tariff." Lacking the space and the attention required to sustain arguments, banners relied on bald assertion. Their limited space also minimized the banners' ability to repeat their messages. By carrying many identical banners, marchers compensated for the short time the voter was exposed to any one of them.

The advance of technology accelerated the demise of the torch parades. Electric lighting dimmed the allure of the torches; by the early 1920s, radio's ready-made audience had minimized the need to use parades to attract political audiences. And while parades drew voters to a central location where the campaign's messages were dispensed, political newspapers insinuated their political pitch into voters' homes.

From their earliest appearance in the colonies, the political power of newspapers was apparent. In 1690 the newssheet *Publick Occurrences* was suppressed by royal dictum. And it was through newspaper that the Federalist papers were transmitted. Newspapers also played an indirect role in precipitating the revolution. One of the earliest British measures to evoke sustained opposition from the colonists was the Stamp Act (1765), requiring that books, official papers, legal documents, and newspapers be printed on stamped paper. Ads were taxed at a rate of two shillings each and newspapers at a penny for four pages. Newspapers protested the act by changing their appearance to that of the untaxed broadsides and handbills, by assiduously reporting hostile discussion of the Act in the legislatures and town mettings, by publishing the tax collectors' names, and by recounting how mobs had hung the collectors in effigy.

From the early days of the presidency, newspapers identified with specific causes and politicians. Alexander Hamilton's *Gazette of the United States* warred with the *National Gazette* which Freneau edited for Jefferson. So open and virulent were Hamilton and Jefferson's published attacks on each other that Washington, appealing to the well-being of the country, urged his two secretaries to make peace.

The systematic use of newspapers as the political forum for a particular candidate for president began in the nation's first contested election in 1796. In 1800, the *Columbian Centinel* observed that "The papers are overrunning with electioneering essays, squibs, and invectives."

Those accustomed to the balanced presentations of the major metropolitan dailies of our time would be shocked by the content and tone of the newspapers of the first half of the nineteenth century. For instance, in 1824 and 1828 newspapers called Andrew Jackson an "adulterer," an "ignoramus," and a "Southerner" who "feared neither God nor man." Charles Hammond, editor of the Cincinnati *Gazette*, asked, "Ought a convicted adulteress and her paramour husband to be placed in the highest office of this free and Christian land?" (Rutland, 1973, p. 118). When his wife, Rachel, died shortly before his inauguration, Jackson blamed the newspapers who had spread slander about her.

Newspapers and pamphlets were major forms of partisan political communication throughout the nineteenth century because they could carry a standardized message to a large audience and, when desirable, could do so pseudonymously. In an era in which public campaigning by presidential aspirants was taboo, the newspapers, handbills, and pamphlets also provided a means of disclosing a candidate's case to the electorate without directly involving the candidate in making the appeal. So, for example, although he did not publicly campaign on his own behalf in the presidential election of 1860, Lincoln did pay $400 surreptitiously to buy a German newspaper in Illinois. He then turned it over to a complicitous editor who agreed to toe the Republican party line. (Shannon, 1959, p. 23).

The contrast between the newspapers of Jefferson's time and the newspapers we retrieve from our doorstep explains a major change in political communication. To reach a newspaper's audience today a politician does not purchase a news organization but instead buys space in a newspaper. Then, newspapers were the tools of a politician or of a party; now they are ostensibly independent of either. The shift occurred gradually. The 1850 census classified a mere 5 percent of the newspapers as "neutral and independent' rather than political, religious, scientific, or literary. By 1880, one fourth were classed as independent, neutral, or local. Ten years later that percentage had reached one third. In the *Editor & Publisher Year Book of 1940,* 48 percent labelled themselves independent; another 24 percent identified themselves as Independent Democrat or Republican, and only 28 percent considered themselves to be either Democrat of Republican (Mott, 1962, pp. 216, 412, 720).

Today, as a general rule, editors and reporters do not mix governmental employment and employment by a newspaper but instead resign one role before assuming another. By contrast the link between party papers and the government in the early days of the republic was a close one. The editor of Hamilton's Federalist press, John Fenno, was the printer to the Treasury; the editor of Jefferson's paper, Philip Freneau, was a clerk in the State Department. Jackson freely dispensed the spoils of office to the editors who had supported his candidacy. This system of rewards was curtailed in 1846 when Congress decided that government printing contracts should be left to the lowest bidder. Politics was removed entirely from public printing in 1860 with the establishment of the Government Printing Office (Mott, 1962, pp. 256–257).

Today we assume that the nominee of either major party may purchase advertising space in any large newspaper, regardless of its editorial preferences or political endorsements. Yet this practice was still controversial in the early decades of this century when Jamse Melvin Lee in his *History of American Journalism* justified the practice on the grounds that "It is a good thing for a Republican to read in his party paper the advertisements of the Democratic Party. The advertisement, being officially prepared, is positive assurance to him that its contents have not been colored or warped by the editorial policies of the paper: it is a yardstick by which he may measure the accuracy of the news reports of the rival party" (Lee, 1917, p. 446).

Although today we associate them with the newspapers and magazines that house them, cartoons were not always the exclusive product of magazines and newspapers. Before the 1870s cartoons could be purchased at publishers' counters or in the streets. The ability of the drawing to create its own reality coupled with caricature's ability to accentuate or impute physicial or psychological attributes creates a potent political form. Cartoons caricaturing the opposition were widely distributed by campaigns.

For example, Jackson is a central figure in the history of political caricature. His colorful personality and humble origins lent themselves to caricature. Shortly before his election, an equally important form of political caricature, lithography, was introduced into the U.S. The lithographic process—drawing with wax crayon on stone, chemically fixing the image, moistening and inking the stone, and repeatedly pressing the image onto paper or silk—made it possible to rapidly reproduce the same image almost limitlessly.

In the 1870s, Thomas Nast demonstrated the power of attack cloaked in caricature when his cartoons of Boss Tweed and the Tammany Ring drove both from office. After sneaking out of the country Tweed was recognized in Spain from one of Nast's cartoons and extradited to the U.S. and a New York jail.

So outraged were California legislators about being pilloried in cartoons that in 1899 they passed an anticartoon law forbidding caricatures that reflected on character. The law was disregarded and unenforced (Mott, 1962, p. 588).

Then as now candidates were idealized by their supporters and vilified by their opponents. The banners carried for Lincoln in 1860 and 1864 show a more handsome man than the one immortalized in Brady's unpublicized photographs from the same period. Similarly, William Jennings Bryan gazing resolutely from the banners of his campaign in 1908 lacks the wrinkles and the jowls but sports substantially more hair than the portly, balding, jowly, wrinkled Bryan captured in the photographs of the day.

Just as their supporters beautified pictures of them, so too Lincoln's and Bryan's opponents caricatured them. The sketches proffered by Lincoln's enemies amply qualified the Albany *Atlas and Argus* claim that he was "the ugliest man in the Union" (Washburn, 1972, p. 181). As Lincoln repeatedly acknowledged, the claims had some grounding in fact. During one of the debates, Lincoln parried Douglas's charge that he was two-faced by saying, "I leave it to my audience. If I had another face, do you think I'd wear this one?"

In 1860, Philadelphia jurist John Meredith Read, fearful that voters were being frightened by "horrible caricatures" of Lincoln, commissioned painter John Henry Brown to paint a flattering likeness of Lincoln, whether be deserved it or not. The resulting portrait was adapted into print for the campaign (Ostendorf & Holzer, 1976, pp. 78–80).

To counter the image propagated by the cartoons and caricatures, Matthew Brady also photographed Lincoln before he delivered his famous address at the Cooper Institute in New York City, 27 February 1860. The photo was then line-engraved in newspapers and lithographed for public display as well as copied on buttons as a visual rebuttal of the hostile claims (Hamilton & Ostendorf, 1963, p. 37). Fortunately for Lincoln, the technology of the period made possible mass production of the photo. In 1859, the carte-de-visite photograph—a paper print from a wet-plate or collodion glass negative—was introduced. It was through the carte-de-visite, mounted in 2 1/4 by 4 inch cards, that Brady's photo became familiar to most Americans in 1860.

Through Brady's lens we see a tall, gaunt, neatly dressed, dignified man, looking directly into the camera. In the photo, Lincoln wears not the suspenders and short pants of a bumpkin but a dark vested suit. Countering the contention that he is crude and uneducated, his hand rested on a book. Brady and some of Lincoln's associates credit his election to that photo (Carpenter, 1867, p. 47). By providing first hand information, the photo enabled voters to gain their own impression of the backwoods lawyer who aspired to the presidency. By creating memorable evidence, the photographs did for visual political communication what songs did for oral communication.

By transforming the candidate's supporters into mobile advertising—bumper stickers, campaign ties, scarves, and buttons today perform the function of nineteenth century badges, buttons, kerchiefs and bandannas. The interpersonal advertising of the last century often invited display, in part, by virtue of its utility.

Through most of nineteenth century, Americans were able to eat on, sleep with, wipe their mouths on, or blow their noses in political advertising, for political aspirants imprinted their likenesses, their slogans, and their promises on bandannas and handkerchiefs, tablecloths and coverlets. Supporters advertised their loyalties and demonstrated their fervor by waving kerchiefs and bandannas in public meetings and by carrying them in private. For example, Ingersoll's nomination of Blaine in 1876 was greeted by a wildly enthusiastic waving of handkerchiefs, and in the Republican convention of 1884 white handkerchiefs fluttered over the heads of the paticipants.

In 1888, Cleveland's running mate, Senator Allen G. Thurman, earned the title "The Knight of the Red Bandanna" by habitually using a red silk bandanna to blow his nose and polish his boots (although not necessarily in that order). His supporters demonstrated their allegiance at the Chicago convention by banding their hats with red bandannas. The red bandanna waved in both the pro- and anti-Cleveland campaign songs of that year. One anti-Thurman song included the line "Old foul bandanna, good-by!" while a pro-Cleveland song enjoined "Wave high the red bandanna." The marriage between bandannas of a certain color and a single candidate was not always as exclusive as that between Thurman (and subsequently the Bull Moose party) and the red bandanna. An 1888 ad offered vendors "The 'Party of Purity' Campaign Handkerchief, made of fine cambric, hemmed and laundered ready for use, full pocket size, fine distinct twin medallion portrait in one corner, of either Republican or Democrat candidates" (Collins, 1979, p. 9). Then as now some advertisers worked both sides of the street.

Because they readily identify their candidate or cause, bandannas are commonplace in the political cartoons of the late nineteenth century, where they often hang from a caricatured candidate's hip pocket or shroud his shoulders. To telegraph the weakness of a cause the bandanna is shown patching a character's pants or hoisted as a distress flag. Bandannas also transmit warnings. An 1888 cartoon in *JUDGE*, showing the bandanna as the sail on a boat sinking under Cleveland's weight, warns,

"The bandanna makes a Very Pretty Canvas, but the Free Trade Passenger is Too heavy."

The twentieth-century offspring of the kerchief and the bandanna are the slogan imprinted neckscarves and ties sold as fundraisers in political campaigns. The kerchiefs and bandannas are a political art form rendered obsolete by paper tissues.

As advertising, the bandannas and handkerchiefs had a singular advantage over the paper napkins printed from the same plates: they survived use. So we find bandannas and kerchiefs but no paper napkins in the memorial signature quilts crafted to eulogize individual campaigns.

Signature quilts, containing cloth signed by the candidate or better still by the president or president-elect, preserved memories of the campaign. Their popularity modified the president's job description to include a tireless hand: as Benjamin Harrison complained, one of the burdens of the presidency was providing signatures for quilts and lunch cloths (Collins, 1979, p. 28). Such quilts were the resting ground for the mementoes of the campaign. Sewn into them were banners, campaign ribbons, flags, bandannas, handkerchiefs, and signature patches.

Any medium that regularly transmitted information to readers, listeners or viewers was ripe for political advertising. The mails were no exception. In the mid-nineteenth centure, patriotic envelopes bearing pictures of American flags, the American eagle, a group of soldiers, or the representation of such American virtues as "unity" appeared. When candidate emblems were popularized and printed on these envelopes, political direct mail was born. Similarly, political postcards suborned the mail to their own ends. Political postcards came into their own in the late 1890s.

Those who pine for presidential campaigns as they were in Jefferson, Jackson, or Lincoln's times and who see our nation's political decline and fall mirrored in the rise of political spot advertising remember a halcyon past that never was. The transparencies, bandannas, banners, songs, and cartoons that pervaded nineteenth century campaigning telgraphed conclusions, not evidence. Their messages were briefer, or in the parlance of 1984, less beefy, than those of any sixty second spot ad. The air then was filled not with substantive disputes but with simplification, sloganeering, and slander. Finally, the absence of a neutral press made it more difficult then than now to identify and assess the competing claims of opposing campaigns.

Radio and television altered what and how presidential candidates communicated to the electorate. In the early days of radio the simple fact of a presidential candidate transported into ones living room was sufficient to gain and hold attention. But as the novelty of the new medium waned and as programming on other channels competed for listeners' attention, hour long speeches gave way to half-hour speeches and half-hour speeches increasingly were bracketed by audience enticing entertainment, often in the form of political songs and skits. As those eager to advertise on the mass medium increased, so too did the cost of thirty minutes of time, a fact that propelled politicians toward choice of shorter segments. The same pattern occurred with television. Where half-hour speeches were the norm in 1952, five minute segments were the politicians' preference in 1956 and 1960. By the 1970s sixty and thirty second spot ads had become the political mainstay.

Whereas in the nineteenth century the short messages of the songs, slogans, and banners had served as lures to draw voters to the message of the political speech, in the seventh and eighth decades of the twentieth century, the shorter messages functioned as ends in themselves. Thirty minute political ads still existed but more often than not the desired audience of undecided voters spurned them for entertainment on the other channels. So, for example, in 1964 more viewers watched "Peyton Place" and "Petticoat Junction" than Eisenhower's "Conversation with Goldwater."

Although thirty and sixty second spots can capsulize a candidate's position on central issues, they lack the time needed to specify the evidence and warrants that lead to that position. What spots do best is telegraph to the electorate the candidate's agreement or disagreement with positions voters already embrace. What they cannot do well is educate the electorate about the desirability of one position over the other or familiarize the electorate with the subtleties of complex matters such as the relationship between the budget deficit and interest rates. Doing either requires longer than sixty seconds. And while a thirty minute message can be as vacuous as a thirty second one, it doesn't have to be.

Nevertheless, if the audience most attracted to a longer message is the educated, committed, partisan audience that will benefit least from the detailed exposition, the candidate's dilemma becomes attracting and holding the attention of the audience inclined to choose "Peyton Place" rather than Eisenhower and Goldwater or *Jaws* rather than Roger Mudd's "Teddy." In 1984, three strategies were tried to resolve the dilemma. The Republicans opened their general election advertising campaign by purchasing the same half hour block of prime time on each of the networks. This use of roadblocking deprived habitual viewers of first run alternatives to the Reagan message. Unlike Reagan's documentary, that of independent Democrat Lyndon LaRouche was aired at 11:30 P.M., well outside prime time. Borrowing a ploy from the networks, LaRouche encouraged viewership with spot ads that functioned as promos. The spots promised that the documentary would provide details about a coming food shortage in America. Spot ads were also used by the National Conservative Political Action Committee and by the Mondale campaign to trigger information seeking. NCPAC included a toll free number. Additional information and appeals for funds were sent to those calling the number. Direct mail lists were created from the addresses gotten through use of the number.

The length of political messages was not the only element in the political equation that changed over the history of broadcasting. The function served by radio changed as well. In 1948 radio was the only mass broadcast vehicle available to carry a politician's message; but by 1956 the amount spent on television ads exceeded that spent on radio. Gradually, network television replaced radio as a mass medium of political persuasion. Radio instead became a medium used to address distinct subgroups of the electorate, farmers and blacks in particular.

Still radio retained an important political role. In 1968 and 1972 Richard Nixon chose radio as the medium on which to issue long addresses. This use revived a traditional political function of radio. Ford adopted the same pattern in 1976. And Carter delivered radio addresses as well at the close of the 1980 campaign. By increasing the newsworthiness of their message, these uses of radio proved a cost-efficient means of increasing printed coverage of a candidate's message. Radio also served some candidate's specific needs. Nixon felt that as a medium radio better suited him and his philosophical discussions of the presidency than did television.

Nevertheless, as television became the country's dominant mass medium, candidates' comfort with it and with advertising on it increased. In 1952 both Eisenhower and Stevenson recoiled at the intrusion of "spot advertising" into their campaigns. Both objected to the notion that complex ideas could be communicated in thirty or sixty second snippets. Both felt uneasy talking to a camera lens instead of a visible audience. Unlike Eisenhower, Stevenson objected to appearing in spot ads in 1952. By 1956 he reluctantly agreed.

From 1952 through 1960 the bulk of broadcast political ads for presidential contenders consisted of the candidate speaking directly to the viewing audience or the viewing audience eavesdropping on the candidate as he addressed a rally. In 1956, in a concession to television's visual nature, both Republican cabinet members and Stevenson's running mate underscored their key ideas with visual aids.

Neither Eisenhower nor Stevenson had any major television experience before the 1952 campaign. By contrast, their successors in the 1960 campaigns had used television ads and, in Kennedy's case, a television documentary in their races for the Senate. Additionally, Nixon had salvaged his political career through the nationally televised Checkers speech and had appeared in ads for Ike in 1956. For Kennedy and Nixon, then, televised advertising was a political fact of life. Both talked to a camera with greater ease than their predecessors.

Throughout most of the nineteenth century when the office was supposed to seek the presidential candidate rather than the candidate the office, candidates did not have to face the delicate task of retaining their public sense of humility while claiming that they were the best person for the office. Surrogates spoke on their behalf. Then, since there were things a candidate could not say on his own behalf without appearing self-serving, surrogates were required even after the candidates took to the stump on their own behalf. Testimonial ads by those who knew the candidate filled this need in both the nineteenth and the twentieth century. As early as 1952, prominent citizens such as Senator Estes Kefauver, nationally known for his investigation of organized crime, praised Stevenson's record as a crime fighter in Illinois. Similarly it was more credible for Harry Belafonte to tell viewers that John Kennedy had a strong commitment to civil rights than it was for Kennedy to make that assertion and more credible for Senator Margaret Chase Smith to testify that Barry Goldwater had voted for Social Security than for Goldwater himself to make that claim in 1964.

Additionally some arguments could be visualized through the magic of television editing that could not be plausibly verbalized. These arguments by association took two forms: one allied positive images with the favored candidate, the other allied negative images with the opponent. Accordingly, in the 1960 campaign, Kennedy's ads juxtaposed him with waving fields of grain, the Liberty Bell, and prospering factories and allied Nixon with joblessness and deserted factories. These negative associative spots were not the misbegotten offspring of television but simply the televised equivalent of a visual argument that was the stock in trade of the broadsides of the last half of the nineteenth century. In these broadsides the favored candidate was painted next to pictures of full factories, contented families, and bountiful harvests; his opponent was allied visually to barren factories, starving families, and empty fields.

Television's ability to edit could join images that had not before coexisted. The nation's first presidential spot campaign utilized this editing capacity when Eisenhower and the persons asking him questions were edited together to form the Eisenhower Answers America spots of 1952. Although the viewer had no way of knowing it, the questioners could not actually see Ike nor he they. Indeed his answers had been recorded before their questions had been asked!

The use to which the Democrats put this ability of television in 1960 was less benign. The Kennedy campaign lifted from the first Kennedy-Nixon debate a scene showing Nixon nodding his agreement to the goals he and Kennedy shared. By the wonders of editing the Democrats injected that scene into a section of the debates in which Kennedy outlined specific controversial proposals.

Had Kennedy proclaimed at the moment before or after the edited insert, "Nixon agrees with me," he would have been lying. Instead the ad showed Nixon seemingly agreeing and thus made the same argument more forcefully. The false inference prompted by this ad demonstrates the danger harbored by television's ability to reconfigure reality.

In 1964 the Democrats and Republicans demonstrated that they understood television's power to create arguments from visual association. The Democrats juxtaposed a child plucking the petals from a daisy with the explosion of a bomb as Lyndon Johnson extolled the value of loving one another; the Republicans abutted scenes of rioting and looting with pictures of Bobby Baker and Billy Sol Estes to preface Goldwater's condemnation of the Democrat's disregard for law and order. Both visual sequences defy conventional logic. Both prompt inferences more effectively than a verbal argument about either peace or morality could.

In 1968 argument by visual association reached a new level of complexity and potential duplicity when patterns of images were created and repeated by the Republicans using still photos. Scenes of the war in Vietnam, of poverty in Appalachia, and of the rioting outside the Democratic convention were intercut with pictures of Hubert Humphrey to visually ally the war, poverty, and the rioting with the Democratic nominee. No such argument is made on the audio track of the ad. To phrase the argument verbally is to reveal its ridiculousness. Even Humphrey's most rabid opponent was unready to argue that he had caused the war, poverty, and social unrest or that he approved of them or was indifferent to them—the three most plausible readings of the visual juxtaposition.

Argument by positive visual association remains a staple of political advertising. In 1976, for example, Ford's campaign argued that America was feeling good about itself and about Ford by intercutting pictures of the Statue of Liberty, tall sailing ships, and picnics with pictures of smiling adults and children and finally by infusing Ford into the rush of pleasant and patriotic images. Carter's campaign visually allied him with great Democratic presidents by dissolving from a picture of FDR to a picture of Truman to a picture of JFK to a picture of Carter as E. G. Marshall opined that a good man can make a great president. In these spots the evidence required to sustain the implied linkage between the associated images is absent. It is absent as well in product ads that link use of the product with beauty, youth, fame, fortune, and friendship. In that they both rely on argument by visual associations, this type of ad sells politicians the way soap is usually sold.

Unlike the ads from 1964 and 1968, the two ads cited as representative of argument by visual association in 1976 are ads *for* a candidate, not *against* an opponent. The public revulsion at the disclosures of Watergate transformed the ads of 1976. In the wake of Watergate no candidate wanted to whisper the possibility that he or she was another Nixon. The guilt by visual association embedded in the Billie Sol Estes Goldwater ad and the anti-Humphrey ad bespoke a willingness if not to overstep the truth then at least to lure the electorate into false inferences. After the light at the end of the tunnel in Vietnam had proven to be that of the advancing enemy and after the Watergate cover-up revealed a second president had lied, use of such tactics raised fears that a candidate who would be president was required instead to quiet. Consequently, positive associative ads of the sort that characterized the Ford and Carter campaigns persevered while ads arguing from negative associations disappeared. At the same time, two new types of political advertisement emerged to carry attacks against an opponent.

Before turning to examine personal witness and neutral reporter ads let me note that most ads that juxtaposed unrelated visual images to prompt false inferences were part of a broader category of attack ads that I call concept or production spots. These attacks ads, in which the candidates do not appear, emerged gradually. In 1956, spots featuring Stevenson did not directly attack Eisenhower's administration. Instead spots starring Estes Kefauver, Stevenson's running mate, took up that burden. By 1960 politicians had realized that one of the ways in which a candidate could damage his presidential chances was to appear unpresidential by attacking his opponent directly. Concept or production spots in which the candidate was unseen, unheard, and hence—the strategists hoped—unblamed for the ad, were assigned that burden. In 1960 Democratic spots attacking Nixon, an unseen announcer asserted that if you wanted underpaid teachers and inadequately supplied schools you should vote for Nixon, but if you stood for strong education you should vote for Kennedy.

In 1964, concept spots asserted that Barry Goldwater would wreck Social Security; the most dramatic and most often aired showed a Social Security card being ripped in half. By contrast, in five minute speeches Johnson spoke in general terms about the need to protect Social Security. Goldwater remained unnamed. In 1968, a Democratic concept spot showed Agnew's name on the television screen as a man convulsed in laughter. In 1972 a man on a girder high above a city was the focus of a Republican ad that suggested that McGovern wanted to put half the country on welfare. For the first time on television in 1972 attack ads were disassociated from their sponsoring candidate not simply by their form but also by their tag. These spots were sponsored not by the Committee to Re-Elect the President but by its offshoot, Democrats for Nixon.

In 1976, the concept spot as a vehicle of attack and the spot that argued by negative visual association were replaced by personal witness ads in which citizens claimed that Carter was "too wishy washy" or noted that he didn't do much as governor. To underscore that these were actual citizens voicing unscripted opinions these Ford attack ads showed the names of their hometowns as they spoke.

Because those testifying are not actors and are expressing actually held opinions, they seem divorced from either candidate. Their statements seem less like attacks than the same comments would in a concept spot or if spoken by the candidate. A number of American commonplace attitudes nurture our disposition to approve of this form of attack, among them, "I may not agree with what you say, but I'll defend your right to say it"or "Everybody's entitled to an opinion." In 1980, rather than return to concept spots to dramatize attacks, Carter—in both the primary and general election—and Reagan—briefly in the general election—used personal witness ads to discredit their oponents.

The second form of attack ad that emerged from the ashes of Watergate I call the "neutral reporter" ad. In both 1976 and 1980 the majority of ads directed against the opponent were either person in the street ads or "neutral reporter" ads. A neutral reporter ad sets forth a series of factual statements and then invites a judgment. These are rational political ads that offer factual data, invite or stipulate a conclusion, and warrant that conclusion. So for example, an ad for Ford in 1976 noted that Carter had promised to do for the federal government what he had done for Georgia. To test Carter's claim the ad invited us to look at the record. It then provided data on the size of government, bonded indebtedness, and other matters that appeared to contradict what Carter had been saying about his record. Similarly Carter, looking directly into the camera, indicted Ford for high inflation and specified its effect on food prices. In 1980 the majority of Reagan's anti-Carter ads on the economy followed this form. Ad after ad simply recounted the inflation rate for such items as sugar and bread or such categories as housing and transportion. Repeating the formula used by Ford against him, Carter responded with an ad that showed the California seal as an announcer noted that Reagan raised taxes and increased the size of government in California. One entire set of Carter's ads in 1980 simply juxtaposed Reagan's statements or statements by others with details about Carter's record.

The majority of the attack ads produced by and for the independent political action committees (PACS) in 1980 fell into the neutral reporter category. The most common form simple quoted a promise Carter made in 1976 and documented that he had not kept it. Of these, the most cogent were the National Conservative Political Action Committee's ads that edited from the Carter-Ford debates specific promises by Carter; the ads froze the frame after Carter stated a promise and printed across the screen the evidence establishing that the promise had been broken. One ad for example, compared the rate of inflation in 1976 and in 1980, another the size of the budget deficit during both years.

As the memories of Watergate dimmed and honesty receded as a criterion by which presidential candidates would be tested, concept spots returned in force in 1984. In the bloody Democratic primaries Mondale attacked Hart in ads whose central characters included a red phone and a handgun. An ad for Hart countered with a burning fuse and the hyperbolic charges that Mondale favored using our boys as "bodyguards" for dictators and as "trading chips." In the general election the red phone reappeared for Mondale. Also on the scene was a roller coaster meant to dramatize the impending collapse of the Reagan recovery. The Reagan campaign contributed a bear who was in the woods in the beginning of the ad but whose existence was questioned by the announcer at the ad's end.

In the closing days of the general election, predictions of a Reagan landslide created a climate in which the Democrats were willing to risk revival of the negative visual association ad. In one ad, children were juxtaposed with missiles as the tune "Teach your Children Well" was sung and Mondale phrased oblique indictments of Reagan.

In place of the careful logic of the neutral reporter ads, 1984 saw a Reagan ad which reduced Mondale's plan for the future to raising taxes and Reagan's to growth, trimming waste and adding jobs.

Personal witness ads survived in 1984. In that campaign the Reagan strategists refined the form of the ad by displaying the speakers' names as they spoke and by contrasting the testimony of a worker in 1980 with testimony of that samer worker in 1984.

The 1984 presidential campaign, then, marked the re-emergence of the concept spot and of argument by negative visual association. It also refined the "personal witness" spot. What these changes suggest is that presidential advertising strategists have available to them certain basic persuasive means but will occasionally abandon some in response to a sensed rejection of them by the elecorate. Other choices are exercised deliberately in response to a felt need on the part of the electorate. So, for example, both Nixon and Humphrey used telethons on election eve 1968, a choice responsive to voters' need for assurance that the person they would elect would be accountable to them in ways in which Johnson had not been.

In 1964, the electorate chose Lyndon Johnson expecting peace; instead it was handed war. In 1968, Johnson's withdrawal from the race denied voters the opportunity to hold Johnson accountable for this betrayal. They required assurances that the next president would be more responsive than Johnson had been. Unsurprisingly, 1968 is the year in which the public was given the greatest chance in paid programming to interrogate the presidential candidates. Nixon and Humphrey both sponsored panel shows. Both held election eve telethons on both coasts. That unprecedented level of access to the candidates was mandated by Johnson's failure to keep what the public took to be his promise of peace. It satisfied a systemic need for reassurance that the next presidency would be an "open" one.

What this cursory overview reveals is that presidential advertising has always been an adaptive art that used whatever resources it could muster from torchparades to roadblocking to invite the attention of its intended audience. Brief, simplistic messages have been a part of American politics since (and perhaps before) the country's first contested election. Finding means of involving would-be voters in more educative forms of both paid and unpaid communication remains a challenge.

• 2 •

An Analysis of Presidential Television Commercials, 1952–1984

L. Patrick Devlin

IN THE 1980 CAMPAIGN RONALD REAGAN RECEIVED almost $30 million in federal funds. He spent $18 million of that $30 million or 60 percent of it on advertising. He spent approximately $13 million of that $18 million on television advertisements. Therefore, 70 percent of the money that Ronald Reagan spent on advertising in the 1980 campaign was spent on television advertising. In 1976 Jimmy Carter spent 74 percent of his advertising money on television. Voters may be voting less, but candidates are spending more and especially spending more on television advertising. Or are they?

An analysis of the spending for television advertising by the 1952 Eisenhower campaign uncovers some interesting comparisons with current spending. In the definitive study of the 1952 Eisenhower television campaign, Wood (1982) estimated that Eisenhower's television spending ranged from $2 million to $6 million when all television time buying—national, state, and local—was factored in. Eisenhower's national network spot buys approximated $1.5 million. In 1980, Reagan's network spending approximated $6.5 million. If these two network spending figures are analyzed in terms of the 1967 base year for constant dollars,

Eisenhower spent $1.9 million on network spots while Reagan spent $2.5 million. If Eisenhower spent a possible total of $6 million while Reagan spent a total of $13 on television ads, Eisenhower actually outspent Reagan $7.5 million to $5.9 million in terms of 1967 constant dollars.

The point is that well-financed presidential candidates always have and always will spend vast sums and a major portion of their budgets on television advertising. Few corporations, aside from Proctor and Gamble, McDonalds, or Miller Brewing, advertise for a full year at the volume of political advertising during the months of September, October, and the first week of November. During a presidential campaign commercials flood the airwaves.

Political commercials come in various time frames. They come in half-hour speeches or biographies. They come in miniprograms, or in four minute and twenty second segments that are sandwiched in before Johnny Carson or right before the evening news. But more commonly they come in sixty second or especially in thirty second segments.

Political commercials can also be categorized as to type or format—documentary, talking head, man-in-the-street, cinéma verité, production idea spot. The format or type of ads will be categorized, examined, and analyzed later in this essay. Before reviewing the changes and consistencies in advertising during the last thirty years, it might be wise to review the purposes or the functions of political advertisements.

The first reason for political advertising is that ads can make an unknown candidate a better known candidate. Examples of unknowns using televisions in presidential races to become knowns is less frequent than in gubernatorial or senatorial campaigns. However, McGovern in 1972, Carter in 1976, Bush in 1980, and Hart in 1984 used television extensively to become better known during their primary campaigns.

Second, ads are often aimed at late-deciding or uninterested voters. Ads are unobtrusive and unavoidable invaders of peoples' living rooms. Ads reach thousands, or in large media markets or across the nation, even millions. Many of these uninvolved voters see little else of the campaign except what they see possibly on the evening news or what they see in these ads. Kaid (1981, p 265) concluded that "political advertising is more effective when the level of voter involvement is low." These late-deciding or uninvolved voters are that crucial 10 to 20 percent of the electorate; normally, they are reached only through television in the last stages of the compaign.

In 1972, a year when scholars Patterson and McClure did their research on the effectiveness of the ads, they found only 18 of 100 voters were late deciders. In 1972 many people had made up their mind. The ads of the 1972 compaign were found to have influenced "roughly three percent of the total electorate" (Patterson & McClure, 1976, p. 135). In 1972 there was a 23 percent spread between Nixon and McGovern in the final tally. Therefore, a 3 percent impact with a 23 percent spread was not much of an impact. Yet in the 1976 campaign there was only a 2 percent disparity between Ford and Carter in the final tally. If the 1976 ads affected 3 percent of the electorate, and there was a 2 percent spread, the efectiveness or ineffectiveness of ads might become crucial.

Third, ads are also used to reinforce supporters and partisans. As partisans watched pictures of Ronald Reagan by the Statue of Liberty or Jimmy Carter standing in front of a gigantic American flag at town meetings, these ads reinforced partisan feelings. For example, partisans watch half-hour programs, but few others do. Only one in twenty people watch half-hour programs, and these are primarily partisans. But their partisan feelings are reinforced, and they may end up giving more money to the campaign through these commercials.

Fourth, ads can be used to attack the opposition. As Reagan's 1980 pollster, Vincent Breglio (1983) maintained, "It has become vital in campaigns today that you not only present all of the reasons why people ought to vote for you but you also have an obligation to present the reasons why they should not vote for the opponent. Hence, the negative campaign, or the attack strategy becomes an essential part of any campaign operation." Therefore, a mix of positive and negative ads are increasingly used to convince voters why they should vote for a candidate and not vote for the opposition candidate.

Fifth, ads develop and explain issues. Research, by Patterson and McClure (1976) has demonstrated that there is more substance and more issue information in presidential ads than in TV news. A 60 second ad has, on average, five times as much issue information about the candidate than a sixty second snippet on the evening news. Hence voters can find out better where a candidate stands by watching his ads than by watching the evening news. And ads have a cumulative effect. In presidential campaigns a multiplicity of ads are used, and these ads are often repeated. Using thirty second time frames voters see ten or twelve ads during the course of a campaign, with five or six of them repeated. So the idea comes across not simply in thirty seconds, but in thirty seconds times the number of times voters ses that thirty second ad and are attentive to it.

Sixth, ads can soften or redefine an image. If a candidate has a reputation for not caring about unemployment or is weak on defense issues, ads can be created which emphasize these positions and the candidate's commitment to these areas. In 1968 candidate Nixon was redefined through TV and in 1976, Jimmy Carter was accused of taking ambiguous stands on issues, so his advertising man created strong, issue-oriented spots to redefine this hazy image.

Seventh, ads are used to target particular demographic groups. This is how ads go hand in hand with polling. Polling shows where potential voters are and ad demographics show how to reach them. For example, women, men, blacks, single mothers, or union members might be targeted voters. Careful time buying before, during, or after key programs such as a hockey game to reach predominantly male voters or the Donahue show to reach predominantly female voters is used. Polling and time buying helps to maximize the potential to reach a particular category of voter.

Eighth, ads cost money, but they can also be used to raise money. Money appeals at the end of half-hour ads or five minute ads often are used. McGovern in 1972 and Anderson in 1980 paid for their television commercials mainly through these appeals at the end of their ads. In 1984, Mondale used a special five minute commercial and beamed it into house parties to raise money. People did in fact send in money so that future ads went on the air.

Ninth, ads are adaptable. They can be made. They can be revised. They can be discarded as the necessities of the campaign change. Multiple generations of spot commercials are extremely common during the presidential campaign, and often several hours of ads using six or seven distinct generations are made.

Tenth, and finally, ads are used because the competition uses them. Few candidates, aside from Jesse Jackson in 1984, can afford to forego commercials. There is an adage in campaigns which states that half of all advertising money is wasted. The problem is no one in a campaign knows which half, so all advertising continues.

Having given some rationale for ads, the focus now will be a review of some prominent types or formats of advertising used in a particular campaign. Many of these types are still in use and are representative of the kinds of advertising seen from 1952 to 1984.

Primitive Ads

The first advertisements examined are labeled "primitive ads." These ads were created in 1952 and 1956.

In 1952 the Eisenhower campaign used three sixty second spots and over 20 twenty second spots with an "Ask General Eisenhower" theme. The "Man from Abilene" spot (Appendix 1) is primitive because the announcer's voice bellowed at the viewer in a way similar to the loud announcer's techniques used in movie theaters during the "March of Time" or "Movietone News." In this spot Eisenhower was ill at ease in front of the camera and his voice and eyes gave him away as an unnatural and uneasy communicator. In the twenty second spots Eisenhower answered a question posed by a voter. Both the rehearsed voter questions and the cue card answers by Eisenhower demonstrate the primitive nature of these 1952 ads.

In 1952, the Stevenson campaign concentrated on half-hour speeches rather than spot commercials. But in 1956 "A Man from Libertyville" (Appendix 2) was created to counteract the 1952 "Man from Abilene‘ approach. However, Eisenhower had been wise enough not to carry grocery bags in his spot. The lesson learned from the Stevenson spot is, if you want to be elected president, don't carry a grocery bag. However, both the Eisenhower and Stevenson ads represent a primitive form of television advertising no longer used in campaigns today.

Talking Head Ads

1960 was the year of the talking head spot. Both John Kennedy and Richard Nixon emphasized ads which had them speaking directly to the viewer.

The talking head format is as much in use in 1984 as it was in 1960. However, there are differences in talking head spots. For example, the Nixon spot (Appendix 3) is much more formal. Nixon is more serious and has a more presidential image. The visual background is blank and concentrated, and complimentary lighting is used on Nixon's face. He is almost angelic. His dark suit and light face contrast with the unphotogenic darkness that Nixon displayed in the debates. In the debate footage he comes across with a five o'clock shadow; these ads were made to compensate for the light suit and dark face of the debates. The Kennedy spot is much more informal. His gestures and his voice are much more conversational, and he had family pictures as a back-drop (Appendix 4). These pictures and plaques are used to give the viewer additional viewing information. Some ad makers want the background to be blank; others want some kind of additional visual information.

Research by Patterson and McClure found it paradoxical but true that a candidate can develop a more favorable image through issue spots which seek to convince the voter that the candidate has positions on civil rights or Medicare and that he can thus handle the difficult problems of a presidency. These issue spots convey a better image than image spots which try to create directly a favorable feeling about the candidate's personal qualities. Research indicates that the best way to make a positive image impression on the voter is to use issues, in this case Medicare or civil rights, as a vehicle or a tool to affect a positive image. The purpose, therefore, for most talking head spots is to focus on an issue and allow the candidate to convey an image impression that he can handle the issues, and most importantly, that he can handle the job of president. Thus an image impression comes across through an issue spot.

NEGATIVE ADS

1964 was the year of the negative ad. Both Goldwater and Johnson emphasized ads that tried to tear down their opponent rather than build up their own positives. Two 1964 commercials are representative of negative commercials made to provoke or bring out negative feelings already within voters. The "Daisy Girl" spot (Appendix 5) was made by Tony Schwartz. It was shown only once and was taken off the air because of the outcry and protest it caused. But this ad had an afterlife through newspaper articles and radio and TV news commentaries about it. The creator of this spot had a philosophy about making good political ads. It was that commercials that attempt to bring something to voters, that is, convey some information and try to bring something new to them, are inherently not as effective as those that try to appeal to something that is already within voters. So the idea is not to get something across to people as much as it is to get something out of people. Nowhere in the Daisy spot is Goldwater mentioned, but the ad evoked a feeling that Goldwater may indeed use nuclear weapons. This distrust was not in the spot, but in the viewer. Similarly, in the Goldwater ad (Appendix 6) many voters already had feelings that we were not a very loved people, and that other countries were using us and burning our flag. This ad used familiar riot footage to reinforce this feeling that was already within many Goldwater-prone voters.

Visual Ads

In 1968, color was first used in presidential commercials to enhance the visual nature of the ads.

The Humphrey ad (Appendix 7) has visual simplicity but little visual variety and excitement. At the beginning of the ad, Humphrey's photo is small and far away, but as the announcer lists his accomplishments his face becomes larger. The Nixon ad people took advantage of the first year of color by creating a series of spots giving life and vitality to well-chosen still photography to give the effect of visual variety to the spot. An example is the "Vietnam Ad" in Appendix 8. Photography in spots is very important because research has shown that people remember the visual more than they retain the specifics of the audio copy. One study found that "80–85 percent of the information that is retained about TV commercials is visual" (Burnham, 1983, p. A6). So good presidential commercials have to be visual.

Production Idea Spots

Television is an excellent tool to convey a memorable idea. In 1972 production spots were created to convey important ideas about candidates. Production spots also allow graphics to be incorporated to make the spot's information more memorable.

In 1972 as other candidates were pictured trudging through the snows in the New Hampshire primary on the evening news, President Nixon was shown on his trip to Russia. Five minute travelogues were created to stress the idea that Nixon was the first president to visit our former enemies China and Russia. These spots stressed that through Nixon we would have a greater chance of peace with our former enemies. However, as McGovern became more the issue in 1972, three anti-McGovern spots were shown more frequently. These negative spots were found by researchers to reach low and moderate interest voters for several reasons (Patterson & McClure, 1976). First, they were perceived as entertaining or funny. If people perceive an ad as entertaining or funny they'll watch it. Secondly, committed vote switchers, that is Democrats who were going to vote for Nixon, had their attitudes reinforced because these idea spots provided reasons for that decision and gave them comfort in knowing that there were many others like them. On the other hand, McGovern voters also got somethng from watching the defense spot (Appendix 9). McGovern voters wanted to reduce military spending; the commercial was consistent with and reinforced their perception of McGovern.

In political advertising, selective perception is constantly working. If pro-Nixon voters view the defense spot they might say, "I knew that about McGovern. That's terrible. That's why Nixon needs to be re-elected to save this country." Undecided voters might look at that defense spot and say "Gee, I didn't know that about McGovern. Is he really going to do that to the Air Force? Is he really going to do that to the Navy?" And McGovern voters look at that defense spot and say, "Right on, George! We need to reduce the military." Selective perception allows different people to take away different ideas from a single commercial.

The "Turn Around" spot (Appendix 10) is also visually important. Like the defense spot it is an idea spot but with greater visual simplicity. Voters did not have to remember a specific McGovern change, not one issue, not one statement from the spot. The idea was that McGovern had switched his stance, and the expectation of future switches was the important idea to get across. And that was achieved through a rotating picture.

When the polls showed that literally millions of Democrats were defecting to Nixon, Tony Schwartz, who created the Lyndon Johnson "Daisy Girl," commercial was hired by McGovern. Schwartz created five spots, of which the "Voting Booth" spot is representative (Appendix 11). This ad, shown only twice, represents the best of what Schwartz classified as an "idea" spot. The real problem for McGovern was millions of defecting Democrats. Schwartz tried to reach them in a catchy, stream-of-consciousness way. You would have to see and listen to this ad several times to get everything because of the speed of the statements. This speed made the ad captivating, yet at times difficult to grasp. Crucial statements such as "This hand voted for Kennedy"; "My father would roll over in his grave"; "The fellas say they are, but maybe they're not"; "My gut feeling, my gut feeling" may not be heard the first time around. These statements represent the kind of emotional feeling that the ad tried to evoke.

Cinéma Verité Ads

Filming a candidate in real life settings interacting with people is a technique called cinéma verité. In 1972, McGovern's principal ad creator, Charles Guggenheim, did not believe in the ethics or in the effectiveness of negative advertisements. Guggenheim was an award-winning documentary film maker who preferred to film McGovern in real settings interacting with real voters. Guggenheim used the cinéma verité technique to show McGovern as a concerned and compassionate candidate. This format allows the ad maker to take footage of a candidate speaking with voters during the course of a day or several days. The footage is then edited down to thirty and sixty second snippets where the candidate concentrates on one issue—in McGovern's case, Medicare (Appendix 12). The technique can also be used to show the candidate shaking hands, listening, and simply being open and communicative with potential voters in group settings.

The Changing Ad Campaign

1976 was the year of the changing spot. President Ford went through three ad makers and three different advertising campaign techniques. And candidate Carter evolved literally from a farmer in a plaid shirt to someone who looked presidential. So 1976 is a good year to examine the changes in presidential campaign advertising.

President Ford used three advertising agencies with different strategies and techniques during his primary and general election campaigns. At first, Ford was portrayed as an effective President who had restored faith in the presidency (Appendix 13). After Watergate and after Nixon's resignation these ads actually had Ford running against Nixon and reinforced Ford as an effective president. But when Ronald Reagan started doing better in the primaries, pressure for changes in Ford's advertising mounted. Ford agreed to air, for the first time in presidential politics, "slice-of-life" advertisements using paid actors in little theater settings which were the tried and true techniques of selling detergents or Preparation H. When I show the "Two Ladies" ad (Appendix 14) to audiences, laughter indicates that presidential candidates cannot be sold like soap or Preparation H: the slice-of-life technique is so blatantly obvious and has too many product advertising associations. In the "Feeling Good" ad (Appendix 15) music is used to create an upbeat mood about the country and its people. Music is often an integral part of the mood setting devices of political ads. If a viewer's toe was tapping to the tempo of this ad, the music accomplished what the ad maker wanted.

In 1976, Carter started by running as a personable outsider (Apendixes 16, 17, and 18). He was the first candidate to run for president wearing a plaid, open-collared shirt in his ads. Carter finished the compaign in a suit, making a series of talking head spots which made him appear presidential.

So in 1976 changes took place in ads. The personable candidate became more presidential, and the president became more personable. Stated another way, Ford started out using his office as his trump card and finishedd by using ads that highlighted his personal qualities. Carter started out by using ads that focused on his casual personableness and finished by using ads that made him appear more presidential.

Most candidates in a long campaign use a multiplicity of ads, and their ad makers create multiple generations of many different types of ads—often too many different types of ads. Ford's media people created almost two hours of varied television advertising. By making and playing so many different spots they negated the impact of their more effective spots.

Documentary Ads

No campaign has emphasized documentary ads more than Ronald Reagan's campaign of 1980. During the 1980 general election campaign, Reagan ad makers wanted to play down the perception of Reagan as an actor and play up the perception of Reagan as an effective governor. The one minute ad (Appendix 19) and a longer four minute and twenty second version were the most heavily played ads of the entire campaign. The ad talked about the accomplishments of Reagan as governor and how as governor he would make an effective president. Partisans did not like the ad because it emphasized things they already knew. But this ad was played over and over again, and it was effective for swing voters or late-deciding voters because its format gave out crucial information.

Man-in-the-Street Ads

Man-in-the-street ads involve real people saying nice things about one candidate and/or nasty things about the opponent. In 1976, Jerry Rafshoon, Carter's ad creator, was on the receiving end of Ford man-in-the-street ads that characterized Carter as wishy-washy. Man-in-the-streets ads are used to reinforce perceptions of candidates that develop from polling. In 1980 Rafshoon wanted to reinforce the perception of Reagan as a scary guy who shot before he thought (Appendix 20). Man-in-the-street ads are excellent reinforcing tools but they are seldom persuasive. Too often the impression from undecided voters upon seeing these types of ads is "you can get somebody to say anything about anybody." However, because these ads do use real people saying real things, many ad makers use them because they think they have a quality of believability about them.

Testimonial Ads

Testimonial ads have prominent politicians, movie stars, or television personalities speaking on behalf of the candidate. The Kennedy testimonial ad (Appendix 21) used a popular star, Carroll O'Connor, to attack Carter's economic policy in an attempt to convey trust for Kennedy. Testimonials by other politicians or personalities and trust were two things Kennedy did not have in abundance during his 1980 campaign. Thus, "Archie Bunker" endorsed Kennedy and said, "I trust and believe in him, folks."

Independent Ads

Independent ads are financed by individuals or organizations separate from the presidential candidates. The real story of the 1980 campaign might not be the candidate ads but the independently financed ads. The ads from the Republican Congressional Committee and the National Conservation Political Action Committee (Appendixes 21 and 22) were representative of ads aired by a host of independent organizations.

All told, the Republican Congressional Committee spent $7 million on television advertising while all of the Political Action Committees spent in the vicinity of an additional $13 million of television advertising. Most of these ads were pro-Reagan and anti-Carter. Considering this additional advertising added together with the Reagan ads, Carter's ad maker, Jerry Rafshoon, concluded that he was actually outspent two or three to one.

Most independent ads are hard-hitting, negative ads. The Republican ads were humorous, but the NCPAC ads were deliberatively provocative. Terry Dolan, national director of NCPAC, wanted ads that created reaction regardless of possible negative reaction. As he said in an interview, "I don't care what Ronald Reagan, Jimmy Carter, or CBS says about our ads. The people we serve are 300,000 throughout the U.S. who could care less about respectability" (T. Dolan, personal communication, September 11, 1980). Independent ads were a potent factor in 1980 as they will be in future presidential campaigns.

SUMMARY

In the early years of presidential spots, 1952 through 1968, there was an emphasis on short spots of twenty or sixty seconds. In 1972 and 1976, the four minute and twenty second was dominant. In 1980 and 1984, the thirty second spot was dominant. So, TV advertising spots have evolved in terms of length, and length preferences depend on other factors of the campaign. Usually, however, a mix of lengths and types of spots are used in a presidential campaign. An analysis of the 1980 Reagan spots illustrates this.

Between Labor Day and Election Day in 1980, Reagan's Campaign '80 ran 255 network television commercials. Seventy-four or 29 percent were five minute spots, forty-one or 16 percent were one minute spots and one hundred-forty or 55 percent were thirty second spots. Of the 74 five minute spots, 60 were versions of the documentary "The Reagan Record." Of the 41 one minute spots, 35 were shortened versions of "The Reagan Record." Of the thirty second spots 10 percent were documentary "Reagan Record" spots, 45 percent were talking head spots, and 45 percent were "Anti-Carter" spots. Thus, of the total commercial allocation by Reagan's Campaign '80, 41 percent were documentary spots, 33 percent were talking head spots and 26 percent were anti-Carter spots (O'Reilly, 1980).

The thirty second spot has become the dominant time frame for political spots. Research on product commercials by Wheatley (1968), Beik (1962), and Sadowski (1972) has demonstrated that thirty second spots are just as effective as sixty second spots in getting the message across. And research by Kaid (1975) on political spots found that "5 minute spots are not significantly more successful than sixty second spots" in the quantity of items recalled in a spot.

Political advertisers have increasingly emphasized the use of the thirty second spot in relation to the sixty second or four minute and twenty second spot. For example, in 1972 Patterson and McClure found only 2 percent of all presidential advertising were thirty second spots while 41 percent of all commercials in 1972 were five minutes in length. In 1980, 55 percent of all Reagan spots were thirty second spots. Going from 2 to 55 percent in eight years is a shift that reflects the fact that stations are set up to sell time, and viewers are prepared to view commercials in thirty second units.

Five minute spots seem to work best as mood pieces to develop feelings through music and emotional appeals or as spots that give biographical or personal information about the candidate. In 1976, Jerry Rafshoon, creator of the Carter spots, became a champion for longer spots and proclaimed, "I'd be very happy if the networks and stations said, 'From now on we'll sell candidates nothing but five minutes' " (Television, 1977, p. 74). In 1976, when Carter was an unknown, Rafshoon used five minute spots in abundance. In 1980, he used fewer of them since, as a candidate moves from an unknown to a known, there is less need for five minute spots.

However, five minute spots are effective money raisers. In 1984 Walter Mondale raised $1.4 million for his campaign by beaming a five minute network commercial into fundraising house parties held around the United States.

In 1984, candidates Mondale, Hart, and Glenn emphasized television commercials in their campaigns. Although Hart's ads were more graphically innovative—using infinity grids, smaller inserted picture frames and peal back frames as the setting changed—all candidates used variations of the historical basics of TV political ads—the talking head, cinéma verité, documentary, and production idea spots. These along with testimonial, man-in-the-street, and negative spots are generic and will be seen over and over again in future campaigns.

Certainly more sophisticated cinematography is in use today than was used in the '50s, '60s, or '70s. Carter's ads in 1980 set a standard for beautifully photographed and produced commercials that Reagan followed in 1984. In Reagan's initial ads of 1984 he is neither seen nor heard. Instead we see beautiful pictures of weddings, hugs, churches, boats, flags, and homes. These ads reinforce the traditional values of love, family, church, community and renew faith in America. Good feelings have been emphasized in ads since 1976 when Bailey/Deardourff did the "I'm Feeling Good About America" series for Gerald Ford. Pictures of America and its people are really attempts at getting the electorate to vote for an idyllic view of themselves. Reagan is not unique in his attempts at ads that use this strategy. However, the fine quality of his ads do indicate that he has raised the technique to a new standard in TV political advertising.

It is difficult to determine the effectiveness of political commercials. Douglass Bailey (1977), who handled the 1976 Ford media, stated, "It is extraordinarily diffficult to look at a political commercial and judge it. Because any reputable agency . . . can produce pretty commercials . . . but to judge their political effectiveness is very hard to do." Aside from trying to separate a commercial's creative merit from its political impact, there is another reason why it is difficult to uncover the effectiveness of political commercials. There is so much happening simultaneously in a campaign it is difficult to isolate the impact of political advertising.

Political ads are but one of the many influences on the outcome of a presidential campaign. Certainly there are other communicative elements—debates, speeches, evening news broadcasts—that affect a campaign, yet campaigns have and will continue to spend a massive amount of their available money on political advertising. Perhaps this historical overview of political will affect more discerning consumers of future persuasive attempts through political advertising.

APPENDIX 1. "The Man from Abilene" (Eisenhower, 1952)

Video	Audio
The title, "The Man from Abilene," appears on screen.	ANNOUNCER: (*Loudly*) The Man from Abilene.
Picture of a small house is superimposed on a map of the U.S.	Out of the heartland of America, out of this small framed house in Abilene, Kansas . . .
Small house dissolves to picture of Eisenhower's face.	. . . came a man, Dwight D. Eisenhower.
Picture of soldiers landing on beaches appears.	Through the crucial hours of D-Day . . .
Picture of Arc de Triomphe dissolves to picture of enthusiastic crowds.	. . . he brought us to the triumph and peace of V-E Day.

"November 4, 1952: Election Day" flashes on screen.	Now another crucial hour in our history. Now the big question.
A man appears on screen and poses a question.	Man: General, if war comes is this country really ready?
Eisenhower appears on screen and answers the man mechanically.	Eisenhower: It is not!
Eisenhower then faces the camera and answers, reading obviously from cue cards.	The Administration has spent many billions of dollars for national defense. Yet today we haven't enough tanks for Korea. It is time for a change.
Picture of soldiers and artillery guns firing appears.	Announcer: The nation, haunted by the stalemate in Korea looks to Eisenhower.
Eisenhower is pictured with other WWII heroes Montgomery and Zuchov and walking with Churchill.	Eisenhower knows how to deal with the Russians. He has met Europe's leaders, has got them working with us.
Picture of Eisenhower talking with world leaders appears.	Elect the number one man for the number one job of our time.
Eisenhower is pictured on the platform at the Republican national convention—hands raised.	November 4th: Vote for Peace! Vote for Eisenhower!
The words "A Paid Political Film" appear.	

Appendix 2. "The Man from Libertyville" (Stevenson, 1956)

Video	Audio
A young man and woman are walking from a car in front of Stevenson. Both are carrying grocery bags.	Announcer: The Stevensons are returning now from a shopping trip in Libertyville. The governor is helping with the groceries.
Stevenson stops, turns, and addresses the camera, holding the bag of groceries in one arm.	That's my daughter-in-law, Nancy and my oldest son, Adlai Jr. He's a student at law school.

	They stay with me during the vacation. I think they live pretty well, but they are learning a lot about something that worries a lot of people in this country. That of course is the high cost of living.
Closeup of Stevenson, still holding grocery bag, appears.	In spite of the Eisenhower promise, the cost of living today is higher than it has ever been before in the history of our country.

APPENDIX 3. "Civil Rights" (Nixon, 1960)

Video	Audio
Nixon sits at a desk, head held high, posture erect, and hands clasped. The wall behind is empty of pictures.	ANNOUNCER: Ladies and Gentlemen, the Vice President of the United States, Richard M. Nixon.
Camera begins to zoom in slowly on his torso and head.	NIXON: I want to talk to you for a moment about civil rights, equal rights for all our citizens. Why must we vigorously defend them? First, because it is right and just. Second, because we cannot compete successfully with communism if we fail to utilize completely the minds and energies of all of our citizens.
Camera now focuses only on the well-lighted face and shoulders of Nixon.	And third, the whole world is watching us. When we fail to grant equality to all that makes news, bad news for America all over the world. Now the record shows there has been more progress in the past eight years than in the preceding eighty years because this administration has insisted on making progress. And I want to continue and speed up that progress.

Picture of Nixon and Lodge flashes on screen.	I want to help build a better America for all Americans.

Appendix 4. "Medicare" (Kennedy, 1960)

Video	Audio
John Kennedy appears on screen, close up, with pictures of family members and award plaques on the wall behind him. Camera begins to zoom out slowly and Kennedy begins to gesture for emphasis with one hand and point a finger forward.	Kennedy: This is Senator John Kennedy, the Democratic nominee for the Presidency of the United States. One of the problems that concerns me most is our failure to meet the problem of medical care for our older citizens. Some of them are in ill health. Some of them are in your family. And yet, under present laws, before they can receive any assitance in the payment of their medical bills which may be expensive, they must take a pauper's oath. They must say that they are medically indigent. I believe that the way to meet this problem is the way that Franklin Roosevelt met it in the Social Security Act of 1935.
Kennedy points the finger again and begins to use his hand with a back hand gesture.	I believe that people during their working years would want to contribute so that when they retire, when they reach the age of sixty-four for men or sixty-two for women, then they can receive assistance in paying their bills.
Kennedy pumps open hand in tempo with each short sentence.	They pay their own way. They live in dignity. They get protection. This is the way it ought to be done. This is the sound way.

	And I can assure you that if we are successful, we are going to pass this bill next January.
Picture of Kennedy, smiling, appears on screen with the caption, "John F. Kennedy for President."	

APPENDIX 5. "Daisy Girl" (Johnson, 1964)

Video	Audio
Little girl stands in a field of flowers, picking petals from a daisy one at a time.	(*Birds chirping*) LITTLE GIRL: One, two, three, four, five, six, six, eight, nine, nine . . .
Camera zooms in for a close up of the girl's face looking up to the sky. The camera continues to zoom in on the girl's eyes.	ANNOUNCER: Ten, nine, eight, seven, six, five, four, three, two, one, zero.
An atomic bomb explodes with a flash; a mushroom cloud forms with billowing fire and smoke.	(*Explosion*) JOHNSON: These are the stakes: to make a world in which all God's children can live, or go into the dark. We must either love each other or we must die.
The words "Vote for President Johnson on November 3" appear on screen.	ANNOUNCER: Vote for President Johnson on November third. The stakes are too high for you to stay home.

APPENDIX 6. "Much Beloved People" (Goldwater, 1964)

Video	Audio
A visual of the Capitol building dissolves smaller, and the words, "We are a much beloved people throughout the world" appear on the screen.	ANNOUNCER: President Lyndon B. Johnson said, "We are a much beloved people throughout the world."

Quick visuals appear: Orientals bear the banner, "Yankee go home" and shake their fists. A banner reads, "Americans go home." Angry people chanting. People running from the police.	(*Pulsating dissonant music*)
Goldwater is sitting in a chair in his living room. Goldwater takes off his glasses.	Goldwater: Is this what President Johnson means when he says we are much beloved? Well I don't like to see our flag torn down and trampled upon anywhere in the world. And I think most Americans agree with me on that. I don't like to see American citizens pushed around, and there is no good reason for letting it happen.
Close up of Goldwater.	All this results from weak, vacilating leadership. We must show the world that we are a mature, responsible people—aware of our rights as well as our responsibilities. And just as soon as we do this, we will resume our rightful role of world leadership which this administration has let go by default.
The words "In your heart, you know he's right" flash across the bottom of the Goldwater close up.	Announcer: In your heart you know he is right. Vote for Barry Goldwater.
The words, "Vote for Barry Goldwater" appear on a blank background.	

Appendix 7. "Ahead of His Time" (Humphrey, 1968)

Video	Audio
A picture of Humphrey appears as a small stamp in the center of a blank background.	Announcer: When he voted for civil rights twenty years ago, a lot of people said he was ahead of his time. He was.

The picture of Humphrey increases in size as Humphrey's accomplishments are stated.

Humphrey's picture now fills the screen as the zoom-in continues to a closeup on Humphrey's face and then a closeup on Humphrey's eyes.

The Humphrey campaign logo, "HHH Humphrey," appears on the screen.

He was ahead of his time when he urged a Nuclear Test Ban Treaty ten years before it was signed. He was ahead of his time when he outlined health insurance for the aged sixteen years before Medicare. He was ahead of his time when he proposed job training for unemployed young people seven years before the Job Corps. He was ahead of his time when he defined Food for Peace five years before the program saw light. And he was ahead of his time when he built up the Peace Corps four years before Congress adopted it. Hubert Humphrey has been ahead of his time for the past twenty years. That's why he is the man that you need for the future. Don't just vote for the right ideas. Vote for the man who thought of them. With Hubert Humphrey it is not just talk. He gets it done.

The preceding was a political announcement paid for by Citizens for Humphrey.

APPENDIX 8. "Vietnam" (Nixon, 1968)

Video

The following pictures are flashed on screen intermittently in synchronization with the drum roll on the audiotape: a helicopter, soldiers firing weapons, soldiers running, wounded soldiers, houses ablaze, bombed houses, a weary-looking soldier, crying Asian women, a medic aiding the wounded, a distraught-looking Asian man, faces of American soldiers.

Audio

(*A drum roll plays intermittently in synchronization with the changing pictures.*)

NIXON: Never has so much military, economic, and diplomatic power been used so ineffectively as in Vietnam.

If after all this time and all of this sacrifice and all of this support, there is still no end in sight . . .

More closeups of the faces of American soldiers appear on screen.	And I say the time has come for the American people to turn to new leadership—not tied to the mistakes and the policies of the past.
Faces of Asian people flash on the screen.	I pledge to you we shall have an honorable end to the war in Vietnam.
A picture of a helmet with "LOVE" painted on it appears on screen, followed by the words, "This Time Vote Like Your World Depended On It," and "NIXON."	

Appendix 9. "McGovern Defense" (Nixon, 1972)

Video	Audio
Three groups of toy marines are pictured.	Announcer: The McGovern defense plan. He would cut the marines by one-third . . .
A hand sweeps away one group of marines.	
Three groups of toy air force figures are pictured.	. . . the air force by one-third.
A hand sweeps away one group of air force figures.	
Four groups of toy sailors are pictured.	He would cut navy personnel by one-fourth.
A hand sweeps away one group of sailor figures.	
A triangle of ten toy planes is pictured.	He would cut interception planes by one-half . . .
A hand sweeps away half of the triangle of planes.	
Ten toy ships are lined-up in rows.	. . . the navy fleet by one-half . . .
A hand sweeps away half of the ships.	

Sixteen toy carriers are in rows.	. . . and carriers from sixteen to six.
A hand sweeps away ten carriers.	
The camera pans the swept-over toy armed forces and then pans the swept-over planes, ships, and carriers.	Senator Hubert Humphrey had this to say about the McGovern proposal, "It isn't just cutting into the fat. It isn't just cutting into manpower. It is cutting into the very security of this country."
President Nixon is pictured on a ship with a naval officer, viewing another ship.	*(Drum roll followed by strains of "Hail to the Chief.")* ANNOUNCER: President Nixon doesn't believe we should play games with our national security. He believes in a strong America to negotiate for people from strength.
The words, "Democrats for Nixon" appear on the screen.	

APPENDIX 10. "Turnaround" (Nixon, 1972)

Video	Audio
A left-profile shot of Senator McGovern appears.	ANNOUNCER: In 1967, Senator George McGovern said he was not an advocate of unilateral withdrawal of our troops from Vietnam.
McGovern's picture rotates right.	Now of course he is. Last year, the Senator suggested regulating marijuana along the same lines as alcohol.
McGovern's picture rotates left.	Now he is aginst legalizing it and says he always has been. Last January, George McGovern suggested a welfare plan that would give a $1,000 bill to every man, woman, and child in the country.
McGovern's picture rotates right.	Now he says maybe the $1,000 figure isn't right.

McGovern's picture rotates left.	Last year, he proposed a tax on inheritances of over $500,000 at 100 percent.
McGovern's picture rotates right.	This year he suggests 77 percent.
McGovern's picture rotates left.	In Florida, he was pro-busing.
McGovern's picture rotates right.	In Oregon, he said he would support the anti-busing bill now in congress.
McGovern's picture revolves around and around.	Last year. This year. The question is: What about next year?
Nixon's face is pictured with the words "Democrats for Nixon."	

Appendix 11. "Voting Booth" (McGovern, 1972)

Video	Audio
A curtain is opened to reveal a man standing in a voting booth. On the panel before him are two levers labelled "Nixon" and "McGovern," respectively. His hand hesitates near the lever and he rubs his fingers in indecision. He moves his finger to his mouth in a pensive gesture. He pulls the lever marked "McGovern."	Man: (*Thinking aloud*) Well, either way it won't be a disaster. What am I looking for? I mean so I'll vote for Nixon. Why rock the boat? I'm not crazy about him. Never was. I've got to make up my mind though. I have to make up my—I don't know about McGovern. I don't have that much time. I can't keep people waiting. The fellas say they are voting for Nixon. They expect me to vote for him too. Me vote for Nixon? My father would roll over in his grave. The fellas say they are, but maybe they're not. Crime—I don't feel safe . . . prices up. My gut feeling . . . don't vote for Nixon. Why am I confused? Who am I measuring McGovern against? My gut feeling. My gut feeling. McGovern.

	This hand voted for Kennedy! I mean, it's just possible McGovern's straight. Maybe he can. (*Whispering*) That's the way.
The words "Democrats for McGovern" appear and remain as a closeup of McGovern appears.	

APPENDIX 12. "Medicare" (McGovern, 1972)

Video	Audio
McGovern is pictured listening to a worker while other workers surrounding them look on.	WORKER 1: I think when most of us fellows get laid off, just paying the insurance wipes us out. That is eighty dollars a month right there.
	McGOVERN: That's right!
	WORKER 2: How do you feel about national health insurance?
McGovern turns to answer Worker 2 as others look on.	McGOVERN: Well it wouldn't cost any more money than what we are now paying on health. The difference is that you funnel it through a national health insurance program instead of letting the individual family pay that cost when they get hit.
McGovern gestures for emphasis.	I know one woman that paid thirty-nine thousand dollars in medical bills when her husband died from cancer. That was what that terminal illness cost her.
The camera focuses on the worker listening to McGovern; then the focus returns to McGovern.	Now she paid it but it broke her. It took her home; it took her savings; it took everything she owned. Under national health insurance the bill wouldn't have been any higher, but it would have been balanced out over the

	whole economy. And I think that's what we ought to do.
"McGovern" appears across the bottom of a closeup of McGovern.	Announcer: McGovern—Democrat—for the people.
The words "McGovern for President Washington, D.C." appear.	The people are paying for this campaign with their hard-earned dollars. Send what you can to "McGovern for President, Washington, D.C."

Appendix 13. "Accomplishment" (Ford, 1976)

Video	Audio
President Ford is pictured, looking out the window of the Oval office.	Announcer: He came to the office of president in troubled times. He began an open administration.
A closeup of Ford at his desk, holding his jaw in a reflective pose, is followed by another closeup of Ford on which the camera zooms in.	Now quietly and firmly he is leading us out of the worst recession in years. Rather than loose promises, he has made hard decisions. Rather than frantic spending, he has had the courage to say "no."
Yet another closeup of Ford in which he is smiling, and his hands are cupped behind his head.	The worst is over. Over two million more Americans are working than at the bottom of the recession. Inflation is cut almost in half.
Ford is pictured at a rostrum with the presidential seal on it. The words "President Ford '76" appear.	President Ford is your president. Keep him!

Appendix 14. "Two Ladies" (Ford, 1976)

Video	Audio
One woman comes out of a store front office with President Ford	

campaign posters covering the front of it. The woman is carrying papers and meets a second woman who is carrying a grocery bag. The second woman speaks first.	WOMAN 2: Ellie! Are you working for President Ford? ELLIE: Only about twenty-six hours a day.
Both women proceed to walk and talk.	WOMAN 2: When did this start? ELLIE: Let me ask you something. Notice anything about these food prices lately?
The women stop in front of a supermarket window with a large price poster displayed.	WOMAN 2: Well, they don't seem to be going up the way they used to.
The camera focuses on the second woman's face as she answers Ellie.	
The camera moves to Ellie's face.	ELLIE: President Ford has cut inflation in half.
The camera moves back to the second woman's face.	WOMAN 2: In half! Wow!
Both women are pictured together; Ellie shrugs her shoulders and gestures.	ELLIE: It is just I'd hate to see where we'd be without him.
President Ford is pictured with the words "President Ford," beneath him.	ANNOUNCER: President Ford is leading us back to prosperity. Stay with him! He knows the way!

APPENDIX 15. "Feeling Good" (Ford, 1976)

Video	Audio
A farmhouse is pictured in lush farm country. A man puts an American flag in front of a rural post office. A child is pictured eating. A man in a hard hat is shown at work. Black children are pictured laughing.	SONG: There's a change that's come over America. There's a change that's great to see. We're living here in peace again. We're going back to work again. It's better than it used to be. I'm feeling good about America. And today is where I'm from.

Video	Audio
A family is pictured with the baby on the father's back.	*(The song continues to play as background while Ford speaks.)*
	Ford: Today America enjoys the most precious gift of all. We are at peace.
The following scenes are flashed on the screen: a baby, a man picking apples, a woman smiling, an old man with a hat and cigar smiling, a woman nodding her head in agreement.	Announcer: We are at peace with the world and peace with ourselves. America is smiling again and a great many people believe the leadership of this steady, dependable man can keep America happy and secure.
President Ford is pictured working at his desk. Then he is pictured with his hands folded behind his head, rocking in his desk chair. Ford is again pictured at a desk, talking and gesturing.	We know we can depend on him to work to keep us strong at home.
Ford is pictured in the back seat of a car, writing on a pad of paper.	We know we can depend on him to ease tensions among the other nations of the world.
Ford is pictured from behind as he speaks.	We know we can depend on him to make peace his highest priority.
A picture of an older couple, hugging and kissing, appears on screen.	Peace with freedom.
A picture of a smiling, young boy appears on screen.	Is there anything more important that?

Appendix 16. "Non Lawyer" (Carter, 1976)

Video	Audio
A peanut warehouse with the name, "Jimmy Carter," painted on the side appears on the screen. A tractor is pictured in the field. Carter appears in a plaid shirt, walking through a field.	Carter: Well now, everybody from Congress who is running for president is a lawyer.

Carter smiles.	I don't have anything against lawyers. My oldest son is a lawyer. But I think it is time to have a non-lawyer in the White House for a change. Somebody that's had to work with his hands. Somebody that's had to run a complicated business.
Carter is shown in a farm field with other workers. Carter scoops peanuts with his hands as they pour down a chute.	
Carter pulls cotton apart in his hands. Then he is pictured sorting peanuts on a conveyor belt. A closeup of Carter in a plaid shirt is shown.	Somebody who has actually had to manage the affairs of a large government. As I have in my own state.

APPENDIX 17. "People" (Carter, 1976)

Video	Audio
Fireworks burst in the sky.	(*Fireworks bursting*)
Carter waves from an open car in a motorcade. The motorcade moves through a large crowd. The camera focuses on a campaign banner which reads "Carter for President."	CARTER: I started my own campaign twenty-one months ago.
Carter speaks at a rostrum.	I didn't have any political organization—not much money. Nobody knew who I was. We began to go from one living room to another, one labor hall to another.
Carter is shown climbing stairs. Carter is shown shaking hands.	Up and down the streets, factory shift lines, barber shops, beauty parlors, restaurants, shaking hands, talking to people, and listening.
Carter is shown shaking hands, talking, and listening. Carter is shown with two men and then with two women. Carter shakes hands with an older farm worker in overalls.	(*Upbeat music comes on as background.*)

Video	Audio
A crowd is pictured from above as it gathers around the back of a train.	
The train pulls out, and people stand along the track and wave.	
The Carter campaign plane, with the name "Peanut One" on its side, appears on screen.	
Carter is shown walking down the steps of his plane.	
Carter shakes hands with people in a large crowd.	
Carter shakes hands with some black people.	
Carter is shown waving.	
Carter is shown shaking hands and smiling as the camera moves in for a closeup. The name "Jimmy Carter," appears to the side of his smiling face.	CARTER: To special intersts, I owe nothing. To the people, I owe everything.

APPENDIX 18. "Reality" (Carter, 1976)

Video	Audio
Carter is pictured facing the camera, wearing a dark suit and tie and speaking.	CARTER: The Republican TV commercials assure us the economy is healthy, inflation is controlled, our leadership is great. But when I look around, I see every trip to the supermarket a shock, cities collapsing, suburbs scared, policemen cut, welfare skyrocketing.
The camera zooms in to show Carter's face close up.	That's reality. Republicans won't face up to it; but we can change it. Americans have done it before, and we'll do it again. It's a long, tough job. It's time we got started.
The names, "Jimmy Carter—Walter Mondale," appear on a screen with a blank background.	

APPENDIX 19. "Reagan Record" (Reagan, 1980)

Video	Audio
	(Music plays.)
Reagan is standing, right hand raised, taking oath as governor of California. The camera zooms in for a closeup of him and of his wife, Nancy, who looks on adoringly.	ANNOUNCER: This is a man whose time has come. A strong leader with a proven record. In 1966, answering the call of his party, Ronald Reagan was elected governor of California—next to president, the biggest job in the nation.
A motorcade led by police motorcycles moves through crowds of people. Reagan walks into the State House.	What the new governor inherited was a state of crisis. California was faced with a 194 million dollar deficit and was spending a million dollars a day more than it was taking in. The state was on the brink of bankruptcy.
Reagan takes a seat at a desk with many microphones on it. Reporters are taking notes. A closeup of Reagan talking appears on the screen.	Governor Reagan became the greatest tax reformer in the state's history. When Governor Reagan left office, the 194 million dollar deficit had been transformed into a 554 million dollar surplus.
Superimposed on a view of the California Capitol are the words, "We exaggerate very little when we say that Reagan has saved the state from bankruptcy."	The *San Francisco Examiner* said "Governor Reagan has saved the state from bankruptcy."
Reagan and Bush are pictured together, and their names, "Reagan and Bush," appear on the screen.	The time is now for strong leadership. Reagan for president.

APPENDIX 20. "Shoots from Hip" (Carter, 1980)

Video	Audio
A man faces the camera and talks as "Sacramento" appears on the screen beneath him.	MAN 1: His problem as governor was the same problem as he has now. Namely that he shoots from the hip.

Another man faces the camera and talks as "San Francisco" appears on the screen beneath him.	MAN 2: He once stated that "if you have seen one redwood tree, you have seen them all."
The Sacramento man reappears.	MAN 1: His statement about "if people are going to have a blood bath on campuses, let's get it over with . . . "
A balding man appears and talks as "Los Angeles" appears on the screen beneath him.	MAN 3: Some of the recent goofs that he has pulled with regard to China . . . .
Another "Los Angeles" man appears.	MAN 4: When you are dealing with a government like Russia . . .
	ANNOUNCER: A lot of Californians feel pretty good about Ronald Reagan, but others feel a sense of continuing concern.
A woman appears as "Sacramento" appears on the screen below.	
A black man from San Francisco appears.	MAN 5: I think he makes a lot of people uneasy. He certainly makes me feel uneasy.
Another San Francisco man appears.	MAN 6: I think he is the kind of guy that shoots from the hip.
The woman from Sacramento reappears.	WOMAN: He did shoot from the hip.
A man from Fresno appears on the screen.	MAN 7: He shoots from the hip.
The first man from Sacramento reappears.	MAN 1: As a governor, it really didn't make that much difference because the state of California doesn't have a foreign policy, and the state of California isn't going to be going to war with a foreign nation. And he was just amusing. But as president, that's scary.
One of the Los Angeles men reappears.	MAN : Well, my decision is made. I'm going to stick with President Carter.

A drawing of Carters appears and the words "Re-elect President Carter" appear in the lower left corner of the screen.	ANNOUNCER: On November 4th, re-elect President Carter.

APPENDIX 21. "Archie Testimonial" (Kennedy, 1980)

Video	Audio
Carroll O'Connor sits facing the camera; he is wearing an open-collared shirt and a leisure jacket.	O'CONNOR: Friends, Herbert Hoover hid out in the White House too, responding to desperate problems with patriotic pronouncements, and we got a hell of a depression. But I'm afraid Jimmy's depression is going to be worse than Herbert's. I'm supporting Senator Kennedy because he is out there facing issues: inflation, sky high prices, an almost worthless dollar, unemployment. I trust Ted Kennedy. I believe in him in every way, folks.
The words "Kennedy for President" appear on a red background with a small picture of Kennedy to the right.	ANNOUNCER: Kennedy for president. Let's fight back.

APPENDIX 22. "Out of Gas" (Republican National Congressional Committee, 1980)

Video	Audio
The camera focuses on a license plate reading "US Congress—Democrat." Then the camera zooms out to picture a large luxury car moving down the street. A Tip O'Neill look-alike is driving as a younger beside him speaks.	YOUNG MAN: Congressman, I think we're running out of gas.

Video	Audio
O'Neill smiles and shakes his head as the younger man appears more nervous. They pass a gas station.	O'Neill: Oh no. Announcer: It isn't as if the Democratic Congress didn't have a warning. They have been told for twenty-five years.
The drive continues with the O'Neill look alike appearing complacent and the younger man more nervous.	Young Man: Congressman, we are running out of gas! Announcer: The last two presidents sent urgent warnings. Young Man: Congressman, look at the gauge.
The car passes a gas station and the young man turns and looks back.	Announcer: The Democrats who have controlled congress for twenty-five years ignored them. They just went blindly down the road.
They continue their drive.	Young Man: Ah, Congressman, this is getting serious. O'Neill: O forget it boy, forget it.
The car is pictured from a distance as it rolls to a stop.	Announcer: The Democrats not only failed to pass a workable energy program, they actually passed laws that cut back on energy explorations here at home, discouraged alternative energy sources, and made us dependent on foreign oil.
The young man mimics the O'Neill look alike and has an "I told you so" expression.	O'Neill: Hey, we're out of gas.
The O'Neill look alike gets out of the car. The words "Vote Republican for a change" appear on the screen below the stopped car.	Announcer: The Democrats are out of gas. We need some new ideas. Vote Republican for a change.

APPENDIX 23. "Why Not the Best" (National Conservative Political Action Committee, 1980)

Video	Audio
A black and white photograph of Carter appears on a table.	ANNOUNCER: In 1976, Jimmy Carter said, "Why not the best?" Let's look at what he gave us.
A photo of Andrew Young appears.	Andrew Young, Carter's UN Ambassador who called Iran's Ayatollah Komeni "a saint": forced to resign after lying to president. (*Camera clicks as if moving frames.*)
A photo of Bert Lance appears.	Bert Lance: also forced to resign.
A photo of Peter Borne appears.	Dr. Peter Borne, the Carter drug expert: forced to resign after supplying drugs to a White House staff member.
Photos appear rapidly of: William Miller Cyrus Vance Hamilton Jordan	(*Camera clicks quickly as each picture appears and another follows.*) ANNOUNCER: And the list goes on.
The words "Ronald Reagan for President" appear on a blue background.	If you want a president whose judgments you can trust for a change, then vote for Ronald Reagan for President.

• 3 •

Fighting Back

American Political Parties Take to the Airwaves

Barry Kolar

Since first coming into the American political scene in the late 1700s political parties have been dynamic, changing organizations, varying from a loose grouping of like-minded politicos to highly organized "machines." While the parties have changed throughout their history, their goal of obtaining increased political power, generally through the electoral process, has changed little. From Jeffersonian Democrats to Reagan Republicans, the pursuit of political power has been central.

But like the parties themselves, the methods of obtaining this power have also changed over time. Journalists, political scientists, and politicians have chronicled these changes, explaining, or at least attempting to explain, why they occurred and what impact they had or would have on the American political scene. Perhaps the greatest change, certainly in recent history, has been that brought about through the growth of mass media, especially television.

During the past three decades television has grown to play a major role in the lives of most Americans. In 1946 there were only eight thousand television sets in America, many concentrated in the Northeast (Sterling & Haight, 1978, p. 377). Since that time, the number of televisions in American households has grown dramatically, to the point where close to 98 percent of all homes have at least one television set (Sterling & Haight, 1978, p. 373). In 1976 there were television sets in more than 70 million homes in America (Sterling & Haight, 1978, p. 377). And Americans are spending more time in front of the tubes. In 1955 the average American household spent 4.5 hours in front of the television each day; by 1975 that figure had grown to 6.26 (Sterling & Haight, 1978, p. 374).

Politicians have taken note of this increase, and the amount of money spent on television advertising has risen almost as fast as the growth of the media itself. The year 1952 marked the birth of national political television advertising with Richard Nixon's famous "Checkers" speech and Dwight Eisenhower's use of sixty second commercials during his campaign (Sabato, 1981, p. 111). From this beginning, television advertising has grown enormously: in the 1964 presidential election, ten thousand spot announcements were made in the top seventy-five markets; in 1968 Richard Nixon and Hubert Humphrey spent a combined $18 million for television; and in 1972 candidates for all levels of office in the United States spent a total of $59.6 million for television ads (Sabato, 1981, pp. 111–14). Political consultants today say that up to 70 percent of each campaign budget is spent on television (Sabato, 1981, p. 190).

This dramatic change in both the way we as a society communicate and the way candidates for office communicate with us had a major impact on American political parties. Prior to television, candidates and parties had to rely upon large numbers of people, using a variety of methods, to communicate information about a candidate or an election. While advertising existed, there was no dominant national medium, no one source that could reach all of the country at one time. Parties developed accordingly, involving large numbers of individuals in organizations often called "machines." While these groups varied greatly in their organizational strength and political power, they did serve as the basic building blocks of the national party with which they were affiliated, performing functions necessary for its survival.

With the growth of television, this has changed. No longer do candidates rely as heavily on individual contact. As is evident from Sabato's information, television now serves as the primary means of reaching voters in national elections (Sabato, 1981, p. 111). Candidates can use television to go directly to voters, without having to rely on political organizational hierarchies or an army of volunteer workers.

While it is evident that television has changed elections, and thus political parties, it is yet unclear how parties are changing to deal with this. Researchers in recent years have seen parties declining in power and influence over voters. A growing number of voters call themselves independents (Pomper, 1975, pp. 18–31) or are willing to vote for candidates of both parties (DeVries & Tarrance, 1972, p. 30). Yet political parties do not seem to be willing to give up their power to television. Instead, parties are changing to adapt to a political world where television is a major influence. During the 1982 campaign season I worked for the National Republican Congressional Committee (NRCC) in its television advertising division. From my experience there, and through information gained by interviewing top mass media officials from both parties, I offer the thesis that American political parties are not declining, but are instead altering their role and function in the electoral process to remain a primary source of information and influence to voters.

LITERATURE REVIEW

With the beginning of empirical research in political science, researchers started studying the American electorate, trying to determine what factors influenced voter decisions. The first efforts, performed during the '40s and '50s, involved a simple survey of voters on what caused them to vote the way they did. Long-term influences were considered central, short-term influences were seen as only playing a small role (Lazarsfeld, Berelson & Gaudet, 1944).

Since these early studies, researchers' methods, like the society they were being applied to, changed greatly. And their findings also changed. Other factors besides partisan loyalty were found to influence voter decisions, causing some observers and political scientists to see a decline in political party power (Pomper, 1975, pp. 38–41; Miller & Levitin, 1976, pp. 90–91). Not all researchers have reached this conclusion. Instead, some cite different types of research and recent changes in the American parties as proof that the parties still exert considerable political power (Sabato, 1981, pp. 290–97).

In the Beginning

The first researchers to look at American electoral behavior were based at Columbia University. They discarded the rational theory of voting which had dominated political thought up to that point (Lazarsfeld et al., 1944). These researchers used a panel technique study to survey voters in Erie County, Ohio, conducting interviews of the same people monthly from May to November. They found the vote decisions of 70 percent of the people corresponded to the vote tendencies prevailing among groups with social characteristics similar to their own. (Lazarsfeld et al., 1944). They also found that the strongly partisan exposed themselves to more political communications than those less interested and that those exposed were more likely to attend to that of their own party. Thus, the authors concluded, the majority of political communcation reached persons least amenable to conversion (Lazarsfeld et al., 1944).

A second generation of researchers working out of the Survey Research Center at the University of Michigan also rejected the rational voter theory, instead saying voting decisions were made based on psychological factors, not social factors (Campbell, Converse, Miller & Stokes, 1960, p. 13). These studies still looked at and placed overriding importance on long-term factors such as party identification for voting decisions. They also said these long-term factors are determined by various attitudes held by the voters.

A Changing World

Since these studies, theory and techniques used to study voting have advanced, and consequently our understanding of electoral decision making has also advanced. We now understand that it is a combination of numerous factors, working in numerous ways, that results in a voter decision. In Nimmo's *Political Communication and Public Opinion in America* (1978), the author writes of American voters as being active, acting towards objects on the basis of the meaning they have to them. Voters interpret campaign stimuli on the basis of their past experiences, present position, and future expectations. This is not to say that voters act rationally; rather, they selectively perceive the parties, candidates, issues, and events, and give them meaning to base their voting decisions. Because voters base their interpretations on campaign stimuli, the campaign takes its form and acquires its meaning for voters through communication. Thus, communication is the important variable of study, not an individual's attributes or attitudes, as early theorists had said (Nimmo, 1978, p. 370).

Along with this development in research and theory there have been important changes in the society being studied. Few recent authors studying the changing role of American political parties fail to note the dramatic growth in television and its influence on voters. The Aspen Institutes' *Guide to Communication Industry Trends* shows just how dramatic the growth of television has been. In 1950, the average American household watched 4.51 hours of television per day. By 1975 that figure was 6.23 (Sterling & Haight, 1978, p. 366). In 1948, only 172,000 homes in America had television sets. By 1976 that figure was 70.5 million, or between 97 and 98 percent of all American homes (Sterling & Haight, 1978, p. 377).

Of the authors who have studied the relationship between the power of political parties and the growth of the media, those writing in recent years have made the strongest statements on the media's influence. Some call television the new political god (Crotty & Jacobson, 1980, p. 67). Others have called the growth of mass media the most important factor in reshaping the electoral scene (Wattenberg, 1982, p. 216).

But even before these authors addressed the issue, and even before television reached its current saturation of American society, some authors recognized the importance of the change they saw coming. Writing in 1942, V. O. Key said the parties' function of managing opinion and representation was being eroded due to the growth in methods available to appeal directly to the masses. And in 1956, Stanley Kelley wrote in *Professional Public Relations and Political Power* about the growth of television and other new mass media. He said the public relations man was using the mass media to organize and direct the actions of the electorate, a duty previously performed by political bosses. "As those who aim at control of government come to regard mass persuasion as their central problem, then the specialist in mass persuasion will rise correspondingly in influence" (Kelley, 1956, p. 210).

In the 1960s, Robert MacNeil chronicled the growth of political usage of the mass media, saying television had become the machine through which American people are "reached, persuaded and normally informed, more extensively and homogeneously than ever before" (MacNeil, 1968, ix). Further, he saw this growth of television as a communications medium causing a radical change in American political communications.

Edward Dryer (1972) concurred, saying that the mass media, by becoming available to an increasingly large audience and by being used by more political candidates and parties, had effectively penetrated all segments of the electorate with electoral information. He concluded that this penetration of information, coming to voters not directly from the party, would erode the stabilizing influence associated with partisan loyalty.

From those works on mass media and politics, one sees a general description of the growing usage of mass media and projections of its effects on politics. Other authors have looked at the situation from a different perspective, focusing on the party and how it has changed during the past few decades. While noting the growing influence of the media, these authors are more concerned with how it and other factors have prompted change in the American party system.

Independent Voters

One of the major trends seen in these works is the development of the independent voter. While not all studies claim mass media is the only cause of voters either not identifying as strongly as before with a party or voting a split ticket, almost all authors agree it is an important factor in this trend.

Several authors use data from the Survey Research Center at Michigan University to document a growth in the number of independent voters in America (Flanigan & Zingale, 1975, pp. 61–63; Miller & Levitan, 1976, pp. 90–91). While these authors still see the parties as important determinants in voter decisions, they also see a growing number of voters who don't identify strongly with any political party.

Gerald Pomper's (1975) study of the data points to a decline in the role of the party in influencing voters. He sees voter decisions being made increasingly on the basis of issues, not parties. Pomper's independent voter is younger, more interested in politics, and of a higher social class than the traditionally viewed independent voter. This voter is also more influenced by the mass media, which Pomper says has replaced the party as the chief source of information for voters.

Warren Miller and Teresa Levitin also look at similar data, focusing on the interrelated concerns of voters and describing how they mesh to form the ideologies of the new politics, with its New Liberals, Silent Minority, and Center groups replacing the parties as sources of identification for voters (Miller & Levitan, 1976, pp. 90–91).

Two other authors who look at the increase in independent voters see less dramatic changes than do Pomper and Miller and Levitan. William Flanigan (1975) says the independent voters are less informed and less interested participants than their partisan counterparts. He points to data identifying parties as remaining the dominant source of both political stability in the U.S. and of political influence on the voter.

Herbert Asher (1980) agrees that parties are still the dominant and stabilizing force in American politics. He says the parties perform a real function in allowing voters an economical method to collect and evaluate data about political affairs and maintain stabillity in the political system. Shifts in political party identification, he says, occur as responses to real world events and that most of those who predict the party's demise are seeing only shifts in degrees in voter identification (Asher, 1980, pp. 63–70).

Another study on the growth of the independent voter was done by Walter DeVries and V. Lance Tarrance. Instead of using survey data on how voters identified themselves, the pair used voting results to identify independent voters. They classify independents as voters who split their votes between candidates from more than one party. Their findings show an increase in split-ticket voting for both president and congress from 3.2 percent in 1920 to 31.6 percent in 1968. This finding is similar to SRC data that shows about one-third of the population identified as independent (DeVries & Tarrance, 1972, p. 30).

Independent Candidates

Another trend seen by researchers is an increase in independent candidates. Several authors have pointed to the use of the mass media, especially television, as a liberator of candidates from political parties (Wattenberg, 1982, p. 216; Emerson, 1982, p. 53; Crotty & Jacobson, 1980, p. 65; and Patterson, 1982, pp. 33–34). Before the country was saturated by television, candidates were forced to go through the party system to reach voters. No other nationwide network of political communications existed (Patterson, 1982, p. 26).

In an article for the Academy of Political Science, Thomas Patterson (1982, p. 26) asserts that the power of the parties declined and that of the media increased in the 1960s when television became a better link to voters than the party. He said the party was never a totally dependable means of reaching voters but that until television came along there was never a more effective method available.

Patterson also notes television as the most effective method of communicating basic politics to voters and the best method of reaching voters who have little interest in politics (1982, pp. 33–34).

In another article for the Academy, David Emerson (1982, p. 53) also writes that candidates have learned they can use the new technology of the mass media independent of the party, thus controlling their own campaigns.

In Martin Wattenberg's book (1982, p. 216) he describes the candidate's ability to establish direct contact with voters as the most important factor in reshaping the electoral scene in recent years. He points to figures showing a decline of party line voting in congressional elections from 1958 to 1978 and information showing a negative relationship between mass media use in political advertising and party salience, regardless of whether or not a strong party organization exists. Much of this advertising, he says, is oriented towards the candidate, not the party (Wattenberg, 1982, p. 223).

William Crotty and Gary Jacobson (1980, p. 65) concur that television has replaced the political party as the primary link between candidates and voters. Not only do they see this as the most common link, but also the best. The authors cite studies showing television to be the most trusted and dependable medium for providing voters with information (Crotty & Jacobson, 1980, p. 67). In addition, Crotty and Jacobson point out that with television replacing parties as the chief link to the American voter, those who understand and control the media are the new powers in politics. "The role of the political parties in campaigns has given way to the technology of television centered campaigns built on polls and run by media and public relations experts" (Crotty & Jacobson, 1980, p. 65).

Masters of the Media

While authors in recent years have made almost a 180 degree turn from their counterparts in the '40s and '50s on the effect the mass media has on voting, few authors have tracked down where the electoral power now lies. There seems to be a consensus, however, that the mass media in the 1980s does play an important role in voting decisions, but the question of who holds and directs this power has not been completely answered.

One early answer came from Kelley who said "To give the public relations man responsibility for the expenditure of campaign funds for the selection and use of the media is to go far towards making him a leading influence in shaping the public image of parties and candidates" (1956, p. 211). Kelley notes that the power does not come to these people without reason. He points to the growing technical and artistic sophistication of the mass media as reasons why someone with special professional skills is needed to be brought into the political process.

A more recent work by Larry Sabato takes what Kelley saw as a potential situation and writes of how it has occurred. Sabato (1981, p. 12) cites survey information from 1972 to 1973 that has shown just how predominant political consultants have become in American electoral politics. The survey showed that 168 of 208 candidates running for state office employed at least one political consultant. Of sixty-seven U.S. Senate candidates sixty-one used consultants. Thirty-eight of forty-two governor candidates used consultants. The author says consultants grew to this stature partly through changes in fundraising procedures that allowed individual candidates to afford paid staff and advisors but mostly through the change in campaigns brought about by the development of mass communications. He traces the modern-day consultant to early campaign strategists and public relations professionals who grew more powerful as the media side of campaigns took a larger and larger role in the overall electoral effort (Sabato, 1981, pp. 10–13). Part of this rise in stature, Sabato writes, is of their own doing. Consultants spend almost as much time developing their own image or mystique as they do for their candidates. In addition, they operate independently of party or interest groups, which both enhances their personal influence on a campaign and weakens the party's influence. Sabato says consultants have developed their role to the extent that they have accumulated unrivaled and unchecked power and influence in a system that is partly their own handiwork (Sabato, 1981, p. 8).

Sabato does point to the National Republican Congressional Committee's operation as an example of how parties can fight back to regain power from consultants. He points to the NRCC's advantage in economy and experience as factors that have lured candidates back to a reliance on party rather than consultants (Sabato, 1981, pp. 290–97).

Another work that suggests the power of media practitioners is a recent book by Edwin Diamond and Stephen Bates (1984, p. 12). The authors interviewed political marketers and top media practitioners to find out how their efforts in producing short political commercials—labeled by the authors as the dominant form of persuasion in American political campaigns today—has affected the electoral process and specific candidates.

Lynda Lee Kaid (1981, p. 250) also stresses the importance of political advertising in modern campaigns. She points out that candidates, or their media consultants, have almost total control over the form and content of political advertising and cites studies showing cognitive and affective responses to political advertising (Kaid, 1981, pp. 262–63). In addition, she notes that even when it was believed that political advertising had only a limited effect on voters, there was a gigantic increase in expenditures from political advertising (Kaid, 1981, p. 282). This suggests that at least among the sources of political advertising, there has for some time been a genuine belief of its effectiveness in influencing voters.

As we can see from reviewing research on electoral politics and the mass media, much has changed since the early studies in the 1940s. Sophisticated research techniques and advanced theories have provided more accurate pictures of what is actually going on in the electoral world. And, perhaps more importantly, the world of electoral politics has changed dramatically. Television beams messages and pictures simultaneously to millions of Americans while not long ago it was possible to reach only a few thousand voters at one time. And consultants draw six-figure salaries advising candidates on how best to get their image across to voters.

Many researchers and observers see the parties as losing political power. The number of independent voters is increasing as are independent candidates. But there also seems to be agreement that parties still hold some real power, either because they provide the basic structure of American politics as Asher (1980, pp. 50–51) might say or because the parties are doing something to change their role in electoral politics as Sabato (1981, pp. 290–97) suggests. Determining how much power or influence the parties actually do have and are able to keep in the coming years are questions that should remain of interest to both the political scientist and the participant in practical politics.

METHODOLOGY

The bulk of the information for this paper comes from interviews conducted with NRCC Communications Director Ed Blakely and Democratic media consultant Bob Hershfeld and from my personal experience as television production coordinator for the NRCC during the 1982 campaign. Along with casual conversations during 1982 with Blakely and then division director Steve Sandler, I conducted a lengthy formal interview with Blakely in December 1982. During this formal interview Blakely traced the history of the committee's television advertising efforts and explained the reasons certain programs were inaugurated and/or dropped. He cited several in-house or privately commissioned surveys to support these decisions. Blakely also supplied statistical information on how many campaigns the party was currently and had been involved in and what role the party played in those races. Further information on the 1984 television program was provided in interviews with Blakely.

Information concerning the television advertising program of the Democratic party also came through interviews. Media consultant Bob Hershfeld provided the bulk of this information in an April 1984 interview.

In addition to these interviews, I was able to use my personal experience with the NRCC as a resource. Along with having access to the NRCC's video library of political advertising tapes, I had the opportunity to travel with the committee's video crew to congressional campaigns across the country, meeting candidates and incumbents, and learning what role they believed the ads played in their campaigns. I was able to see the inner workings of the committee, observing how decisions were made on advertising approaches and styles, and how campaign efforts were coordinated through the national committee.

This combination of information obtained by interview and personal experience within the program provides timely insight into what American political parties are doing to combat a perceived decline in influence. This information provides, at one point, a different perspective from voter surveys on the role parties are playing in influencing voters. At the same time, it provides additional knowledge on the communications sources, a part in the communication process often ignored in political communcation research in general and political advertising research inparticular (Kaid, 1981, p. 253). Knowledge of this source activity aids in the understanding of the political communcation process and ultimately the role political parties are playing and will play in the American political process.

Republicans Pioneer the Airways

Richard Nixon had resigned the presidency and Watergate was a household word. Democrats scored big wins in 1974 House and Senate races, and '76 wasn't much better for Repuplicans; Gerald Ford lost and Jimmy Carter won. As Republican campaign strategists approached the 1978 elections, they knew something had to be done to change the image of both the party and its candidates.

That something eventually became America Today, a first ever national media campaign paid for by the Republican party to promote the Republican party and its officeholders as honest, caring people. The project was conceived by party officials, and much of the creative and production work was done by the National Republican Congressional Committee staff.

Along with America Today, the NRCC in 1978 also launched a program of producing television and radio advertisements for individual congressional candidates. The aim of this program was to provide expertise and professionally produced television commercials for a fraction of the cost candidates would have to pay an ad agency.

Both programs proved so successful that the party expanded them to the point that the NRCC media division's budget for 1984 was $2.5 million, up from $750,000 in 1978. A stable of writers, producers, media buyers, cameramen, and video tape editors made up the division's twenty-one member staff, and almost $1 millino in editing equipment was installed to put the NRCC's facilities on the same level as Washington area production houses. In 1984 the NRCC produced ads for more than 115 candidates.

As further proof of the program's success, it was imitated by the Democratic National Committee. Starting with a series of institutional or brand ads in 1982, the Democratic party steadily expanded its national media program, adding editing facilities in 1983 and producing another series of national ads for the 1984 election.

Officials from both parties are firm believers in their media programs and what they do to help elect candidates. In a day when the number of people who identify with either party is declining (Pomper, 1975, pp. 31–35) and more people are likely to vote a split-ticket ballot (DeVries & Tarrance, 1972, p. 30), party officials see the institutional or brand ads as giving an image or an identity for their party, something voters can rally around and become loyal to. And the ads produced for individual candidates tie them to the national party organization early. If the campaign ads are seen as playing an important role in the election, this further reinforces the tie between candidate and party.

Nationally televised institutional advertising and televised candidate advertising are becoming important functions of the national parties. While most political scientists and observers agree that the parties have declined in influence over the past few decades, due at least in part to the emergence of television, we now see the parties using this very instrument as a means of reclaiming influence over voters and candidates. Their ability to function, in part, as a media service agency could determine the role American political parties will play in future elections.

It Began with American Today

A survey conducted during the 1976 election told Republican party officials something they didn't want to hear—being labeled a Republican was hurting their candidates. The survey showed that even the party's strongest candidates were losing 5 to 10 percent of the vote because they were identified as Republicans. To alter that, party officials decided something drastic had to be done before the 1978 elections.

The director of communications for the NRCC then was Jay Bryant. He and a group of consultants got together in 1977 to develop a program that would both improve the image of the Republican party and build party credibility, so its candidates could later address issues. Another function of the American Today series was to break the stereotype of all Republicans being like Richard Nixon or rich, country club members.

Television was chosen as the medium for the thrust because of its ability to reach large numbers of people and to convey an image. Bryant decided the ads would focus on personal concerns of average people; nothing political wouls be presented. Polling determined specific wants and needs to be addressed in the spots. The ads features incumbent Republican congressmen, dressed casually, addressing mostly consumer problems. In one ad, a congressman was going through a CPR course, while in another a congressman gave tips for planning and enjoying a family vacation.

Many of the ads also tried to get feedback from viewers, with an offer for additional information free of charge. On the vacation planning ad, the committee offered a free travel map to anyone who wrote in. The series of five minute ads were distributed to fifty-eight stations in eighteen markets and ran in cycles of three weeks on, two weeks off, from January to August of 1978. Total production cost was $1.5 million.

The ads were pre- and post-tested in Evanston, Illinois, and Cedar Rapids, Iowa. Robert Teeter's Marketing Opinion Research firm study of the ads found they were successful in producing changes in the evaluation of the GOP. The study found viewers' favorable impressions of the Democrats had declined 3 to 13 percent on rating scales for nine attributions, and that Republicans were viewed as more caring than had previously been believed (Teeter, 1979, pp. 38–39).

In October, the second portion of the NRCC's 1978 effort began. Four 30 second spots were produced and distributed that portrayed Republicans presenting an alternative view on four major campaign issues. This program was to be an extension of America Today, with the party's stronger image and credibility making its view of the issues more easily accepted by voters. About $10,000 to $15,000 was spent in producing these four spots and $200,000 was spent to buy air time. A final $15,000 was spent to purchase election eve air time for a five minute address from NRCC chairman Rep. Guy Vander Jagt.

On to 1980

With some success at the polls—the Republican Party picked up twelve congressional seats, three Senate seats and six governorship—and survey results showing the ads were part of the reason the GOP made these gains, Republican officials began plans in 1979 to expand the program for the 1980 presidential and congressional elections. The first project developed by the NRCC in 1979 was a series of ads called "Issues of the '80s." These spots, which presented Republican views on various issues, were test marketed but dropped when communications director Jay Bryant left the committee.

With "Issues of the '80s" put by the wayside, probably the most well known GOP ad program was begun. The three Republican campaign committees—The National Republican Congressional Committee, the Republican Senatorial Committee and the Republican National Committee—organized and funded the Republican Marketing Group to produce and air institutional campaign ads beginning in January 1980. Originally, the project was budgeted at $4.5 million for production and media buying, but it was later to nearly $10 million.

To produce the Vote Republican for a Change campaign, the GOP brought on Steve Sandler to head the NRCC's communication division. Sandler had extensive experience working in product advertising for a major New York ad agency along with a background in political campaign work. In addition to Sandler, the Marketing Group hired Jim Killough as a consultant to help produce the ads. Killough had done the institutional ads for the Tory party in England in 1979 when the conservatives and Margaret Thatcher swept into power. Humphrey, Browning, and MacDougal originally was selected as the Marketing Group's ad agency to place the ads.

When the Vote Republican for a Change campaign was first conceived, it was to be a national advertising effort composed of three two-week waves of commercials. The first wave, beginning in January, was to be made up exclusively of attack ads. A second wave, beginning in April was to be divided between ads attacking the Democratic party and ads pointing to the positive side of the Republican party. A final wave, beginning in July, was to be made up of all positive ads. This strategy lasted through the first wave of ads. That's when party officials received results from test marketing that showed the ad's effects were far surpassing their expectations. More money was pumped into the program and more attack spots were produced.

In probably the best remembered ad in the campaign, an actor resembling House Speaker Thomas P. "Tip" O'Neill rumbles down the road recklessly in a big black sedan, ignoring a passenger's fears that the car is running out of gas. When the car finally stalls, the announcer says the Democrats have run out of gas and urges viewers to "Vote Republican for a Change."

Several of the ads attacked Democrats for hurting working people. In conversations set in repair shops and offices, actors decried the hardships Democrat-induced inflation caused them. One ad featured an unemployed steel worker in Baltimore walking through an empty factory talking about being out of work and asking, "If Democrats are so good for the working people, how come so many people aren't working?" Interestingly enough, this same out-of-work steelworker appeared in a 1982 Democratic ad denouncing his 1980 appearance and offering his support to Democratic candidates.

In all, fourteen televisions advertisements aired nationally during the nine-month period leading up to the 1980 presidential and congressional elections. The ad campaign consisted of one five minute ad and a variety of sixty second, thirty second, and ten second commercials. Most of the two-week waves consisted of buys in forty-eight to fifty-two selected television market areas and some network broadcasts. Each market had between twelve and twenty spots aired per wave with a higher frequency in selected market areas during the final two weeks of the campaign. One casualty of the campaign was the Humphrey, Browning, and MacDougal agency which the Marketing Group fired midway through the program because the Marketing Group didn't believe their account was big enough to receive the amount of attention from the agency they wanted. After the agency was fired, the ads were produced and distributed by NRCC, RNC, and RSC staff.

The ad program was lauded by advertising experts and political consultants who credited the campaign as being one factor in the GOP's 1980 sweep in which Ronald Reagan captured the presidency and the party regained control of the Senate and gained thirty-three seats in the House of Representatives.

Disorganization and Disappointment in 1982

With the success of the 1980 ad program, Republican officials were anxious to continue the effort into the 1982 election season. Talk around the NRCC focused on how to pick up the necessary House seats to take complete control of the Congress. With fund raising running ahead of schedule, the Marketing Network began plans to start airing ads in October 1981.

These ads were different from those first appearing in 1980. Instead of attacking Democratic policies, these ads were scheduled to begin appearing at the same time that President Reagan's economic program and income tax cuts were going into effect. All three ads aired promoted the Reagan economic program. The first ad was of joggers running in a distance race, working hard and struggling to the finish. The announcer voiced over copy explaining that the road to economic well-being in the country was not an easy one, but that with hard work and courage the Republican economic program would bring about a healthy economy. A second ad showed a line of blue collar workers at a pay window. One worker asks if there has been a mistake in his paycheck: he has been given too much money. A voice from above informs him that it is no mistake, but the result of the Republican tax cut. The third ad featured an animated character called the Federal Tax Bite that went around causing economic hardship until being leashed by the Republican party.

About $1.3 million was spent to produce and air the three ads nationally. The ads were created and produced by the NRCC with outside production and distribution help. After these ads appeared, the Marketing Group planned to continue their media effort with waves of ads appearing regularly until the 1982 election. But a reorganization of the Republican National Committee caused the marketing group to break up, so until March 1982 the party was off the airways.

In March, the RNC and NRCC again united to televise campaign advertising (the Republic Senatorial Committee lacked funds to continue in the cooperative group). The two committees hired the New York ad agency Korey and Kay, hoping a smaller agency would give them better service than Humphrey, Browning, and MacDougal. Korey and Kay produced two spots for the committees. In one, a judge reads the Democratic party's will, which leaves deficits and inflation to the American public. In the second spot, a family climbs into a dusty, long-stored camper now that the Republicans have restored economic health to the nation. The committee spent $1.5 million buying time for the spots and $145,000 for production costs and a retainer fee for the ad agency.

Officials from both committees were unhappy with the spots and with Kory and Kay, so shortly after the ads appeared, the agency was fired and each committee began its own separate media program. The RNC hired media consultant Hal Larsen to produce ads for spot market buys, while the NRCC hired Bailey Deardorf to produce a major national ad campaign.

The results of the two programs were quite different. The RNC's most widely distributed spot was of an elderly postman delivering social security checks, defending President Reagan and the Republican party against charges that they were out to cut social security. The Bailey Deardorf spots were all man-on-the-street ads using the tagline "stay the course." Shot mostly at the World's Fair in Knoxville, Tennessee, the spots featured a variety of people saying they believed it was best to stick with President Reagan's economic policies, to give him a chance. In all the ads, the slogan, "stay the course," was repeated. The NRCC spent between $3.5 to $4 million to air the spots, with some money for the project coming from the RNC and RSC.

The Program Continues in 1984

As the 1984 presidential and congressional elections approached, Republican strategists took stock. The election of 1980 had provided them the best of all possible worlds, i.e., they were the party out of power designing an advertising campaign to attack the Democratic presidential and congressional dominance. By 1982 things had changed since Republicans now controlled both the presidency and the U.S. Senate. A simple attack on the "ins" was no longer possible. Still Republicans were able to suggest in 1982 that the ills of the nation would be cured if voters returned a Republican House as well as Senate. Voters did not comply. But, 1984 was the worst of all possible worlds; Republicans had to devise a way of calling for a Republican controlled House and Senate while at the same time trying to defend the Republican administration in the White House.

To meet this problem Republicans hired the Tusday Team for consultation. Working with the Republican National Committee and the NRCC (but only briefly with the Republican Senatorial Committee) the team designed a $12 million nationwide advertising campaign. The televised campaign was three-pronged. First, to put the onus on a Democratically controlled House of Representatives there were "wedge" ads. They attacked Democrats by focusing upon legislative proposals which had Republican administration backing, and which had won majority support in the Republican Senate, but which had been stalled in the Democratic House. The call for a balanced budget amendment was one example. Second, a series of televised ads dealt with the "fairness" issue, i.e., attempted to respond to Democratic charges that Republican policies were insensitive and unfair to blacks, Hispanics, women, and others. A third televised ad campaign sought to attract what Republican opinion polls indicated as a promising constituency, namely, people eighteen to twenty-four years of age expressing growing support for Republicans. In addition to televised ads directed at these three areas there were also political commercials on radio and special advertising inserts placed in the Reader's Digest.

Candidate Advertising: A Humble Beginning

The early production of candidate advertisements was not as well planned or sophisticated as the effort put together for the national media campaigns. The NRCC had for years been involved in consulting individual congressional campaigns on how to raise money, organize workers, handle public relations, and other aspects of running a campaign. But their involvement in the production of television and radio ads in the 1978 election came more by accident than by plan. Several candidates that year, like any year, had a need for writing and technical expertise in television, but had little money to pay for it. Slowly, NRCC communication division staffers started doing work for candidates, mostly with equipment they had on hand for filming events on Capitol Hill. When the election finally rolled around, the NRCC had produced spots for eight candidates. The efforts drew praise from candidates and party officials, who saw the project as a tool for getting low cost yet quality television advertising for candidates who had to operate on a limited budget.

1980: A Major Effort

Before the 1980 election season, NRCC executive director Steven Stockmeyer and other party officials agreed to expand the candidate advertising program to make available full service writing, production, and postproduction to incumbents and congressional candidates. The committee recruited four college students to train in an extensive six-month school, teaching advertising, television production, creative services, writing, polling, research, and media buying. After the training course, the four were sent into the field as producers under the supervision of their division head Steve Sandler and assistant director Ed Blakely.

The result was a massive expansion of the 1978 effort. In 1980, the NRCC provided radio and/or television services for 115 candidates (52 challengers and 63 incumbents). In television services, the NRCC did the creative work for 41 candidates (26 challengers and 15 incumbents), taped or filmed commercials for 80 candidates (33 challengers and 47 incumbents), and edited spots for 69 candidates (38 challengers and 31 incumbents). The NRCC spent more than 441 hours shooting tape or film for candidates and edited 309 separate commercials. The NRCC also did the media buying for 37 candidates (24 challengers and 13 incumbents).

Again, much of the ad work was done for candidates considered to have a chance of winning but who lacked money. The expansion of the program aided more of this sort of candidate and was seen as a factor in the Republican Party's gaining thirty-three seats in the House in 1980. Many of the candidates elected in the 1980 sweep were those who benefited from the candidate advertising service.

A good example of how the candidate advertising program worked in 1980 can be seen in the Jack Fields campaign in Houston. A former president of the student body at Baylor, Fields was only three years out of law school when he challenged seven-term incumbent Bob Eckhardt in the eastern Harris County district that included a substantial blue collar work force along with several Republican suburbs. As was the case in many of the races handled by the NRCC, a three-person production crew spent several days in Houston traveling with Fields as he campaigned, shooting some prearranged scenes and some extemporaneous campaigning.

The raw footage was edited down to a series of commercials at the NRCC studios in Washington and distributed to Houston stations by

NRCC media buyers. In a race where both candidates raised and spent large sums of money—Fields raised $800,343, Eckhardt $454,253 (Ehrenhalt, 1983, p. 1464)—the expertise and saving brought about by the NRCC was credited by Fields as providing a key advantage in a race decided by fewer than five thousand votes.

Uncertainty in 1982

The year 1982 was difficult and confusing for the NRCC as it approached its candidate advertising program. Redistricting of congressional districts had altered many established districts, sometimes even pitting incumbent Republicans against each other in primary elections. And, through delays from court cases and state legislative battles, redistricting left some states up in the air as to which candidates would be running in which districts and which districts would be winnable and which wouldn't. Because of these problems and the resulting uncertainty as to which candidates to focuse on, the NRCC's effort in 1982 was neither as organized nor as widespread as in 1980. Party officials tried to save on production costs by bringing candidates to Washington instead of sending production crews into the field. The committee experimented with donut spots, commercials which dealt with a specific topic and could have cuts from various candidates inserted. The NRCC also experimented with regional ads, focusing not on specific races, but on regions that had common problems. Before the project was dropped, the committee produced two regional spots. One was taped in South Dakota and dealt with the problems facing farmers in the Midwest. Congressman Clint Roberts, who had at one time auditioned for the role of the Marlboro Man, was taped at a farm auction, discussing the grain embargo, how it had hurt farming, and what he and the Republican party were doing to help farmers return to prosperity.

The other spot was taped in a bar in Youngstown, Ohio, at a time when unemployment in the blue collar city was running high. Popular Republican representative Lyle Williams bellied up to the bar, drank a few beers with some out-of-work steel workers, and discussed President Reagan's economic program and how he and other Republicans were working to make industry strong again.

But neither the regional ads nor the donut ads were believed to be as effective as the plan used in 1980, and by July the division again started sending its television crew on the road to different campaigns. Before November 3, the committee had provided radio or television services to ninety-two candidates (forty-eight incumbents and forty-four challengers). Forty-six candidates had television ads produced for them by the NRCC, while fifty-five had spots edited at the committee's facilities. Two hundred twenty-seven television commercials were produced by the committee, and air time for spots was purchased through the NRCC by forty-three candidates.

Despite these efforts, the Republican party was not able to duplicate its 1980 effort and suffered a net loss of twenty-six seats in the House of Representatives in the 1982 general election. However, the NRCC's efforts affected several races, including two involving incumbents.

In Alabama's second congressional district Bill Dickinson had been serving as a representative since 1964. During that time he rose to the position of ranking Republican on the Armed Services Committee, a key position under the Reagan administration. In 1982, with former Governor George Wallace leading the ticket in Alabama, Democrats pitted Wallace's former press secretary and president of the State Public Service Commission against Dickinson. Late in the summer Wallace was gaining strength and Dickinson was in trouble.

While Dickinson's race wasn't originally scheduled for NRCC help on television advertising, the committee was called in on short notice to produce a series of ads showing the congressman active in the district and active in Washington, bringing key military projects to the district. Dickinson went on to win by only 1,386 votes out of 165,194 cast (Ehrenhalt, 1983, p. 20). The ability of the NRCC to come into the campaign late and provide quality television spots with less than a one week turnaround was considered important by campaign officials in securing the victory.

Another congressman in trouble also benefited from a series of political ads shot in his district and produced by the NRCC. Arlan Stangland was first elected to Minnesota's seventh district in a 1977 special election. Since that time, he had never earned more than 52 percent of the vote in his traditionally Democratic district (Ehrenhalt, 1983, p. 816).

The ads cast Stangland as a farmer with a strong tie to the area's Norwegian heritage. One ad produced for Stangland is a good example of how much influence the media professional can have in a campaign. The congressman had supported legislation to help open shipping on the Great Lakes to farmers in transporting grain. Through the efforts of writer/director Steve Sandler, this effort was turned into the "The Stangland Plan," an exciting, dynamic plan to move grain to the markets. Stangland won by 1,192 votes out of 215,316 cast (Ehrenhalt, 1983, p. 817).

More in '84

Republican efforts in campaign advertising in 1984 can be summed up in the phrase, "more and sooner." The committee added more writers and producers to the staff. By June of that election year the video crew had already traveled to various states to shoot footage for upcoming ads. In 1984 the committee produced, wrote, or marketed ads for more than 115 candidates; and twenty-five candidates received full advertising programs, from planning and writing to taping, editing, and placing.

A Democratic Response

Reviewing the 1980 election, Democratic party officials realized the Republican party had gotten the jump on them in 1980 with their national television advertising program. They were determined that would not happen again in 1982 and hired media consultant Bob Hershfeld to develop a national television advertising effort of their own. Since then, the party has invested more than $1 million in production facilities and has expanded its national advertising efforts.

In 1982 Hershfeld produced a package of five television commercials and three radio ads with assistance from media consultant David Sawyer. Party officials credit the ads with helping create doubt about the Republican party's programs and ultimately allowing Democratic candidates to pick up twenty-six seats in the House of Representatives.

All five of the television ads were attack spots. One ad showed a social security card being cut into pieces while the announcer described how Republicans were trying to cut social security programs. A second ad attacked the Republican economic program as being trickle-down economics, with most going to the rich and little to the poor. Two ads dealt with unemployment, one that showed a modern unemployment line dissolving into one from the 1930s. A second featured the unemployed Baltimore steelworker who was featured in the 1980 GOP ads. This time, he denounced Republican economic policies and defended the policies of the Democrats. The final ad was an elephand in a china shop, destroying social programs created by the Democratic party.

Production costs for the ads totaled about $75,000, and the Democratic party spent about $1.2 million to target the ads to ten industrial states with high unemployment. In addition ten state party organizations funded the airing of the ads in their states. The ads were also available for individual candidates to use in their campaigns.

The Democratic party continued a national advertising effort in 1984 and started producing television ads for individual candidates. A package of four institutional ads was produced and received a favorable testing in the Washington, D.C., market in March. Airing began after the Democratic convention.

Candidate advertising also began in 1984 with a slightly different structure than the Republicans use. Instead of hiring writers, producers and directors on staff, the Democratic party provided facilities for use by candidates and their media consultants. The Democratic party's Media Center opened in February with an investment of about $1 million in equipment.

DOES PARTY PLUS TV EQUAL SUCCESS?

Both major political parties have invested more than $1 million in video production equipment and have hired full-time staffs to do nothing but prepare and produce television ads for the party and its candidates. Since 1980, the budget of the NRCC's communication division has increased steadily from $750,000 to $2.5 million, with almost all of it spent for television advertising. Obviously both parties believe in using television advertising and believe it's successful. While both institutional and candidate advertising involves many of the same people in the parties, officials believe the two play related but separate roles in electing candidates and strengthening the parties.

When talking about the institutional and brand ads, both Blakely and Hershfeld spoke about building an image for their parties—something voters can identify with. Blakely said it is a primary function of the party to develop a positive image of itself. And Hershfeld said the ads provide a common theme for Democrats to rally around: "When people see the party as an influential organization with common themes, then candidates can rally behind it." Attack ads, Hershfeld said, create feelings of doubt about the other party. Both agreed television is the most effective method to translate image to voters.

As for the candidate or product ads, Hershfeld and Blakely both talk about benefits on a nuts and bolts basis. With a full-time staff working year-around on political ads, Blakely said his people can produce a better product than ad agencies that usually deal with consumer products. And the NRCC can produce the ads at a lower cost.

In an average race, Blakely said, the NRCC can write, shoot, and produce a television advertising package for about $5,000. An ad agency would charge $20,000 to $25,000 for the same effort. Campaigns also save on the placement of the ads. Agencies typically charge a 15 percent commission of the total cost of the media time bought. Charging by the hour for its media buying, the NRCC cost would compare to about a 2 percent commission, Blakely said.

In addition to these savings, campaigns are more likely to be able to obtain the services when strapped for money. The Congressional committees can donate $5,000 per election (primary and general) which can be given in cash or in services. The national parties can donate $5,000 per election plus $18,000 for the general election, which can also be funneled through the congressional committee in cash or services. Because of this, a campaign can produce—the way the Republican party program is set up—a complete television advertising package without spending any funds raised by itself. This can be a key advantage in the early stages of a campaign when funds are short. In one campaign in 1982, the party produced ads for a struggling candidate in Rhode Island using this funding procedure, hoping the appearance of the ads would spur support and additional contributions to the campaign.

Despite the capacity for these savings, Blakely said it's not the party's desire to put ad agencies or media consultants out of business. "It's not a good idea to stifle free enterprise by monopolizing all the races," he said. "But in campaigns where we could win but for a lack of money, it removes a problem. This is where we function best."

Hershfeld agreed that the primary benefit of having production facilities for candidate advertising is financial. "In the long run," Hersheld said, "the technical center is in the best interest of the party. Production time is vry expensive especially around election time. Opening the Media Center allows us to have media at a lower cost."

In the ever-changing world of electoral politics few things remain constant. Power shifts from one group to another; themes, issues, and images come in and go out of vogue. Wars are waged, hostages taken, and crimes committed. One thing that does seem to remain constant is the motivation, the quest for political power that underlies the efforts of those involved in politics. For national political parties this is especially true.

Their ability to elect candidates, to be a source of influence on the American voter, is their raison d'etre. Without this ability, their role in the American political system is diminished and their very existence threatened.

Numerous political scientists and journalists writing in recent years have ventured that the parties are indeed diminishing in stature and see their role in the American political system declining. While many of these authors point to the growth of government-provided services, a better-educated electorate, and several other factors as causing this decline, more agree that changes in the way we as a society communicate is an important factor is causing the decline. Since the 1950s we have seen a tremendous growth in the one medium that is capable of broadcasting a message simultaneously to millions of Americans throughout the country. Not only does television have this ability to reach a broad and diverse audience, but it is able to reach it with emotional, personal messages, to draw a reaction more real and intense than was ever possible with the printed page.

The effect of this on political parties has been dramatic. No longer are party organizations the primary source of information or point of contact between candidate and voter. Television news reports nightly the actions of candidates from both parties, and the candidates' advertisements provide the voter with a look at the personal side of candidates, as well as how they stand on issues of public concern. Voters don't see Joe Smith as simply the Republican candidate for office; they can see him as the handsome thirty-four-year-old family man who has a pretty wife, opposes abortion on demand and the MX missile, and believes in preserving family values.

Studies of voters conducted since television has become the predominant form of mass communication have found increases in the number of voters who consider themselves independents rather than party loyalists (Pomper, 1975, pp. 18–31) and increases in the number of voters who vote a split ticket (DeVries & Tarrance, 1972, p. 30). Along with this, researchers point to a growing independence among candidates. Politicians can use television to go directly to the voter, bypassing party hierarchy and organization and giving themselves a sense of freedom from obligation to the party. Both of these trends tend to support the thesis that the influences of American political parties is declining.

Despite the emergence of these two trends, it is too soon to sound the final death knell for American political parties. First, parties are still influential. And second, parties are changing, adapting to a changing world, to preserve their political power.

After the 1982 election all federal, elected officials identified themselves with one of the two major parties (the retirement of Virginia Senator Harry F. Byrd, Jr. removed the only independent from the U.S. Congress). All governors identify themselves as either a Republican or Democrat (Ehrenhalt, 1984, v–xiv). And no independent or third party candidate has made a serious challenge to the presidency in recent years. As Herbert Asher (1980, pp. 50–51) says, parties are still the dominant and stablizing force in American politics.

And, as we can see from the preceding pages, both major political parties are attempting to change and adapt new strategies and techniques in order to function in the television age. The Republican party has made the greatest efforts, producing and airing institutional and candidate ads since the late 1970s. The Democratic party is following suit. Beginning in 1982, the party produced and aired institutional advertising. In 1984 it continued its national advertising program on behalf of the party and, in addition, provided full scale technical facilities for individual candidates to use in their own campaigns.

The two types of television ad programs attack directly the trends seen as threats to political parties. Institutional or brand ads, those that build an image rather than asking for a specific response, are targeted at giving voters a concept of what a Republican or a Democrat is. With an image of the party established in the voter's mind, it follows that he or she would then be more likely to identify with and vote for a specific party. Ads produced by the GOP tend to show the party as economically responsible and as favoring a strong national defense. Democratic ads, meanwhile, attempt to present the party and its elected officials and candidates as compassionate and interested in the well-being of all citizens.

While the institutional ads attempt to give voters an image of the party to identify with and support, thus combating the growth of independent voters, the candidate ad program attacks the growth of independent candidates. By providing technical expertise and facilities at a price considerably less than that available in the private sector, the party can help to elect more candidates of party officials' choosing and develop a tie with those candidates who use the service and are elected.

Together, the use of institutional ads and party-produced candidate ads is growing as both major parties strive to retain political power. Because the programs address the two specific trends of decline confronting the parties and because the parties seem committed to continuing and expanding these efforts, it appears that television will not be the destroyer of the American political party system. Rather, it seems more likely that the parties will adjust to television much as they have adjusted to other changes in the political world throughout their history.

• 4 •

Corporate Advocacy Advertising as Political Communication

George Dionisopoulos

FOR ALMOST A WEEK DURING 1979, the attention of the world was riveted upon the events which came to be known as the accident at Three Mile Island. The reactor cooling towers of the Unit Two reactor were pictured on the cover of *Time* magazine. The cover called the accident "America's Nuclear Nightmare." Before awakening from this nightmare, America witnessed several incidents which many believed would undermine public confidence in the nuclear power industry. Before the crisis was declared "over," the public witnessed Pennsylvania's Governor Richard Thornburgh's order to evacuate all preschool children and pregnant women from Harrisburg; arguments by officials of the Nuclear Regulatory Commission (NRC) concerning the explosive potential of a hydrogen bubble in the reactor core; and a CBS newscast on March 30, in which Walter Cronkite intoned, "the world has never known a day quite like today" (Sandman & Paden, 1979, p. 44), and warned of "the remote but very real possibility of a nuclear meltdown at the Three Mile Island atomic power plant" (Farrell & Goodnight, 1981, p. 287).

Many people perceived the accident at Three Mile Island as "the beginning of the end for nuclear power in this country" ("The Nuclear Nightmare," 1979, p. 8). The end of the accident at Three Mile Island marked the beginning of a public relations crisis in which the industry perceived itself to be "on trial" before a court of public opinion ("Atomic Power's Future," 1979, p. 23): the future of the industry would depend upon the outcome of that trial. In response, the atomic power industry undertook a corporate advocacy[1] campaign to "[recapture] public confidence" (Hyde, 1979, p. 14). This paper examines part of that campaign.

Specifically, this paper examines the industry's use of newspaper advertisements during this campaign.[2] As will be illustrated, these ads were attempts by the industry to exert what is termed here "definitional hegemony" over the post–Three Mile Island situation. That is, they were aimed at affecting public images and defining salient issues in order to help secure favorable public policy decisions. They were, in effect, political communication.

Public Policy and the Industry's Perceived Need to Gain the Support of Public Opinion

The term "public policy" can convey several meanings. For example, public policy could be thought of as a guideline, or a framework within which the government acts. Or public policy might indicate a type of philosophy, such as "political conservatism," that undergirds government action. Some theorists conceive of public policy as legislation. For example, Nigro and Nigro (1977) wrote that "[Public] policy is made by the legislature in the form of laws and is carried out by the executive branch" (p. 9). However, Anderson, Brady, and Bullock (1978) offered an excellent operational definition for the term public policy. They wrote that public policy was simply "what governments do" (p. 6). After Three Mile Island, the industry was concerned with what the government was going to "do" about atomic power in the United States.

Defining the exact relationship between public opinion and "what governments do" is regarded as a "major difficulty . . . within the democratic process" (Woll, 1974, p. 9). This is especially true because it is often the case that "very few groups and individuals participate in the process of defining public interest in a particular area" (Woll, 1974, p. 9). However, while the relationship between public opinion and public policy is "neither as simple nor as direct as was once assumed" (Anderson, 1975, p. 81), scholars agree that public opinion does play a role in "mapping the broad boundaries and directions of public policy" (Bullock, Anderson, & Brady, 1983, p. 13). From this viewpoint, the public is viewed as "a natural resource full of potential power to be harnessed" (Farrell & Goodnight, 1981, p. 298).

This appears to have been the perspective of the atomic power industry following Three Mile Island: that public opinion would hold the key to the future of atomic power (Gartner, 1979; Taylor, 1979; Bukro, 1979b; Burnham, 1979b). From this perspective, the industry's postaccident problems were viewed as being "social and political" in nature (Burnham, 1980, p. F9). There was a feeling that the future of atomic power would be determined by public opinion, "not by electric utilities, nor by environmentalists or scientists" ("Nuclear Energy," 1980, p. 52).

The necessity of securing public opinion was echoed throughout the media. For example, the "leading topic" at the 1979 meeting of the American Nuclear Society was described in the *Chicago Tribune* as the "survival of the U.S. nuclear industry" (Bukro, 1979a, p. 6). The Atlanta gathering of nuclear scientists and engineers was told that the atomic power industry was "at the mercy of public sentiment" (Bukro, 1979b, p. 3). Since the "leading assessment" at the conference was that "the fate of nuclear power in this country now rests on public opinion," the "logical course of action" was "to sway public opinion" (Bukro, 1979a, p. 6).

The perceived importance of the industry's recapturing of favorable public opinion after Three Mile Island cannot be overemphasized. Evidence indicates that during the period following the accident the political fortunes of the industry depended upon its ability to cultivate public opinion. Carl Walske, president of the Atomic Industrial Forum, was quoted as stating, "It has been hard enough keeping Congress supportive with a majority of people behind us." Walske felt that if public opinion ever shifted against the industry "we would probably see all kinds of restrictive legislation in Congress" ("Nuclear Energy," 1980, p. 57). Additionally, some members of Congress who had recently endorsed nuclear power as a viable energy option were reevaluating their positions. One of these, Chairman of the House Interior Committee, Arizona Congressman Morris Udall, stated after Three Mile Island, "We may have rushed headlong into a dangerous technology without sufficient understanding of the pitfalls" ("The Nuclear Nightmare," 1979, p. 19). Udall later predicted that the issue of nuclear power would be the "centerpiece of politics in 1980. It has a potential all its own" ("Hell No, We Won't Glow," 1979, p. 17). Further political ramifications of Three Mile

Island were predicted by a nuclear industry lobbyist in Washington: "our good friends [in the House] are going to be perhaps more cautious" ("The Critical Problem," 1979, p. 28).

So, after Three Mile Island the industry perceived that public opinion would determine the fate of atomic power in this country. As such, public reaction to the accident became linked to the survival of the nuclear industry. The industry's perspective maintained that supportive public opinion would lead to supportive public policy decisions. From this perspective, the atomic power industry can be studied as a type of "actor" within the political environment.

The Atomic Power Industry as a Political Actor

Studying the atomic power industry as a "political actor" lends insight into the way the industry employed its rhetoric to help gain public opinion support. However, this insight can be highlighted by an examination of the environment in which this rhetoric was to function.

The Character of the Political Environment

This paper is grounded in the belief that the political environment consists of three basic elements. The first and most basic element is "conflict" over some valued resource (De Jouvenel, 1963, p. 189). That is, a political environment or situation involves multiple and conflicting demands addressed to a politically scarce resource. Bennett (1975) wrote that "political scarcity" is defined in terms of "how many people want how much of what exists. Scarcity is *created* from the calculus of 'how many' who want the 'how much.' " Thus, political scarcity is "created through valuation and demand while [natural scarcity] need not be" (p. 26).

The object of the demand can be a tangible entity like property or mineral rights. However, it can also be, as in the case of corporate advocacy advertising, a set of tangibles such as the ideas or belief systems of a "target audience." Within the political arena "the symbolic flexibility provided by culture, social arrangements and human imagination provides that almost anything can become a political resource" (Bennett, 1975, pp. 26–27).

The second element of the political environment is that disputes become political conflicts when they are "unsolvable." That is, no "effective computational procedure (or algorithm) is available by means of which a solution can be found, which dissolves the problem" (De Jouvenel, 1963, p. 189). However, even though political conflicts are, by their very nature, unsolvable, they are approached as though they are conventional problems. That is, a political actor will use "rhetoric and symbolic redefinition" to "recast the basic terms of conflict" (Bennett, 1975, p. 28). These definitions become successful "by virtue of the fact that the original points of conflict have been translated into, or placed in the context of, terms which mitigate or transform the original sense of conflict" (Bennett, 1975, p. 39).

When political actors seek to transform the original terms of the political confict, they are actually attempting to transform the unsolvable political conflict into a solvable problem. That is, they are constructing political issues. The third element of the political environment concerns the nature of these political issues.

Virtually all scholars who have addressed the concept of issues agree that issues are "ideational constructs rather than material objects: they do not share an existence apart from the mind" (Hunsaker & Smith, 1976, p. 147). However, although they are intangible, issues serve an indispensable function in that they are "the building-blocks of argument" (Newman, 1961, p. 51). The issue functions as a "resting place of the controversy" (Thompson, 1972, p. 136); or that "point in controversy which acts as a focus or center for opposing contentions" (Nadeau, 1958, p. 59). This symbolic nature of issues is especially important within the political environment.

A political actor possesses a great deal of latitude in determining the structure of an issue (McBath & Fisher, 1969, p. 19; McCombs & Shaw, 1977, p. 15). The ability to capitalize upon this opportunity and thus redefine an issue is "the cornerstone of political success." This process involves a " 'setting up' [of] a political equation in such a way that a selected public will likely visualize a desired 'solution.' Before people can extract information from an environment (and convert it into such things as attitudes, behaviours, etc.), the information must be in 'extractable' form. [Thus,] the nature of political consciousness is inextricably linked to the rhetoric . . . in the political environment" (Bennett, 1975, pp. 40–41).

While some members of the public are able to "generate stable attitudes about political matters, relatively few people have the cognitive analytic ability to generate abstract categories with which to organize, compare, and project political information." In the absence of the public possessing the necessary abilities, "politicians are in the business of providing the contexts within which information can be conveniently extracted and categorized" (Bennett, 1975, p. 41).

A large measure of political activity consists of trying to define situations in ways that are beneficial to the actor. Graber (1976) observed that much of politics "consists of defining political situations in specific terms and linking them to valued or unvalued goals in order to make them attractive and to be fought for, or unattractive and to be opposed" (p. 176). She stated that when political actors publicly offer definitions, "they create new perceptual realities for receivers who accept [the new definitions]." In turn, these new perceptual realities "become prisms through which future information is filtered and shaped" (Graber, 1976, p. 53).

In other words, when political actors define an issue, they determine the frame of reference or "the perspectives from which it will be viewed and evaluated" (Edelman, 1964, p. 131). In constructing and offering definitions, political actors place the "facts and concepts which have been selected for political attention" within some kind of verbal context. The ability to determine this context for the public "permits the politician to encourage others to view the world from his perspective and act accordingly" (Graber, 1976, p. 48).

Thus, a political actor's successful ability to define an issue translates into a type of power exerted through what is termed here "definitional hegemony." The term "hegemony" is selected because it suggests a limit to the application of this power. Corporations cannot exert absolute control over situational definitions. However, they can exercise what Nadel has termed, "a high degree of domination relative to other" actors in the situation (1976, p. 18).[3]

The argument here is that the atomic power industry perceived itself in a political situation following Three Mile Island. The accident had juxtaposed dynamically the public-as-consumer and the public-as-victim, and thus had reinvigorated the unsolvable twentieth-century problem of attempting to balance the need for power against the safety of the public. The atomic power industry viewed itself as being in conflict over the scarce symbolic resource of public opinion. The industry responded as a political actor by employing its advocacy rhetoric to define the relevant issues and thus exert definitional hegemony over the situation.

STRATEGIES OF ISSUE DEFINITION

The atomic power industry's rhetorical effort after Three Mile Island focused upon two major arguments. The first maintained that nuclear power was necessary to meet America's need for energy; the second concerned the relative safety of nuclear power. These two arguments provided the backdrop against which the nuclear power industry attempted to define the issues raised by Three Mile Island.

In defining the issue of the need for atomic power, the industry employed a strategy of transcendence and defined the issue of the need for *nuclear* energy against the higher hierarchical frame of projected energy requirements. In so doing the industry's rhetoric argued that there was a "nuclear imperative for this country" (Hertsgaard, 1980, p. 270). This need for energy was underscored by events far removed from Three Mile Island. During 1979, the United States embassy in Teheran was seized, and the United States stopped importing oil from Iran. OPEC increased the price of oil to twenty-three dollars a barrel, and there were long lines at the gas pumps in service stations. None of these events went unnoticed by the atomic power industry or the public.

The instability of event in the Mideast was used effectively to dramatize the need for alternative energy sources. Robert E. Kirby, president of the Westinghouse Corporation was quoted in the *New York Times* as saying that the United States was hanging "in the winds of fortune, held high by the thin line of ships bringing foreign oil to our ports and refineries" (Burnham, 1980, p. F9). He went on to warn that the American public was going to "have to choose . . . between some tough alternatives. Alternatives like inflation, higher unemployment, no economic growth and national insecurity" (Hertsgaard, 1980, p. 271). In an article entitled "Nuclear Energy: Survival at Stake," Dr. Edward Teller (1980) was quoted as saying that "current events in the Middle East underscore the absolute folly of eliminating the nuclear option" (p. 52). John Simpson, who headed Westinghouse's nuclear program from 1953 till 1974, went as far as to emphasize the transcendent issue of energy need at the expense of minimizing the importance of the issue of purifying safety. In November of 1979, at the industry meeting in San Francisco, Simpson stated: "You know, even if we killed hundreds of people a year, we'd still have to have nuclear. There's just no other way. The Russians could paralyze this country overnight by wrecking the Middle East oilfields. The United States just can't stand for that" (Hertsgaard, 1980, p. 270).

There could be no denying that the accident at Three Mile Island had raised the issue of safety. Following Three Mile Island, public opinion polls consistently revealed that the safety of reactors had become a major concern (Mitchell, 1980, p. 34). The industry responded to this situation by engaging in what can be understood as a rhetorical strategy of purification.

Harrell and Linkugel noted that the strategy of purification "implies a previously established image or ideology has somehow become tarnished through attack or some sort of redefinition" (1978, p. 271). Prior to the accident, public acceptance of atomic power had been premised upon a faith in the technology of the safety devices. Three Mile Island had called the public's "technological faith" into question, and thus had "tarnished" the public image of nuclear power in this country. To address this problem, the industry's rhetoric attempted to purify the image of nuclear power. It attempted to define the safety issues raised by Three Mile Island along two lines. First, the industry embarked on a concerted effort to remind the public that, when all the hysteria was over, *no one had died* at Three Mile Island. This element of the industry's rhetoric blamed the media for sensationalizing the accident. The second perspective held that the industry had responded to the accident and was correcting itself. Toward that end, the industry argued that the important safety issues of Three Mile Island concerned how the industry could learn from the accident to improve safety technologies for the future.

In summary, after the accident at Three Mile Island the atomic power industry faced an uncertain future. Perceiving that the public would play a major role in determining that future, the industry attempted to secure the support of public opinion—and thereby, favorable public policy decisions—by offering publicly "industry definitions" of the relevant issues. The first was the industry's argument that this country had a "need for energy," and that the need had an underlying "nuclear power imperative." This issue involved the industry's use of the rhetorical strategy of transcendence. The second issue concerned safety and involved a rhetorical strategy of purifying the public's technological faith in atomic power.

Some time after the accident the media began to carry evidence that the atomic power industry was mounting a public relations campaign aimed at responding to the damage caused by Three Mile Island. In June of 1979, public relations executives within the nuclear power industry met in San Francisco to learn the details of the industry's upcoming campaign. On 7 June 1979, the *San Francisco Chronicle* reported that the "top executives of America's nuclear industry are planning a nationwide public relations campaign . . . to pump up sagging public support for nuclear power." The *Chronicle* reported that this effort was "a direct outgrowth" of Three Mile Island (Taylor, p. 1). This "nucler energy campaign" to "promote the $100 billion industry whose image. . . . sagged [after] the Three Mile Island accident," was necessary "to convince the public that the country faces an energy disaster in the 1990s without nuclear energy" ("Utility Execs to Hit the Road," 1979, p. A2).

To "argue their case" (Thimmesch, 1979, p. 2), the industry embarked on an ambitious corporate advocacy campaign to exert definitional hegemony over the issues raised by Three Mile Island. The next section of this paper examines the industry's use of newspaper advertisements during this campaign.

The Atomic Power Industry's Use of Newspaper Advertisements

A major portion of the industry's post–Three Mile Island advocacy effort was aimed at disseminating the industry's message through the medium of newspaper advertisements. In the sociopolitical environment which followed the accident, executives of the major television networks felt that much of the industry's rhetoric was too controversial. As a result, the medium of television was closed to the industry (Burnham, 1979c, p. B11). The medium of newspapers, however, was open, and offered the industry a way to aim its message at the general public. (See the Appendix for a list of industry advertisements).

Through the use of these newspaper advertisements the industry attempted to assert definitional hegemony over the situation by addressing directly the public perceptions of the accident at Three Mile Island and of nuclear power generally. This rhetoric transformed the indeterminacies of the situation "into a determinant and coherent structure" and thus offered the American public a perspective for "interpreting and acting in the situation" (Consigny, 1974, p. 179).

This paper examines first, those ads emphasizing the industry's transcendent need argument and second, those which focus primarily on the purification safety issue. However, as will be demonstrated, often these two rhetorical strategies are combined within these ads.

Newspaper Advertisements and the Transcendent Strategy: A "Need" for Atomic Power

During the summer of 1979, OPEC oil sold for twenty-three dollars a barrel. That represented an increase of ten dollars in a single year. The summer months also saw the problem of a gasoline shortage as drivers had to cope with long lines at the neighborhood gas station. For many in this country, the summer months are associated with an increased use of the automobile, and that naturally means more public gasoline consumption. The summer's high pump prices, coupled with the inconvenience incurred trying to get fuel, provided the backdrop against which industry ads dramatized the argument that there was a need for nuclear power in this country.

On 25 June 1979, a full-page advertisement was placed in the *New York Times* by "the stockholders of ConEdison." ConEd's ad had a drawing of several cars lining up to buy gas. Above the drawing, a sentence in bold print read, "While you're waiting on line think about this . . . Last year, ConEdison burned enough fuel oil to make one billion gallons of gasoline. Wouldn't you like some of that in your tank?" (p. A11).

The text of this ad addressed readers who were unsure about the Indian Point nuclear plants. These readers were told to "consider" the fact that to "replace the power produced by Indian Point 2 and 3 would take fuel oil that could make 20 percent of the gasoline used by New York City and Westchester motorists." After assuring motorists with "gasoline problems," that "we're on your side," this ad said that since "your car can't run on . . . nuclear energy, [it] doesn't make any sense for us to burn your gasoline." The ConEd ad closed by asking those readers who agreed to "write and tell your elected representatives. Or let us know." After all, "One way to help solve the energy problem is to use the right fuel for the right purpose."

On 1 August 1979, the *New York Times* carried another advertisement using the theme of the energy/gasoline shortage. Placed by the American Nuclear Energy Council, this full-page "image" advertisement had a drawing of a gasoline pump. A long line of cars was waiting to buy fuel, but across the pump was a sign reading "NO GAS." In bold print beneath the drawing a headline proclaimed, "Nuclear power is part of the answer."

This ad assured the reader that the "severity of the energy crisis is real" and that the "long lines at the gasoline pumps this summer were only the beginning if we do not move to reduce our nations dependence on foreign oil" (p. B16). The text of the ad asked the reader to consider several facts concerning nuclear power. These facts were an impressive collection of statistics related to the production of energy through nuclear power. For example, one fact stated that America's seventy-two nuclear plants "produced energy equivalent to 1.3 million barrels of oil a day," and that was the equivalent to "enough gasoline to fuel 17 million cars—for a full year," and another observed that when the 126 nuclear plants "under construction or on order" were completed, nuclear power could "provide the energy equivalent of more than 4.5 million barrels of oil a day."

Employing a concise summary of the industry's transcendent strategy, the ad stated that the nuclear industry was "participating in the national effort to make American energy safe and self-sufficient." After all, nuclear energy was "a proven technology" that was "available *today* to help meet our nation's energy requirements, to help end dependence on foreign oil, and to help ease our balance of payments problem." The ad concluded by stating "Now is the time to use [nuclear power.]"

On 8 November 1979, the Committee for Energy Awareness (C.E.A.)[4] placed full-page advertisements in several major newspapers across the United States (Hertsgaarg, 1980, p. 271). In the *New York Times,* the *Los Angeles Times,* the *Washington Post,* the *Washington Star,* and the *Boston Globe,* readers were asked the rhetorical question, "Where is the Energy to Come From? (*Washington Post,* p. A17). This ad stated that the demand for electricty was rising 4 percent a year. Since President Carter had declared "that the U.S. will cut by almost half the amount of foreign oil we import," the country had to find alternative sources of energy. After explaining that solar power was "a long way off," and dependence upon coal alone would not solve the problem, the ad concluded that "nuclear power must be part of the answer."

The C.E.A. observed that there were enough uranium reserves "in this country alone to fuel all of the nuclear reactors now in existence—as well as those planned for construction between now and the year 2000—for their entire lifetime." It was a "telling fact" that "most other industrialized nations—from the Soviet Union to Japan" were "moving towards greater reliance on nuclear energy." Only the United States was "slow to move toward energy self-sufficiency." The ad's final paragraph stated a "lesson" that "should by clear to us now: America cannot afford to be dependent ever again on *any* one source of energy. That is why nuclear power is so very important." The ad closed with the transcendent claim "Nuclear Power. Because America Needs Energy."

This ad was the first nationwide media effort by the Committee for Energy Awareness. It employed a direct rhetorical strategy of transcendence in an attempt to redefine the nuclear power debate as a question about energy need.

On 1 February 1980, another C.E.A. advertisement employed the transcendent rhetorical strategy. Under the headline "Which Side Do You Believe?" (*New York Times,* p. A9), this ad stated that there were two sides to the "issue of nuclear power," and that both sides felt "strongly that their position is correct." The fact that people were "bombarded with conflicting views and statements from numerous self-proclaimed energy experts" made it "difficult for Americans to form a responsible position on whether our country needs this source of energy."

However, when one "consider[ed] the *sources* of the loudest anti-nuclear noise," it became clear that "The Issue Isn't Just Nuclear," it was, instead, one of "growth vs. no growth." On one side of the controversy was "a host of actors and actresses, rock stars, aspiring politicians and others who think America has grown enough." Often these were the same people who had "been against the development of geothermal energy in California . . . stopped new hydro-electric plants in Maine and Tennesse . . . blocked a new oil refinery for southern California . . . opposed new pipelines to deliver natural gas to the East . . . fought the building of more coal-fired plants . . . and opposed President Carter's plan for developing synthetic fuels program." The ad wondered "what they are *for,* and how they propose meeting America's energy needs."

On the other side of the dispute were organizations such as the AFL-CIO, the NAACP, the National Governor's Conference, Consumer Alert, "and many more." These groups recognized "that America's need for electric power is growing at a rate of 4% each year." There was also the fact that the health and safety record of nuclear technology had been "endorsed by a vast majority of the *scientific* community—including such organizations as the National Academy of Sciences, the World Health Organization, the American Medical Association, and the Health Physics Society." The ad admitted that the atomic power was not "risk free," but the "overwhelming evidence" was clear: "nuclear power is at least as clean and safe as any other means available to generate electricity—more so than most."

In a concise summary of the industry's tanscendent framework, the final paragraph of this ad said that the "real question in the nuclear debate" was, "Where will Americans get the electicity that is needed if not in part from nuclear power?" The ad observed that this question was "the one for which the anti-nuclear leaders have no answer." This ad closed with the transcendent claim, "Nuclear Power. Because America Needs Energy."[5]

In summary, these ads are interesting for several reasons. First, they demonstrate clearly the industry's use of transcendent need strategy. This strategy attempts to transform the debate concerning the future of nuclear power into a debate concerning projected energy needs, and the industry aimed this rhetoric at a kind of general audience that would be able to identify with the need for increased energy. In fact, the last ad establishes for the reader a simple dichotomy concerning the atomic power question. On one side is no atomic power and no growth; on the other side is atomic power with growth. As a group, these ads evidence a kind of patriotic appeal since atomic power is identified as a way to achieve energy independence from OPEC, an independence already underway in "other industrialized nations."

There is also within these advertisements a strong emphasis on the facts. In each of these ads the reader is implored to "consider the facts" or the "overwhelming scientific evidence." The industry's presentation of these facts dramatizes the serious need for atomic power in this country. However, some evidence indicates that the industry's facts may not have been complete while others may be inaccurate.

For example, some of the institutional support claimed in the C.E.A.'s February 1 advertisement had been the subject of earlier investigation in 1979. In May of 1979 the *New York Times* reported that the "pro-nuclear position of unions and their leaders" was based on more than just the fact that more electricity meant more jobs. There was also the very important consideration that the jobs of many union members were involved with the "building, maintaining and providing fuel for nuclear plants." In fact, privately, some union leaders had expressed "strong reservations about the future of nuclear power," but they supported it because "their first responsibility was to the job security of their members" (Shabercoff, 1979, p. B13). The industry advertisement neglected to mention these "facts" in connection with the AFL-CIO endorsement of atomic power.

The *Times* reported that one of the sponsors of the NAACP support statement, Mrs. Margaret Bush Wilson, had been appointed to the board of directors of Monsanto Corporation "after she became NAACP board chairman in 1975." Mrs. Wilson, of course, "denied accusations that she has been unduly influenced by her association with Monsanto Corporation." The chairman of the NAACP's energy committee, James E. Stewart, was a retired vice president of an energy company in Oklahoma. He also denied "that his association with the industry had any effect on his activities on the committee" (Johnson, 1979, p. A8) Here again, these "facts" were omitted from the advertisement.

There is also evidence to suggest that the facts providing the foundation for the industry's transcendent strategy were inaccurate. During the 1970s the demand for electricity had "not grown as fast as expected," and that had "left the energy cart racing a bit ahead of the horse." In fact, the 4 percent increase in energy quoted in these ads was actually a severe drop from an earlier projected increase of 7 percent (Graham & Rowe, 1979, p. A10). By 1979, the nation's utilities had the capacity to "produce 32 percent more power than is required on the hottest day. The optimum would be somewhere around 29 percent" (Graham & Rowe, 1979, p. A10).

The *New York Times* echoed the sentiment that the atomic power industry's claims of an "urgent need" for more plants could not be sustained. This article illustrated that atomic power plants generate "nothing but electricity," and electricity "accounts for only about a tenth of 'end use energy'—that is consumed by final users of various forms of energy" (Wicker, 1979, p. A19). In fact, only "three percent of our total energy comes from . . . [atomic] plants" (McGrory, 1979, p. 32), and according to energy consultant Dr. Vince Taylor, "replacing all oil and gas now used for electricity production with nuclear power would reduce oil consumption by only about 12 percent." Taylor estimated that this would "stave off critical oil shortages by less than five years" (Wicker, 1979, p. A19).

The *Bulletin of the Atomic Scientists* stated also that conversion to atomic power would have a "minor effect on our ability to replace foreign oil. [Because only] about 10 percent of oil consumption is used in generating electricity" ("Nuclear Power in 1980," 1980, p. 18). In fact, although atomic power provided about 13 percent of the country's electricity in 1979, it provided less than 5 percent of the country's total energy. So, in order to be "factual," industry statements such as "Where is the Energy to Come From?" or "Nuclear Power. Because America Needs Energy," probably should have substituted the word "electricity" for "energy."

But these ads are of further interest for what they did *not* say. Specifically, these ads make no mention at all of the accident at Three Mile Island. In fact, most of these ads mention only rarely the issue of safety. Nuclear power is referred to as a "proven technology," or as an "available technology," but there is only slight reference to it as a "safe technology." One possible explanation for this is that many of these advertisements, most notably those placed during the summer of 1979, may have been prepared prior to the accident at Three Mile Island. Another possible explanation would be because there were other newspaper advertisements that dealt specifically with the industry's purification saftey issue. An examination of these ads constitutes that next section of this study.

Newspaper Advertisement and the Strategy of Purification: Purifying Technological Faith

On 7 May 1979, less than two months after Three Mile Island, the Edison Electric Institute, an "association of electric companies," placed a full-page advertisement in the *New York Times.* Entitled "Three Mile Island Update: Reassesing the Risks," the greater part of this ad focused on the audience's image of the safety issues raised by Three Mile Island. The ad addressed itself to "setting straight" a "regrettable error" that had emerged from the accident (p. A22). The Institute quoted Roger Mattson, Director of the Nuclear Regulatory Commission's Division of Systems Safety, as saying that the concern over the danger of the hydrogen bubble explosion during the accident "was entirely undeserved. . . . There never was any danger of a hydrogen explosion in that bubble." The ad congratulated the N.R.C. for trying "to set the record straight, although this statement was not reported widely."

After reminding the reader of the "great influence" public perception of Three Mile Island would have "on the contribution of nuclear energy to solving this country's energy problems," the ad went on to explain that the industry was responding to the challenges posed by the accident. "Since the first hours after the accident at Three Mile Island began, nuclear power plant operators all over the nation have been analyzing their procedures and equipment, learning from the experiences of the accident."

Here is an example of the industry's juxtaposition of passive and active language. In industry newspaper advertisements emphasizing the safety issue, the accident was referred to using a more passive language style. In this ad the events are referred to as the accident "at Unit II of the Three Mile Island nuclear generating station"; it was not the "Three

Mile Island accident." However, the fact that the industry was responding to the lessons of Three Mile Island was highlighted in more active language. The industry response was portrayed as active, industry-wide, and immediate as members of the industry "analyzed" and "learned" from the "experiences of the accident."

Another subtle element at work in this advertisement involves the credibility of the media. The statement within the ad that the N.R.C.'s effort to "set the record straight" was "not reported widely" carries with it the unmentioned implication that the media were not telling both sides of the Three Mile Island story. By subtly questioning the willingness of the media to report evidence that the accident was not as dangerous as originally reported, this ad begins to establish for the reader some doubt concerning the accuracy of media information.

The Edison Electric Institute's ad was the first attempt by an industry trade association to offer an industry "definition" of events connected with Three Mile Island. The Institute's ad offered a limited redefinition of the actual events connected with Three Mile Island. However, the response of the industry was portrayed as being immediate, industry-wide, and "active."

On 31 July 1979, another industry advertisement addressed directly the purification issue of safety. Appearing in *The Wall Street Journal,* this ad was a two-page spread featuring a question and answer format with Dr. Edward Teller, a long-time supporter of atomic power. Paid for by Dresser Industries, this ad began with the headline, "I Was the Only Victim of Three Mile Island" (pp. 24–25).

Beneath the headlines was a short essay in which Teller stated that after the accident at Three Mile Island he had gone to Washington "to refute some of the propaganda that Ralph Nader, Jane Fonda, and their kind are spewing to the news media in their attempt to frighten people away from nuclear power." Teller explained that he was seventy-one years old," and the strain of working twenty hours a day "was too much." On 8 May, Teller suffered a heart attack. He continued, "You might say that I was the only one whose health was affected by that reactor near Harrisburg. No, that would be wrong. It was not the reactor. It was Jane Fonda. Reactors are not dangerous."

Teller felt "compelled to use whatever time and strength are left to me to speak out on the energy problem," and he affirmed that "nuclear power is part of the answer to that problem." He stated that he had "worked on the hydrogen bomb and on the safety of nuclear reactors" for the same reason—"Both are needed for the survival of a free society."

Teller observed that Americans were "just beginning to recognize the impact of the world's growing energy shortage." Such things as gasoline lines, electrical brownouts and higher prices were "minor irritants." But they were "nothing compared to what may lie ahead. In a struggle for survival, politics, law, religion and even humanity may be forgotten. When the objective is to stay alive, the end may seem to justify the means. . . . When our existence is at stake, we cannot afford to turn our backs on any source of energy. . . . When it comes to generating electricity, we especially need nuclear power." Teller went on to say that, despite "what Nader and Fonda and their friends . . . would have you believe," nuclear power was "the safest, cleanest way to generate large amounts of electrical power." Teller observed that that position was not simply his opinion, "it is a fact." Teller then assured readers that the "lessons learned at Three Mile Island" would make "the nuclear generation of electricity even safer."

Toward the end of his introductory essay, Teller stated that he once was asked "how I would like for my grandson, Eric, to think of me and my life's work." Teller explained that Eric was nine years old, and although "he beats me at the game of GO," he [Teller] was still "enormously fond of him." Teller admitted that he had not thought about how Eric would evaluate the life's work of Dr. Edward Teller. But he had given a "great deal of thought" to whether Eric would be alive in the next century, "and whether he would be living in freedom or slavery." Teller concluded that if Eric was "living under Communism, he will know I was a failure."

The balance of this advertisement presented a series of questions and answers as Teller "attempted to respond briefly to some of the questions which people ask about nuclear power." The questions and answers covered a variety of topics, but most concerned issues related to the safety of atomic power. For example, "Can a nuclear reactor explode like an atomic bomb?" or "What about the effect of an earthquake on a nuclear plant?" Teller's answers to questions of this type were always reassuring: nuclear technology is reliable.

Clearly the industry strategies of purification and transcendence are interwoven throughout this advertisement, and there is a continued reliance on presenting "the facts." But Teller's introductory essay sets a tone for the reading of the entire ad. This essay is flavored by apocalyptic doomsaying with its ominous visions of the future. On one hand is Dr. Edward Teller, reliance on nuclear, power, and "politics, law, religion and humanity." On the other hand is Ralph Nader, Jane Fonda, no atomic power, and little Eric growing up as a Communist.

This advertisement engendered its own controversy within the media. On 17 August 1979, a *New York Times* editorial raised some questions concerning information in the *Journal* ad. One question concerned a "noteworthy omission" in the ad. As mentioned previously, this ad was paid for by Dresser Industries. During the events at Three Mile Island, "a valve stuck open . . . and contributed to the accident. . . . It would have been nice of Dr. Teller or the advertiser to have identified the manufacturer of that valve: Dresser Industries" ("Propaganda," 1979, p. A24).

The *Saturday Review* also questioned some of Teller's information. In an article entitled "Q & A That Raises More Q's Than A's," the *Review* pointed out that Dr. Teller's statement about being the "only victim of Three Mile Island" was "remarkable" considering that the N.R.C. "estimated that at least 10 people will die of leukemia or other forms of cancer as a result of the accident at Three Mile Island" (Cousins, 1979, p. 10). The *Review* article reminded readers that a decade ago, Dr. Teller had recommended that all atomic reactors be built deep underground for safety reasons and now was insisting that "reactors are not dangerous."

These two newspaper advertisements addressed specifically public reaction to the accident at Three Mile Island. Both offered industry definitions, or more precisely, redefinitions of the events connected with Three Mile Island. Unlike most of the need advertisements mentioned earlier, both the Edison Electric and the Dresser Industries advertisements exhibited a strong interrelation of the industry's strategies of purification and transcendence. That interrelation was to continue in most of the industry's ads emphasizing the purification safety issue.

On 15 November 1979, a week following its first ad, the Committee for Energy Awareness again place a full-page advertisement in several major newspapers across the United States. In this ad readers were informed of the industy's side of "What *Really* Happened at Three Mile Island." This ad began by acknowledging the "troublesome disorder" surrounding the events at Three Mile Island (p. 32). In fact, this disorder was presented visually by a pictorial collage of several newspaper and magazine stories concerning the accident. Terms such as "China Syndrome," "Melt-down," and "Nuclear Nightmare" were highlighted within the collage.

The text of the ad reiterated the disorder surrounding the events at Three Mile Island. "You've heard it called a 'catastrophe' . . . a 'disaster' . . . and 'the week we almost lost Pennsylvania.' " The ad further observed that opponents of nuclear power had offered the events at Three Mile Island as proof that nuclear power plant construction should be halted. However, before "allowing opponents of nuclear energy to deprive us of still one more source of energy," there were some "important facts which every American deserves to know." The ad's presentation of these "facts" employed the rhetorical strategy of purification to offer the audience a new perspective from which to view Three Mile Island.

The new perspective redefined the accident so that the reader would perceive that the technology had *worked,* not that it had failed. "When malfunctions occurred at Three Mile Island, the containment dome did exactly what it was supposed to do; it prevented the release of any harmful amount of radiation into the atmosphere." This ad emphasized also that the concept of "redundant safety systems" was used in every nuclear power plant—"even if one system fails, there are others to prevent any harm to the public or environment."

This ad went on to state that, since the accident, the industry was working to make nuclear technology even better. "Lessons have been learned from [Three Mile Island]—and are being used to improve nuclear power's unsurpassed safety record." The ad concluded by telling the reader that depsite all the confusion surrounding the events at Three Mile Island—"One thing is certain: what happened at Three Mile Island does *not* justify a halt to nuclear power development. . . . The system worked. And we've moved to make it work even better."

There are interesting elements at work within this ad. For example, not only does this ad offer the American public the "facts" concerning Three Mile Island, but it offers facts which "every American deserves to know." Thus, it gives the impression that these "facts" have been, until now, kept from the public. Even the title, "What *Really* Happened at Three Mile Island" suggest that the public's image of the accident is not in accordance with the "facts."

This advertisement evidences also the subtle juxtaposition of passive and active language. Consider for example, the sentence concerning the containment dome at Three Mile Island. "When the accident happened at Three Mile Island, the containment dome did exactly what it was supposed to do: it prevented . . ." The sentence employs passive language in reference to the accident, but portrays actively the fact that the dome worked. This ad also portrays actively the response of the industry to the "lessons" of Three Mile Island. Examples include phrases such as, "we moved to improve reactor safety," or the closing lines of the text: "The system worked. And we've moved to make it work even better."

A still more polemic attempt to purify the meta-image of the industry was an advertisement placed by Commonwealth Edison in the *Chicago Tribune,* on 18 March 1980. This ad began with the dramatic title, "Exploding Three Mile Island." This ad referred also to the "explosive hydrogen bubble." Emphasizing the confusion and troublesome disorder of the situatin at Three Mile Island, it stated (p. 6): "Pennsylvania looked like it might be blown off the map any minute, turned into a radioactive no-mans-land. 'Permanently unihabitable' was the way they said it in the movie *The China Syndrome.* That's the trouble. A lot of people said a lot of things. And a lot of it just wasn't true. Not even close."

In its effort to "correct" these "untruths," the Commonwealth Edison ad offered the public a new disposition concerning the events at Three Mile Island. This ad states that the hydrogen bubble ("Bubble, nothing. The implication was a time bomb, ticking away.") was never in any danger of explosion. Unlike the earlier ad by Edison Electric, the Commonwealth Edison ad explained *why* the bubble could not explode. After a brief, layman's description of how the cooling system of a pressurized-water reactor works, the ad gave a three sentence summary of what transpired during the accident. The main point of the summary was to illustrate that there was no oxygen in the hydrogen bubble and then to state a basic principle of high school physics: "what nobody bothered to tell you at the time was that without oxygen, hydrogen can't explode." Referring to Mattson's 1 May admission that the bubble never really posed a danger, the ad lamented, "That never made headlines."

Having addressed the issue of the hydrogen bubble, illustrated the biased reporting of the news media, and questioned the credibility of the "experts" who even suggested there was a danger in the first place, this ad went on to argue that even if a meltdown had occurred, "it wouldn't have spelled disaster for Pennsylvania. It couldn't have." Attempting to purify further the public's image of atomic power, the ad reminded the reader that in the event of a meltdown the containment building would have limited the extent of the problem. After all, it was not "just any building, [but] an immense fortress with an enormously thick floor. Eleven feet of solid concrete reinforced with steel"—the technology was sound.

The ad argued that the "point of it all" was that "Three Mile Island and nuclear power itself deserve a fairer shake. A second look minus the hysteria, the hyperbole, the half-truths, and the untruths. They deserve a close, careful reading of the facts." When all the indeterminacies of the situation were made clear—through the industry's presentation of the "facts"—"the safety system worked." After all, although "we've experienced the worst accident in the twenty-two years America has been using nuclear energy . . . it wasn't the apocalypse. No one died. And except for the stress of being scared stiff, no one was injured." The ad concluded by referring to its title and saying that what really exploded at Three Mile Island "were myths."

The strategy employed in the Commonwealth Edison ad sought to purify the public image of nuclear power by redefining the events at Three Mile Island as an exemplary symbol of the reliability of atomic safety technology. Also, this ad made explicit reference to the "facts" pertaining to Three Mile Island and nuclear power in general. Further, it presented these facts as if someone or something were trying to keep them from the American public. Phrases like "what nobody bothered to tell you," and "that never made headlines," emphasize the idea that the "facts" about Three Mile Island were either kept from the public or were distorted.

But this ad is interesting also because of what it did not say. In this ad there was no reference to the "lessons" of Three Mile Island, nor any statement saying that the industry had moved to make the technology better. Instead there was an effort to purify the image of the technology at Three Mile Island. This effort was grounded in an almost blanket assertion that, because of this technology, the accident did not present a significant danger.[6] The structural integrity of the containment dome made the "meltdown theory" a "fallacy," and since "no one died" the only real "danger" was people being "scared out of their wits" by "the hysteria, the hyperbole, the half-truths, and the untruths."[7]

Observations Concerning this Rhetoric

After the "nightmare" of Three Mile Island, the public relations problems facing the nuclear power industry were considerable. From the industry's perspective, the problems presented by Three Mile Island were critical, and they had to be resolved favorably. Toward that end, the industry's newspaper advertisements attempted to exert definitional hegemony over the postaccident situation by offering industry definitions of the key issues and images to emerge out of Three Mile Island.

The "experts" who were so worried about a catastrophe were recast in light of their mistakes concerning the "explosive hydrogen bubble." The accident itself was redefined as being "not really as bad as the media lead people to believe." In fact, far from being a reason to abandon nuclear power, the accident at Three Mile Island was hailed by the industry as "proof that the safety technology works." Finally, the accident was redefined further as a "learning experience" that would result in an even safer nuclear industry in the future.

Observations concerning this rhetoric are provided by examining some of the dominant images which permeate it. One is the public image of the industry. Efforts to improve the damaged public image of the industy portrayed the industry as possessing a high moral character. This morality was displayed by industry's consistent claim that it was presenting the facts about nuclear power. There is a constant emphasis upon the position that the truth resides within the arguments of the industry. The reader, this rhetoric implies, has been denied access to the facts. The image contained in this rhetoric would lead an audience to believe that there was a truth pertaining to nuclear power that somehow had been kept from the American people.

This element of the industry's rhetoric can be considered less than candid. Much of the material it presented as fact was really nothing more than the industry's interpretations of much-disputed data. The industry's portrayal of itself as the "champion of truth" was at best an over-simplification, and at worst a hypocritical deception.

Another element of this rhetoric's moral tone is that it suggests that the only force standing between our standard of living and a halt to progress—if not a destruction of our way of life—are the brave men and women who are striving to keep nuclear power alive. That is, the industry portrayed itself as a modern Horatius in a struggle that would determine the future of "progress" in America.

This rhetoric further enhanced the industry's public image by offering a simplistic portrayal of the antinuclear movement. These advertisements constructed for the reader an image of the antinuclear power movement as a conglomeration of "movie stars," "aspiring politicians," and leftover radicals. The redefinition offered in this rhetoric would lead a reader to believe that there were no reasonable members of the scientific community nor committed members of the middle class who opposed nuclear power.

Another important image of this rhetoric pertained to the accident itself. As stated previously, much of the rhetoric in this campaign focused on redefining the public's image of what transpired in Pennsylvania.

From a general perspective, this element of the industry's rhetoric is disturbing because it appears to deny how truly dangerous a problem occurred at Three Mile Island. There are references to the fact that it was a "bad accident," or a "big problem," but the overall tenor of these advertisements maintained that it wasn't as bad as indicated in the press.

While denying the true danger of the accident, this rhetoric seemed also to minimize much of the psychological and physical costs associated with the accident. Whether the hydrogen bubble could have exploded or not does not alter the fact that the experts thought it could explode. The fact that the technical experts were wrong provides little reassurance to consumers of a product where faith in the technology is the main selling point.

On a more specific level, an element of the industry's rhetorical image of the accident seems almost paradoxical in nature. That is, the image of Three Mile Island as a "learning experience" comes very close to labeling this accident as a positive element. If the first Three Mile Island is a good learning experience, what of a second such accident, or a third? As Schuyten (1979) wrote in the *New York Times,* there is a "unique quality that sets nuclear power apart from other technologies" (p. D9). While some scientific endeavors can proceed by trial and error, nuclear power cannot. With reactors situated in populated areas, accidents are intolerable, and attitudes such as "we learn from Three Mile Island and proceed" seem a bit shallow.

Finally, the portrayal of atomic power as a key element in the quest for energy independence played a significant part in the atomic power industry's campaign for definitional hegemony over the postaccident situation. The events in the Middle East in 1979 helped to foster a sociopolitical environment in which this argument would be well received. However, here again, evidence suggests that this redefinition is less than candid. The production of electricity through atomic energy had very little impact upon the total energy picture of the United States. Further, while atomic power has some effect on the amount of coal burned, it has little effect on the amount of oil this country imports. But by employing such terms as "saving the equivalent of (so much oil)," the definition constructed leads an auditor to believe that atomic power can be instrumental in helping America to achieve independence from OPEC.

The industry's newspaper advertisement campaign offered readers redefinitions concerning the industry, the accident, and the role of atomic power in America's quest for energy independence. Offered as facts, some elements of these images were actually little more than the industry's interpretations of much-disputed data.

Conclusion

The *New York Times* observed that the 1980 Presidential campaign was being "spared the agitations of Three Mile Island." California Governor Edmund G. Brown, "the one Presidential candidate who tried to make an issue of the threats of nuclear power," had to drop out "because of a lack of public interest in him," and even the Pennsylvania primary did not treat Three Mile Island or atomic power as an issue (Clines, 1980, p. D14). In fact, by October the opposition to atomic power had diminished noticeably (Starr, 1980, p. 54), and in November the issue of nuclear power did not play a major role in determining final vote tallies. Congressman Udall's prophecy had not come to pass.

Concerns about definitional hegemony imply that much is at stake. The federal government constitutes a major element of corporate America's operating environment. That fact means that corporations have a vested interest in the structure and development of political issues pertaining to public policy decisions. Corporate advocacy advertising allows corporate America to exert influence over the dimensions of political issues by "grass-roots lobbying" (Nadel, 1976, p. 65) in the "marketplace" of ideas.

This paper examined corporate advocacy advertising by the atomic power industry as an effort to assert definitional hegemony over the post–Three Mile Island situation. The concept of defintional hegemony and its relationship to the development of political issues demands further attention by scholars of political communication.

Appendix. Corporate Advocacy Newspaper Advertisements

American Nuclear Energy Council. Nuclear power is part of the answer. *New York Times,* 1 August 1979, p. B16.

America's Rural Electric Systems, If you like the gasoline shortages of the 70s, you'll love the electrical power shortages of the 80s and 90s. *New York Times,* 23 September 1979, p. E19.

America's Rural Electric Systems. You can't stockpile kilowatts for lean years. *New York Times,* 21 October 1979, p. E21.

Committee for Energy Awareness. Where is the energy to come from? *Washington Post,* 8 November 1979, p. A17.

Committee for Energy Awareness. What *really* happened at Three Mile Island. *Washington Post,* 15 November 1979, p. A32.

Committee for Energy Awareness. We get more radiation in our living rooms than from nuclear power. *New York Times,* 10 January, 1980, p. B7.

Committee for Energy Awareness. Which side do you believe? *New York Times,* 1 February 1980, p. A9.

Commonwealth Edison. Exploding Three Mile Island. *Chicago Tribune,* 18 March 1980, p. 6.

Commonwealth Edison. Radiation and the future of Kimberly Michelle Mayberry. *Chicago Tribune,* 12 October 1980. p. 8.

Con Edison. While you're waiting on line think about this. *New York Times,* 25 June 1979, p. A11.

Con Edison. OPEC has raised your electric bill again. Are you ready to fight back? *New York Times,* 6 August 1979, p. A18.

Dresser Industries. I was the only victim of Three Mile Island. *Wall Street Journal,* 31 January 1979, pp. 24–25.

Edison Electric Institute. Three Mile Island update: Reassessing the risks. *New York Times,* 7 May 1979, p. A22.

Edison Electric Institute. An open letter to President Carter from the people who manufacture America's electricity. *Washington Post,* 15 July 1979, p. E8.

Edison Electric Institute. Saving leftover electricity. *New York Times,* 26 October 1979, p. 67.

Edison Electric Institute. The electric companies agree with the Kemeny Commission's message on nuclear power: Proceed, but proceed with caution. *New York Times* 2 November 1979, p. A32.

Edison Electric Institute. The safety of nuclear power plants is our top priority, too. *Washington Post,* 19 December 1979, p. A25.

Stockholders of New York State's Investor-owned utilities. Mr. President, we hear you. Here's a way to help free New York State from OPEC. *New York Times,* 26 July 1979, p. A20.

• 5 •

The Televised Political Spot Advertisement

Its Structure, Content, and Role in the Political System

Leonard Shyles

That the outer man is a picture of the inner, and the face an expression and revelation of the whole character, is a presumption likely enough in itself, and therefore a safe one to go on.

—Schopenhauer

There is nothing imaginable so strange or so little credible that it has not been maintained by one philosopher or other.

—Descartes

The dramatic increases in the proportion of campaign costs devoted to televised political advertising is well documented, thus highlighting the increasingly important role of such messages in American politics. The literature has also reported conventional wisdom and intuitive impressions of campaign workers who assert that some presentational devices are better suited to image creation of the candidate while others are better suited to underscoring campaign issues. Past communication research however, has not investigated empirically the validity of these intuitive impressions concerning presentational devices and their suitability to images and issues. This chapter reports research which analyzed the content of thirty and sixty second televised spot advertisements for the 1980 American presidential primaries in terms of candidate images, campaign issues, and selected methods of presentation; regularities were discovered in the audiovisual treatments used to present candidate images and campaign issues. In addition, this chapter reports, among other things, the results of a post hoc test designed roughly to determine the practical utility of the findings.

Growth and Use of Political Advertisements: A Justification and Rationale for a Research Program

The use of televised political spot advertisements in presidential politics has proliferated since their debut in the 1952 races, spreading to the early primaries and even in caucuses in the 1980 and 1984 campaigns, thus broadening their application significantly from the days before television was considered basic to politics. Pragmatic arguments in favor of using spot announcements in political campaigns have been that spots are a practical application from the lessons of repetition research in brand-name advertising, aie a low cost-per-thousand purchase, could reach undecideds and nonsupporters rather than only those voters already in favor of the candidate, and permit a modular approach to regional and statewide campaigns, especially in critical, undecided areas (Ogden & Peterson, 1968, pp. 192–93; Patterson & McClure, 1973, pp. 7–8; Minow, Burch, Corcoran, Heard, & Price, 1969, pp. 2, 15).

The expanded use of short spot announcements within the spectrum of political broadcasting has been evidenced by newspaper and trade journal reports as well as by full-blown studies (Monow et al., 1969, pp. 7–9). The authors of *Voter's Time,* a report on campaign costs, specifically note the "tremendous growth in the popularity of 'spots' " and attribute such growth to two factors: "They enable a candidate to reach a large number of viewers at a relatively low cost, . . . and they allow him to address people he could not reach by any other means" (Minow et al., 1969, p. 15).Specifically, Minow and Burch report that political candidates during 1968 spent more than three-quarters of their total television budgets on spots, amounting to twice that spent by candidates in 1964 for the same purpose (Minow et al., 1969, p. 16). They added that "expenditures for all other television time in the 1968 . . .

campaign changed hardly at all from the 1964 level" (p. 16). This information was in agreement with the Federal Communication Commission's *Survey of Political Broadcasting* for the primary and general election campaigns of 1968, which reported that

> The trend towards purchasing commercial spot announcements continues. In 1968, of the $49.3 million political charges by radio and TV stations, only 9% was for program time and 91% was for the spot announcements. . . . (In 1964, 81% of the $30.4 million station charges was for spot announcements.) More than five million political announcements were broadcast by the radio and TV stations in 1968. (FCC, 1969, p. 2)

Thus, during the 1960s a shift toward greater use of short, spot announcements occurred.

In support of this trend over a twelve-year period was a series of quadrennial studies of election financing, which chronicled campaign expeditures in presidential politics and other levels of government (Alexander, 1966, 1971, 1976). In his 1972 study of campaign financing, Herbert Alexander explained how the Federal Election Campaign Act of 1971

> affected broadcasting in several significant ways. . . . The law limited the amounts candidates for federal offices could spend on . . . television . . . to ten-cents time the voting-age population of the geographical unit covered by the election, or $50,000, whichever was greater. Second, it restricted candidates to spend no more than 60% of their media expenditures on broadcast advertising. (1976, p. 318)

Yet even with the artificial, legal noneconomic federal ceiling placed on broadcasting practices in the 1972 election, "presidential and vice-presidential candidates . . . spent slightly more for announcement time than for program time: $2.5 million for announcements and $2.4 million for programs. This differed from 1968 when $4.6 million was spent on program time and $4.2 million on announcement time. On local stations . . . over three times as much was spent on announcement time as on program time" (Alexander, 1976, p. 333). Furthermore, Alexander observed that on nonnetwork television, for primaries and general elections candidates at all levels spent $29 million on announcements and $3.2 million for program time, a ratio of nine to one, as compared to six to one in 1968 (Alexander, 1976, p. 335). Thus the trend toward greater use of short spot announcements appeared to have continued into the decade of the seventies.

Campaign spending for the 1980 presidential primary campaigns further accents the trend toward increased use of spot advertisements. ABC News reports that the 1980 primaries were to that time, the most expensive in history (ABC News, July 13, 1980). The Chicago *Tribune* (Television advertising, 1980) reports that spending on advertisements for the 1980 Iowa precinct caucus prior to any of the 37 primaries had already cost seven of the nine candidates over $300,000. Perhaps the single most significant expenditure of the 1980 primaries was the investment by former Texas Governor John B. Connally of over $10 million (New York Times, 1980), at least one-quarter of which was estimated to have gone for spot announcements. The New York *Times* reports that in 1980, "John B. Connally raised an spent $11 million, but had won only one delegate by the time he quit the presidential race. The ambitious advertising campaign began with spots . . . about the economy and national defense . . . [but] soon gave way to folksy stuff" (Anderson at crossroads, p. 4:4E).

The presidential primary campaigns for 1984 have kept pace with this trend. Edwin Diamond and Stephan Bates report in their timely and fast-reading book *The Spot* that in 1984, Senator John Glenn of Ohio had by January already committed over $3 million for a series of spots "intended to accentuate the differences between" former Vice President Walter Mondale and himself (1984, p. 21). Further, Walter Mondale's campaign organization had "entered 1984 with some $9 million—to Glenn's $6 million—and, under the terms of campaign finance law, got an additional $3 million in federal money" (Diamond and Bates, 1984, p. 27). As it turned out, the Mondale campaign needed every penny, because no sooner did it compete successfully against opponent Glenn, who dropped out shortly after "Super Tuesday" in March of 1984, than it was faced with a series of fearful campaign threats by Colorado Senator Gary Hart, who ran a vigourous and expensive campaign often featuring negative spots casting frontrunner Mondale as a slave to special interests.

While the spots made on behalf of Glenn, Mondale, and Hart account for the major share of those made and used during the 1984 primaries, it should be noted that *every* other major Democratic candidate, including Florida Governor Reuben Askew, South Carolina Senator Ernest Hollings, former South Dakota Senator George McGovern, California Senator Alan Cranston, and even the charismatic Reverend Jesse Jackson used spots to reach voters. Hence in 1984 the televised spot continues consistently to remain the campaing organizations' single largest broadcasting expense.

Value of Political Advertisements and Emergence of the Image/Issue Controversy

In spite of their increased use by candidates and their organizations the value and impact of televised political spots remains largely unknown. Concern about their rightful role (if any) in the political process has led to controversial sustained debate: Has the electorate been informed by thirty and sixty second spot announcements? Have these tightly structured miniextravaganzas presented candidates so that the electorate can significantly better judge issue positions and candidates' personal qualities to lead than they could without these messages? As the Twentieth Century Fund Commission has asked; "Specifically, does a series of short "spot" announcements contribute as much to the voter's knowlede of the issues and of the candidates as longer programs where issues are discussed and candidates are exposed to view?" (Minow, et al., 1969, p. 2). Debate over the quality and value of political spots stems from ideological concern that democracy better proceeds from an electorate that is better informed: "the democratic process requires open forums for political ideas and the widest possible dissemination of information . . . [F]ostering the development of commercial-like campaign spots rather than rational political discussions may in time subvert the democratic process" (Minow, et al., 1969, p. 17). Patterson and McClure, (1973) further describe the concern over the alleged detrimental effect of political spots on the political system: "conflicting claims are made about the impact of televised political spots. Critics contend that televised ads fail to provide the voters meaningful information, that they degrade the electoral process by selling candidates as if they were soap, that they emphasize image-making while ignoring political issues" (Patterson and McClure, 1973, p. 7).

Other writers who seem to agree that televised political spots are preoccupied with images at the expense of issues recount the emergence of the "TV candidate" as the product of "image-merchants and media specialists" (Devlin, 1973, p. 18; O'Keefe & Sheinkopf, 1974, p. 403). As early as 1958, New York *Times* columnist James Reston expressed the image-issue controversy: "Instead of the old-fashioned emphasis on what a candidate thinks, or what he says, the emphasis now seems to be on how he looks, especially on television, and on what kind of personality he has" (Rubin, 1967, p. 32). In 1968, Robert MacNeil criticized political commercials as featuring image at the expense of issue: Political commericals "are intended to influence us vividly and emotionally in as short a time as possible. They imply that the ingredients of a political decision can be encapsulated like the ingredients of any trivial commercial decision. They reduce the complexities of public life to a formula cunningly devised to cure everything. . . . They are so indefensible by any criterion of public service that politicians do not even pretend otherwise" (MacNeil, 1968, p. 194).

While observers like MacNeil excoriate political spots due to preoccupation with image content, there are some who see image material as useful for voters. Joseph Napolitan, campaign worker for over fifteen years when he wrote his impressions of modern election planning, viewed the "personality and personal characteristics of the candidate" as "much more important than his stand on specific issues" (Napolitan, 1972, p. 154). Therefore, he does not frame his views on the image emphases in spots as pejoratively as others.

Still other writers have removed the pejorative connotation totally, and have evaluated image material concerning candidates positively, claiming that information about the image of the candidate has been perhaps more important for the electorate to have than issue information. Ogden and Peterson, for example, have argued that

> The presidential candidate must convince the American people that he can lead the nation. He must establish confidence in his competence, honesty, judgment and maturity. He must demonstrate warmth, humane understanding, and concern about people. . . . His qualities as a person and as a leader are far more important on the whole than are the stands he takes on particular issues . . ." (Ogden & Peterson, 1968, p. 16).

Finally, Comstock and his colleagues (Comstock, Chaffee, Katzman, McCombs & Roberts, 1978) conclude that television continues to play an ever-increasing role as informant to the electorate with regard to shaping "images and views on issues, both of which have probably increased in their importance in voter decision-making" (p. 362). Thus, the spectrum of views regarding the content and value of political spots and the importance of their image and issue content has been quite broad and has constituted a controversial and vigorous debate among scholars, campaign workers, and other observers.

Problems of Resolving the Image Controversy in Televised Political Commercials

Resolving the controversy over the value of image content in televised political commercials is difficult, in part, because the "image" concept has been used in two legitimate but categorically different ways in the literature. In addition, the "image" concept has been alternately cast as stimulus-determined and/or receiver-determined in various research settings, and this has further confounded meaningful interpretation of findings concerning the nature of political images.

"Image" as Graphic Representation

The term "image" has been used in one sense to mean the visual likeness of the candidate. Here, "image" has been close to the meaning of "image" when used in the field of photography; "image" in this sense has been similar to a visual impression, a graphic representation.

Boorstin (1972) used this sense of "image" (though not exclusively throughout his writing) when he talked of the Graphich Revolution: "Man's abilty to make, preserve, transmit, and disseminate precise images—of print, of men and landscapes, and events, of the voices of men and mobs, now grew at a fantastic pace. . . . Still more revolutionary were the new techniques for making direct images of nature" (p. 13). In this passage, Boorstin credits the Graphic Revolution with making it possible for images to be multiplied and vivified by machines which create accurate replicas of face, form, and voice and with disseminating them as well. The term "image" in this graphic sense, then, has obvious application to the televised spots in modern political campaigns.

With specific reference to political spots, Wyckoff (1968) uses "image" in a graphic sense to distinguish between straight-talk-to-the-camera formats versus more complex production techniques using still pictures, fast cutting and music. In Wyckoff's view the more static the treatment, the less "image," while the more complicated the production techniques, the more "image". In this use of the term, "image" is clearly linked to selected methods of presentation used by the candidate's production team.

"Image" as Candidate's Character

But another sense of "image," quite different from image as graphic presentation, has been the wholly legitimate and more frequent usage of the term to refer to the character attributes of candidates. From the standpoint of political communication research, this use of "image" may be likened to a loose modern construction of Aristotle's ethos concept or to the "source credibility" of the candidate. More precisely, the "image" of a candidate in this sense refers to the candidate's received or projected personality traits and character attributes. Most such research pertinent to candidate image has focused on this latter usage of the term. Most such research concludes that "trustworthiness is a factor common to the image of all candidates" (Philport & Balon, 1975, p. 184). In assessing political images or character attributes of candidates, semantic instruments (including the semantic differential and Q-sort lists, for example) are often used to tap the personality traits perceived by respondents (hence a great deal of this work falls into a media effects tradition). The terms found most often in addition to trustworthiness are terms such as honest, experienced, intelligent, wise, strong, active, serious, true, and optimistic (Kraus, 1962, pp. 262, 276, 295).

Douglas (1972, p. 10) analyzed responses to seventy-four pairs of semantic differential items about political figures and named factors like trust, achievement, drive, credence, among others. Some scholars have used adjective lists to assess images of political candidates, and the image terms used included mature, fair, hardworking, and active (Nimmo & Savage, 1976, p. 66). Much past political image research has found regularities in the attribution of personality traits to candidates by respondents, clustering around such adjectives or constructs as honest, intelligent, strong, trustworthy, friendly, fair, ethical, and the like. Finally, Suci's semantic differentiation of candidate images in the 1952 presidential campaign (Osgood, Suci & Tannenbaum, 1971, pp. 104–24) has been judged to have "considerable subsequent validation" in the realm of candidates and their images (Nimmo & Savage, 1976, pp. 60–61) with other, more recent studies reflecting images of political candidates through factors named evaluative, assertive, trustworthy, and leader; McCroskey's factor analytic work on "source credibility" offers similar findings (McCroskey, 1966, pp. 65–72). It is clear from the foregoing, that when "image" has been used to refer to personality traits of candidates, the term has invariably referred to some cluster of character attributes of the candidate. Candidate image, viewed in this way, has been related most often to descriptions like trustworthy, expert, competent, honest, etc. The term "image," then, when used in this sense, has referred to "semantic character attributes of political candidates."

If we recognize a difference in the meaning of "image" when used to refer to graphic methods of presenting candidates (visual display), versus character attributes of candidates, then we can begin to assess more accurately the relationship between images and issues in televised political spots; perhaps then some of the controversy regarding the value of image and issue content of candidates in televised political advertising can be resolved.

Two Models of the Image Construct

Image scholars have described two image models—one, a source projection model which has viewed the message output of candidates as the origin of candidate images; the other, a perceptual balance theory which has held that images are the product of the modifying selective biases and cognitive predispositions of the receiver (Nimmo & Savage, 1976, pp. 31–32; Freeman, 1980, pp. 7–10). This latter view has been more popular with empirical media-effects researchers who have concentrated mainly on receiver variables and measure in the design of their studies (Kaid & Sanders, 1978, p. 57; Hofstetter & Zukin, 1979, p. 106; Hofstetter, Zukin, & Buss, 1978, p. 562; Atkin, Bowen, Nayman & Sheinkopf, 1973, pp. 209–24).

However, some researchers have investigated the perceptual balance principle and the stimulus-determined image theories, and have interpreted their findings in support of the stimulus-determined alternative. McGrath and McGrath (1962) have concluded that "perceptions of political figures are stimulus-determined rather than perceiver-determined for a large number of attributes. Thus, there seems to be much support for the image-theory of political perceptions" (p. 246).

The overall findings of research have indicated that whereas there has been value in both the source-projection model and the perceptual-balance model in image research, neither one has been sufficient by itself to account for candidate imagery. The content of candidate images has probably been the product of projections emanating from candidate stimuli as well as from the predispositions of receivers.

Compared to the perceptual-balance theory so often used as a basis for inquiry, the source projection model has been used too conservatively and too infrequently as a theoretical orientation to fruitful image research of political candidates. However, the continuing growth in the use of televised political spot advertisements by presidential candidates over the last twenty years by itself justifies inquiry into the nature of such messages and their impact on the electorate; the additional sustained controversy and heated debate surrounding their content and value for the electorate and the role they play in the political system further justifies systematic inquiry.

Systematic analysis of image and issue content of televised political spots becomes increasingly important when we realize, as Shneidman (1963) has noted that "we are a nation of millions of television sets; we are a nation of almost constant political elections and of intense political interests. . . . Television influences our elections and our international relationships, and it is extremely important for us to know more about the television stimuli that our own political leaders transmit" (p. 178). If the recommendation by Shneidman that we learn more about the nature of the political stimuli our leaders transmit was important in 1978, it is even more important for our political health in 1984. As political spots continue to proliferate on the national scene, it becomes increasingly important to try to understand better the structure of the messages aimed at voters during our modern political election campaigns.

The Issue Concept in Political Research

With regard to the notion of "issue" in political research, it can be stated at the outset, that the issue concept has been viewed in the literature as more stable than the image concept and has therefore been easier to define. Numerous studies of the effects and content of televised political advertising and of political content generally, have presumed that agreement exists with respect to what constitutes issue information (Patterson & McClure, 1974, pp. 3–31; Kaid & Sanders, 1978, p. 57; Hofstetter & Zukin, 1979 p. 106; Hofstetter, Zukin, & Buss, 1978, p. 562). It has generally been taken for granted that "issue" has referred to "specific policy" stands (Kaid & Sanders, 1978, p. 60). Most often, the notion of issue has been related by listing those topics which have been tied to the civic concerns of the citizenry. Patterson & McClure (1974) include political corruption, government spending, military cutbacks, bussing, welfare, and tax structures as part of a battery of issues they used to judge the television network's performance in contributing to voter knowledge (p. 11). Other researchers have included the topics of gun control (Kaid & Sanders, 1978, p. 51), the legitimate exercise of police power (Hoffstetter, Zukin & Buss, 1978, p. 567), and such issue categories as social welfare, racial and civil liberties, law and order, agriculture, natural resources, labor and management relations, economic, consumer business, and international affairs (Hofstetter, 11976, p. 80). From the literature dealing with issues in political and public affairs programming, it has been apparent that what has counted as issue material have been those references to topics "linked to the national interest" (Hofstetter & Judge, 1974, p. 12). A reasonable definition of "issue," then is that offered by Hofstetter in his content analytic work dealing with network news coverage and political affairs programming. Issues are defined as "current topics linked to the national interest."

In the past, the image-issue controversy, precipitated in part by political spots, has been ambiguously articulated by political observers. Such ambiguity has been typified by the statement that televised political spots provide images of the candidates at the expense of issues. In statements like this, it is not clear whether critics are condeming spots because they focus on character traits of the candidates at the expense of issues, or because they are preoccupied with stimulating graphics at the expense of issue and / or character content useful for informed choice.

In order to clarify these criticisms and find out whether any of them are true, and in order to avoid ambiguity in referring to the "images" of political spots, the convention is therefore adopted that when graphic images are implied, the phrase used in place of the term "image" will henceforth be "methods of presentation," while when character traits are meant, the term "image" itself will suffice. Based on the foregoing rationale, the research reported here has as its purpose to describe the image and issue content of televised political commercials and then to analyze the relationship between such content and those methods of presentation employed in its expression.

To explore this via content analysis, rationales explicating the constructs of "image," "issue," and "methods of presentation" (offered in Shyles, 1983, pp. 333–43; Shyles 1984a; 1984b) were developed which permit justifiable, operational definitions amenable to reliable quantification.[1] This chapter will mainly concern itself with the role of audiovisual elements in political advertising since it is here that the greatest dependence still seems to lie with intuitive impressions and somewhat limited anecdotal accounts offered by campaign workers and some researchers.

Rose and Fuchs (1968), for example, mention the use of editing, orientation of candidate to camera, setting, and cinéma verité (employing "old home movies" and "candid" shots of the candidate) as some of the techniques used to express images and issues (pp. 247–55). They note the use of montage and music as well as locales of the candidate to be additional variables for political announcements, and distinguish between "straightforward issue-oriented films" and those with a "more artful approach" (p. 257), better suited, supposedly, for conveying images of candidates.

Political consultant Robert Goodman also offers similar impressions and philosophy concerning methods of presenting candidates. Variables Goodman thinks are important in presenting images and issues include the candidate's wardrobe, camera angle, editing or cutting rate, locale of the candidate, the use of music, and the juxtaposition of the candidate with other citizens (Dybvig, 1970, pp. 92–94, 97, 180, 188–89).

Finally, Gene Wyckoff (1968) offers similar impressions on types of formats or styles of presenting candidates for television which lead one to suppose that some devices may be more associated with image appeals while others may more closely relate to issues. Wyckoff includes the use of rapid editing, music, and other techniques intended to feature candidate images rather then specific issues.

But beyond anecdotal reports of campaign workers and researchers concerning effective graphic styles, very little empirical investigation of assumptions has taken place. At the same time, ironically, virtually no political media-scholar will fail to assert the importance of visual design in televised propaganda; yet compared to the ongoing research programs of other communication fields involving visual considerations, there has been relatively little detailed analysis of the iconic meaning of televised political messages. This research has as its objective to begin just such a program of analysis using televised political advertising content, under the assumption that attention to audiovisual elements is of essential importance if we are to understand more fully the role of television in presidential politics.

In related fields of study one finds much attention to visual design. Roland Barthes writes about the rhetoric of graphic images and presents semiotic, critical analyses of visual media using copious examples from photojournalism (1977). Susan Sontag (1977) attaches great importance to the role of pictoral design in her explanation of cultural symbolism. Fiske and Hartley (1978), closer to home, present criticism employing the notion of "meaning systems" and "dominant codes" generally at work in television drama and entertainment formats as well as in product advertising. Randall Harrison (1981) refers to a "technical lexicon" used by cartoonists to code messages in iconic fashion for newspaper readers.

Arthur Asa Berger (1984) presents accounts of visual and iconic imagery and meaning in a number of settings (except that of political television) including pop art, comics, poetry, photography, sports, and a wide variety of other life forms of which visual media are an integral part. Sol Worth (1981) devoted his entire scholarly career to the study of visual aspects of communication, including the development of a semiotic of film, and an explication of symbolic strategies in the design of visual media and the application of ethnographic and anthropological frameworks for creating and understanding visual rhetoric. All of these writers and researchers grounded their work in the same semiotic traditions shared by such writers as Langer, Morris, Ogden and Richards, Peirce, Cassirer, Gombrich, Kracauer, Metz, Nichols, Eco, and Saussure.

For years, education researchers have engaged in an ongoing effort to develop design principles which could help to maximize effectiveness of audiovisual materials used in instructional television modules and other audiovisual teaching aids (Anderson, 1972, pp. 43–63). In addition, researchers have attempted to discern the impact of different presentational schema on film audiences (Isenhour, 1975, pp. 69–80); other have found source credibility judgements to be affected by camera angle differences in the presentation of televised messages (McCain, Childberg, & Wakeschlag, 1977, pp. 35–46). Still others have analyzed the construct of imagery into perceptual and symbolic modes in order to try to learn about what influences subjects' pictorial learning abilities. (Fleming, 1977, pp. 43–62).

While this litany of past research is by no means complete, nevertheless it is representative to the extent that it accurately reflects great general concern for visual rhetoric but little empirical inquiry focusing on the structure of such messages. Such work on the structure of the visual rhetoric of televised political advertising is attempted here in order to identify the value such information might have for enriching our understanding of the contemporary political scene.

To analyze the content and relationships (if any) between the semantic images and issues of televised political spot advertisements and the methods of presentation which such messages use, 140 thirty- and sixty second political commercials were analyzed from nine campaign organizations from January to June of 1980. The distribution and frequency of advertisements in the analysis are listed in Table 1 by candidate, party, and last office held.

Reports of the proportions and frequencies of image and issue mentions for groups of commercials by party and candidate have already

TABLE 1

DISTRIBUTION AND FREQUENCY OF ADVERTISEMENTS BY CANDIDATE, PARTY

CANDIDATE	LAST OFFICE HELD	TOTAL NUMBER OF ADS	NUMBER OF 30 SECOND SPOTS	NUMBER OF 60 SECOND SPOTS
John B. Anderson (I)*	Rep., 16th Dist. Illinois	24	21	3
Howard H. Baker (R)	Senator, Tennessee	14	12	2
Edmund G. Brown, Jr. (D)	Governor, California	7	3	4
George Bush (R)	CIA Director	22	21	1
Jimmy Carter (D)	President, U.S.	18	13	5
John B. Connally (R)	Secretary, Treasury	14	11	4
Phil Crane (R)	Rep., 12th Dist., Illinios	9	9	0
Edward M. Kennedy (D)	Senator, Massachusetts	26	19	7
Ronald Reagan (R)	Governor, California	5	5	0
Party				
Republican		89	79	10
Democrat		51	35	16
TOTAL		140	114	26

*R = Republican, D = Democrat, I = Independent. (Anderson was designated Independent because he declared his independent candidacy before the primary period was over).

appeared elsewhere (Shyles, 1983; Shyles, 1984a, b). as have similar measures for the methods of presenting candidates within the spots. Therefore, the focus here is simply to describe the variables of interest in terms of all commercials coded (the total sample called the population and treated as the census) and then to evaluate whether there are distinct image and issue styles (or codes) operating in the presentation of candidates and campaigns.

RESULTS OF CONTENT ANALYSIS—ISSUES

Table 2 reports the frequencies, proportions, and descriptive statistics across nine issue categories for all political advertisements. From Table 2 it is clear that the total number of issue mentions for all commercials was 649, nearly 20 percent of which belongd to the national well-being category. Next was the economy, with nearly 13 percent of issue mentions. Inspection of the means and standard deviation scores in Table 2 reveals that most thirty second spots contained approximately between one and seven issue mentions.

Overall, the most salient issues (those most frequently coded) were

TABLE 2
FREQUENCIES, PROPORTIONS, AND DESCRIPTIVE STATISTICS OF ISSUE MENTIONS IN NINE CATEGORIES FOR ALL ADVERTISEMENTS

	N*	%*	MEAN**	S.D.
Carter's Record	16	2.5	.11	.48
Domestic	66	10.2	.43	.86
Economy	84	12.9	.54	1.01
Energy	77	11.9	.46	1.35
Federalism	61	9.4	.41	.76
Foreign Policy	77	11.9	.48	1.05
Gov't Management	74	11.4	.46	.88
Nat'l Security	65	10.0	.41	.94
Nat'l Well-Being	129	19.8	.79	1.24
Total	649	100.00	4.10	2.76

*Based on 140 ads, time = 83 minutes.
**Based on halved values for 60 second spots.

those associated with national well-being, the economy, foreign policy matters, energy issues, and government management concerns. These results were generally consonant with the political climate during the primaries and were not surprising; during the campaign, the nation was at odds with soaring inflation and unemployment, and/or, Mideast and foreign policy crises (high OPEC prices, the Iranian hostage crises, and the Russian invasion of Afghanistan). Hence it is fitting that these results should accrue. From a methodological standpoint, these results are comforting.

Images

The image profile is no less comforting. Table 3 reports for image mentions the same statistics as those reported in Table 2 for issues. As Table 3 shows, the total number of image mentions for all commercials was 383, over 30 percent of which belonged to the experience category. Next was the competence category with just over 15 percent of image mentions. Inspection of the means and standard deviation scores in Table 3 reveals that most thirty second spots contained approximately between one and four image mentions. (A narrower range than that scored for the issue variable).

TABLE 3
FREQUENCIES, PROPORTIONS, AND DESCRIPTIVE STATISTICS OF IMAGE MENTIONS IN EIGHT CATEGORIES FOR ALL ADVERTISEMENTS

	*N**	%*	MEAN**	S.D.**
Altruism	27	7.0	.16	.44
Competence	58	15.1	.39	.65
Experience	117	30.5	.74	1.22
Honesty	43	11.2	.30	.61
Leadership	40	10.4	.27	.59
Personal	8	2.1	.06	.23
Strength	39	10.2	.26	.55
Other Qualities	51	13.3	.34	.71
Total	383	100.0	2.51	1.88

*Based on 140 ads, time = 83 minutes.
**Based on halved values for 60 second spots.

Overall, the most salient images were those associated with experience and competence, an outcome that accurately reflects a nearly unanimous view by candidates during the campaign that the Carter administration succeeded most in demonstrating general ineptitude; such a view was held by opponents of the incumbent from both major parties. Candidates roundly criticized the administration for an indecisive foreign policy as well as for ineffective governing on the domestic front. (For example, commercials made on behalf of George Bush emphasized repeatedly in an announcer's tag that George Bush would "be a President we won't have to train," while Governor Brown's commercials called for a change in leadership in order to avoid further "bumbling" away of our world prestige. Senator Kennedy's spots also referred frequently to mistakes of the Carter administration.) Although there were significantly fewer image mentions coded than issue mentions (in part an artifact of method, a point that will be discussed later), and although images were generally harder to code than issues, these results tend to reflect accurately views about the Carter presidency current during the campaign.

Audio Treatments

Table 4 reports the times, proportions of time, rates in seconds per minute, and descriptive statistics of selected audio variables for all advertisements. As shown, the voices of candidates, by a substantial margin, were present over all other audio material with 46.4 percent of time

Table 4
Minutes, Proportion of Time, Rates in Seconds Per Minute, and Descriptive Statistics Associated with Selected Audio Methods of Presentation for All Advertisements

	Minutes*	%*	Rate*	Mean**	S.D.**
Voice Announcer	19.5	23.5	14.1	7.57	8.66
Voice Candidates	38.5	46.4	27.8	13.86	10.77
Voice Citizen	11.7	14.0	8.4	3.98	8.55
Voice Famous	4.9	5.9	3.5	1.62	5.90
Music	7.8	9.4	5.7	2.78	7.94
Crowd Sound	4.1	5.0	3.0	1.57	4.93

*Based on 140 ads, time = 83 minutes.
**Based on halved values for 60 second spots.

devoted to them. Announcer's voices were heard nearly a quarter of the time, followed by citizen's voices (14 percent) and music (10 percent). The total for all audio treatments sums to a precentage greater than 100 percent because music at times accompanied voices. Clearly the dominant audio formats for many political spots contain voices of candidates, announcers, and citizens with a comparatively minor role played by music, crowd sounds, and testimonials by famous people.

Inspection of the means and standard deviation scores in Table 4 reveals that most thirty second spots contained approximately between three and twenty-five seconds of candidates' voices while only rarely did such spots feature more than seven seconds of crowd sounds; it was rare to find music for more than ten seconds.

Video Treatments

Table 5 lists time, proportions of time, rates in seconds per minute, and descriptive statistics of selected video treatments for all advertisements. As shown, neutral camera angles were present over 70 percent of commercial time with live action interior locales present over half the time. Nearly half the time (46.4 percent) talking candidates were shown; they were formally dressed 43.4 percent of the time. Over a quarter of the time, candidates were directly oriented toward the camera (so that they appeared to be looking directly at the viewer). Exterior locales were offered over a fifth of the time, as were candidates oriented indirectly to the camera. Furthermore, a transition rate of just over seven per minute was recorded. Inspection of the means and standard deviations reveals that thirty second spots rarely contain more than 18 seconds of candidates directly addressing the public. One can characterize the thirty second spot as often containing from 6 to 27 seconds of live interiors, between 2 and 24 seconds of formally dressed candidates, and 4 and 24 seconds of visuals of talking candidates. Only rarely does a thirty second, political spot contain more than seven transitions (which, intuitively, seems to be significantly lower than that which generally accrues for contemporary spots advertising products).

Descriptively, then, we have a profile of the images, issues, and graphic devices used in political, spot commercials. We may now move to determine what presenatational styles (if any) are uniquely associated with image and issue expression. Through the use of correlational, multiple regression procedures, it has already been reported elsewhere (Shyles, 1984b) that there are indeed unique image and issue audio/vis-

Table 5

Minutes, Proportions of Time, Rates in Seconds Per Minute, and Descriptive Statistics Associated with Selected Video Methods of Presentation for All Advertisements

	Minutes	%[a]	Rate[a]	Means[a]	S.D.[b]
Live Action Footage					
Talking Candidate	38.5	46.4	27.8	14.08	10.07
Talking Citizen	12.0	14.4	8.7	4.14	8.60
Talking Famous	5.3	6.4	3.9	1.75	5.93
Non-Talking Non-Candidate	6.8	8.2	4.9	2.61	4.89
Non-Talking Candidate	4.1	4.9	3.0	1.38	3.56
Other Visual Treatments					
Neutral Camera Angle	59.5	71.6	43.0	21.01	7.76
Non-Neutral Camera Angle	6.0	7.2	4.3	2.38	5.45
Still Candidate	6.1	7.4	4.4	2.26	5.10
Still Non-Candidate	12.6	15.2	9.1	4.71	6.55
Transitions[c]	598.0	—	7.2	3.84	2.85
Context, Orientation and Dress					
Candidate Direct to Camera	21.1	25.4	15.2	7.74	10.54
Candidate Indirect to Camera	17.3	20.8	12.5	6.26	9.02
Live Exteriors	18.5	22.3	13.4	6.66	9.77
Live Interiors	43.1	51.9	31.2	16.71	10.39
Candidate Formal Dress	36.0	43.4	26.1	12.98	10.47
Candidate Informal Dress	5.8	7.0	4.2	2.08	6.45

[a]Based on 140 ads, time = 83 minutes

[b]Based on halved values for 60 second spots.

[c]Raw frequency given with rate and descriptive statistics.

ual codes operating in televised political spot advertisements. Correlation (Pearson r) coefficients (see Table 6) computed for each spot between all presentation variables and total issue mentions (composite score) as well as between all presentation variables and total image mentions (composite score) reveal that issues are presented in formats which feature direct-to-camera-talking-heads of candidates in formal dress. By contrast, image expression, it is found, is negatively associated with voices and visuals of candidates directly oriented to the camera; instead, images tend to be accompanied by still pictures of candidates with visuals

TABLE 6
PEARSON *R* CORRELATION COEFFICIENTS COMPUTED ACROSS ALL ADVERTISEMENTS BETWEEN PRESENTATION VARIABLES AND COMPOSITE SEMANTIC ISSUE AND IMAGE SCORES(N = 140)

VARIABLES	ISSUE*	IMAGE*
Voice Announcer	−16	19
Voice Candidate	45	−48
Voice Citizen	−36	43
Voice Famous Person	−06	02
Music	−19	05
Crowd Sound	01	00
Talking Candidate	45	−41
Talking Citizen	−36	44
Talking Famous Person	−05	04
Non-Talking Non-Candidate	−04	−18
Non-Talking Candidate	−05	08
Neutral Camera Angle	17	−08
Non-Neutral Camera Angle	−15	02
Still Candidate	−16	28
Still Non-Candidate	−12	18
Candidate Direct to Camera	49	−38
Candidate Indirect to Camera	−08	−03
Live Exterior	−16	13
Live Interior	24	−20
Candidate Formal	42	−27
Candidate Informal	00	−14
Transition	−15	18

*Decimal points deleted.
The correlation between composite semantic issue and image scores was −.26.

and voices of citizens; voices of announcers and higher transition rates are also associated with image expression.

Multivariate and linkage analysis (McQuitty, 1957), in addition to simple correlations, similarly indicates that issue spots tend to use relatively straightforward formats featuring formally dressed candidates talking directly to the camera, while image spots tend to use a more slickly packaged format featuring still pictures of candidates in rapid succession with announcer voice-overs, testimonials by citizens and famous persons, and stirring music. (Shyles, 1984b). In other words, there are unique image and issue codes operating in political advertising.

TESTING THE PRACTICAL UTILITY OF IMAGE AND ISSUE CODES

If it is true that some presentational styles promote issues and others promote images, then it should be possible to state with better than chance accuracy where high and low issue and image scores may be found simply on the basis of presentational styles observed. Simply stated, this means that in commercials where only issue formats are observed, high issue scores and low image scores should accrue; likewise, in commercials where image formats are dominant, one should expect high image scores and low issue scores.

A post hoc test was performed to find out whether knowing about production styles can help in predicting image and issue orientations in televised political advertisements. A rough point evaluation system was used to rate commercials' image and issue content either high, medium, or low *based solely on their presentational formats.* This was done as follows: commercials were evaluated by comparing the proportion scores of a subgroup of spots (either by candidate or party) to those of the population of all commercials analyzed.

If the score for an "image-related" presentation variable within a candidate's group of spots was greater than that scored for the population and if the variable was related to image mentions by all correlational analyses (simple r's, linkage analysis, and multiple regression procedures), then an image score of +2 points was awarded to that candidate's group of commercials for that variable. If the proportion score surfaced across only two analyses, a score of +1 was awarded. For future reference, presentational variables that correlated positively with image scores, negatively with issue scores, and which appeared dominant across all three correlational analyses are henceforth designated "primary image-related variables," while those that emerged in only two analyses are designated "secondary image-related variables."

For variables correlated similarly with composite issue scores, in like manner either +2 or +1 points is awarded. Conversely, −2 or −1 points are awarded for primary and secondary presentation variables whose proportion scores are lower than those scored for the population. Finally, all issue-related points are summed to a single value, and in the same way, a single image value is obtained.

This was done with each candidate's group of advertisements. Four issue-related variables (the primary ones included voices of candidates, candidates presented in formal dress, and candidates oriented directly to the camera) and seven image-related variables (the primary ones included voices of announcers, still pictures of the candidate, and high transition rates) were viewed as the key presentational elements related uniquely to issue and image content, respectively. Table 7 lists the sum of all points for primary and secondary issue- and image-related, audiovisual variables based on scores for groups of commercials by candidate compared against those of the population. As table 7 shows, the spots of candidates Anderson, Brown, and Crane received the highest possible point evaluation total for issue related variables (all three received a +7 rating), while the commercials of candidates Connally and Kennedy received the lowest possible ratings (−7). As for the image variables, Brown's spots were rated lowest (−10); Baker and Carter's spots were relatively high (both a +6 image rating). It should be noted that the ranges of possible scores for any group of spots for issue-related variables is 14 points (from −7 to +7), while that for image-related variables is 20 points (from −10 to +10).

Next, the ranges of obtained evaluation scores for the audiovisual variables purportedly related to issues and images were broken into three equal intervals designated low, medium, and high. Then, *actual* issue- and image-mention rates were similarly classified for groups of spots by candidate in order to test predictions of the type, "Since candidate X's commercials received a low score for image-related variables, then the *actual* image mention rate will also be low."

Table 8 displays the actual issue- and image-mention rates per commercial minute comparing groups of commercials by candidate and the totality. As shown, the spots of Brown, Crane, and Reagan had the highest actual issue-mention rates (with scores of 14.9, 10.7, and 10.4, respectively) while those of candidates Carter and Connally had the highest image-mention rates. (The range of scores for actual issue men-

TABLE 7

IMAGE AND ISSUE RELATED AUDIO-VISUAL VARIABLES WITH POINTS AWARDED BASED ON PROPORTIONS BY CANDIDATES' SPOTS COMPARED AGAINST THOSE OF THE POPULATION*

	CANDIDATES								
	ANDERSON	BAKER	BROWN	BUSH	CARTER	CONNALLY	CRANE	KENNEDY	REAGAN
Issue Related Variables									
Primary									
Formal Dress	+2	+2	+2	0 −2	+2 0	0 −2	+2 0	0 −2	+2 0
Voice of Candidate	+2	+2	+2	+2 0	0 −2	0 −2	+2 0	0 −2	0 −2
Candidate Direct	+2	−2	+2	+2 0	0 −2	0 −2	+2 0	0 −2	+2 0
Secondary									
Visual Talking Candidate	+1	−1	+1	0 −1	0 −1	+1 0	0 −1	0 −1	0 −1
Subtotal	+7	+4 −3	+7	+4 −3	+2 −5	0 −7	+7 0	0 −7	+4 −3
Issue Evaluation Net Total	+7	+1	+7	+1	−3	−7	+7	−7	+1

Table 7 (cont.)

	Candidates								
	Anderson	Baker	Brown	Bush	Carter	Connally	Crane	Kennedy	Reagan
Image Related Variables									
Primary									
Voice of Announcer	0 −2	+2 0	0 −2	+2 0	+2 0	0 −2	0 −2	+2 0	+2 0
Still Candidate	0 −2	+2 0	0 −2	+2 0	0 −2	+2 0	0 −2	0 0	0 −2
Transitions	0 −2	+2 0	0 −2	+2 0	+2 0	0 −2	+2 0	0 −2	+2 0
Secondary									
Music	0 −1	+1 0	0 −1	+1 0	+1 0	+1 0	0 −1	0 −1	0 −1
Live Non Talk Candidate	0 −1	+1 0	0 −1	0 −1	+1 0	+ 0	0 −1	0 −1	+1 0
Visual Talk Citizen	+1 0	0 −1	0 −1	0 −1	+1 0	+1 0	0 −1	+1 0	+1 0
Visual Talk Famous Person	0 −1	0 −1	0 −1	0 −1	+1 0	0 −1	0 −1	+1 0	0−1
Subtotal	+1 −9	+8 −2	0−10	+7 −3	+8 −2	+5 −5	+2 −8	+4 −4	+6 −4
Image Evaluation Net Total	−8	+6	−10	+4	+6	0	−6	0	+2

*Numbers designate a proportion score for a variable greater than or less than that scored for the population.

TABLE 8
RATE OF ACTUAL ISSUE AND IMAGE MENTIONS PER MINUTE COMPARING CANDIDATES AND POPULATION

POPULATION AND CANDIDATES	RATE	
	ISSUE	IMAGE
Population	7.8	4.6
Anderson	7.4	4.7
Baker	8.0	4.6
Brown	14.9	2.5
Bush	7.0	4.2
Carter	6.2	6.2
Connally	5.7	6.4
Crane	10.7	2.7
Kennedy	7.5	4.4
Reagan	10.4	1.6

tions was from 5.7 to 14.9; for image mentions, the range was from 1.6 to 6.4). Actual issue- and image-mention rates by candidates were designated high, medium, and low, and the number of times that high, medium, or low classifications were correctly identified for actual issue- and image-mention rates based solely on audiovisual variables, was finally computed.

In using scores based on presentation variables for a rough prediction of high, medium, or low issue- and image-mention rates, the data consist of "dichotomous outcomes of independent Bernoulli trials having constant probability of success" of one-third. (Hollander and Wolfe, 1973, p. 15). In this case, correctly predicted outcomes are classified as successes. Successful predictions are compared to the overall number of trials in order to determine whether the probability for success is greater than one-third; the binomial test determines the alpha level associated with the outcomes.

Table 9 shows, by candidate, the scores for all issue- and image-related presentation variables, the predicted location of issue- and image-mention rates within three levels of classification, the actual location of such rates, and the outcomes of each prediction. As Table 9 shows, overall it was possible to predict correctly the classification level of actual issue- and image-mention rates in nine out of eighteen cases. "Under the

TABLE 9

SCORES FOR ALL ISSUE AND IMAGE RELATED PRESENTATION VARIABLES, PREDICTED AND ACTUAL LOCATIONS OF ISSUE AND IMAGE MENTION RATES WITHIN THREE LEVELS OF CLASSIFICATION, AND OUTCOMES OF PREDICTION BY CANDIDATE

GROUPS OF SPOTS BY CANDIDATE		POINT EVALUATION SCORE	PREDICTED LOCATION	ACTUAL LOCATION	*OUTCOME OF PREDICTION
Anderson	Issue	+7	High	Low	False
	Image	−8	Low	Medium	False
Baker	Issue	+1	Medium	Low	False
	Image	+6	High	Medium	False
Brown	Issue	+7	High	High	True
	Image	−10	Low	Low	True
Bush	Issue	+1	Medium	Low	False
	Image	+4	High	Medium	False

Carter	Issue	−3	Low	Low	True
	Image	+6	High	High	True
Connally	Issue	−7	Low	Low	True
	Image	0	Medium	High	False
Crane	Issue	+7	High	Medium	False
	Image	−6	Low	Low	True
Kennedy	Issue	−7	Low	Low	True
	Image	0	Medium	Medium	True
Reagan	Issue	+1	Medium	Medium	True
	Image	+2	Medium	Low	False

*Number of successes = 9, number of trials = 18.

hypothesis that there is no basis for discrimination, the probability *p* of success is one third, whereas a basis of discrimination would correspond to values of *p* that exceed one third" (Hollander & Wolfe, 1973, p. 17). Staticstically speaking, we consider the binomial test where $n = 18$ trials, $p = 1/3$, and the number of successful outcomes = 9. The alpha level associated with this outcome is .07. Hence there is evidence approaching the .05 alpha level of significance that presentational formats are useful for distinguishing issue and image orientations in televised political spot advertisements.

DISCUSSION

There is little value in processing political data through a set of empirical tests if one fails to anchor the significance of the study in terms of contemporary political communication theory. What do our findings tell us about politics and the political landscape? What knowledge do we gain from these data about the nature of politics and the contemporary political system?

First, the findings of this study indicate that there are measurable regularities in the structure of televised political advertising which uniquely accompany symbolic content in the communication of images of candidates or campaign issues to the electorate. Such an outcome is especially striking to the extent that one may interpret it as contrasting sharply with contemporary writing about the nature of communicated, political phenomena which currently springs from a constructivist, interpretive perspective. Edelman's position, for example, on the verifiability and factualness of political phenomena is that while "both scientific and political language are always open to interpretation and that the distinction between them is tenuous . . . it is interpretations that have [political] consequences" and "not 'facts.' " Edelman states further that usually there is no way to establish " 'correctness' [of interpretations] because unobservable premises and values inevitably play their parts. But even if there were a way, such proof would be politically irrelevant. . . . Correctness in a positive sense is a useless concept and a misleading one for [political] analysis. . . . There are no essences; just language games, as Wittgenstein contended."[2] Yet it seems that establishing the plausibility or "correctness" of political interpretations is not only desirable but essential and necessary (even if not in the extreme positivist sense of discovering "essences") if we are to modify or increase our knowledge of political phenomena.

If there are regularities within the genre of televised political spot messages between its "structural qualities" (or iconic dimesions) and its symbolic content, it indicates that at least some political phenomena may be amenable to corroboration or be in some way amenable to "correct" or "plausible" interpretation. This would put in question the universality of the constructivist view, which, in the extreme, leads to an autistic interpretation of Lippmann's famous "pictures in our heads" thesis. Cronkhite (1984) notes Gibson's observation that "persistent autistic construction of perception is unlikely because any organism that consistently constructed its perceptions independently of reality would, in Spence's memorable phrase, 'come from a long line of extinct ancestors.' Thus Gibson's position is that perception is veridical—that it preserves stimulus characteristics" (p. 57). Cronkhite adds humorously later that

> should a persistent constructivist survive long enough without walking into a truck while constructing his way across a busy street, his fellow citizens will likely take him into protective custody to relieve him of the need to perceive veridically. Once he is certified to be constructing his perceptions independently of reality, the state will award him a rent free rubber room in the Psycho Chateau. Such an arrangement will be no inconvenience to the hard-core constructivist, since he will simply fancy himself to be a satyr gamboling about a climate-controlled forest in pursuit of wood nymphs, or whatever other social construction of reality happens to tickle his autism. (P. 58)

Although the topic of perception differs from that of politics, Cronkhite's views on veridical perception and interpretation of meaning can also help political communicologists separate the plausible from the preposterous when applying dramatistic and constructivist concepts. There is nothing here that says political perceptions must necessarily be isomorphic between senders and receivers (or even with "reality"); what is affirmed is the presence of some stable correlates (or codes) between iconic presentations in televised political spots and their symbolic content. While political perceptions may be interpreted, political stimuli do not stop being political when some aspect of them becomes more predictable or well-known. It may be difficult to tell when political negotiations between labor and management are charades rather than conducted in good faith, but that does not mean that charades equal good faith.

Although people often experience negotiation through the interpretation of their observations, experiences, impressions, and perceptions, and these interpretations often have significant consequences, it is still of value to look for corroborating evidence (in the form of subsequent action on the part of agents, for example) which will "correct" or modify interpretations in line with future developments. In this spirit, the present analysis confirms through separate means the anecdotal and impressionistic accounts of campaign workers who have claimed that some graphic devices are used for campaign issue expression while others are used to convey candidate images in political campaigns.

There may be statements in the reporting of political developments which are not easily open to radically different interpretations but rather fit into the class of statements more clearly designated "correct" or "incorrect." For example, when the news media reported correctly that Ohio Senator John Glenn failed to run first in any of the 1984 democratic primary races in which he participated, the activity of reporting presupposed some commitment to the veracity of the thing reported. The news organization stood to lose credibility if they were wrong, as was the case when John Hinckley shot President Reagan, and it was reported that Press Secretary James Brady was killed—the report was false due to the "incorrectness" of the interpretation of events by the reporter. ABC news anchor Frank Reynolds, registered his dissatisfaction with the bogus story demanding "Let's get it nailed down, somebody." Accordingly, we don't just interpret; we interpret something. Similarly we don't just report; we report something. Statements may still be "political" that are known to be accurate. It is not a necessary prerequisite of a political statement that it be ambiguous, enigmatic, or a Rorschach test of constructivist interpretation; some interpretations are better than others. Even if there are no essences but just language games, as Wittgenstein contended, we can still invoke methods for checking our interpretations against subsequent behavior of the players. It is in the spirit of more finely tuning, modifying, updating, and confirming our beliefs (even political ones) that we appeal to findings, reward "good" reporting, engage in double-checking, perform measurements, and look for corroboration to see if we need to alter the pictures in our heads.

If we relied solely on generating the pictures in our heads, instigated by no stimuli except those which we automatically engendered by rubbing our closed eyes, our beliefs would never have the chance of becoming political. It is only when we experience the world around us that we hold the view that accurate reporting is a viable alternative; while docudrama may wink at the truth, it is not merely winking. Bastardization presupposes an original, knowable enough so that we can recognize the cheap imitations. As Cronkhite (1984) says, "Autistic perception becomes noticeable—and interesting—only as a figure against a ground of veridicality" (p. 68).

It is the object of veridical perception which, it is hoped, has been illuminated in this analysis of the structure of the genre of televised political advertising.

Limitations and Future Research Directions

The foregoing analyses of the images, issues, and methods of presentation of political spots allow concluding remarks to be made within certain limits. One may question from an empirical standpoint, for example, the harsh judgment of some critics that political commercials emphasize image-making while ignoring political issues. Contrary to this belief, this study indicates that political advertisements do contain and emphasize references to both political issues and candidates images (649 issue references coded as compared to 383 image references). Clearly some political commercials do not ignore issues. In addition, some aspects of the image-issue controversy may be resolved in part as a result of this study; findings support the view that semantic issue and image content is present in televised political spot advertisements, and that such material does vary in unique ways with respect to selected methods of presentation.

However, it must be kept in mind that this study addressed only semantic (verbal and textual) image and issue phenomena and did so from a composite frequency measure rather than from a conceivably equally valid time-based measure of visual candidate imagery. Candidate image phenomena, more than campaign issue phenomena, reside in the video portion of political commercials. Future studies need to assess the image content located in this domain.

Further, issue-mention rates were considerably higher than image-mention rates throughout the coding process; this was due to the explicit nature of the operational definitions of semantic issues and images which were used. There were cases where image terms appeared in an advertisement, but were not coded into any image category because they did not explicitly refer to a current, presidential candidate. An example of this occurred in the case of some Reagan spots where the candidate says, "We have the ability . . . talent . . . drive . . . imagination. Now all we need is the leadership." Each one of the qualities mentioned were potential image terms, but none were coded because they were not explicitly ascribed to a current candidate. Therefore, the lack of explicit reference to a current candidate kept these image terms out of the analysis.

The rigor of the operational definition of what constituted a codeable semantic image term was sorely felt at times, but it was decided to keep the cirteria rigorous so that there would be less chance for questioning how much was being read into the data that may have been more an artifact of interpretation than content.

There was an obvious limitation of generalizability to all televised political spot advertising. Since these data were only from the 1980 primaries, generalizing the results to general elections and past and future campaigns is tenuous. However, the methods developed here can be used to assess images, issues, and presentational methods in other campaigns. There will always be the need to refine issue and image categories, and there is the possibility of new production techniques being adopted. Minor refinement in the measurement of such variables should allow for the possibility of conducting future research similar to the present effort.

• 6 •

Political Advertising and the Meaning of Elections

Richard Joslyn

> As candidates and parties clamor for attention and vie for popular support, the people's verdict can be no more than a selective reflection from among the alternatives and outlooks presented to them. Even the most discriminating popular judgment can reflect only ambiguity, uncertainty, or even foolishness if those are the qualities of the input into the echo chamber. . . . Fed a steady diet of buncombe, the people may come to expect and to respond with highest predictability to buncombe. And those leaders most skilled in the propagation of buncombe may gain lasting advantage in the recurring struggles for popular favor.
>
> —V. O. Key, *The Responsible Electorate*

> Normatively speaking, consent from ignorance can never by genuine, no more so than conversion by the sword. Pragmatically speaking, an ignorant citizenry is dangerously unready when the time comes for choice, the key citizen choice being election.
>
> —James David Barber, *Race for the Presidency*

Televised political advertising is one of the major components of contemporary campaigns for public office. Television commercials consume a significant share of a campaign's financial resources and creative energies, they are being used by an increasing number of candidates for elective office, and the American public undoubtedly sees more of them than ever before. In short, the televised commercial makes an important contribution to the "information flow" of the modern campaign.

Despite the importance of political advertising, social scientists have been slow to study and appreciate this form of campaign communication. Much more attention has been devoted to understanding the campaign behavior of journalists and voters than of candidates, and political advertisements have been dismissed as empty or inconsequential rhetoric. Although scholars have gleaned fresh insights into the electoral process by analyzing the political rhetoric of party platforms (Ginsberg, 1972), candidate debates (Ellsworth, 1965; Kraus 1968; Bishop, Meadow, & Jackson-Beeck, 1980; Miller & MacKuen, 1979) and campaign speeches (Page, 1978; Fenno, 1978), this has not been true for campaign commercials. In fact, it is truly ironic that a form of campaign communication developed with such care and expense by campaigns and seen by so many voters has been the subject of such little systematic analysis. (Two recent books, by Diamond & Bates [1984], and Jamieson [1984] are welcome exceptions to this general observation.)

The main thesis of this chapter is that televised political commercials reveal much about the nature of the American electoral process. By studying the appeals that are generally made in commercials, one can learn about the nature of electoral choices, the educative effects of campaigns, and the meaning of electoral outcomes.

Theoretical Overview

There are a number of important controversies and disagreements about the nature of contemporary U.S. elections. These disagreements involve many of the most important aspects of the electoral process, including the content of the campaign's information flow, the educative effect of campaign communication, the voter's decision-making calculus, and the message that may be inferred from an electoral outcome. These disagreements are so extensive that it is possible to identify four major approaches to American elections.

One approach, the *prospective policy choice* approach, holds that elections are an opportunity for voters to contrast the opposing policy intentions of candidates and to choose the candidate most similar to their own policy preferences. According to this approach, electoral choices center on the evaluation of policy positions, and election outcomes may be considered "mandates" for the policy promises of victorious candidates.

A second approach—*retrospective policy satisfaction*—argues that elections give citizens a periodic opportunity to evaluate recent programmatic decisions and social conditions and to decide whether the incumbent candidate or party has performed satisfactorily. The message that is sent by the electorate, according to this view, is one of general preference for either continuity or change, as indicated by whether or not the electorate "throws the rascals out."

A third approach deemphasizes the policy significance of American campaigns and finds instead that the electoral process magnifies the importance of the "fit" between the role expectations for particular public offices and the personal characteristics of candidates. This *benevolent leader* approach rejects the notion that electoral outcomes reveal the policy preferences of the public and instead asserts that elections reveal the leadership qualities that are preferred and selected by the American public. Any policy consequences of electoral choices, by this logic, are more likely to be unintended than intended and more likely to be secondary to the electorate's search for public officials with desireable personal attributes.

Finally, a fourth approach treats elections as a particular type of political *ritual.* This approach holds that it is the campaign more than the outcome which is significant and that the electoral choices made by voters are not nearly as consequential as the effects campaigns have on the public. According to this view, elections serve to legitimate prevailing political values and beliefs, reinforce identification with the political community, and bolster support for the political system. In sum, elections permit political elites to shape the attitudes and behavior of the public.

These are four very different perspectives on elections.[1] Each one has much to commend it and is consistent with some body of evidence. Each of the approaches contains assertions about the content of campaign information, the educative impact of the campaign, and the meaning of election outcomes. Since televised political advertising is an important component of a campaign's information flow, it may be used to shed some light on the accuracy of each of these four views.

The remainder of this chapter will be devoted to an evaluation of the extent to which each of these four approaches is consistent with the world of televised political advertising. I will attempt to answer this question by specifying the types of appeals that are consistent with each approach, illustrating the use of these appeals in specific commercials, and measuring the prevalence of different appeals in television commercials in general. At the conclusion of this analysis we should have a better idea of how persuasive each of the four approaches is and of how political commercials delimit the meaning of American elections.

Data

The following analysis will be based on a sample of 506 televised political commercials. The sample cannot be defended as a random or representative sample of all ads ever shown on television; it is purely a convenience sample consisting of all of the television commercials the author has been able to locate and analyze to date. The sample does consist of ads from a variety of years, offices, parties, competitive situations, and outcomes (see Table 10). It is hoped, therefore, to yield a more general picture of television advertisements than has been attempted before. In the remainder of this chapter, these 506 ads are used to illustrate and evaluate the campaign appeals consistent with each of the four approaches to elections.

The Content of Televised Political Commercials

Prospective Policy Choice Appeals

The electoral process glorified in civic texts is an opportunity for voters to compare the policy promises of candidates so that the voters can vote for the candidate who best approximates their own policy preferences. This view of the electoral process places a premium on candidates revealing future-oriented public policy promises that are specific, detailed, and distinctive.

Political scientists are not nearly as naive and idealistic as the authors of civic texts. However, they too place a normative value on candidate rhetoric that reveals specific policy proposals and distinguishes one candidate's policy preferences from another's. In fact, over the past few years a considerable amount of commentary on presidential elections has bemoaned the dearth of such specific policy promises while occasionally finding some evidence that the amount of this type of campaign discourse is on the rise.

Although many political scientists believe in the normative value of specific future-oriented policy promises, the discipline is deeply divided over empirical estimates of the amount of such rhetoric that candidates

Table 10
Attributes of Commercials in the Sample

Political Party	
Democrat	313
Republican	179
Other*	14
Year in Which Ad Was Shown	
1960–1967	38
1968–1975	205
1976–1984	257
Other*	6
Office Contested	
President	179
U.S. Senate	205
Governor	74
U.S. House	28
Other	20
Status of Candidate	
Incumbent	167
Challenger	225
Open Seat	94
Other*	20
Outcome	
Won	328
Lost	152
Other*	26
Type of Election	
General	385
Primary	112
Other*	9

*Includes missing data

actually use. On the one hand, a number of accounts of recent presidential elections have observed that presidential campaign rhetoric has become increasingly policy-oriented, that candidates are more willing to reveal specific policy proposals, and that the policy preferences of at least the major-party presidential candidates have become sufficiently distinct. Reviews of the 1964 election, for example, found that the candidates provided "sharply contrasting philosophies of government" with Goldwater in particular providing "an ideological stimulus" and a "meaningful test of liberal-conservative sentiment" (Field & Anderson, 1969; Pierce, 1970). A review of the 1968 election argued that the candidacy of George Wallace "was reacted to by the public as an *issue* candidacy" (Converse, Miller, Rusk, & Wolfe, 1969); and reviews of the 1972 election claimed that candidate "issue positions were unusually sharply defined" (Stimson, 1975) and that the election marked the end point of a twelve-year process during which there was an "upgrading in the quality of political rhetoric and debate" and an "increased articulation of the ideological differences between the parties" (Miller, Miller, Raine, & Brown, 1976). This position was summarized nicely in a major study of U.S. public opinion that argued that candidates have shown an increased willingness to present voters with "meaningful bundles of issues," with positions "on the liberal-conservative continuum that [are] both unambiguous and fairly far from the center," with "issue choices," and with a "coherent set of issue positions" (Nie, Verba, & Petrocik, 1976). The net result of these studies has been to suggest that candidates are increasingly offering meaningful, clear, and distinct policy proposals to the electorate.

On the other hand, a number of political scientists have argued that campaign rhetoric is far more typically cliche and image-oreinted than policy-oriented, and that what passes for candidate discussions of public policy alternatives is usually vague and ambiguous. Benjamin Page (1978) in his comprehensive review of presidential campaign rhetoric, concluded that

> the most striking features of candidates' rhetoric about policy is its extreme vagueness. The typical campaign speech says virtually nothing specific about policy alternatives; discussions of the issues are hidden away in little-publicized statements and position papers. Even the most extended discussions leave many questions unanswered. In short, policy stands are infrequent, inconspicuous and unspecific. Presidential candidates are skilled at appearing to say much while actually saying little. (Pp. 152–53)

And Murray Edelman (1964) argued two decades ago that "most campaign speeches consist of the exchange of cliches among people who agree with each other. The talk therefore, serves to dull the critical faculties rather than to arouse them." This debate raises a significant empirical question about the frequency with which candidates reveal policy promises, intentions, or preferences.

Candidates *do* reveal future-oriented policy proposals in televised spot advertisements. Furthermore, occasionally these proposals are quite specific, though not very detailed, given the constraints of a thirty or sixty second presentation. In 1964, for example, Barry Goldwater took a very specific position regarding the draft in one of his television advertisements:

> I want to end the draft altogether and as soon as possible. In order to keep this nation strong and keep the peace, our military services need trained volunteers. We must attract men and women who will dedicate their careers to the military services. And we'll attract them with good pay, good career opportunities, and real security for their families. The present draft system is dangerously outmoded, it's wasteful, and it's unfair to our young people. What we need is a good professional corps, which has real pride in its service to the cause of peace and freedom.

In 1976 Fred Harris, then a candidate for the Democratic presidential nomination, revealed a specific policy promise regarding domestic oil prices. "We've got to have immediate price controls on all of these monopoly industries, rolling back the price of domestic crude oil to January levels, not taking the lid totally off the price of domestic crude oil as President Ford wants to do, but going after them under the antitrust laws to bring down these prices naturally too through competition." And in 1976 both Jimmy Carter and Gerald Ford took specific policy positions in two of their advertisements. Jimmy Carter opined that "we need a nationwide, comprehensive, all-inclusive, mandatory health insurance program" in one ad while Gerald Ford revealed that he wanted to increase the personal income tax exemption from $750 to $1,000 in another.

Nonpresidential candidates also occasionally reveal specific policy promises. Bennett Johnston, during his 1978 campaign for reelection as a U.S. Senator from Louisiana, revealed that he was "cosponsoring a bill to reduce federal income taxes 30 percent across the board, which would drop rates back to where they were before inflation raised them"; Henry

Jackson, in his 1982 bid for reelection, used a commercial in which he said that "we could save the taxpayers over six billion dollars by converting 747s instead of buying fancy new C–5s;" Walter Mondale, in his 1972 capaign for election to the U.S. Senate from Minnesota, spelled out the details of a piece of legislation on pension funds he was supporting; and in 1970 James Buckley, candidate for the U.S. Senate from New York, revealed in some detail why he was opposed to a troop withdrawal from Vietnam.

As the previous examples indicate, it is possible to reveal a specific policy preference in a brief televised campaign commercial. However, the simple fact of the matter is that very few commercials contain this sort of appeal. Of the 506 ads studied here, only twenty-four—or 5 percent—contained this type of content.

Perhaps it is unreasonable to expect candidates to reveal detailed, specific policy proposals within the constraints of televised commercials. What if we relax our criteria a bit and consider appeals which contain policy proposals but which lack the detail and the specificity of those just considered? While the specificity of a policy promise is clearly an imprecise judgment, it is possible to distinguish between specific and less-specific policy positions.

If we relax the criteria for a policy promise, many more candidates can be said to have used this type of appeal in their television advertisements. In 1960, for example, John Kennedy aired this commercial: "The Republicans say that they're considering doing something about distressed areas. Yet the Congress has passed bills twice, and each time the administration has vetoed them. Next year the Congress will pass them again, and if elected president I will fight for them and sign them." In this case the candidate reveals a specific policy position, provided the viewer knows something about the piece of legislation to which Kennedy is referring. The candidate does not provide the details himself but rather relies on the "stored information" of the citizenry to provide a context for the appeal.

Numerous candidates have revealed policy proposals at this level of specificity. Barry Goldwater, in 1964, said he would "cut down government spending and move to keep down the size of government too." George Wallace, in 1968, said he would "turn back the absolute control of the public school system to the people of the respective states . . . stand up for your local police and firemen in protecting your safety and property . . . and halt the give-away of your American dollars and products to those nations that aid our enemies." And Gerald Ford, in 1976, said "I don't think the $15,000 a year taxpayer ought to get any more tax increase. That group in our taxpaying public ought to get a decrease."

Nonpresidential candidates also make this kind of policy appeal. In 1972 Walter Mondale aired an ad in which he said "I think we've got to have some kind of national health insurance program that takes the sting out of getting sick and makes health a matter of right and not what we do today." In 1970, U.S. Senator Phil Hart made the following policy promise: "You say you haven't got the money—the President's vetoing housing and education bills. It isn't immature to say you've got your priorities out of whack. We can delay getting to Mars, we could even have delayed, I suppose, getting to the moon. Our long-term survival more importantly hinges on how we take care of the problems of the neighborhood than on getting seven more pounds of moon rock back."

In 1970 Sander Levin, a candidate for Governor in Michigan, revealed that his position regarding pollution control was that "the primary responsibility for stopping big pollutors must belong to state government. The governor should make sure it's the polluter, not the taxpayer, who pays to clean up our state." And Paul Sarbanes, 1982 candidate for reelection to the U.S. Senate from Maryland, aired this ad about the social security system:

> Franklin Roosevelt wanted to provide security for older people in their retirement years. Is that a fundamental objective of this society? Is that what a decent society oughtta be all about? I think it is. And if someone comes along to me and says, "Well, we're gonna cut the old people and their retirement in order to give a big tax break to the very rich." I mean my response to that is, well, what kind of sense of priorities is that?

Ten percent of the ads in this sample contained these *fairly* specific policy promises. This kind of appeal, then, is twice as prevalent as the more specific policy promises. The two kinds of appeals combined, furthermore, show up in no more than 15 percent of all the commercials analyzed.

Is it possible that this analysis has underestimated the prevalence of prospective policy positions? Surely candidates talk about policy alternatives more often than has been suggested so far. It is true that candidates raise policy choices in many more commercials than have been analyzed so far. However, in these other ads the mention of an issue is not accompanied by the revelation of a policy *position* or policy *preference.* Rather, the candidate's appeal is so vague or ambiguous as to prevent the viewer from using it as the basis of a policy choice or to hold a public official accountable for political actions.

A few examples should clarify this distinction.

Richard Nixon (1960—U.S. President) on national defense:

NARRATOR: Mr. Nixon, what is the truth about our defenses? How strong should they be?

NIXON: Well, they must be strong enough to keep us out of war; powerful enough to make the Communists in the Soviet Union and Red China understand that American will not tolerate being pushed around. That we can, if necessary, retaliate with such speed and devastation to make the risk too great for the Communists to start a war any place in the world. We have this kind of strength now and we are getting stronger every day. We must never let the Communists think we are weak. This is both foolish and dangerous. And so I say let's not tear America down; let us speak up for America.

NARRATOR: Vote for Nixon and Lodge November 8th. They understand what peace demands.

Barry Goldwater (1964—U.S. President) on foreign policy:

WOMAN: I'm Mrs. Hustler, and I have a question for Barry Goldwater. I'm concerned about communism, and it's spread throughout the world. You know, as the years go by, they gain more ground all the time, and as time goes on the matter is going to get much worse. I'd like Mr. Goldwater to tell me his thoughts and ideas on how we can stop the spread of communism throughout the world.

GOLDWATER: Well, the first thing we can and should do is to rebuild and revitalize our whole system of alliances. Top priority must go to repairing the damage done by this administration to the great North Atlantic Treaty Organization, which to me is the greatest peace-keeping force ever devised by free men. Our allies will know that, once again, America wants to work with them as equal partners, in the cause of freedom and peace.

NARRATOR: In your heart, you know he's right. Vote for Barry Goldwater.

Walter Mondale (1984—U.S. President) on international trade:

MONDALE: . . . I believe in an open, international, competitive environment. Playing on a level table. But I'm not a sucker, and I think the American people want their President to stand up for the American economy, American workers, American businesses, and American farmers again. And I intend to do that.

Narrator: Mondale, for President.

Dick Stone (1974—U.S. Senate) on the issues:

Stone: I'm Dick Stone. As your United States Senator I'll work with other senators who believe in keeping America strong. A fiscally conservative America. An America which takes care of Americans first. I believe in a workable policy of environmental improvement, consumer protection, and a strong health care program. I want to be your hard working United States Senator.

Narrator: Dick Stone is there when you need him. Democrat.

Edward Kennedy (1970—U.S. Senate) on medical care:

Narrator: A Massachusetts town meeting on a hot summer evening.

Man: You know, with the rising costs of medicine and hospitalization, do you think the government should be stepping in to investigate these all and program along this line, Senator?

Kennedy: The whole health area, which means some seventy billion dollars a year that is expended by federal, state, local, and individual taxpayers, is the fastest failing business in the country. I think we oughta devise a system which increases the total manpower, health manpower, in this country and, secondly, devise a better delivery means for health services to the people of this country. So that better health will not be just a privilege of the few, but will be actually a right for the many.

Narrator: Kennedy. Kennedy of Massachusetts.

What is striking about these bogus policy appeals is that they are without risk to the candidates and are a considerable distance from the types of policy alternatives that public officials face. They are more similar to consensually held *values* than they are to *policy promises,* and they are hardly the sort of appeal with which anyone could seriously disagree. Almost everyone is in favor of a strong national defense, a revitalized NATO alliance, a competitive international marketplace, consumer protection, and a better health care system. The policy question is more typically how to accomplish these objectives, a question on which this type of appeal is silent.

Policy appeals of this type are more prevalent in political commercials than are the more specific policy promises discussed above. Twenty-two percent of these ads contain only this type of policy appeal—a greater percentage of the ads than accounted for by the specific and fairly specific ads combined (see Table 11).

In short, the ideals of the civics book authors and the hopes of political scientists are seldom met in this form of campaign communication. Although a future-oriented consideration of public policy questions is often present in televised campaign commercials (all the ads considered so far represent 37 percent of the total sample) candidates more often reveal a riskless, ambiguous, vague policy promise than a specific one. Consequently, it would be difficult for the public to use this form of campaign communication to make the sort of future-oriented comparison of policy preference revered by the prospective policy choice approach.

Retrospective Policy Satisfaction Appeals

Elections are not only an occasion for citizens to compare and evaluate the policy promises of candidates. They also provide an opportunity for the public to evaluate *past* policy performance and to reward or punish incumbent parties and candidates. Indeed, a considerable portion of campaign rhetoric is devoted to assessing social, economic, and political progress (or lack therefore); evaluating the impact of public policies; and arguing over whom to hold responsible for political events and conditions.

Retrospective appeals seldom ask the electorate to contrast the specific policy promises of candidates. Instead they ask citizens to look backward in time and to decide how satisfied they are in general with the policy actions of public officials or with the "state of the union." The

TABLE 11
COMMERCIALS IN WHICH POLICY INTENTIONS ARE REVEALED

	n^a	%
Specific Policy References	24	5
Fairly Specific Policy References	52	10
Vague, Ambiguous Policy References	111	22
Total References to Future Policy Decisions	187	37

[a]Total n = 506

focal point of this evaluation is usually the incumbent party or candidate, and the voter's choice is whether to stick with or turn out the incumbent. Twenty years ago V. O. Key (1966) noted this retrospective nature of electoral choices:

> As voters mark their ballots they may have in their minds impressions of the last TV political spectacular of the campaign, but, more important, they have in their minds recollections of their experiences of the past four years. Those memories may be happy ones or they may be memories of dissatisfaction with what government has done or left undone.
>
> The impact of events from the inauguration of an Administration to the onset of the next presidential campaign may affect far more voters than the fireworks of the campaign itself. Governments must act or not act, and the action or inaction may convert supporters into opponents or opponents into supporters.

Retrospective judgements are furthered by candidates when they place blame and claim credit for policy decisions and political conditions. Such appeals may not, and usually do not, contain any indication of what a candidate would have done differently or what the candidate would propose doing in the future. Nor are such appeals necessarily careful about holding public officials responsible only for those policies or conditions on which they exerted some influence. What this type of appeal does do, however, is ask citizens the question Ronald Reagan asked repeatedly in 1980: "Are you better off today than you were four years ago?"

A number of electoral observers have argued that it is easier for citizens to make retrospective than prospective policy choices. Not only is performance more concrete than promises, but information is more abundant and credible about past and current conditions than about the impact of specific policy proposals.

> Voters aren't sure of their policy preferences because they don't know, and can't easily find out, just what the effects of alternative policies would be. But they do know their basic goals and values, and can rather easily in their daily lives get some information about whether times are good or bad in terms of these values. (Page, 1978, p. 194)

And,

> The prospects for the future may generally tend less to engage the voter or to govern his actions. Those prospects tend to be hazy, uncertain, problem-

atic. Voters may respond most assuredly to what they have seen, heard, experienced. Forecasts, promises, predicted disaster, or pie in the sky may be less moving. (Key, 1966, p. 52)

Candidates contribute to retrospective policy evaluations with their televised commercials in three different ways. One is through *credit-claiming.* Candidates frequently claim credit for personal achievements and for the improvements in social, economic, or political conditions. Incumbent Presidents and Vice Presidents, for example, claim credit for social conditions or improvements in social conditions during their administrations, as these excerpts illustrate:

1960 Richard Nixon campaign:

NIXON: Americans are working at better jobs for more pay than ever before. And we must continue this sound growth to stay strong and to keep the peace.
NARRATOR: Vote for Nixon and Lodge November 8th. They understand what peace demands.

1964 Lyndon Johnson campaign:

NARRATOR: When you're in the voting booth on November 3rd, keep this in mind. America is stronger and more prosperous than ever before and we're at peace. Vote for President Johnson November 3rd. The stakes are too high for you to stay home.

1976 Gerald Ford campaign:

NARRATOR: Here's what the people of New Hampshire are saying about President Ford.
1ST MAN: Well, I think President Ford has done an excellent job in the past two years in the White House. I think he's turned the economy around, which was very necessary.
1ST WOMAN: I think he tries very hard to put his programs over and to do what he thinks is necessary to restore the economy and I think he's really helped it a lot. . . .

Presidential non incumbents, of course, do not have a record of policy accomplishments as President to point to. Most presidential aspirants, however, have some political achievements for which they can claim credit. So, for example, in 1976 Democratic presidential contenders Jimmy Carter and Henry Jackson each claimed credit for actions taken while holding nonpresidential, elective office:

NARRATOR: Jimmy Carter is one Democrat who's proved he can manage government. Listen.
CARTER: When I was elected governor, we had 300 agencies or departments in the Georgia bureaucracy. We abolished 218 of them.
NARRATOR: Jimmy Carter unscrambled a bureaucratic mess during his term as Governor. He can do it as President. Jimmy Carter knows that working Americans are paying for government's inefficiency, and he'll eliminate waste. Vote for Jimmy Carter.

1976 Scoop Jackson campaign:

NARRATOR: Who do the big oil companies attack with newspaper ads because he fought to keep prices down? Shriver, Sanford, Harris, Wallace, Udall, Shapp, Carter, Bayh? Nope, Senator Scoop Jackson. Whose amendment helped thousands flee Eastern Europe for freedom in the West? Bayh, Shriver, Wallace, Udall, Shapp, Carter, Sanford, Harris? Nope. Senator Scoop Jackson. Who authored most of the landmark legislation to protect our environment? Carter, Sanford, Harris, Shapp, Wallace, Shriver, Bayh, Udall? Nope, Senator Scoop Jackson. Let's have a President who does something. Elect Senator Scoop Jackson while there's still time to save the 70s.

Occasionally (and only occasionally) candidates claim credit not for personal accomplishments but for the achievements of their party. In this highly unusual ad from Hubert Humphrey's 1968 presidential campaign credit is claimed for the policy enactments of the Democratic party.

NARRATOR: What have the Democrats ever done for you? Well, let's think about it. Your kids are getting a better education today because Democrats have given schools needed federal aid. And when school is out, your kids won't have to wander the streets—Democrats have paved the way for them to get good summer jobs. You've got more money today for those little luxuries, because Democrats worked hard to push through a higher minimum wage. You don't have to worry about supporting your mother today and she needn't worry about being a burden on you—thanks to social security and medicare. Quite an accomplishment? You know it; and you only heard a minute's worth. What have the Democrats ever done for you? Think about it. . . .

This is a rarity. The credit that is typically claimed by candidates is personal rather than partisan. This is in keeping with the individualistic, entrepreneurial campaign style of contemporary American electoral politics in which the focus is generally on the candidate as an individual political actor rather than on the candidate as a member of a political party. Although there is nothing legal or technical that prevents a candidate from engaging in *partisan* credit-claiming, our political culture and the reward/incentive structure among politicians do not encourage such appeals.

Incumbent executives of other types—most notably governors and mayors—are also not bashful about claiming personal credit for programmatic success in their television advertisements. In 1978 then governor of Iowa Robert Ray claimed credit for atracting new jobs to Iowa and encouraging existing companies to expand there; in 1978 then governor of Ohio Jim Rhodes claimed credit for enacting policies to assist senior citizens and for supervising snow removal during a winter blizzard; in 1974 then governor of Kentucky Wendell Ford claimed credit for reducing the sales tax, streamlining the state government, enacting a statewide kindergarten program, and developing an energy policy; in 1974 then governor of Ohio John Gilligan claimed credit for attacking consumer fraud, providing increases in state support for the public schools, improving the treatment of the disabled and mentally ill, enacting a reduction in the property taxes paid by senior citizens, and improving safety in the workplace; in 1966 then governor of New York Nelson Rockefeller claimed credit for improving the roads and water quality in New York State; and in 1970 then governor of Texas Preston Smith claimed credit for increasing state educational expenditures. Obviously "running on one's record" is a favorite pastime of incumbent executives.

Incumbent legislators also often claim credit. However, the achievements they publicize are more varied and less programmatic. Sometimes legislators do claim credit in their commercials for authoring pieces of legislation as did Jennings Randolph in 1972 (the 26th amendment, granting the right to vote to eighteen to twenty-one year olds); Lawton Chiles in 1976 (the Sunshine Bill); Warren Magnuson in 1980 (a job training program and consumer labeling law); Henry Jackson in 1982 (the sale of surplus federal land); and Bob Griffin in 1966 (the Landrum-Griffin Act). In addition, legislators also sometimes claim credit for legislation they have supported or worked to defeat: Congressman John Jenrette, "fought to keep the Emergency Jobs Bill and the Public Works Bill . . ." and "worked for bills to create jobs in the railroading and construction industry"; and Senator Bennett Johnston voted against the Consumer Protection Bill, "to cut excessive government spending"; and for "legislation to save the family farmer."

There are also other dimensions of credit-claiming available for incumbent legislators, since they are representatives as well as law-makers. Incumbent congressmen also spend much time and breath claiming credit for exercising power within the legislature and for performing important services for their constituencies. A couple of examples will suffice to illustrate this point:

Exercising influence within the legislature:

NARRATOR: We're lucky that Bennett Johnston ranks second on the Senate Energy Committee. He'll be the next chairman.

JOHNSTON: Last year the House of Representatives passed the President's energy bill. It would have been devastating to Louisiana. Taking our gas North, doubling our utility rates, closing Louisiana industries. But in my committee we turned it around. Now we've got an energy bill that's good for the country, and good for Louisiana.

NARRATOR: Keep Bennett Johnston on the job in the U.S. Senate.

CHURCH: Idaho is a farm state and I spend much of my time in the Senate on farm problems. Over the years I've learned from the farmers themselves what these problems are. I've worked to curb excessive foreign imports of meat and dairy products . . . and to make government support programs, as in the case of wheat and sugar beets, work as well as possible. But experience has taught me that the real . . . of the farmer doesn't lie in government supports but rather increasing his own bargaining power in the marketplace. I'm working for legislation which will free the farmer of government control while strengthening his own capacity to obtain a fair price for his product.

NARRATOR: Seniority gets things done in Washington and Frank Church is Idaho's senior Senator. In fact, Frank Church is one of the country's senior Senators. Vote for Frank Church—a Senator the whole country respects.

Constituent service and bringing "goodies" home to the district:

NARRATOR: Idleness is a greater enemy to Indiana and the nation than any other force on earth. But when machines are going jobs are created, wages are paid, and America has prosperity. Last year, Senator Vance Hartke helped bring to Indiana $500 million of federal contracts alone. Senator Hartke's aware of the needs of Indiana's business and industries that helped build the longest and strongest period of prosperity known in

Indiana history. Large or small business, as long as it's good for Indiana's economy, Senator Hartke is there to help them. Alcoa, U.S. Steel, Goodyear and Kaiser . . . contracts have all been assisted by Senator Hartke. The Senator also brought aid to Indiana's limestone, coal and oil industries. In his second term Senator Vance Hartke will continue to work for increased business and job opportunites for all of Indiana. Re-elect Vance Hartke, U.S. Senator.

NARRATOR: When the federal government cut off highway construction funds, Senator Bayh promised to do something. $15.2 million in highway funds were restored to Indiana. The promising young Senator kept his promise. Senator Bayh for Senator.

Of the television ads analyzed here, 23 percent contain a credit-claiming appeal. Therefore, credit-claiming for past accomplishments is more prevalent in televised spots than the revelation of specific or fairly specific policy promises.

Candidates also encourage retrospective judgments through *blame-placing.* This type of appeal is the flip-side of credit-claiming and is one in which a candidate or party is blamed for some policy failure, decision, event, or worsening of conditions. These appeals are often made by challengers and represent some of the so-called "negative" or "attack" advertisements.

There are many ways of attempting to make an election a referendum that punishes a candidate for past actions and current policy dissatisfaction. One is to criticize an individual for specific actions, as these ads attempt to do:

NARRATOR: This is a Clark McGregor doll. Wind him up and he votes no for the people of Minnesota. On raising the minimum wage of $1.25 McGregor voted no. On new housing for the elderly, no. On improving farm prices, no. Does McGregor ever vote yes for the people of Minnesota? No. One man has always voted yes for you. Humphrey. You know he cares.

1ST NARRATOR: You're trying to figure out how to pay your bills.
2ND NARRATOR: U.S. Senator John Heinz isn't worried. He's a millionaire.
1ST NARRATOR: You're worried about keeping your job.
2ND NARRATOR: Heinz voted for huge tax breaks for the rich and big business.
1ST NARRATOR: You're worried about putting your kids through college.
2ND NARRATOR: Heinz voted to cut student loans.
1ST NARRATOR: You're worried about retirement.
2ND NARRATOR: Heinz voted to cut minimum social security benefits.

1st Narrator: We think it's time to stop the Senator's party. Common sense for Pennsylvania. Cyril Wecht for Senate.

Narrator: Pete Flaherty wants you to believe he cut taxes while he was mayor of Pittsburgh. The truth is that after he was elected mayor, Flaherty rammed through the Pittsburgh city council a 20 percent increase in property taxes, and a 40 percent increase in his own salary. He took Pittsburgh so far into debt that the city's credit rating has dropped twice since he left office. So the question is this: Can the man who drove Pittsburgh to its knees put Pennsylvania back on its feet? The one man who can is Dick Thornburgh.

Another way of placing blame is by attempting to hold a public official responsible for worrisome or worsening conditions. In the following ad, blame is placed not for any specific action by the public official but for social conditions regardless of the official's specific role in them. In many ads, in fact, public officials are blamed for a failure to act rather than for a decision that did not turn out well.

Narrator: For twelve years, during the lifetime of most of our children, New York State has been governed by one man. In twelve years, we've increased the air pollution in our cities by 60 percent. After twelve years, two thirds of our population lives near polluted water. The Hudson has become a sewer, the Niagara River a drain for a poisonous mercury. Every twelve months we've spent a half a billion dollars on highways while transit fares increased 20 to 50 percent each year. In twelve years we've turned our back on reality. In twelve years we've become the victims of political neglect. Do we need four more? Vote Goldberg, Patterson.

In recent years, the blame-placing ads appearing on the nation's airwaves have taken on a new appearance; they have become quite partisan rather than candidate-oriented. First the Republicans in 1980, and then the Democrats in 1982, produced advertising campaigns which attempted to hold the other party responsible for the nation's ills. The Republicans fired the opening salvo in 1980:

Worker: I used to work here along with a lot of other people. Nearly a year ago, they closed the plant for good. I'm one of the millions of people in this country who have lost their jobs. And we've got something to say to the Democrats: you've been running Congress; you've been running the economy. So we've got just one question. If the Democrats are good for working people, how come so many people aren't working?

NARRATOR: Let's get America working again. Vote Republican. For a change.

The Democrats answered back in 1982:

NARRATOR: Two years ago we trusted the Republicans to mind the store in Washington. They promised us they'd bring prosperity and respect America's heritage of fairness. Instead, they're crushing the hope of our elderly, of workers, small business, farmers, and a generation's dreams. The Republicans have made a mess of things. Now, they want to throw their weight around our state. Only one thing stands between them and us: The Democrats. Democrats stand for fairness.

Partisan blame-placing has also been attempted at the state level. In this ad, the Democratic candidate for governor in Wisconsin places blame on the Republicans.

NARRATOR: A Wisconsin political quiz. You have sixty seconds to answer the following questions:

In the last six years, which party has twice raised taxes after promising no tax increase? The Republicans.

Which party was responsible for eliminating $322,000 in funds for campus security? The Republicans.

Which party refuses to enforce antipollution laws against Wisconsin's big industries? The Republicans.

Which party claimed a three million dollar surplus in 1968 and a twenty-nine million dollar debt sixty days later? The Republicans.

Which candidate for Governor led the fight to raise the sales tax to 4 percent? Olsen.

Which candidate best promises a real change for Wisconsin? Lucey. Nov. 3rd.

And in this ad, consisting entirely of scenes of zoo animals, the Michigan Republican party chastizes the Democrats for their policy failures and ineffectiveness:

NARRATOR: Have you noticed how the Lansing Zoo, otherwise known as the Democratic State Legislature, is such a sleepy place? Maybe that's why it took them thirteen months to lower the tolerance levels on PBB. And after four years they still haven't passed a jobs placement bill. On the energy crisis the Democratic legislature just couldn't quite summon the energy to do anything. Maybe they need a good long rest. It looks like it.

Blame-placing is, like credit-claiming, a prevalent type of commercial appeal. 23 percent of the ads analyzed here contain an attempt to blame a public official or political party for some political act or social condition. When credit-claiming and blame-placing are considered together 44 percent of the ads contain an attempt to either claim credit, place blame, or both.

The third way in which candidates contribute to retrospective judgments is by drawing attention to social problems or conditions that are in need of correction. This type of appeal does not claim credit or place blame for past actions or current conditions but it does attempt to increase the salience of political issues or conditions which are worrisome. In that respect they are like the blame-placing appeals but they lack an attempt to place blame on any specific political actor. The following ads illustrate the way in which this type of appeal focuses the voter's attention on social, economic, or political problems without any indication of what the candidate would do about the issue in the future:

NARRATOR: Crimes of violence in the United States have almost doubled in recent years. Today, a violent crime is committed every 60 seconds; a robbery ever 2½ minutes; a mugging every 6 minutes; a murder every 43 minutes, and it will get worse unless we take the offensive. Freedom from fear is a basic right of every American. We must restore it.

CARTER: The Republican TV commercials assure us the economy's healthy, inflation's controlled, our leadership is great. But when I look around I see every trip to the supermarket a shock, cities collapsing, suburbs scared, policemen cut, welfare skyrocketing. That's reality. The Republicans won't face up to it, but we can change it. Americans have done it before and we'll do it again. It's a long, tough job; it's time we got started.

HART You don't have to be a young revolutionary to say something's wrong. We think that we're the healthiest people in the world—best medical system. Truth is, we're eighteenth among twenty-three of all the developed nations. We can do better than that.
NARRATOR: Phil Hart, the senior Senator from Michigan.

Ads which attempt to raise the salience of a political problem without necessarily giving any indication of what ought to be done about the issues in the future, are just as prevalent as credit-claiming and blame-placing ads. In fact, 21 percent of the ads analyzed here mention social conditions or problems in this way.

Televised campaign commercials clearly promote retrospective judgments by voters and, hence, electoral choices that are a referendum on past policy performance and current policy satisfaction. This is done by claiming credit, placing blame, and raising issues about past and present conditions and performance. Over half (60 percent) of the ads in this study attempt to promote retrospective judgments (Table 12) while only 15 percent of the ads reveal the information necessary for a prospective policy choice. If these ads are at all indicative of the content of all televised campaign commercials, it would suggest that this information flow is far more conducive to retrospective than prospective judgments.

Sometimes candidates combine retrospective policy satisfaction and prospective policy intention appeals in the same advertisement. In the ads that follow, for example, the candidate raises a political, social, or economic problem or condition and then couples this with some hint of what ought to be done in the future. In the first Lyndon Johnson criticizes Barry Goldwater for his vote on Medicare and then takes a fairly specific policy position on this same issue, and in the second Claude Kirk combines a list of Florida's problems with a somewhat vague future-oriented policy promise.

NARRATOR: On September 1st 1964, Senator Barry M. Goldwater interrupted his vacation cruise and headed for shore in a big hurry. Destination: Washington, D.C. He arrived just in time to cast his vote: NO. Then he turned around and headed back. Senator Goldwater flew across the continent twice, almost 6,000 miles, to vote against a program of hospital insurance

TABLE 12
RETROSPECTIVE POLICY SATISFACTION COMMERCIALS

	n[a]	%
Credit-claiming	114	23
Blame-placing	117	23
Issue-raising	104	21
Total retrospective ads[b]	305	60

[a]Total $n = 506$

[b]These totals are less than the sum of the first three rows because an ad may contain more than one type of retrospective policy satisfaction appeal.

for older Americans. As he said in the *Atlantic Constitution* on January 26th, 1963, "I've got my own medicare plan. I've got an intern for a son-in-law." Flip answers do not solve the problems of human beings. President Johnson wants a program of hospital insurance for older Americans. He is determined to see this program passed in the next Congress. Vote for President Johnson on November 3rd. The stakes are too high for you to stay home.

NARRATOR: Had enough high prices? Fed up with the tax happy, free spending ultraliberals? Tired of the high cost of living and the declining value of your dollar? What can you do to help bring prices down? Elect Claude Kirk governor.

KIRK: I pledge to resist on every level the liberal society planners who've brought on the inflation that today strangles all of those living on low and fixed incomes. But I need your help, I need your vote to keep the ultraliberals out of Tallahassee.

NARRATOR: Vote for the man with the plan. Vote Kirk, Governor.

Combining retrospective and prospective policy appeals in the same commercial is quite rare. Only 8 percent of the advertisements analyzed here contained such a combined appeal, primarily because of the scarcity of specific or fairly specific policy promises to begin with.

In general, then, most programmatic statements made by candidates encourage a retrospective evaluation of policy decisions and effects and the assignment of responsibility for those actions and consequences. Much more unusual is candidate rhetoric which permits the contrasting of policy preferences or intentions. This would seem to indicate that the policy-centered meaning of elections is much more likely to be retrospective than prospective, performance-oriented rather than intention-oriented, and based on global satisfaction and assignment of responsibility rather then issue comparison and proximity. It is difficult to see how the notion of a policy mandate is furthered by televised commercials except insofar as the electorate reveals a general preference for continuity or change.

Benevolent Leader Appeals

A third approach to elections is the *benevolent leader* perspective. From this viewpoint the significance of election campaigns is not to be found in their programmatic content, either past or future. Rather, the electoral process provides the electorate with an opportunity to select those public officials who possess the personality traits appropriate for the role to which they aspire. While some of those personality traits might be indirectly related to the policy preferences and intentions of public officials (e.g., prudence as indicative of the likelihood of committing U.S. troops into a no-win situation), it is the correspondence between the personas of candidates and the role expectations the public has for different offices which is of more central concern.

It is this perspective on elections more than any other that has been implicitly assumed to prevail in the world of televised political advertisements. Commentary on "packaging" candidates and the "image" campaigns of media consultants usually has in mind the presentation of candidate personas. Television, because of its visual component, is assumed by many to be uniquely effective in transmitting "information" about the personality traits of candidates.

To what extent are televised advertisements consistent with the "benevolent leader" approach? It is clear that most of the commercials studied here include information which might be used by the viewer to form an impression of the personalities of candidates. What if we confine our attention, however, to the explicit, verbal attempts to persuade the audience that a candidate possesses specific personality traits? Though such an approach will yield a conservative estimate of the prevalence of "the benevolent leader" it has the virtue of relying more on the explicit content of the ad itself than on the message-received impression transaction between the ad and the audience.

Of the 506 ads studied here, 290 (57 percent) contained an explicit reference to the personal attributes of candidates. Across these 290 ads over 100 distinct attributes were mentioned. An analysis of these attributes indicates that most of these mentions may be understood as representative of six clusters of personality traits.

One cluster of personal attributes frequently touched upon in campaign commercials has to do with a candidate's *compassion.* References to concern, caring, and compassion form the core of this personality cluster. Also included within this grouping are attributes which indicate compassion by one's deeds—through adjectives such as protective and helpful—and attributes which indicate compassion in one's thoughts and beliefs—through, for example, sensitivity and understanding. Though the term "understanding" can mean a number of different things, the context in which it is used in the ads coded here makes clear that it is understanding of people's problems, concerns, and values that is at issue.

The two ads presented below are good examples of those that attempt to persuade the electorate that a candidate is compassionate.[2] In the first, Edward Kennedy states explicitly that Warren Magnuson is compassionate, and in the second the message is delivered via a jingle for Lamar Alexander, a then-Republican candidate for governor of Tennessee.

KENNEDY: This is Senator Edward Kennedy of Massachusetts. When I came to the United States some six years ago the man I looked to for real leadership in that body was your own Warren Magnuson. He's a man of great power in that body, but he uses his power compassionately, humanely, and for the interests of the people, not only of this state but of the nation. I hope you'll send him back to the United States Senate where he belongs.

If the right man was there, with care and understanding,
Walkin' arm in arm and hand in hand,
Talkin' face to face to get to know us better
Wouldn't it be great, if the right man was there?
Wouldn't it be great, with Alexander there.

Table 13 shows the number of references to compassion in the 506 ads analyzed here. Most of the references are to a candidate's caring,

TABLE 13
REFERENCES TO CANDIDATE COMPASSION IN TELEVISED SPOT ADS*

Core Attributes	
Compassion	12
Concern	6
Caring	20
Relationship with others	
Protective	2
Helpful	2
Personal Characteristics	
Understanding	14
Sensitive	3
Total	59

*6% of all 931 personal attributes coded.

compassion, and understanding. The total represents 6 percent of all of the personal attribute references coded.

A second cluster of personality attributes mentioned in political commercials involves a candidate's *empathy* with the public. The core characteristics within this cluster are empathy, being in "touch," or being "one of us." Empathy can be demonstrated with thought or belief—via reference to rapport, listening, being common or down-to-earth, and being altruistic or public-regarding—or with actions—via reference to being dependable or responsive.

The two ads presented below attempt to establish a candidate's empathy with the citizenry. At stake is the ability of the candidate to put himself in the people's place and identify with their problems, concerns, hopes, and fears. In the first ad, Dale Bumpers is portrayed as in touch, trustworthy, responsive, and understanding, and in the second Jimmy Carter is someone whose experiences give him a special empathy with those who work for a living.

NARRATOR: Dale Bumpers cares enough to stay in touch with the people. And his accomplishments for Arkansas prove you can trust his judgment.

BUMPERS: Who do you think will listen to you? Who do you think will be the most responsive to your needs? Who do you think understands your problems best and will work the hardest to solve them? That is an issue.

NARRATOR: Elect Dale Bumpers your Senator. He'll listen to the people of Arkansas.

NARRATOR: Jimmy Carter knows what it's like to work for a living. Until he became governor he put in twelve hours a day in his shirt-sleeves during harvest at his farm. Can you imagine any of the other candidates for President working in the hot August sun? That's why Jimmy Carter has a special understanding of the problems facing everyone who works for a living. America needs someone like this as President. Vote for Jimmy Carter in your Democratic primary.

Table 14 shows the references to empathy in the spots analyzed here. Most of the references are to a candidate being "in touch," "one of us," dependable, responsive, and public-regarding. All together, references to empathy constitute 16 percent of the personal characteristics coded.

A third dimension of "benevolent leader" portrayals involves a candidate's *integrity*. Here the core values are honesty, integrity, trustworthiness, fairness, and decency. Integrity in one's speech or actions is

Table 14
References to Candidate Empathy in Televised Spot Ads*

Core Attributes	
Empathy	24
In touch, one of us	25
Accessible	1
Empathy demonstrated with actions	
Dependable	24
Responsive	17
Empathy demonstrated by thought, belief	
Listens, easy to talk to	15
Rapport	3
Public-regarding	32
Altruistic	4
Common, down-to-earth	6
Washington outsider	1
Total	152

*16% of all 944 personal attributes coded.

evidenced by being candid, genuine, sincere, open, and forthright. Integrity in one's thought or belief is presented by portraying a candidate as principled, moral, ethical, independent, or honorable.

The next three ads illustrate the presentation of integrity. In the first, three "persons-on-the-street" assert that Jimmy Carter is honest, in the second Archibald Cox gives a testimonial to Morris Udall's honesty, and in the third Bennett Johnston attempts to portray himself as honest and candid.

Narrator: On September 23rd, more than half a million Georgians voted for Jimmy Carter.
1st Woman: I believe he will be honest in all of his decisions.
1st Man: I just think he knows the state of Georgia. He knows the people, he knows what it's all about.
2nd Woman: Jimmy's honest and he's capable of developing the potential that Georgia seems to have.
2nd Mand: I think he's a really sincere and honest man. That's the reason I voted for him. . . .

NARRATOR: Vote for Jimmy Carter again November 3rd in the general election. Half a million Georgians can't be wrong.

COX: What kind of man can help restore our confidence and remind us that we can have the country we want to have? Certainly, it's only a man of character, only a man of openness, integrity, courage, and honor can do those things. I'm confident that Morris Udall is such a man.
NARRATOR: Elect Mo Udall President.

JOHNSTON: Some politicians think they can fool all the people, all the time. The position they took yesterday is changed today and forgotten tomorrow. They'll tell you whatever they think you want to hear. Well, that kind of politics is a thing of the past. The people of this state want straight talk, not false promises; honesty, not arm waving. Integrity and hard work—that's what we need in the United States Senate.

In Table 15 we can see that explicit references to honesty, integrity, trustworthiness and candor predominate in the portrayal of candidate integrity. Together such references constitute 17 percent of all personal references.

A fourth cluster of personal attributes frequently used in political commercials contains references to the *activity* level of the candidate. Vigor, energy, drive, initiative, enthusiasm and hard-working represent the core of this cluster. Related attributes include ways in which an individual manifests activity—through, for example, one's dedication, commitment, purpose, conviction, confidence, and sense of urgency—and ways in which a candidate's activity level affects other people—through, for instance, dynamism and inspiration.

The two ads presented below illustrate verbal attempts to demonstrate action. In the first, Frank Church is presented as a hard worker, and the second asserts that Lee Hamilton is young, energetic, and aggressive.

NARRATOR: Isn't it great to have a senator who works as hard as you do? Vote for Frank Church. A Senator the whole country respects.

SONG: Come on, you Hoosiers, look at our progress
In just a hundred and fifty years
We now are building a new Indiana
Cause we're the modern pioneers.

NARRATOR: This is Congressman Lee Hamilton; young, energetic, aggressive. A Congressman who gets things done for the people of the new ninth district. Reelect Congressman Lee Hamilton. . . .

TABLE 15
REFERENCES TO CANDIDATE INTEGRITY IN TELEVISED SPOT ADS*

Core Attributes	
Integrity	14
Honesty	51
Trustworthy	16
Ethical	3
As demonstrated by personal thought and deed	
Honorable	2
Principled	6
Independent, independent-minded	7
Conviction	3
Humane	2
Fair	8
Decent	1
Moral	5
As demonstrated with speech	
Candid	8
Forthright	10
Clear	9
Specific	2
Outspoken	3
Open	7
Genuine, sincere	4
Total	161

*17% of all 944 personal attributes coded.

Table 16 shows the explicit, verbal references to a candidate's activity level. Activity is demonstrated mainly through references to being hard-working, effective, active, dedicated, and committed. All together there are 121 references to activity representing 13 percent of all personal references in these ads.

A fifth grouping of personal attributes in political commercials focuses on the *strength* of the candidate. The core of this cluster is indicated by such adjectives as tough, strong, firm, solid, steady, stable, decisive, consistent, and courageous. Related concepts assert that a candidate

TABLE 16
REFERENCES TO CANDIDATE ACTIVITY IN TELEVISED SPOT ADS*

Core Attributes	
Drive	1
Enthusiasm	1
Energetic	4
Active	18
Vigorous	3
Hard-working	35
Initiative	1
Effective	33
Effect of activity on others	
Inspiring	1
Dynamic	1
Personal indications of activity	
Dedicated	9
Committed	6
Purposeful	3
Conviction	1
Crusader	1
Urgency	1
Striving	1
Confidence	1
Total	121

*13% of all 944 personal attributes coded.

possesses "inner" strength—through persistence, determination, and perseverence—and that a candidate demonstrates strength in his relations with others—by being demanding, for example. Strength is also portrayed by presenting a candidate as powerful and "a fighter."

The next two ads illustrate candidate strength. In the first, Bill Bradley draws an analogy between the dogged determination of Senator Don Riegle and one of his former teammates on the New York Knicks, and in the second Eleanor Roosevelt delivers a testimonial to the strength, conviction, and power of John Kennedy.

Narrator: It was a tough fight in the Congress to save social security. Senator Bill Bradley talks about Senator Don Riegel's leadership.

Bradley: And, frankly, Don Riegel became the leader of that effort. And, you know, I had a previous profession as a basketball player and we used to say that someone was in someone's face like, say, DeBusschere, for example. And nobody could score because he was dogged and determined. And in my view Don Riegel played that role on the minimum benefit. He led the fight and he was successful.

Narrator: Senator Don Riegel. He fights for Michigan.

Narrator: Here is a message from Mrs. Eleanor Roosevelt.

E. Roosevelt: If we are to be the spokesmen for a free world, we must begin at home by ensuring all our people regardless of race, religion, or national origin equal opportunity under law and under God. When you cast your vote for president of the United States, be sure you have studied the record. I have, and I urge you to vote for John F. Kennedy, for I have come to believe that as the president he will have the strength and the moral courage to provide the leadership for human rights we need in this time of crisis. He's a man with a sense of history.

Narrator: Vote for John F. Kennedy for president.

Table 17 shows the references to candidate strength in this sample of ads. The prevalent attributes are being tough, strong, steady, courageous, powerful, and a fighter. All together 145 or 15 percent of the personal references in these ads are to strength.

A sixth cluster of personal attributes appearing in political commercials relates to the *knowledge* possessed by candidates. The core of this cluster involves references to being knowledgeable, smart, enlightened, wise, intelligent, prudent, sensible, thoughtful, reasonable, rational, practical, and so forth. A related dimension of knowledgeability emphasizes possessing appropriate types of experience. Adjectives such as seasoned, savvy, well-rounded, respected, and senior suggest this aspect of knowledge. A different aspect of knowledge involves the type of creative intelligence suggested by such terms as creative, innovative, ingenious, imaginative, insightful, and instinctive.

The two ads presented below illustrate the portrayal of candidate knowledge. The first comments on Lyndon Johnson's prudence, and the second on Don Riegle's thoroughness and reason.

Narrator: The Constitution does not tell us what kind of man a President must be. It says he must be thirty-five years old and a natural-born citizen. It

TABLE 17
REFERENCES TO CANDIDATE STRENGTH IN TELEVISED SPOT ADS*

Core Attributes	
Tough	14
Strong	24
Firm, solid, steady, stable, sure	14
Serious	1
Decisive	6
Consistent	11
Courageous	16
Relationship with others	
Powerful	10
Demanding	2
Insistent	1
Fighter	30
Aggressive	1
Bold	3
Personal strength	
Determined	4
Persistent, tireless, inexhaustible	6
Perseverant	2
Total	145

*15% of all 944 personal attributes coded.

leaves the rest to the wisdom of the voters. Our presidents have been reasonable men; they have listened. They have thought clearly and spoken carefully. They have cared about people, for the pieces of paper on which they sign their names change people's lives. Most of all, in the final loneliness of this room, they have been prudent. They have known that the decisions they make there can change the course of history or end history altogether. In crisis and tragedy, we have found men worthy of this office. We have been fortunate. Vote for President Johnson on November 3rd. The stakes are too high for you to stay home.

NARRATOR: Senator John Glenn talks about Senator Don Riegle.

GLENN: He's known as being very thorough, and so when he gets into committee work or when he's trying to debate something on the floor that is either for

Michigan or for the country as a whole, people listen. People listen because they know that he has some rationale on his side that's been well-thought-out. He goes to work in committee and buttonholing individual Senators and explaining his position to them; that's the way leadership's exerted in the Senate.

Narrator: Senator Don Riegle. He fights for Michigan.

Table 18 shows the references to candidate knowledge in this collection of ads. Explicit references to experience, knowledge, and creativity

Table 18
References to Candidate Knowledge in Televised Spot Ads*

Core Attributes	
Knowledgeable, know-how	30
Smart, wise, intelligent, enlightened	12
Prudent, sensible, reasonable, careful	15
Practical, common sense	8
Thoughtful, sound judgment, clear thinker	8
Rational, planner	2
Open-minded	1
Educated, expert, sense of history	5
Attributes related to personal experience	
Experienced, tested	36
Respected	10
Seasoned	1
Savvy	1
Senior	2
Well-rounded	1
Competent, able	9
Attributes related to intellectual creativity	
Creative, innovative, ingenious, imaginative	23
Far sighted, visionary, dreamer	12
Insightful	1
Deep, complicated	2
Instinctive	2
Total	181

*19% of all personal attributes coded.

predominate, with numerous other references to intelligence, common sense, prudence, competence, and vision. The total number of references to knowledge—181—is the highest of any of the six attribute clusters and constitutes 19 percent of all the personal attributes exhibited in the ads.

Once these six attribute clusters have been accounted for, some 125 (13 percent) other personal attributes remain. Few of these recur with any regularity, nor do they define any other meaningful attribute clusters. Most of them are highly specific to a particular candidate or represent candidate characteristics other than personal ones. For example, such references as businessman (7), economist (2), father (6), farmer (2), statesman (2), ambassador (2), lawyer (4), vigilant (1), quiet (1), humorous (2), optimistic (6), impressive (2), proud (3), humble (3), and successful (3) are included in the "other" category.

Table 19 summarizes the distribution of references to a candidate's personal attributes across the six attribute clusters. There we see that references to knowledge are the most frequent, followed by references to empathy and integrity, and less closely by references to activity and strength. References to compassion are by far the least prevalent in the sample of ads.

As the analysis indicates, "benevolent leader" ads are one of the most prevalent types of televised commercial message. In fact, of the 506 ads considered here, over half (57 percent) contain some *explicit* attempt

TABLE 19

PERSONAL ATTRIBUTES MENTIONED IN TELEVISED SPOT ADS*

	NUMBER OF REFERENCES	%	NUMBER OF ADS CONTAINING REFERENCES	%
Compassion	59	6	31	11
Empathy	152	16	55	19
Integrity	161	17	86	30
Activity	121	13	74	26
Strength	145	15	90	31
Knowledge	181	19	90	31
Others	125	13	68	23
Total	944	99%		

N = 290 ads, 57% of the total of 506

to communicate a candidate's persona. This estimate is probably a conservative one since it ignores more implicit, exclusively visual attempts to transmit character traits. Consequently, this is undoubtedly one of the most typical uses of televised political advertising. As a result, televised ads increase the likelihood that electoral choices will be based on nonprogrammatic considerations.

Elections-as-Ritual Appeals

A fourth perspective on elections and the conduct of election campaigns might be called the *ritualistic* approach. Though admittedly a minority viewpoint among political scientists, the ritualistic approach holds that what is significant about election campaigns is not the choice made by voters but the conduct of the campaign itself. To these observers elections are rituals, that is, a type of motor activity which is the occasion for the celebration of one's identity and an opportunity for the reinforcement of cultural norms and values. The political discourse that takes place during election campaigns, to this school of thought, is more significant for the agreement between candidates and the articulation of consensually held beliefs, than for any programmatic or personal contrasts between candidates. To the ritualist, campaign rhetoric which is characterized as "empty"—because of its ambiguity, reliance on cliché, or use of cultural symbols—is not empty at all but filled with meaning. The meaning, however, is more typically the reinforcement of cultural myths and the reassurance of the citizenry than the presentation of distinctive, contrasting, and thought-provoking views.

What types of political commercials would be consistent with the *ritualistic* perspective? Generally, commercials which do not make any pretense of offering contrasting policy promises, retrospective judgments of policy successes or failures, or portrayals of the personas thought to be appropriate for a particular public office might be consistent with elections-as-ritual. More specifically, commercials which articulate cultural myths or values with which few are likely to disagree, commercials which rely upon the symbols of a political community, and commercials which are minimelodramas would be consistent with the ritualistic perspective.

We have already encountered one type of campaign commercials consistent with the ritualistic view. Many of the commercials containing prospective policy preferences, we saw, contained messages that were so vague and ambiguous as to reveal little to the public and to leave a public official uncommitted to any specific course of action. These commercials, which we saw constituted 22 percent of the total sample, commit a candidate to such policy positions as firm diplomacy, sound fiscal policy, responsible government, opposition to wasteful spending and the like. Such promises, one suspects, are utterly without risk to the candidate and engender little resistance or disagreement from the public. Consequently, they are likely to be comforting instead of challenging, reassuring rather than bothersome, and familiar more often than unfamiliar. I presented examples of these ads in the section dealing with prospective policy messages with the intention of clarifying, by means of contrast, the nature of those policy promises. In terms of an approach to elections, however, these vague policy promise commercials are consistent with an approach to elections emphasizing the importance of vacuous rhetoric.

A second type of commercial consistent with elections-as-ritual is one which contains many of the elements of melodrama in an attempt to tell a story about the candidate or the campaign. Since thirty or sixty seconds is not a very long time in which to develop a melodrama, political commercial melodramas are exceptionally truncated and simplistic. Nonetheless, many advertisements have used the elements of intensified peril, conflict, suspense, and villainry to communicate a message.

The most famous, and earliest example of such a minimelodrama was the Daisy spot of 1964. The spot attempts basically to frighten people by suggesting that the selection of the president may well have an effect on the likelihood of a nuclear war. The ad also provides a heroic portrayal of Lyndon Johnson, leaving it to the viewers to identify the villain:

CHILD'S VOICE: 1, 2, 3, 4, 5, 7, 6, 6, 8, 9, 9

DOOMSDAY VOICE: 10, 9, 8, 7, 6, 5, 4, 3, 2, 1, 0

JOHNSON: These are the stakes; to make a world in which all of God's children can live or to go into the dark. We must either love each other or we must die.

NARRATOR: Vote for President Johnson November 3rd. The stakes are too high for you to stay home.

The theme of a nuclear war has actually been fairly prevalent in political commercials. What is notable about these ads, and the reason for discussing them here is that they do not contain a discussion of the policies related to nuclear war nor even of the personality traits of candidates germane to the probability of war (as some benevolent leader commercials do). Rather, they merely articulate people's fear of nuclear war and imply or state explicitly that one ought to vote for a particular candidate because of that fear. The following ad, aired by Lyndon La-Rouche in 1976, is both illustrative of this genre and exceptional for its blunt presentation.

LAROUCHE: It is no exaggeration to say that if Jimmy Carter were to be elected on November 2nd this nation would be committed to thermonuclear war probably no later than the summer of 1977.

Candidates also play upon other fears or negatively valued stimuli in their television commercials. Communism, for example, is a favorite subject, with candidates often implying that if one is opposed to communism than one should vote a particular way. The following ads illustrate this tactic.

TEACHER: Hand over your heart, ready, begin. (Scenes of young children reciting the pledge juxtaposed with Khruschev's belligerent threats against the U.S.)

GOLDWATER: I want American kids to grow up as Americans. And they will if we have the guts to make our intentions clear, so clear they don't need translation or interpretation, just respect for a country prepared as no country in all history ever was.

NARRATOR: In your heart, you know he's right. Voter for Barry Goldwater.

NARRATOR: When it comes to spending taxpayer's money, Senator James Sasser in a master. Take foreign aid. While important programs are being cut back here at home, Sasser has voted to allow foreign aid to be sent to committed enemies of our country: Vietnam, Laos, Cambodia, Marxist Angola, and even Communist Cuba. You can bet James Sasser is making a lot more friends abroad than he is here in Tennessee.

CASTRO LOOK-ALIKE: Muchísimas gracias, señor Sasser.

Dissent or disorder is also a prevalent fear on the part of the American people and, as the ad below shows, has been used to make a not-so-subtle appeal for votes.

NIXON: It is time for an honest look at the problems of order in the United States. Dissent is a necessary ingredient of change, but in a system of government that provides for peaceful change, there is no cause that justifies resorting to violence. Let us recognize that the first civil right of every American is to be free from domestic violence. So I pledge to you, we shall have order in the United States.

Sometimes ads communicate a melodramatic message by focusing on a villain and implying that one's opponents are associated with that villainy. As we have already seen, Communist leaders often play the part of the villain, as do dissenters and protesters. Other villains, however, are more campaign-specific. In the next two 1982 ads, villainy is ascribed, in turn, to federal bureaucrats and the National Conservative Political Action Committee. Although there may be serious public policy issues lurking behind these melodramas, the commercials themselves do little to further an appreciation of such issues on the part of the viewer.

NARRATOR: Everywhere you look these days the federal government is there, telling you what they think; telling you what they think you oughtta think; telling you how you oughtta do things; setting up rules you can't follow. I think the federal government is going too far. Now, they say, if you don't take the portable facility along with you on a roundup, you can't go. We need someone to tell 'em about Wyoming. Malcolm Wallop will.

NARRATOR: During the next few weeks you're going to see some distasteful television commercials by some Washington promoters specializing in lies and half-truths. NCPAC has joined James Collins in an attack on Senator Lloyd Bentsen. NCPAC is the same organization that said it could elect Mickey Mouse, that brags that NCPAC can lie through its teeth, and the candidate it helps stays clean. So when you see those ads, remember, NCPAC and James Collins are not trying to build, they're trying to destroy. And that's not the way we do things in Texas.

The third type of commercial consistent with the ritualistic approach is one in which candidates attempt to use positively valued icons of the American political culture to their advantage. Although candidates often make certain that American flags, pictures of the White House, the presidential seal, Mount Rushmore, and the Statue of Liberty appear in their advertisements, the commercials dealt with here have positive cultural symbolization as the centerpiece of their message. In the following examples, Walter Mondale speaks out in favor of rural, small-town America; and Glenn Beall relies upon a celebration of the circumstances surrounding the writing of the Star-Spangled Banner.

MONDALE: It's not just the figures, it's the commitment; whether we believe in small communities, whether we believe in family farmers, whether we believe that people ought to live in communities where they know each other. And I don't . . . I'm not against big cities, but I think there ought to be a choice and increasingly there isn't any choice. I think there's a deeper issue; I think this country has to ask itself whether we really believe in rural America.

NARRATOR: Once in an hour of strife and danger, a young Marylander strained for a glimpse of a flag. The answer greeted him from these ramparts. A century and a half later, another Marylander pauses, reflecting on those events. His name is Glenn Beall. His roots are deep in Maryland. What has much of the strife this flag has seen been all about? Glenn Beall thinks its been a struggle by a people who demand the right to choose who will govern *for* them, not *over* them; men who will represent them. Glenn Beall knows how Marylanders feel about their flag, their state, about the kind of country they want this to be. That's why Maryland needs Glenn Beall in the United States Senate.

In 1980, two presidential candidates offered contrasting attempts to associate one's candidacy with positively evaluated icons of American culture. Edward Kennedy, during the primary season, delivered this message over film footage of a rocket lift-off (the ad was entitled "Apollo").

NARRATOR: Have we lost the spirit that put man on the moon? The spirit that enabled us to solve the toughest problems and meet the greatest challenges? Or do you believe that spirit is still in us, that we have the greatest resources, technology, and minds of any country in the world and that with strong leadership we can put those . . . to work and let that spirit. . . . Ted Kennedy, because we've got to do better.

KENNEDY: This is the country that put mankind's footprints in the valley of the moon, and I say that we can meet our challenges in the 1980s.

Ronald Reagan uttered these words from a podium set up in Liberty Park in New Jersey with the Statue of Liberty in the background:

NARRATOR: Labor Day, 1980. Governor Reagan speaks to the people of the nation.

REAGAN: Beside that torch that many times before in our nation's history has cast a golden light in times of gloom, I pledge to you I'll bring new hope to America. This country needs a new administration with a renewed dedication to the dream of an America, an administration that will give that dream new life, and make America great again. I want more than anything I've ever wanted to have an administration that will, through its actions at home and in the international arena, let millions of people know that Miss Liberty still lifts her lamp beside the golden door.

Approximately 40 percent of the ads in this sample could be considered consistent with the elections-as-ritual approach. About half of these are the vague policy promise ads illustrated earlier in which candidates practice the "art of ambiguity." The other half are ads in which candidates play upon the hopes and fears of the American people, attempt to associate their opponents with various villains, or associate themselves with positively evaluated elements of our political culture. As those who have articulated this approach have suggested, ads of this type are more likely to comfort or frighten the public than to permit a choice between competing and distinctive promises, records, or personas. Although these ads do not contain "empty" or meaningless rhetoric, their contribution to civic education is not what we usually expect of election campaigns.

CONCLUSION

"The time is now" (as the Reagan campaign was fond of saying in 1980) to reflect on the typology of political commercials that has been presented and illustrated. I began this essay by arguing that an analysis of political advertisements could help us evaluate the empirical accuracy of four quite different perspectives on elections. The frequency distribution of advertising types may be used to indicate which approaches are the most consistent with the information flow of paid televised spot commercials. This determination will also enhance our understanding of the educative value of election campaigns, the nature of the public's electoral choice, and the meaning of electoral outcomes.

The most prevalent type of appeal made in televised political commercials is the benevolent leader appeal (Table 20). By my conservative estimate, based only on the explicit, verbal content of ads, 57 percent of these ads contained references to the personal attributes of candidates. If one were to utilize a less conservative approach and consider the uses to which these ads might be put by their viewers, this estimate would undoubtedly increase appreciably. Many ads contain nonverbal cues germane to perceptions of personal attributes although these were not included in this particular analysis.

Benevolent leader appeals focus on the personality traits rather than the programmatic actions, policy intentions, or political values of candidates and attempt to accomplish a correspondence between the role expectations for a public office and the persona of the candidate. Further-

Table 20
Summary of Ads Consistent with Four Approaches to Elections[a]

Prospective Policy Choice	15%[b]
Specific Policy Preferences (5%)	
Fairly Specific Policy Preferences (10%)	
Retrospective Policy Satisfaction	60%
Credit-claiming (23%)	
Blame-placing (23%)	
Issue-raising (21%)	
Benevolent Leader	57%
Elections-as-Ritual	40%
Vague, ambiguous Policy Preferences (22%)	
Melodramatic } 24%	
Positive inconography }	

[a]Total n = 506

[b]The percentages in this column do not sum to 100 because an ad may be consistent with more than one approach. The same is true of the precentages for the subcategories of the Retrospective Policy Satisfaction and Elections-as-Ritual ads.

more, a limited repertoire of traits (compassion, empathy, integrity, activity, strength, and knowledge) are used by admakers time and again to persuade the electorate that a candidate's character is right for the job.

One suspects that benevolent leader advertising accomplishes little programmatic education since policy alternatives or preferences are generally absent from these ads. Instead, what educative value there is to these ads lies in the electorate's perceptions of the personal traits of candidates and the correspondence between persona and the requirements of a particular public office. Occasionally a personal trait may be used by citizens to draw inferences about the policy preferences of candidates; generally, however, this proves difficult to do.

As a result of the type of information presented in benevolent leader commercials, the electorate is encouraged to view elections as a choice between people rather than between political belief systems. Since electorates cannot predict with certainty the public policy questions that will face a newly elected public official, selecting public officials based on their personal attributes makes a certain amount of sense. However, it also increases the chances that the electorate will select public officials who are unlike-minded in a programmatic sense.

As a result of the political learning and the understanding of electoral choices encouraged by benevolent leader appeals, it is difficult to see how the resulting electoral outcomes could generally be viewed as policy mandates of any sort. If the echo chamber contains electoral communication that is impoverished in terms of the discussion of public policy alternatives, then the electorate can hardly intend very much programmatically by their selection of public officials. Instead, election outcomes more typically indicate the type of person preferred by the American electorate for the public offices at stake. As Fenno has pointed out regarding U.S. congressmen, the public is often more interested in selecting someone they can trust than in choosing someone with whom they are likely to agree programmatically.

This is a troubling discovery. For one suspects that the type of political learning and electoral choice encouraged by benevolent leader appeals is shallow and transitory. Furthermore, since the public often has a minimal opportunity to reality-test benevolent leader claims, the opportunities for deception and distortion by admakers are worrisome. Finally, and most important, transforming election campaigns into an exercise in benevolent leader selection is a severely delimited form of public choice. As Page has pointed out, one hesitates to consider such a process consistent with democratic governance.

> Even if . . . the electoral process casts up a paragon of benevolent leadership every time, we would still have to ask whether it is not a debasement of language to call this democracy. It has about it a flavor of citizen abdication, of giving up on instrumental benefits of government and settling for the symbolism of a father figure or a dignified elected monarch.
>
> In isolation, certainly, the selection of a benevolent leader is a weak sort of democracy. "Rule by the people" must concern the substance as well as style, and the connections between presidential personality and the policy performance, while significant, are not sufficient to dictate in detail what government does. *Only in conjunction with other processes* of democratic control does the selection of an appropriate presidential personality take on normative importance [emphasis added]. (P. 265)

The second approach to elections consistent with the content of televised campaign commercials is the retrospective policy satisfaction approach. Sixty percent of the ads analyzed here contained the past-oriented credit-claiming, blame-placing, and issue-raising appeals consistent with a retrospective policy judgment. These ads present "the record" for the electorate's evaluation and ask the voters to decide whether to "throw the rascals out" or give the incumbents "two, four, or six more years." In retrospective voting, it is the electorate's overall policy satisfaction which is important, along with the electorate's decisions about whom to hold responsible for what. Future actions are not discussed nor future intentions revealed with this type of campaign communication.

Advertising of this type has considerable educative potential. Although admakers are not always careful about who is blamed for or credited with what, retrospective ads can give voters a policy-oriented information base upon which to cast a vote. Policy decisions are presented, defended, and explained; causal explanations are advanced and debated for social and political phenomena; and public officials are held accountable for previous promises and actions. Although there is ample room for deception, oversimplification, and distortion by admakers when they interpret the "record," the debate undertaken in retrospective ads tends to be fairly concrete, engaging, and focused on the incumbent's conduct in office.

Retrospective appeals also encourage the electoral choice to be seen by voters as a programmatic one. That is, it is the incumbent's policy decisions and preferences that are the subject of scrutiny and the focal point for the electorate's decisions. One problem with this type of campaign rhetoric is that it often leads to an electoral choice situation which is unbalanced—that is, much is known about the incumbent's policy behavior while little is known about the challenger—and the electorate is in a position of accepting or rejecting the incumbent without a full appreciation of what the alternative will bring. But at least the choice may be seen as a programmatic one, and the basis of the choice is one about which information is fairly plentiful (though often confusing and contradictory) and concrete.

Retrospective appeals also permit election outcomes to have a measure of programmatic meaning. If the electorate does learn something about the incumbent's policy preferences (in the past) and uses that as the basis for electoral choice, we could infer programmatic satisfaction or dissatisfaction from the election result. This does not mean that the electorate is sending a message about their future-oriented policy preferences, however, since they typically do not know what they will be getting if they elect the challenger. But retrospective policy satisfaction appeals do permit electoral outcomes to reveal a more limited policy-oriented message: whether the electorate generally prefers policy continuation or change.

A third approach to elections—elections-as-ritual—also receives some support in our analysis of advertising content. Forty percent of the ads were found to contain content consistent with this approach. These appeals were not nearly as prevalent as the benevolent leader and retrospective appeals, but they are frequent enough that they ought not be ignored.

The educative value of elections-as-ritual appeals lies in their ability to legitimize prevailing values, norms, and beliefs; reinforce the political identities of the public; and revitalize support for the system. In other words, election campaigns do not just inform citizens about candidates, parties, and policies; they also inform them about themselves, their regime, and their political community. Because of the prevalence of elections-as-ritual appeals, we would expect contemporary U.S. election campaigns to exhibit a significant integrative effect by increasing belief in the political norms, myths, values, and identities shared by most members of the polity.

Similarly, elections-as-ritual appeals partially reorient the nature of electoral choice away from a choice between parties or candidates to a choice involving participation in the process itself. In other words, the significant choice exercised by the citizen is less clearly one candidate versus another than a choice between expressing support for the electoral process—by voting—or withholding that support.

Electoral outcomes cannot possibly—if this type of appeal predominates—reveal very much about the governmental preferences of the electorate. Since elections-as-ritual appeals do not give voters a policy-oriented information base from which to choose between candidates, electoral outcomes lose that meaning as well. Instead, elections are an opportunity for a political community to relegitimize its existence, social structure, norms, and values and to deflect or manage citizen discontent, conflict, or restiveness. The message sent by voters exposed to elections-as-ritual appeals is more likely to be one of quiescence versus dissent or reassurance versus discontent.

The approach to elections which receives the least support in this analysis of political advertising is the *prospective policy choice* approach. Only 15 percent of the ads discussed here are consistent with that approach, by far the least prevalent of the four types considered. Televised ads simply do not typically provide the public with the information flow necessary to permit the public to learn very much about the contrasting "bundles" of policy promises, preferences, or intentions represented by candidates. As a result televised political advertising interferes with seeing elections as a choice between alternative policy futures and prevents election outcomes from representing the electorate's "mandate" for a particular program of governmental action.

The prospective policy choice approach has taken a beating lately from many different directions, contrary to the fond hopes of many political scientists. Candidate rhetoric in general (Page, 1978), news coverage of election campaigns (Patterson & McClure, 1976; Patterson, 1980), and the behavior of the electorate all suggest that election campaigns may seldom be understood in terms of future-oriented policy mandates. This analysis of televised political advertising confirms that judgment as well.

This is a particularly distressing conclusion, for it is the prospective policy choice approach which is the most clearly consistent with prevailing notions of democratic theory. Most versions of democratic theory posit the importance of the "enlightened understanding" of the populace and the availability of "effective participation" by that populace. Were the attributes of the prospective policy choice approach observed empirically in our political system we would have some assurance that our electoral process enhances both enlightened understanding and effective participation. In the absence of evidence that this is the case, however, we are forced to ponder the possibility that our electoral process does not enhance the type of information-holding and political choice that are the most clearly and directly consistent with democratic theory.

Just because a political system has an electoral process does not insure that that process enhances civic education and provides the citizenry with meaningful, political choices. In fact, this analysis of the information flow of modern campaigns casts considerable doubt on such a presumption. The world of televised, campaign commercials is much more likely to delimit citizen understanding to perceptions of candidate personas and the recognition of cultural icons and values than to an apreciation of policy alternatives; much more likely to restrict elections to choices between competing images of candidate personalities, unbalanced perceptions of incumbent and challenger records, or a choice between participation or nonparticipation than to a choice between competing programs of governmental action or political belief; and much more likely to reveal a truncated message-as-sent by the electorate than a message rich with preference or guidance for a future course of governmental action.

• 7 •

Elements of Videostyle

Candidate Presentation through Television Advertising

Lynda Lee Kaid and Dorothy K. Davidson

Because the impact of paid television advertising on the American electoral system has escalated, it is important to identify the ways political candidates present themselves in television ads. Such presentation, or videostyle, plays a crucial role in shaping the political environment. Candidates do not control events, but they can and do structure the discussion of them. The unique characteristics of television (and the unique legal position of political ads) offer the candidates opportunities to control the way their images are defined, creating clear consequences for representative government.

The Importance of Political Advertising and Candidate Images

Television is now the dominant medium for candidate-to-voter communication in most state and national elections. Through television news where 65 percent of the electorate receives most of its public affairs information (Roper, 1983), through television documentary programming, through occasional televised debates, and through televised advertising, voters receive information about the personalities and public images of candidates, their stands on issues, and their qualifications for office. Of the various ways to transmit messages through television, only one is under the direct and complete control of the office seeker—advertising. In fact, an estimated 50 to 75 percent of the budget in major campaigns goes to finance the production of and to buy time for electronic advertising (Patterson, 1983).

Some scholars still believe that the media have a minimal effect on the voter, a perspective that grew out of the early voting studies (Lazarsfeld, Berelson, & Gaudet, 1944; Berelson, Lazarsfeld, & McPhee, 1954; Campbell, Converse, Miller, & Stokes, 1960). However, more recent studies suggest that mass media in general (Kraus & Davis, 1976) and political television advertising in particular affect the attitudes, thinking, and behavior of voters substantially (Joslyn, 1981; Kaid, 1981; Goldenberg & Traugott, 1980). Even the more traditional voting models (Campbell, et al., 1960) acknowledge the potential impact of short-term issue and image forces on vote decisions, and some scholars now suggest that *candidate image* has become one of, if not the most important element in a voter's decision in the American electoral system (DeVries & Tarrance, 1972; Nimmo & Savage, 1976; Markus, 1982).

Scholars and practitioners have argued that television images of candidates are unique in part because of the medium's visual element (Patterson & McClure, 1976) and also because of the sense of "intimacy" it conveys (Lang & Lang, 1968). Political spotmaker Tony Schwartz (1973) believes that television is a private, "undress" medium, so intimate that many viewers actually feel that the stimuli they experience through television are more real than firsthand, face-to-face encounters. McGinniss (1969) observes that on television a candidate does not need ideas; it is "his personality viewers want to share" (p. 22). Thus, "style becomes substance" (p. 23). In such contests, issues per se have limited meaning except as convenient mechanisms for projecting an appropriate image (Dybvig, 1970; Denton, 1982). Thus, when candidates use television to project themselves to voters, they engage primarily in a form of pseudointerpersonal communication in which they use television's visual element and its capacity to induce intimacy to portray themselves as they believe voters wish to see them. Their methods of self-portrayal make up their videostyles.

COMPONENTS OF VIDEOSTYLE

Not every political candidate will present himself through television in the same way. As Nimmo and Savage (1976) suggest, "The contender for elective office is an actor playing a political role which voters perceive as leader and/or as politician, and each has a characteristic style that reflects the candidate's performance and/or personal qualities" (p. 46).

In the study of political campaigning and advertising, researchers have virtually ignored the *style* of presentation. Other than the anecdotal narratives of campaign media consultants, no attempt has ever been made to explain the components of a candidate's videostyle. This is particularly puzzling since some experimental research clearly indicates that different styles and types of political commercials influence voter evaluations of candiates (Brownstein, 1971; Kaid & Sanders, 1978; Meadow & Sigelman, 1982).

The study reported here is the first attempt to describe systematically the style of political commercials. Videostyle in political advertising combines three major factors: (1) verbal content; (2) nonverbal content; (3) film/video production techniques.

Verbal Content

The verbal content of political advertising has received some attention in recent years. Early studies analyzed commercials and their likely effects somewhat impressionistically (Rose & Fuchs, 1968). Devlin's (1973, 1977, 1982) careful explications of content and strategies in the commercials used in the 1972, 1976, and 1980 presidential campaigns provide useful information.

The verbal content of commercials aired in the 1972 presidential campaign has been analyzed systematically. McClure and Patterson (1976) reported that 42% of these television commercials concentrated on the issues; another 28% contained substantial information about issues. Hofstetter and Zukin (1979) found that 85% of the ads contained some information about issues. These two studies cannot be directly compared because their coding procedures differ. Nonetheless, they indicate that a substantial portion of the candidates' advertisements contained information about issues.

Using a convenience sample of ads from presidential, gubernatorial, senatorial, and congressional campaigns, Josyln (1980) also found some emphasis on issues. He noted, however, that, even though nearly 77% of the ads contained some information about issues, only 19.9% presented specific positions of the candidates.

It is not surprising that many commercials contain information about issues but that few present substantive policy positions because media consultants proclaim that issues are important only as a means of selling image (Wyckoff, 1968; Napolitan, 1972; Schwartz, 1973; Chagall, 1981; Sabato, 1981). Consequently, the individual characteristics of candidates also make up an important portion of the verbal content of television advertisements. Nimmo and Savage (1976) have suggested that typical attributes ascribed to candidates include honesty, calmness, activeness, intelligence, independence, friendliness, and good television personality. Joslyn (1980) found that candidates valued similar qualities since they portrayed themselves in their ads in terms of leadership, honesty, concern, responsiveness, strength, determination, perseverance, vigor, and purpose. Shyles (1983a) studies the ads of the 1980 presidential primary contenders and found that the qualities they mentioned most often were experience, competence, honesty, leadership, strength, and altruism. A preliminary analysis of the dominant themes of senatorial campaign commercials found that incumbents used record and experience most frequently, and challengers used trustworthiness and general competence (Davidson, 1981).

Clearly, it is possible to ascertain the semantic / verbal content of political television commercials. To date, however, no project has systematically applied content analysis categories to a well-selected sample of commercials or considered the verbal content together with nonverbal content and production techniques.

Nonverbal Content

The verbal content of a commercial is only a small part of its message, yet researchers have virtually ignored all else. Nonverbal content can include both the visual elements and audio elements that do not have specific semantic meaning (sounds, voice inflections, etc.). Given that one of television's unique features is its visual nature, it is amazing that so little attention has been paid to this facet of television advertising in politics. The possibilities for considering such content may seem endless, but previous research on the importance of nonverbal messages verifies the particular importance of some of these possibilities, with some research actually indicating that the mere existence of a video image reduces recall of audio information (Warshaw, 1978; Garramone, 1983).

Communication researchers have long acknowledged the importance of nonverbal and visual cues in message reception (Birdwhistell, 1970; Burns & Beier, 1973), and political scientists have maintained that such content must be considered when evaluating televised messages (Adams, 1978; Blankenship, 1983). Burgoon (1974) identifies several dimensions of nonverbal behavior that affect reception of communication messages, including *kinesics* (visual aspects of behavior such as movement, gestures, facial expressions); *paralanguage* (word emphasis, voice quality), *physical appearance*, and *environments and objects* (placement and choice of surroundings, color, etc.).

In fact, several researchers have argued that many of these elements are particularly important to the way politicians present themselves. In discussing political language, Graber (1981) contends that television's emphasis on visual information has "restored non-verbal symbols to a primacy previously enjoyed only in the preliterate age of human history" (p. 212). Nimmo (1974) discusses this distinction between verbal and nonverbal content of images as the difference between *object language* and *protolanguage*, and he contends, as have other scholars (Graber, 1981; Edelman, 1964), that much of America's political symbolism rests upon protolanguage. A candidate's nonverbal behavior or protolanguage can be interpreted as indicating his thoughts and positions (Nimmo, 1974). Thus, it plays an important part in his image-presentation style. For instance, Frank (1977) studied the nonverbal and paralinguistic behavior of Humphrey and McGovern in a 1972 primary election debate in California and identified patterns of behaviors for each candidate.

Numerous examples in the history of the American electoral system imply a strong relationship between nonverbal messages and the projection and reception of a candidate's image. To many, Richard Nixon's pale skin and five o'clock shadow, combined with heavy perspiration, made the vice president appear tense and ill-at-ease during the 1960 television debates (Nimmo, 1974). John Mitchell's excessive blinking signified tension in the Watergate hearings. Ed Muskie's tears in New Hampshire indicated weakness.

Perhaps the major reason scholars agree that the nonverbal content of messages must be considered is their belief that receivers weigh nonverbal cues more heavily than verbal ones. Burgoon (1980) summarizes the literature on this point by saying, "the overwhelming conclusion has been that the nonverbal channels carry more information and are more believed than the verbal band, and that visual cues generally carry more weight than vocal ones" (p. 184). Goffman (1959) maintains that this is true because others believe that verbal expressions are more easily controlled and orchestrated by the speaker.

Goffman (1959) argues that the audience holds the advantage in the communication process because the "arts of piercing an individual's efforts at calculated unintentionality seem better developed than our capacity to manipulate our own behavior" (p. 9). Goffman, however, did not envision the capacity to edit so finely that a presentation can be perfected and polished, controlled and rehearsed, timed and staged. In fact, television advertising may actually supply the candidates with a communications channel through which nonverbal and (more believable) behavior can be controlled. In television advertising, the candidates can rehearse their messages over and over again until they "get it right," until they have the exact presentation of self through nonverbal, as well as verbal, characteristics. If the tie is not straight (personal appearance), or the background is not the right color (environment and objects), or eyes shift at the wrong moment (kinesics), or the voice becomes too intense or high-pitched (paralanguage), they can always redo the commercial until it presents just the right video image.

Film and Video Production Techniques

Film and video production techniques affect the presentation of nonverbal messages, and one could argue that they are a part of the *environment and objects* dimension of nonverbal presentation. However, because production techniques can be used to modify the projection of most verbal and nonverbal content, they are treated here as a separate factor in videostyle.

The impact of film and video techniques has been more the object of speculation than of serious study. Some of the accepted, though not tested, assumptions of campaign media specialists are solely intuitive, but some techniques result from the perspective of well-known film theorists, such as Eisenstein (1948). The most commonly discussed techniques include camera angles, cutting techniques, use of music, use of sound-on versus sound-over approaches, live (or natural) versus staged settings, and various special effects.

Camera shots and angles have probably received the most systematic investigation. Closeup shots are thought to produce a warmer, more intimate image of the subject, calling attention to detail and creating more emotional involvement (Battlin, 1964; Primeau, 1979). Long shots, on the other hand, make the candidate appear more remote, less personal. Frank (1973) found that the greater number of closeups of McGovern in the network evening news about the 1972 campaign created a warmer image for him.

Low camera angles (creating the effect of looking up at the candidate) may contribute to perceptions of strength, dominance, importance, and potency. A high camera angle, on the other hand, places the viewer in the position of looking down at the subject, implying weakness and unimportance. The results of research on this point are mixed, however. Mandall and Shaw (1973) found that low angles increased the potency and activity perceptions of a state government official. Others have found that a high angle increased the source credibility of a newscaster, with best results achieved from a variation of high and low angles (McCain, Chilberg, & Wakshlag, 1977).

Film and video cutting techniques also affect viewers. Quick cuts between pieces of action increase the tempo or create tension or expectations (Battlin, 1964; Primeau, 1979). Such techniques are common in political spots designed to create excitement (Dybvig, 1970) or to focus on candidate image (Meadow & Sigelman, 1982).

Music sets a different mood from spoken words (Rosenfeld & Civikly, 1976). At least one political spotmaker, Robert Goodman, considers music a preeminent part of political commercials, maintaining that it generates emotion and has independent effects on mood and image perception (Dybvig, 1970).

The use of sound-on versus sound-over audio is an important production decision. Actually seeing and hearing a candidate speaking himself (sound-on), rather than hearing the candidate's or an announcer's voice imposed over other video, is thought to create a more real, more immediate impression. Frank (1973) drew similar conclusions when studying the 1972 network news campaign coverage. Similar effects are often hypothesized for live versus staged settings. The former technique is an offshoot of the film genre *cinéma verité,* and is thought to leave a more believable impression with the viewers.

Little research exists on the impact of special effects in political television commercials. Such techniques range from simple superimpositions of visual images to split screens, special dissolves, and complicated computer graphics. No research on political commercials has seriously investigated the impact of such variables.

Candidate and Contest Characteristics

The content of television commercials and the patterns of style they display provide the dependent variables for our analysis. Describing the components of videostyle—in terms of verbal, nonverbal, and production content—is important. Variations in style are expected, and these variations are most meaningful when they can be placed in a general theoretical context. The literature on congressional elections suggests the importance of examining differences between incumbents and challengers.

A large proportion of representatives and senators are returned to office every election year. Until recently House incumbents had a higher return rate than Senate incumbents (Vogler, 1983). Hibbing and Brandes (1983) discuss two kinds of explanations for the difference. The institutional explanation focuses on factors such as the two-year term of House members. Despite the complaints of many representatives that this forces them constantly to run for reelection, the two-year term may actually help their chances because they remain more consistently visible to their districts. House members are also thought to have a greater ability to perform services for their constituents, producing a "grateful" electorate which returns them to office. In contrast, senators are considered to have greater visibility on tough policy votes, and senatorial races may attract better challengers since it is a more prestigious office.

The second type of explanation focuses on the difference between constituencies in the House and Senate. The statewide senatorial race must appeal to a larger population, and cover a geographical area not amenable to personal contact with voters, implying a greater reliance on the media. The larger area of a state may also translate into more partisan competition and greater heterogeneity than may be found in a congressional district.

Despite these very significant differences between the House and Senate, Westlye (1983) suggests that races for the Senate may be more similar to elections to the House than many have supposed. According to his analysis, of state-level surveys, a substantial proportion of senatorial elections are low-key races in which one candidate is unable to marshal the resources necessary to mount an effective challenge. Therefore, some of the research on incumbent advantage in races for the House may be generalizable to races for the Senate.

Attempts to define incumbent advantage have attributed it primarily to behavior *in office* rather than to the incumbent's performance *during the campaign*. Cover and Brumberg (1982) demonstrate the positive influence of congressional mail on constituents' awareness and evaluation of their congressmen. Parker (1980, 1983) argues that the advantage of incumbents results partly from their ability to focus attention on their job performance and provide mostly positive information to voters about their activities. Parker's and Cover and Brumberg's findings may apply less to senate races since senators tend to be treated as more "newsworthy" than congressmen, and thus, have less control over the information their constituents receive.

Kostroski (1978) has defined incumbent advantage in senatorial elections. He argues that incumbency serves as an alternate voting cue to party. Incumbents enjoy a high success rate in their bids for reelection because (1) they have more substantial political skills, experience, and organization since they went through the process before; (2) they have greater name recognition since they have been in office for six years; and (3) they have more political clout within the party through patronage, fundraising activity, prestige, and favors.

Jacobson (1975) explicitly draws the link between incumbent advantage and broadcast campaigning. In his sample of senatorial races, only thirteen of seventy-seven incumbent senators lost. Nine of the thriteen lost to challengers who spent more on radio and television than they did. Jacobson does not untangle whether challenger spending is a response to a weak incumbent or a cause of weakness. He analyzes aggregate data about campaign expenditures. This study goes beyond this initial link between media spending and incumbent advantage to determine whether incumbents and challengers present themselves differently. Rather than focusing on the behavior of the incumbent in office, it focuses on the behavior of both candidates during the campaign, specifically, their videostyles.

Videostyle, then, describes the verbal, nonverbal, and video-production content of political spot advertising and relates types of videostyle to incumbent advantage. These relationships should explain why candidates for the U.S. Senate adopt particular styles of presenting themselves.

METHODOLOGY

Sample

The sample consisted of fifty-five commercials from three United States Senate races in 1982. The commercials present both candidates in each race (or six candidates), and they are the work of four producers of political media. All of the races pitted a Republican incumbent against a Democratic challenger.

The cases were selected for analysis on the basis of (1) availability of data, (2) ability to hold constant certain characteristics of the candidates, and (3) ability to hold constant certain contextual variables (i.e. region, presence of an incumbent in the race, etc.). The content analysis examined the verbal, nonverbal, and production characteristics of the ads. The only context variable we included was status of the candidate—incumbent versus challenger. Other contextual data on the races is considered, including interviews with the candidates and producers. This paper is a look at the content analysis of the ads and an effort to determine some of the components of videostyle and to suggest ways in which the political environment (in this case, status of the candidate) shapes videostyle.

The candidates shared some important characteristics. Three were attorneys; the other three worked in science, education, and agriculture. They ranged in age from thirty-five to fifty. Four had run in at least one prior statewide race, but two had not.

Coding

Trained research assistants, using a written codebook and printed coding sheets, coded each commercial independently. Garramone (1983) demonstrates that the presence of a visual image reduces the ability of viewers to recall audio information. Therefore, coders viewed the commercials first without the audio and ranked the themes pertaining to candidate qualities (trustworthiness, competence, issue positions, issue valence associations, ideology, partisanship, personal attractiveness, and group identification). The categories used to code the verbal content of each commercial were derived from earlier studies of voting behavior (Kinder, Peters, Abelson, & Fiske, 1980), incorporating the findings of Berlo, Lemert, and Mertz (1969–70) on source credibility and Davidson (1982) on candidate evaluation. The resulting categories consisted of qualities that describe how a candidate seeks to be perceived by voters. Earlier pilot studies suggested that some qualities are more likely to be presented visually than verbally. Thus, coders were asked to rank qualities of the visual message and qualities of the verbal message separately. After ranking the visual themes, coders listened to each commercial without watching it and again ranked the candidate qualities in terms of their importance in the verbal message. Following these ranking procedures, each coder coded the other items discussed below while viewing and listening to the spot simultaneously.

Categories for nonverbal content were developed by selecting the components of nonverbal communication that are most applicable to the presentation of political candidates—kinesics, paralanguage, physical appearance, and environment and objects. This paper reports the results of the coding of candidate eye contact with the audience, the identity of the speaker in the ad, candidate attire, and setting. Actual coding of nonverbal content was fairly extensive and detailed, including facial expression, gestures, body movement, fluency, rate of speech, pitch variety, accent or dialect, staging, and interaction with inanimate objects.

Television production characteristics were also considered. Items coded and presented in this paper include type of spot, film technique, and length of spot. Coding validity was checked by having both coders code a subsample of the spots and calculating agreement between them. Where disagreements existed, coders reviewed the items in question and recoded them if necessary. This procedure yielded intercoder reliability of 100 percent for items reported in this paper.

Commercials of Senatorial Candidates

Most of the commercials of the senatorial candidates were twenty to thirty seconds long (76%). Only 22% were sixty seconds, and only one ad was two to five minutes. The spots represented a variety of types, the most popular of which was the introspective spot (24%). Introspective spots focus on the candidates and show them reflecting on the campaign, their jobs, their philosophies of government, or their reasons for running. The candidate may or may not be alone.

Other common types of ads include the opposition-focused spot (22%) and the testimonial (20%). The opposition-focused spots attack the opponents, their records, or their campaign tactics. The attacks need not emanate directly from the candidates. Testimonial spots show people reacting to the candidates or show individuals or groups endorsing them in the form of discussions of their virtues or their records in office.

The issue-dramatization spot (18%) illuminates, emphasizes, or portrays an issue or problem. It may also imply a solution. The documentary spot (7%) is usually long and describes the lives of the candidates or their activities in office. A few spots did not fall clearly into any of these categories and were coded "other." This category included staged press conferences or the responses of candidates who had been attacked, etc.

Most of the spots focused postively on the candidates, that is, they emphasized their virtues (which may imply negative things about the opponents but not state them overtly). Approximately 73% of the spots in our sample were candidate-positive; 27% were opponent-negative. An opponent-negative focus explicitly attacks the character, record, or campaign of the opponent and may imply that the candidate is better. Given all of the attention in the press to the use of negative advertising in the 1982 elections, it was surprising to see the small proportion of spots which were, in fact, negative. However, the number of negative ads produced by a candidate does not necessarily reflect how often each ad was aired or its impact. The story of the Daisy Girl spot produced by Lyndon Johnson's campaign in 1964 (aired once but creating such a furor that it was actually broadcast later on the news) is common knowledge. In fact, in the 1984 Democratic primaries the network news repeatedly aired either excerpts or entire commercials of the major candidates. Thus, the proportion of negative ads produced by the candidates does not necessarily reflect the tone of the campaign.

The substantive content of these very diverse commercials was more difficult to assess and compare. Coders ranked the extent to which the visual and the audio message of each commercial stressed trust, competence, issue positions, issue valences (associating self with a postive issue), personal attractiveness, political party, group affiliations, and ideology.

Issues occurred rarely in either the visual or the audio content of these commercials. For instance, only 11% of the ads contained a video presentation of an issue position, and only 20% contained an audio issue position. Issue valences fared somewhat better, ranking first or second in the audio portion of 60% of the advertisements.

Political party, as expected, was hardly mentioned in the visual or the audio aspects of the commercials. Only one commercial in the entire set mentioned it at all. Trust and competence both occurred more frequently as messages. Trust was ranked first or second in the video content of 47% of the commercials, and competence was ranked first or second in 58% of the audio messages.

Candidate Status and Videostyle

Incumbency has figured so largely in electoral contests of the past several decades that it provided an important first step in looking for types of videostyles. Matched-sets data also made this a viable approach. Consequently, each of the verbal, nonverbal, and video-production-technique variables coded in the content analysis was compared to determine its use by incumbents and challengers. The results disclose definite patterns of style whose characteristics depend on a candidate's status, as shown in Table 21.

Challengers used considerably more short, twenty and thirty second commercials than incumbents, who favored the longer, sixty second ad. In fact, 96% of all challenger commercials were of the shorter length. A chi square test shows these differences to be significant ($X^2 = 10.725$; $p = .004$).

Testimonial ads were the backbone of the incumbents' advertising strategies (28%), and introspective ads were second (24%). Challengers, on the other hand, preferred to attack the opponent/incumbent (35%), while engaging in some introspection (23%). Incumbents and challengers both chose to dramatize issues, but overall, the differences between their uses of types of commercials were not statistically significant.

However, there was a statistically significant relationship between candidate status and focus of the advertisements ($X^2 = 7.149$; $p = .05$). Incumbent spots were usually candidate-positive (90%). Challenger spots were almost evenly split between candidate-positive ads (54%) and opponent-negative ads (46%).

The production style of the ads also revealed interesting differences between incumbents and challengers. Challengers generally used a cinéma verité approach (42%); incumbents opted for a heavy use of slides with printed words and symbols superimposed (38%). Incumbents rarely produced commercials in which the candidate was the face-on star (3%), but challengers used this approach more often (23%). Incumbents did, however, use more animation and special production techniques than challengers. Overall, the differences in production style were statistically significant ($X^2 = 11.505$; $p = .042$). This may reflect the incumbent's better ability to raise money and thus produce "slicker" spots.

The ways in which candidates choose to interact with the camera, the viewer, and their environment are important aspects of their styles. Here, the coding considered the eye contact of the candidate, attire, the setting of the commercial, and who was speaking to the audience/voters in the commercial.

Challengers generally chose to speak for themselves—in 46% of their commercials the candidate himself was the dominant speaker (see Table 1, page 32). This was true in only 21% of the incumbents' spots.

Table 21
Television Spot Characteristics of Incumbents and Challengers

	Incumbent ($n = 29$)		Challenger ($n = 26$)	
Film/Production Style[a]				
Cinéma verité	7	(24%)	11	(42%)
Slides with print	11	(38%)	7	(27%)
Candidate head-on	1	(3%)	6	(23%)
Someone else head-on	5	(17%)	2	(8%)
Animation/special production	4	(14%)	0	
Combination	1	(3%)	0	
Type of Commercial				
Testimonial	8	(28%)	3	(12%)
Introspective	7	(24%)	6	(23%)
Opposition attack	3	(10%)	9	(35%)
Issue dramatization	6	(21%)	4	(15%)
Other	5	(17%)	4	(15%)
Setting[b]				
Formal indoors	9	(41%)	9	(47%)
Formal outdoors	1	(5%)	3	(16%)
Informal indoors	7	(32%)	2	(11%)
Informal outdoors	5	(23%)	5	(26%)
Speaker[ab]				
Candidate	6	(21%)	12	(47%)
Announcer	8	(28%)	10	(39%)
Combination	9	(31%)	1	(4%)
Other	6	(21%)	3	(12%)
Dress[b]				
Formal	16	(67%)	7	(44%)
Casual	5	(21%)	9	(56%)
Varied	3	(13%)	0	
Eye Contact[ab]				
Almost always	3	(14%)	8	(53%)
Sometimes	5	(23%)	4	(27%)
Almost never	14	(64%)	3	(20%)
Length of Commercial[a]				
2–5 minute	1	(3%)	0	
20–30 second	17	(59%)	25	(96%)
60 second	11	(38%)	1	(4%)
Focus of Ad[a]				
Candidate-positive	26	(90%)	14	(54%)
Opponent-negative	3	(10%)	12	(46%)

[a]Indicates chi square test is significant: $p < .05$.
[b]Indicates fewer than 55 in totals for some variables due to inapplicability of some content categories to particular spots.

Incumbents more often employed announcers as speakers, used other persons as speakers, or tried some combination of self, announcer, and other. This difference was statistically significant ($X^2 = 9.486$; $p = .023$).

Given this finding, it is not surprising that incumbents "almost never" engage in direct eye contact with the camera/audience (36% of their commercials). Challengers, on the other hand, looked at the camera/audience "almost always" (in 53% of their spots) ($X^2 = 8.519$; $p = .036$).

Differences in the way candidates dressed were not as dramatic, although variation was noticeable, if not statistically significant. Incumbents dressed much more formally (wearing suits and ties in 67% of their spots). Challengers wore more casual attire (rolled-up sleeves, sweaters, shirts, and jeans) in 56% of their spots. This difference in formality of dress is clear, even though, in general, incumbents and challengers both chose "formal indoor" settings for their commercials. Incumbents did, however use "informal" settings, both indoors and outdoors, more often than challengers, although the differences in settings are not statistically significant. Perhaps incumbents are trying to seem "closer" to constituents, whereas challengers are trying to appear "senatorial."

As mentioned above, the diversity of content in the verbal messages made comparisons difficult. Because rank ordering was used and because so many different categories were utilized, these data were not not subjected to any statistical testing. However, incumbents stressed competence much more frequently both in their visual and their audio messages. Competence was the first or second most important message in 38% of their visual messages and in 69% of their audio messages. The corresponding percentages for challengers were 8% and 46%. No apparent differences in emphasis were placed, visually or verbally, on trust, personal attractiveness, issue position or valence, political party, or ideology.

DISCUSSION

These preliminary findings clearly validate the hypothesis that videostyles among candidates differ. In fact, the very similarity of the appeals that candidates made in terms of image, issue, party, or ideology suggests that they are all saying essentially the same things to voters. The differences lie in how they say it, how they present themselves.

A pattern definitely emerged in comparing the videostyles of incumbents and challengers. Based on this candidate/contest variable alone, two distinct videostyles with the following characteristics can be identified:

Incumbent Videostyle. In general, the incumbent (1) uses longer commercials; (2) uses more testimonials; (3) uses more candidate-positive focus; (4) uses more slides with print; (5) dresses more formally; (6) is represented by an announcer or other voice; (7) verbally and visually stresses "competence."

Challenger Videostyle. In general, the challenger (1) uses more opposition-negative focus in ads; (2) uses cinéma verité style; (3) uses ads where candidate appears "head-on"; (4) uses more frequent eye contact with camera and audience; (5) dresses more casually; (6) speaks for self more frequently—is not represented by surrogates.

Personal interviews conducted with the candidates and the producers provide some insight into the strategies and theories behind media campaigns. The interviews were conducted from November 1982 to June 1984 and lasted between one and three hours. All of the interviewees were informed that no names would be used in this or any other analysis. The project was briefly described as a study of political advertising in U.S. Senate elections.

Producers of the ads were asked questions focusing on (1) how they think voters evaluate candidates; (2) how much control the candidate exercised over the campaign; (3) whom they perceive as the targeted audience; and (4) whom they perceive as the candidate's natural constituency (see Davidson & Kaid, 1984, for excerpts of other interviews).

Challenger Strategies

A common theme among the producers for all of the candidates was the development of media strategy in stages. The stages, however, differed for incumbents and challengers. Producer One worked for a Democratic challenger in a state that is heavily Republican. He is interested in politics and has done media work for other candidates in the state. He is the president of his own advertising firm, which works principally on commercial accounts. The 1982 race was the first senatorial race he handled. He was brought onto the campaign staff initially as a consultant to an out-of-state producer—buying time and doing graphic work only. Because of delivery problems with the out-of-state producer, Producer

One eventually took on all the media production work, except for two spots produced by another friend of the candidate.

Producer One talked in terms of an overarching goal of the campaign. Though he did not explicitly say that the spots tried to make the candidate appear "senatorial," the implication was there.

INTERVIEWER: Could you give me an overview of your strategy?

PRODUCER: I was called in in February or March and nothing was done until much later. Our overall strategy was to make sure that number one, [A] was never embarrassed.

INTERVIEWER: What do you mean by that?

PRODUCER: That he didn't ever get put in the position of saying something, particularly in the media, that he didn't mean. To make sure that he was never physically or intellectually embarrassed.

. . . Every piece was aimed at everyman. That's exactly the way we were trying to buy it, for every man. What we were trying to express is "you've got a guy in there who's never home, doesn't know what's going on, and you've got a chance to elect a guy who's from here, understands the problems, and cares."

Producer Two came from out of state to handle the race of candidate B. Like Producer One, Producer Two faced the seemingly impossible task of getting a Democratic challenger elected in a state with a Republican majority. Although it is possible for a Democrat to win statewide (several Democrats have been elected governor), the legislature is controlled by the Republicans. The state has voted overwhelmingly for Republican presidential nominees since 1964.

Producer Two discussed media strategy in terms of "hurdles" of information which the candidate had to overcome in educating the voter. The initial need was to establish recognition of the candidate. Second, the aim was to provide positive information about the candidate. Finally, the overriding concern in all the information presented was to make the candidate appear senatorial. Producer Two explicitly discussed what looking "senatorial" consisted of—in both visual and audio terms.

Could you give me an overview of your strategy?

rm name] were the pollsters. [B] seemed to have two things against
e, he wasn't known. So the first wave was radio and just hammered
his name and accomplishments. One thing we did while shooting

was make him look dignified, experienced, a little older than he was. We put him in traditional blue suit and tie.

In [state name] TV doesn't reach everywhere. So we used a lot of radio. For him [the candidate] to come out punching would have been a mistake. We started out positive. You want people to look at your candidate as if they are already in that position. So I tried to make him look senatorial where possible. We had spots with the governor and with him all dressed up, head-on. The family spot we did because that's important in [state name].

We did, I did, all the filming in August. We started working on image and issues. They got all the positive spots, except agriculture, early. The initial rotation was eleven, but the governor spot. In each one he (the candidate) identified himself in the tagline. I think you get more information in an ad than almost any place. Shortly after that we started going with the testimonials, to show that he had done something.

Producer Three had extensive and varied political experiences before taking on the senate race. He had worked on several presidential campaigns and community development projects doing everything from organization and management to media production and political advising. At the time of the senate race he had been in the state about seven years, working in various capacities for the candidate. At the time of the interview he was on the candidate's staff, but he was considering moving on to another project. Producer Three faced a less difficult task than Producers One and Two because he was working for a Democratic challenger in a state that is Democratic two to one. Despite this raw advantage in party registration, the Democratic party had a history of poor organization, and at one point the Republican party managed to control the entire congressional delegation. With the assistance of the national party organization and through a massive fundraising effort, the Democratic party had begun to modernize several years prior to the 1982 race and had slowly regained strength.

Producer Three spoke in different terms of the tradeoff between positive and negative advertising and the stages of the campaign. For Producer Three, issues played a prominent role in the definition of strategy. However, it was not the candidate's positions on the issues that were most important. It was the juxtaposition of his stands on issues with his attacks on the incumbent's record. The sequence of information fed to viewers involved alternating positive and negative information about the candidate and his opponent throughout the campaign, rather than holding off on attacks until the end.

INTERVIEWER: Could you describe your strategy?

PRODUCER: You can find out how voters feel at a particular time and they will reply to you in political terms. You look at what you think the poll results mean, decide what positions you can live with, and look at your opponent's positions and figure out where he went wrong. We had five issues—social security, environment, jobs, education, and defense.

We got our production values from Tony Schwartz. I think he's right. The campaign should be an issues campaign and if you have nothing to say about them [the issues] you ought to go into another line of work. Mainly we used full face shots of [C] where he said, "My name is C and . . . " talked about the issue. We had negative education spots of [opponent's] record on all five issues. We ran two tracks—[C] positive and then we'd trail it with the [opponent] negative. We started positive over a ten-day run in September. His [C's] style is so cool that people forget who he is. When he finished being [in office] only 48% knew who he was. Of those 48% they all thought highly of him. One of [C's] assets was that he came from a middle class family that has a gift for making money, which he didn't have any particular use for, and he was willing to spend on a senate race. We didn't have a problem with needing money and not having it.

There's a different dynamic in a state this small. There is an ethic that says you can take someone on on the issues, but not personally.

The importance of the negative track of advertising in C's campaign cannot be overstated. His ads contained more negative material than either of the other challenger's spots. The sequence of transmitting messages is also important. Rather than spending weeks leading up to the attacks of the incumbent by establishing name recognition of the candidate, and then establishing a "positive field" of information about the candidate, C immediately led off with positive and then negative ads which contrasted his views with his opponents. Thus, C was able to control the agenda and set up the choice of voters on his own terms.

Each of the challenger's producers was concerned with the availability of money and with timing the entrance into the campaign. The producers also made a conscious effort to meld the visual and verbal elements of the spot and to avoid presenting contradictory information about the personality and issues of their candidates. Each producer expressed these concerns in a unique way, and some emphasized one element more than another. Producer One was chiefly concerned with preventing mistakes or "embarrassments" to the candidate. Producer Two focused on countering the candidate's youthful appearance by creating a "senatorial" look. Producer Three emphasized early attacks on the incumbent to define the candidate's image relative to his opponent.

Incumbent Strategies

For incumbents, creating awareness, increasing name recognition, and acquainting voters with the candidate are generally not strategic necessities. Incumbents begin their races at or above the "threshold of awareness." Popular incumbents begin their races at or above the "threshold of affection." In these races, mobilization is the only hurdle faced during the campaign, and the incumbent may be more concerned with the weather than with his opponent. Incumbents' media efforts were directed toward increasing voter "comfortableness with the candidates" or "reconnecting them emotionally with the state." One producer worked for two of the incumbents studied. Content analysis of his work and his comments on strategy prompt the argument that producers have a formula into which they plug any and all candidates. However, the races he handled differed strategically, and some of the themes varied, reflecting the individual assets and weaknesses of the two candidates. These factors and the small number of cases preclude generalizations about distinct producer styles. (See Davidson and Kaid, 1984 for a more extended discussion of the tension between candidate and producer for control over the content and production of political spots.)

Producer Four lived and worked in the state in which his candidate was running. He had worked on two other statewide races and had extensive political experience, including a short stint in Washington, D. C., working on press relations before the 1982 senate race. He occasionally worked out-of-state, but concentrated his efforts within the state as a means of building his consulting firm. He handled both political and nonpolitical advertising but seemed to prefer the political.

The affective orientation of the political spot became much more apparent in the comments of the producers who worked for incumbents. Producer Four detailed how he achieved a "natural openness" in the spots, an openness that did not come easily to his candidate.

Interviewer: Could you give me an overview of your strategy?

Producer: We didn't write the strategy or participate in strategy development as much as we like to. Our advertising we recommended to them [the campaign manager and candidate]. We took part of their strategy, and our recommendations, and worked together on it.

> We had two concepts that we felt needed to be sold to the people of [state name]. People in [state name] need to feel comfortable about the candidate, that he will do the right thing, and they need to feel that he won't be an embarrassment. They need confidence in his ability. Going in we had poll data that said people were confident but didn't feel very comfortable about him. We wanted to reinforce the confidence in him and develop that feeling of comfort with him. The reasons they weren't comfortable was that he has a national agenda, he tends to be very strident. The research shows that people thought he was arrogant. It was really clear. I'll give you one example. When his opponent announced, the polls showed a horse race, dead even. His opponent was ahead with women by 10%. He's [opponent] a mountain climber, good looking, a friend of [famous person].
>
> We went on the air earlier than any other campaign in [state name]. We wanted to show a different side of [D] that people had never seen before. The campaign nicknamed two ads "hearts and flowers" ads. They didn't talk about issues, didn't give any reasons to vote for [D]. No makeup, no script, they had candid shots, really pretty pictures. We tried to present [D] as a dedicated family man, warm, caring, human being. We had thirty to forty hours on audiotape of him talking. We would interview him late at night and got some nice tender moments. Late at night he gets reflective. If you just listened to the ad it makes no sense. It's just excerpts from the audiotape. But it all flows.
>
> In April/May we did the first flight. The first flight was 2 two minute spots, the hearts and flowers. Then we took a poll and [D] led by ten points. That's a twenty point change. And we had moved women. We occasionally saw some slippage, and then we'd insert the ads.
>
> In phase two we had found a good formula so we didn't want to change it. It was dedicated to reinforcing the confidence thing. But we didn't talk about pocketbook issues, we talked about people issues. Four ads were produced, three were aired. One was never aired. It was a guy with muscular dystrophy or something. [D] got him a job. One was home health care. The other was crime; the other was [pollution]. All of those were that same style—semidocumentary with real people, no makeup, no scripts. The handicap and [pollution] were real people. Crime was an interview with a police chief. The old people were hard to do; we had to go find some. Most of them are in pretty bad shape, so it took awhile to find one well enough to do it.

Producer Four emphasized the casework the senator had performed and created a more intimate image of him. Producer Four was perhaps most explicit in detailing his efforts to touch voters emotionally. Information about the candidate was clearly peripheral to the need to make voters comfortable with him. There was tension between "pocketbook issues" and "people issues," and pocketbook issues were ignored. The senator's accomplishments on national issues and his concern with a national agenda were muted by the focus on his service to constituents. The logic behind this strategy is obvious. Taking positions on national issues may win the support of some but is certain to antagonize others. On the other hand, nearly everyone values serving as ombudsman for the downtrodden or the bureaucratically harrassed.

Presenting this kind of information about the senator accomplishes two things. First, it "warms up" his image, making him seem more compassionate, more caring, less arrogant. Second, it creates a setting in which opponent attacks on the incumbent are likely to backfire, causing the opponent's negative rating to rise.

Producer Five, unlike Producer Four, did not live in either of the states in which he was working. Producer Five has worked in a large number of races, congressional, gubernatorial, senatorial, and local. Prior to 1982, however, he had not handled candidates in either state [E] or state [F]. In 1982 Producer Five worked on five campaigns simultaneously.

Producer Five discussed strategy in much the same way as Producer Four. He focused attention on casework as a means of increasing voters' feelings of closeness with the senator and increasing identification. Producer Five also noted a contrast between the senator's "real" personality and the media strategy designed to make him more "lovable."

> [E] didn't do anything that emotionally. He's very goal-oriented, just did his homework. That's important, especially in a state like [state name] where people tend to be fairly emotional. Our strategy was to come up with spots that put him in [state name], as opposed to Washington, with real people in [state name], saying and doing things with real people.
>
> There were three spots in the first tier, a sixty second beauty . . . it talked about [E] and [state name] as one and the same; had pretty music and nice shots, some excerpts from interviews, it was one of the most effective spots. It was shown first in May—preprimary. The second spot was an issues laundry list—"accomplishments." It was supposed to remind people of his accomplishments on [state name] related issues. It was a thirty second spot. The last spot in the tier was "reassurance." It was our early effort to set up a positive field on the issue of social security. It was designed to innoculate people against social security attacks, so people wouldn't believe attacks.
>
> The second tier took specific problems and had [E] solve them. We used actual casework examples. Picked issue subject areas that were of obvious importance to more than a few peopl—social security, retirement,

disability, water in the southeast, the flood retention dam. It was an effort to carry reconnection with the state a step further, solving specific problems of specific people.

. . . The first two stages were designed to make him lovable. [Opponent] was doing a strident attack on [E] in personal appearances . . . from late September on. Our inclination was to beef up his biography, keep our strategy. [The pollster] argued for attack. We didn't want to because it's dangerous for an incumbent. It's more accepted for a challenger to attack an incumbent.

We thought about a quiz spot—which candidate will do this? By early October the extent of the slide for [E] was such that it looked like he would lose. In a series of conference calls with [E], his pollster, and the campaign manager, we were persuaded to do a negative attack. We stopped the bleeding a little bit with radio spots—they called into question [opponent's] tactics. [Opponent] pulled his spots off the air, but didn't stop. The hardest was a social security attack. It became evident that we couldn't avoid attacks. Nobody questioned [opponent's] attacks, nor reporters asked why. He succeeded in setting up a negative atmosphere. Once that atmosphere is in place positive media doesn't work. We did an attack on [opponent]. . . . Two things happened. First, it was so out of character with the [E] campaign. People were unaware that [E] was in a slide. Up to that point [E] had been a good guy. The spots proved to be, in retrospect, not inaccurate, but sufficient gray area existed that questions of accuracy could be raised.

Questions were raised by the press and [opponent] as to accuracy. We considered pulling them [the ads]. We did make one correction. The campaign staff argued that they were accurate. What they were was *legal.* They [the ads] were perceived as bad sportsmanship. The perception was that the spots were wrong.

Producer Five used the same basic apprroach for candidate F as he did for candidate E. The media campaign aimed to increase voter identification with and attachment to the incumbent. The ads were set in the incumbent's state, and they relied on the testimonial format.

For [F] an overview would be very similar to [E]. Both were regarded as someone who had moved from their constituency for whatever reason. The strategic necessity was to reconnect them with the state. We did spots that talked about [F's] accomplishments, the state of [state name] and what he thought of it, pictured him in the state, and casework. We used more casework in [state name] because we had better access to cases and less of a need to attack. Cases were beautiful, made to order, and countered the opponent's argument. A heavy preponderance of the cases were on social

> security or railroad retirement or pension. The [name] case had a high profile in the state and worked very well. It pushed him [F] on the [F] law. We were also able to use Reagan—[state name] is largely Republican—Reagan cut a spot for [F] also.

Producer Five used the same basic strategy in states E and F. In state F, however, the opponent was never able to mount an effective attack, so there was no need to adjust the ads produced. In anticipation of a strong attack, Producer Five had prepared some negative spots. The candidate returned one of these to the producer because he perceived it as inaccurate.

Summary and Conclusions

Videostyle is the way candidates present themselves to voters through televised advertising. The study of videostyle is in part inspired by the work of Goffman (1959) and Fenno (1978). Goffman's work focuses on the presentation of self in everyday life. Fenno describes the interpersonal interaction between members of the House of Representatives and their constituents. Mass communication, as in broadcast campaigning, places different constraints on the presentation of self than interpersonal communication. Mass communication through television is aimed at large heterogeneous audiences; messages are transmitted rapidly and simultaneously to each member of the audience; and there is little opportunity for audience feedback. After initial contact, the candidate controls the message. In contrast, interpersonal communication typically involves small, homogeneous audiences; messages are transmitted slowly, and there are opportunities for immediate audience feedback. The candidate and the audience share control of the message.

Television advertising also provides the opportunity for someone other than the candidate to define the situation and control the candidate's presentation. The final distinctive feature of videostyle involves the audience. People watch commercials because they lead into or out of a program. Thus, the audience is inadvertent. It is also typically passive. Viewing spots requires no effort. Indeed, one must make an active effort to avoid receiving a candidate's message, either by turning the channel or leaving the room. Krugman and Hartley (1970) provide evidence that some types of advertising have their greatest effect on uninvolved, uninterested voters. They focus on what is "caught" rather than "taught" in a process termed "passive learning." Although Fenno (1978) and Goffman (1959) examine the verbal and the nonverbal components of the presentation of self interpersonally, the study of videostyle additionally explores the use of special production techniques. Nonverbal behavior is difficult to control in an interpersonal setting; however, advertising offers candidates and producers more opportunity to project the nonverbal message self-consciously.

The content analysis presented here demonstrates that the verbal and nonverbal messages and production techniques of incumbents and challengers differ significantly. There are more than two videostyles, though on the basis of three state races only these two are identified here. The task now is to identify the other styles within this broad category and assess the impact of competing styles on the electorate.

Two themes run throughout the comments of the producers. First, producers both for challengers and incumbents are preoccupied with reaching the voter/viewer emotionally. Their aim is to make the constituency feel something—"comfortable," "confident," "an emotional connection."

Producers make few references to reaching the voter/viewer cognitively, and these tend to revolve around the need to establish awareness of the candidate. Even the effort to increase recognition of the candidate, however, carries with it the association of the candidate's name with positively held values.

Even candidate C's producer, who spoke at length on the issues and their importance, for the most part did not present his candidate's positions on the issues. He did, however, attack the incumbent's record specifically and contrasted these attacks with the challenger's positive value associations on key issues.

The second theme which stands out in the interview excerpts is the producer's need to consider the environment in which he is working. Each state possesses its own unique political heritage, traditions, and taboos. Different political contexts create different strategic needs, and the expectations of constituents place constraints on candidate styles.

Several directions for future research on videostyle are clear. First, more in-depth analysis of the interactions between matched sets of candidates may enhance understanding of shifts in strategy. Candidates do not operate in a vacuum. They are attentive to the reactions of their opponents. They react to attacks with counterattacks. What makes some negative advertising effective and other negative advertising backfire?

Second, assessing the impact of competing styles on voter decisions is imperative. Candidates are attentive to the reactions of their constituents. Mass communication delays feedback. One could even argue that the burden of obtaining audience reaction falls on the candidate. Candidates have adopted, in some cases, elaborate schemes for finding out how voters are responding to their messages. The increased use of tracking and panel designs in election polling is one reflection of candidates' concern with audience reactions.

• 8 •

Political Commercials and Candidate Image

The Effect Can Be Substantial

Donald T. Cundy

The Ubiquity of Television[1]

The television set has become a nearly universal feature of our society. Recent evidence indicates that almost 99 percent of all American households have at least one, and more than half have two or more (Sabato, 1981, p. 117), a penetration rate which virtually elminates the possibility of significant variation by age, race, income, or any other major demographic characteristic.

Television also seems to be perceived as a very credible source of information. Ongoing polls by the Roper organization have indicated that sometime around the middle sixties, television surpassed newspapers as the major and most trusted source of the American public's information about what's going on in the world (Roper, 1983.) At a more directly political level, the Roper polls have also shown that in the U.S., people are about two and a half times as likely to name television over newspapers as the medium through which they become most acquainted with candidates for national political office. A majority also said that TV provides the clearest understanding of the candidates and the issues (Roper, 1969; Keating & Latane, 1976).

THE RISE OF PAID POLITICAL ADVERTISING

Politicians were quick to exploit paid television advertising as a means of controlled communication with the electorate. Following Eisenhower's initial use of spots in the 1952 presidential campaign, paid political advertising grew at a phenomenal rate and now occupies a prominent position in virtually every contested race for major political office in the U.S. today.

The percentage of total campaign spending devoted to television advertising underscores the importance of the medium to modern political campaigns. In 1980, Carter and Reagan each spent close to two thirds of their $29.4 million budgets on advertising. Approximately $13 million of that was spent on TV (Devlin, 1981). At the subpresidential level, the NRCC's (1979) post-1978 study of campaign expenditures showed that paid media costs averaged about one third of the total budget for a major political campaign, though variations all the way from 15 to 70 percent were apparently not uncommon. Similarly, Traugott (1984) found that candidates in contested races for the U.S. House of Representatives in 1982 spent an average of about 25 percent of their total campaign budget on television advertising and related costs.

THE DOMINANCE OF THE SPOT COMMERCIAL

As the use of paid political television advertising has grown, it has moved increasingly toward short thirty and sixty second spot commercials and that approach now dominates this form of electronic communication almost to the exclusion of the longer documentary approach pioneered by Guggenheim. Reagan spent $10.4 million, or 80 percent of his 1980 TV budget on spots (Devlin, 1981), and it has been estimated that the thirty to sixty second variety now comprise between 75 and 90 percent of all paid TV political advertising (Sabato, 1981, p. 124).

Joslyn (1981) has argued that given enough funding, exposure to this form of political communication is almost involuntary for anyone who watches television, and there is some compelling evidence to support his view. Using survey data from Wisconsin and Colorado respondents, Atkin, Bowen, Nayman & Sheinkopf (1973) discovered that following saturation campaigns for governor in each of those states, about 75 percent of the respondents claimed they could recall seeing at least some TV advertising. More detailed analysis showed that the primary determinants of exposure were simply the amount of daily viewing time and the availability of each candidate's ads. Sheer pervasiveness of the spots tended to overwhelm any sort of selective attention factor.

Similarly, Surlin & Gordon (1976) report that in their study of Atlanta and Philadelphia residents, 93 percent of the former and 91 percent of the latter indicated they had seen at least one advertisement about either Nixon or McGovern during the 1972 presidential campaign. Of the exposed groups, 99 percent of the Atlantans indicated they had seen an advertisement on television, as did 98 percent of their Philadelphia counterparts. Newspapers and radio were not even close.

EVIDENCE FOR THE EFFECTIVENESS OF POLITICAL SPOT ADS: SUGGESTIVE, BUT INCONCLUSIVE

The evidence presented thus far makes it clear that (1) television viewing is pervasive in America, (2) major candidates for elective office spend a great deal of money on television advertising, and (3) televised political ads are seen and heard by a lot of people.

Do these massive advertising expenditures have any appreciable effect? Early pioneering efforts such as the work of Lazarsfeld, Berelson & Gaudet (1944) (which preceded the arrival of televised political commercials) suggested that the role of the media was largely limited to reinforcement rather than conversion.

Later work has indicated that the impact of the media goes beyond mere reinforcement. Though not without controversy, there has, for instance, been increasing support for the general agenda-setting function of the mass media (see, for example, the pioneering work of McCombs & Shaw, 1972). Recently, experimental evidence presented by Iyengar, Peters, & Kinder (1982) has made a rather convincing argument for the agenda-setting function of the network evening news, along with the relevance of that agenda to viewer judgments of presidential contenders.

Evidence for the impact of televised political spots is not as strong—research in the area has been relatively limited and the results suggestive, but inconclusive. Lack of better alternatives has often forced reliance upon relatively crude aggregate indicators, correlational inference, or indeterminably atypical populations of college students.

These qualifications not withstanding, the findings have tended to be positive. Palda (1973) used government records of the campaign spending of parties and candidates in the 1966 and 1970 Quebec elections and found a significant relationship between television advertising expenditures and electoral outcomes. Wanat (1974) used a similar procedure and found a significant positive correlation between political broadcast advertising and a candidate's percentage of the vote in primary elections for the U.S. House of Representatives.

Joslyn (1981) took a different but parallel tack and related FCC data on the partisan balance (i.e. ratio) of broadcast advertising expenditures in a state or district to whether or not respondents in the corresponding political unit of the 1970, 1972, or 1974 SRC/CPS surveys reported crossing party lines in their vote for congressional and senatorial candidates. Multivariate analysis showed that the partisan balance of media advertising expenditures was the third best predictor of voting loyalty/defection—behind party identification and incumbency. Mulder (1979) used much the same approach but expanded his research design to include a panel survey of voters during the 1975 Chicago mayoral campaign. He found modest, but consistent and statistically significant correlations between reports of exposure to political advertising, vote intention, and a number of other campaign issues.

Other studies have dealt with some combination of issue, knowledge acquisition, and/or image. Hofstetter, Zukin, and Buss (1978) examined national survey data and found that exposure to political advertising, local TV news, and campaign discussion were all correlated with respondent information level, particularly among the less politically interested and involved.

Atkin and Heald (1976) interviewed a random sample of voters from a Michigan congressional district and found that frequency of viewing TV political commercials correlated .34 with their measure of campaign knowledge. The relatively uninformed voters also displayed a significant correlation between viewing frequency and an operational measure of liking for the candidate.

POLITICAL ADVERTISING AND CANDIDATE IMAGE: CONFLICTING EVIDENCE

There is yet another body of research on the impact of televised spot commercials that has focused much more directly on the image aspect. In a very broad sense, a candidate's image could be defined as the voters' subjective impressions of the individual (Boulding, 1961). At an operational level, image is usually used to refer to the personal traits of the candidate: such things as sincerity, honesty, experience, knowledge, leadership, etc.—though often grouped into different subsets of one type or another.

While there is some disagreement on the nature and extent of the role played by image in determining voting behavior, virtually no responsible scholar denies that the image component can be significant. Given that significance, can political advertising exert an appreciable influence on the substance, intensity, and/or direction of the candidates image? Patterson's earlier statements (Patterson & McClure, 1976) have been primarily negative: "In presidential politics, advertising image-making is a wasted effort. All the careful image planning—the coaching, the camera work, the calculated plea—counts for nothing." (p. 111).

This conclusion was apparently based largely on the fact that in their study of the 1972 presidential election, images of Nixon and McGovern showed very little change through all the weeks of political advertising and newscasts until the voter made up his or her mind which candidate to support. After that, the images changed substantially (just how the voter came to that decision in the first place, or what factors were involved, were never directly considered). The authors did, however, acknowledge in a footnote (#8 for chapter 6) that television advertising might indeed have some effect on voter images of the candidates for offices below the presidency.

Patterson and McClure's 1976 work presents some valuable information and insights, but the downplaying of the role of television advertising in image formation is questionable for a number of reasons. First, there is the prominence of image in the comments of Patterson's later (1980) study respondents—one cannot help but wonder where those images came from. Second, the unequivocal nature of the conclusions (including the distinction between presidential and lesser offices) appears to exceed the limitations of the data. Third, it seems rather implausible that political advertising is capable of exerting a significant impact on the vote, information levels, and general affective responses to the candidate, as suggested by the research cited earlier, yet somehow acquires massive impotence with respect to image. Fourth, the evidence from several other studies dealing specifically with the relationship between political advertising and image formation (two of them experimental) is consistent with the earlier references and to varying degrees, incompatible with a number of the conclusions presented in Patterson and McClure's 1976 work.

Wattenberg (1982), for instance, combined data from the 1978

SRC/CPS election study of congressional districts with information about media expenditures in those same districts the same year (the media expenditure data was obtained from the work of Goldenberg and Traugott, 1979). He found strong indications of a relationship between mass media advertising and candidate image.

Keating and Latane (1976) conducted three separate experimental studies with undergraduate psychology students. The purpose was to examine the persuasive impact of a political message presented live, on television, audio only, and written. The results showed that the medium of communication had no effect on change in audience agreement with the positions advocated in the message, though there were consistent and significant effects on the image of the candidate. The live presentation was most effective in this regard, followed by the TV version. Both the live and televised presentations were significantly more effective than the written or audio ones.

Finally, Meadow and Sigelman (1982) produced a series of their own television commercials about a real candidate for Congress and then applied an experimental design to undergraduate psychology students to examine the differential effects of various styles of commercials. Confounding factors make some of their conclusions questionable, but they did find significant effects on such image dimensions as "warmth" and "humaneness."

Thus, the bulk of the evidence available at this time runs counter to the major thrust of Patterson and McClure's (1976) conclusions about political advertising and image. Most of the studies suggest that televised political spots can have an impact on the image of political candidates. Nevertheless, it must also be acknowledged that the evidence on both sides has been less than compelling.

THE PROBLEM AT HAND AND A DIFFERENT METHODOLOGICAL APPROACH

Part of a larger project dealing with the impact of various forms of television communication on voter image formation, the portion of the research effort presented in this report attempts to obtain a more definitive estimate of the extent to which a paid political spot commercial can or cannot affect the image of a candidate for elected political office. Deciding how to go about accomplishing both this and the other goals of the project in a way that would yield meaningful results was not a simple matter. Some fundamental, methodological problems had to be considered.

There are presently two dominant techniques for conducting research in the social sciences—the survey and the controlled experiment. Each have major advantages and major problems. A properly conducted survey has high external validity—that is, it is likely to be a very good representative cross section of whatever universe the researcher is interested in. On the other hand, it has low internal validity in that even with a panel design, the researcher does not control, and hence cannot manipulate, the independent variable(s). As a result, the researcher must often rely on measures of covariation that may or may not reflect causation.

The major advantage and disadvantage of the experiment are essentially the reverse of the survey in that, if properly done, it provides a strong basis for making causal inferences. On the other hand, a host of practical factors generally impact in such a way that the approach is is generally weak in external validity, ie. the ability to generalize to larger populations of interest. Most of the studies cited earlier in the discussion suffer from one or more of these difficulties.

Our solution to this problem was to adopt a quasi-experimental approach (for a good introduction and overview see Cook & Campbell, 1979). The essential difference between our approach and a true experimental design is that we did not have random assignment of individuals to experimental conditions; rather, we had random assignment of small groups (generally ranging from five to ten people). Those small groups were obtained by contacting virtually every club (or any other organized entity that met together as a group) in a 2,500 square mile area of a midwestern state and asking them if they would be willing to participate. If they agreed (over 90 percent did), they were randomly assigned to one of the experimental conditions. Since the groups were small, problems that can arise from lack of individual random assignment were minimized.

Each experimental group was exposed to two messages: (1) the "treatment" condition, which consisted of a short (thirty-eight second) message about a fictitious Congressman by the name of Bob Landers or (2) what is often referred to in television news parlance as a "fluff" piece, in this case a rather innocuous thirty-seven second message about an equally fictitious individual named Alan Scott. Scott had supposedly been the victim of some friends' harmless, but embarrassing humor involving his fiancée and some puppies his dog had recently given birth to.

The fluff piece said nothing about the personal attributes of Scott beyond the fact that he was a 35 year old bachelor and "local man." Bob Landerrs, on the other hand, was identified as an incumbent 38 year old Congressman who had been recognized by his peers for having the highest attendance rate in Congress for ten of the last eleven years; had been reelected to the U.S. House of Representatives in the last election with the largest plurality ever received by a candidate from his district; had become known for his central role in legislation dealing with truth in advertising and campaign reform; and had recently been singled out and publicly recognized by his Congressional colleagues for his integrity and accomplishment in that body.

The spot began with a lead-in by an announcer and was followed by a fade-out to a full length profile of Landers while a voice in the background recited the virtues listed above. At the end of the spot, the announcer's voice clearly stated "Vote for Bob Landers for Congress", while a highly visible white crawler passed across the bottom of the screen with the words "PAID FOR BY CITIZENS FOR BOB LANDERS." In the fluff piece, a picture of Scott was shown over the newscaster's right shoulder while the announcer was talking. In both cases, only the announcers said anything.

To help maintain authenticity, the scripts were both written by a professional television newsstation manager. Two professional radio news announcers from a distant large metropolitan area alternatively acted as the newsperson or the spot announcer. The subjects presented as Landers and Scott were each private citizens and both of them were also from an entirely different section of the country than the experimental subjects. These precautions were taken to avoid any complications that might have arisen from prior subject familiarity with the persons shown in the various treatment conditions.

We also wanted to minimize the impact of any atypical responses that might have resulted from the idiosyncratic characteristics of a particular stimulus individual. To do that, the persons we presented in the political spot and fluff pieces were randomly switched from one data collection session to the next. The same procedure was followed in presenting the spot announcer and newsperson.

The result was that for half the subject groups, individual A was the Congressman and B was the object of the fluff piece. For the other half, the situation was reversed and similarly for the spot announcer and news person. Therefore, each news and story subject appeared in both experimental conditions (a two by two repeated measures factorial design).

Later, in analyzing the data, the two halves were merged, thereby yielding an averaged response, less subject to individual vagaries. Both story subjects were of nearly identical height (about 6 feet), very close to the same body build, almost the same age (thirty-six and thirty-seven), and wore blue suits.

The data collection itself took place wherever the subject groups happened to be getting together—from private homes to the back meeting rooms of restaurants, club houses, hospital meeting rooms, or what have you. In each instance, a twenty-one inch video monitor was set up on the top of a five foot stand and connected to a three-quarter-inch video recorder capable of playing the color video tapes that were used.

We were also very concerned about "demand characteristics" (see for example Orne, 1962)—any kind of cues or signals in our presentations that might give the subjects some idea of what we were looking for, or how they might be "expected" to respond, as opposed to what those responses might otherwise have been. To do that, the groups were led to believe that the research was being done to provide data for the master's thesis of a graduate student in psychology in a nearby university (a true statement) and that the object of the research was to learn more about how people form "first impressions' of individuals they have never met before (also a legitimate part of the research effort).

Prior to the presentation of the video tapes, the subjects were simply told that they would be seeing some people that had been video taped from television programs in another city some time ago. It was also emphasized that the subjects of the tapes were unknown to the experimenters (the main investigator was always introduced as a "helper" to the graduate student), that there were no right or wrong answers, and that the subjects should feel free to respond solely on the basis of their feelings or intuition—they didn't have to have any reasons and shouldn't feel obligated to conform to any normative standards.

After a practice session on how to use the measuring technique we had adopted for the research (see discussion in the following section on measurement), the subjects were shown video stills of Scott, Landers, and the news announcer and asked to rate them on eight different dimensions (always presented in random order for each individual subject). One of the dimensions was physical appearance, defined as "good-looking"; the others were personal warmth, strength under pressure, honesty, intelligence, dependability, fairmindedness, and overall liking or disliking for the story subjects.

The first seven image dimensions were chosen because a number of them frequently appear in studies involving candidate evaluation (see the image and image-related studies listed in the preceding literature review) and because they showed strong relationships to "likeability" (our eighth experimental dimension) in Anderson's (1968) classic study of 555 personality trait words. Three of them—honesty, dependability, and fairmindedness—were directly involved in the content of the political commercial.

Every attempt was made to keep the data collection sessions as relaxed and natural as possible. The subjects often laughed and chatted among themselves during the presentations and in nearly every session at least one person would express concern that he/she couldn't remember who one or more of the people were. When this happened, the person was told it didn't matter whether the identity of the stimulus persons was remembered or not, the individual should just go with his/her feelings of the moment and not worry about who was who or how he/she might have evaluated any particular individual earlier in the session.

MEASUREMENT PROCEDURES

The category scaling techniques typically used for measuring strength of opinion in social science research all share a number of serious drawbacks: first, the limited number of categories forces respondents to lump some items together, even if they can distinguish between them; second, the measurement is really only ordinal and most of the more powerful statistical procedures require at least interval level data; third, by offering a predetermined number of categories, no matter how many or few, the investigator is to some extent forcing the respondent to adopt a system of discrimination at some unknown degree of variance with that individual's own internal propensities or preferences, thereby introducing further distortion and error variance (Lodge & Tursky, 1979).

A few decades ago, the psychologist S. S. Stevens (1975) was faced with a similar dilemma as he attempted to measure subjective impressions of the sensory intensity of physical stimuli. His response to the problems he faced in that area of psychophysics was to develop a new measurement technique—commonly referred to today as "magnitude scaling." Since that time, the technique has been successfully adapted to the measurement of a wide variety of social stimuli, including political phenomenon (Ekman, 1962; Shinn, 1969; Wyler, 1971; Lodge, Cross, Tursky, Tanenhaus & Reeder, 1976; Tryon, 1977; Baker, 1977; Coleman & Rainwater, 1978; Moskowitz & Chandler, 1979)

While certainly not a panacea, magnitude scaling has a number of virtues. Among them are that it offers a ready means of checking to see whether respondents are using the technique correctly (criterion validity) and the fact that it yields true ratio scales. Such a sclae not only provides much richer information than the ordinal level category scales typically employed by social science researchers, it also allows for the legitimate use of the more powerful statistical techniques presently available.

Thus, at a practical level, our choice of this method of scaling not only provided us with an extremely sensitive measuring instrument, it also allowed us to speak meaningfully about the exact magnitude (10%, 54%, −110%, etc.) of the changes produced by our experimental manipulations, something that has not been accomplished in this area of political communication research before.

Immediately prior to every experimental session, the subjects completed two practice pamphlets that familiarized them with two different modes of magnitude scaling procedures (line production and numerical estimation). This dual mode approach to both the practice sessions and later the experimental session gave us the means of determining whether individual respondents were using the scales correctly (via what are known as cross-modality matching procedures—see Lodge, 1981).

Following the familiarization sessions, the subjects were shown the video stills of the two stimulus individuals (ninety seconds each) and during that time proceeded to evaluate those persons on the seven attribute dimensions previously described. They were then shown the stills a second time (fifteen seconds each) and asked to give their overall like/dislike reactions. This was followed by a presentation of the taped political spot and fluff pieces (thirty-eight and thirty-seven seconds respectively), after which, there was a third showing of the video stills (forty-five seconds each) while each of the subjects indicated their posttreatment impressions of the stimulus persons on the same seven traits.

They were then told that since some people found it easier to express their feelings in the second of the two modes of responding they had practiced earlier (whether number or line estimation), they would now be given a chance to do it that way too, and the stills of the three stimuli persons were shown a fourth time. That was followed by a last general like/dislike evaluation. (At this point, it was no longer necessary to show the video stills, as the subjects were by now very familiar with the stimulus individuals: rather, the latter persons were just described as the man with glasses, the one with darker hair, etc.).

Each respondent then filled out some general demographic information and subsequent to that, was strongly encouraged to express any additional thoughts or feelings he or she might want to share (either verbally or in writing), given the opportunity to ask questions, and the session came to an end. The explanation and data collection portion of the proceedings generally took somewhere between thirty-five and forty minutes and the follow-up discussion session about ten to fifteen minutes. To the best of our knowledge, not a single participant was ever aware of the political aspect of the study.

The data presented in this report is derived from a subset of two replications of the basic research design. That is to say, two replications of four experimental conditions (2 separate individuals in the spot commercial × 2 separate announcers). Seventeen different randomly assigned groups were required to fill all these conditions and achieve the total usable *n* of 109.

As suggested earlier, the small size and multiplicity of different groups required to complete each experimental condition of the study have the virtue of helping to minimize the drawbacks inherent in a quasi-experimental design lacking random assignment of individuals to treatment conditions. It does not eliminate the problem. Therefore, we took the additional precaution of following the generally accepted procedures set out by Lord (1967, 1969) and based our analysis on a pre- and posttreatment difference in means strategy that concentrates on the magnitude and direction of the change in the dependent variables, rather than on their absolute values.

One final methodological/measurement step involved the use of a reference standard. Prior to making judgments of how much of each of the experimental traits the subjects thought the stimulus persons had, they were asked to indicate their individual impressions of how much of each one the "average person" possessed. Once we had that "average person" value, we were able to effect a sort of standardization of all the subject ratings by dividing each of their judgments of the amount of a given trait he or she thought the two stimulus persons had by his or her corresponding average person estimate (a legitimate procedure with magnitude scales). Thus, the average person always acquired a value of one and we were able to compare the judgments of different individuals in a meaningful way. The ratio properties of the magnitude estimates also enabled us to talk in terms of the politician being considered, say, 85 percent as honest as the average person, etc. One additional advantage to using a magnitude scaling procedure is that there are literally no theoretical limits to the values that can be assigned (any limits are self-imposed); therefore, possible ceiling effects are minimized.

Sample Characteristics

As indicated earlier in the methodology section, our desire to avoid relying on an indeterminably atypical group of college students (usually about the only available pool for large scale random assignment of individuals to treatment conditions) as a sample population led us to opt for a quasi-experimental design instead of a purely experimental one.

Our hope was to get as diverse and representative as sample of the population of the area as we could. To that end, we contacted every conceivable group in the vicinity—from mothers of twins to the business women's association; from a local sportsmen's club to the Kiwanis, stamp collectors, La Leche, a diabetic organization, Knights of Columbus, and TOPS (Take Off Pounds Sensibly), to name just a few.

The results were quite supportive. The sample was 56% female and 44% male with an age range from eighteen to eighty-seven. Fifty-five percent of the respondents were eighteen to forty-four years of age and 45% were older with 10% over sixty-five. Sixty-three percent of the groups were married, 7% divorced, 6% widowed, and 24% had never been married. Occupationally: 26% were business owner / managers; 25% were clerical workers, skilled laborers, foremen, or some sort of supervisors; 22% listed themselves as housewives; 12% were students, 4% unskilled / service workers, and 11% retired.

Gross annual household incomes were also widely distributed. Fifteen percent of the respondents indicated less than $11,000 a year and 10 percent $50,000 per year or more. The mean was approximately $26,000.00. Minorities constituted 6 percent—very close to the actual area percentage. The one noticeable bias (compared to area census figures for adults eighteen years of age or older) was in education. Twenty-seven percent of the respondents indicated they had never gone beyond high school or trade school, 38 percent claimed some college, and 35 percent claimed at least a four year degree. The latter figure is somewhat high for the area.

All in all, the sample showed wide diversity across virtually every demographic characteristic and those background characteristics were remarkably close to area census figures. It is true that all of these people shared one common differentiating characteristic—that of belonging to an organization of some type. The data does not, however, give us any reason to believe that this factor exerted any systematic biasing relationship relative to the focus of the study.

Criterion Validity

Figure 1 presents the results of the criterion validity test based on cross-modality matching of the data from the initial practice pamphlets. If the subjects are scaling properly, the ratio of the means of the logs produced by number estimation and line production should approach the value of 1 as well as producing a straight line power function when graphed on log-log paper (Stevens, 1975). We should also expect the two measures to be highly correlated—somewhere around the .98 level or better (Lodge, 1981).

The data obtained for this study easily meet these criteria. Figure 1 presents the results of the cross-modality matching procedure for the line production and number estimates. The individual deltas represent the means of the logs (computed from ratios to a fifteen centimeter standard and analogous to the geometric mean of the raw data) plotted against log scores on the vertical and horizontal axes. The dashed line depicts a curvilinear relationship, but that is only because software limitations in the graphing procedures did not allow for the production of log-log ruled coordinates. When plotted on such coordinates, the relationship does become linear as it should. Note also, that the slope exactly equals the expected value of one (depicted by the solid line in the graph) while the cross-modal, product-moment correlation is .991.

The product-moment correlation between the actual ratios of the practice number stimuli and the geometric means of subject perceptions of the relative magnitude of those stimuli obtained from their line production efforts was .9997, with a slope value of .91. Similarly, the correlation between the actual ratios of the practice line stimuli and subject perceptions of their relative magnitude expressed through number estimation was .9893, with a slope value of .89 (slopes modestly less than unity are fairly common in this type of calibration task—see Lodge, 1981).

Slightly over eight percent (8.4) of the original pool of respondents did not scale individually at a level of .866 or better (75 percent shared

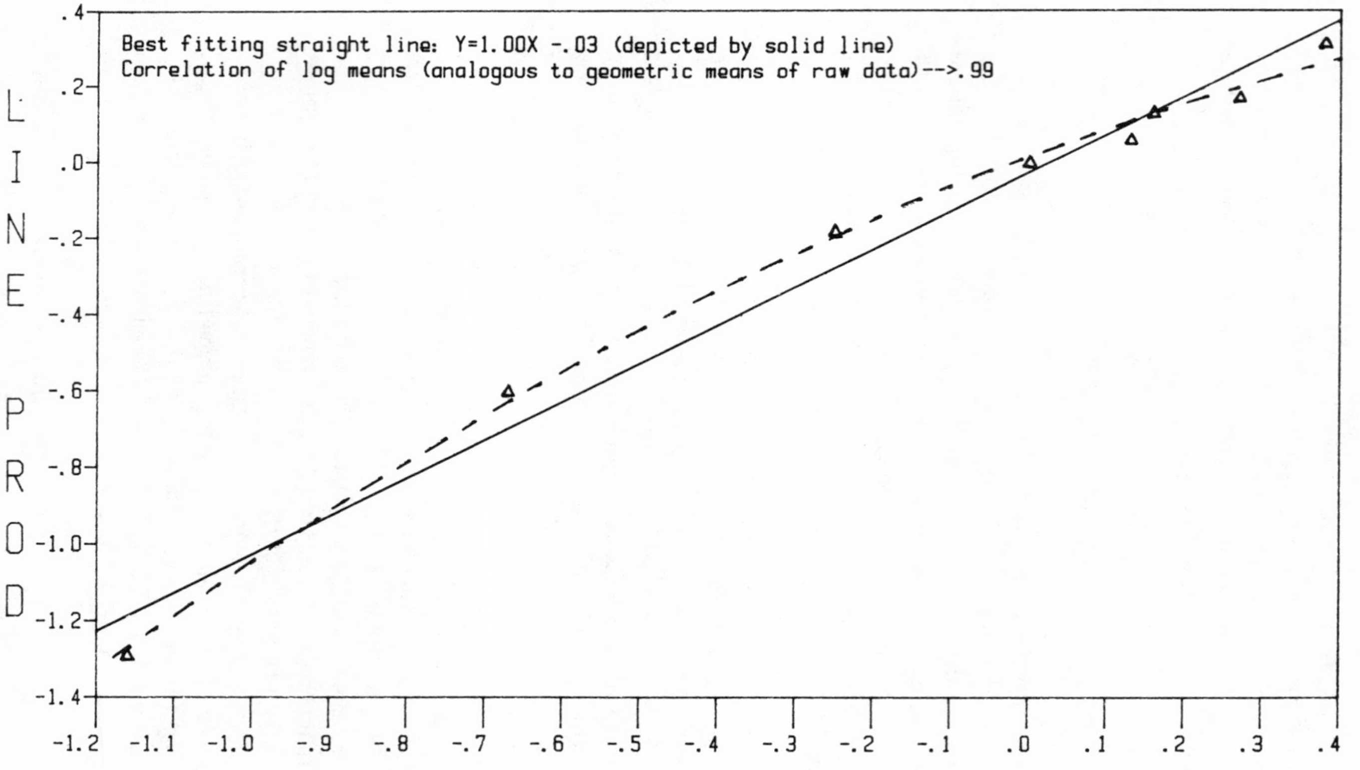

Figure 1. Criterion validity: number estimation versus line production. Deltas are base 10 logs plotted on standard arithmetic coordinates due to graphics software limitations. Logs computed from ratios to a 15 centimeter standard. N = 109.

variance) and were removed from the rest of the analysis. Of the remainder, nearly 90 percent produced a number estimation/line production product-moment correlation of .93 or higher!

The Results: Televised Spot Commercials Can Impact Significantly on Candidate Image.

Some Standards of Comparison: Looks and Warmth

Two of the seven specific traits the subjects were asked to evaluate were "how warm" and "how good-looking" they thought the stimulus persons were compared to their idea of the average individual. Figure 2 presents the results in terms of the percentage change in subject perceptions following exposure to the political commercial and fluff piece, as compared to their perceptions prior to exposure.

The objective physical attributes of the stimulus persons were of course invariant throughout the experimental sessions. Correspondingly, we see that while there was some increase in the evaluations of both the politician (Bob Landers) and the fluff person (Alan Scott), they were not statistically significant (nor were the differences between the two stimulus persons).

The results for warmth are much more interesting. This factor was

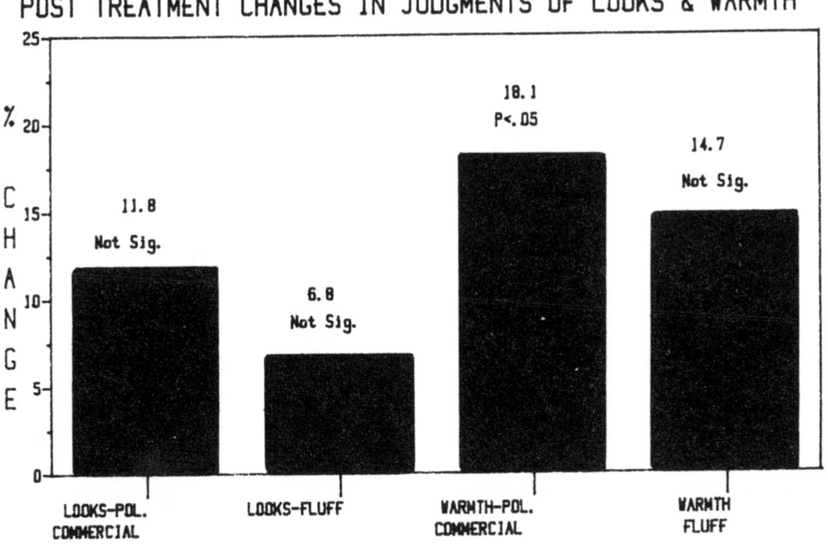

Figure 2. Posttreatment changes in judgments of looks and warmth. Data represent a composite of the same two white males as stimuli.

never directly referenced in either of the experimental presentations, yet there was an average increase of 18 percent in judgments of the personal warmth of Landers the politician, an increase that was significant at the .05 level (two-tailed T-test). Our best guess is that after the respondents heard all the other good things about him—his prominent role in legislation dealing with truth in advertising, campaign reform, integrity, and so on, some of them consciously or unconsciously (one of the virtues of line production and picking up the data pamphlets immediately after the subjects finish with them is that unlike numbers, it's hard for subjects to remember what they did before with any degree of precision) decided he must also be a warmer person.

Judgments of the personal warmth of Alan Scott, the fluff person, also increased—almost 15 percent, though that increase was not statistically significant. (The lack of significance in this instance is primarily a product of a relatively large variance in the change scores.) Our postexperimental discussions with the respondents strongly suggest that for some people, the fact that he had a dog somehow suggested personal warmth. For a roughly equivalent number of subjects it apparently had no such impact, hence the greater variability and resulting lack of statistical significance.

Role Attributes: Intelligence and Strength under Pressure

Neither of these image dimensions were directly manipulated in the experimental treatments. They were included—partly as an aid in disguising the real purpose of the study, partly because they often turn up in one form or another in studies of candidate image and, in the case of intelligence, ranked very high on Anderson's (1968) list of the "likeability" of personality-trait words (seventh out of 555). Courage—something reasonably close to strength under pressure—ranked eighty-fourth. The results for these two image dimensions are presented in Figure 3.

The changes illustrated here are quite striking. The mean judgment of the intelligence of Landers, the politician, posted a 23 percent increase over preadvertisement perceptions, and strength under pressure made an average gain of 34 percent. Both of these increases are not only very large in absolute terms, they are highly significant statistically and indicate a substantial degree of subject consensus (the coefficients of variation were both less than .40).

The postexperimental debriefing session comments of the subjects, along with additional data outside the scope of this report, strongly

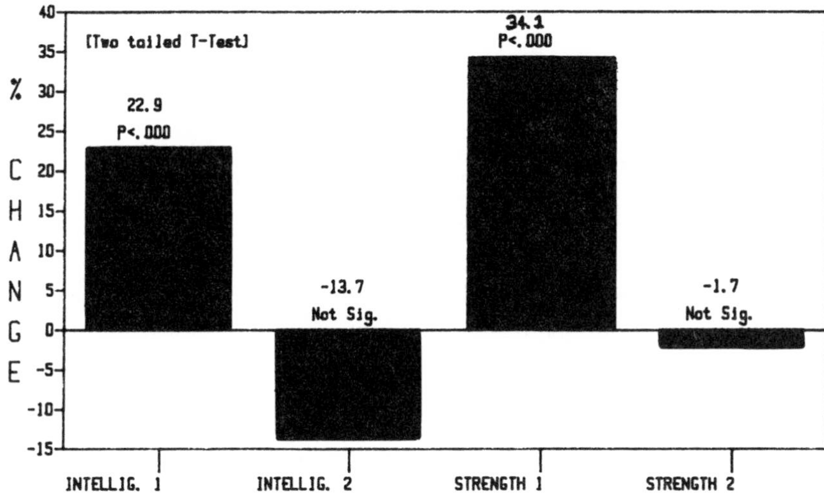

Figure 3. Posttreatment changes in judgments of intelligence and strength under pressure. Data analyzed by two-tailed tests of significance.

suggest that much of the postadvertisement increases on both these dimensions were a function of the role expectations of the respondents—though the spot did mention "accomplishment" and some subjects apparently felt that it took intelligence and strength to achieve what he did. Nonetheless, there were clearly preexisting ideas as to the intelligence and strength under pressure possessed by a Congressman and simply learning that it was the stimulus person's vocation was enough to trigger those evaluations.

In contrast to the political commercial condition, the small drop in judgments of the strength under pressure of Alan Scott in the fluff piece is so slight it should probably be viewed as no change at all. On the other hand, the drop in the mean perception of his intelligence is noticeably larger—close to 14 percent and approaching statistical significance—why? Once again, our postexperimental debriefing discussions helped shed some light on the matter.

Recall that prior to their first evaluation of the two stimulus persons, the subjects were told that these were individuals who had been taped from television programs in another part of the country. Apparently, this led some of the respondents to expect somebody important (and intelligent) or the person wouldn't have been on TV! Later, when they viewed the fluff piece presenting Scott as just an ordinary person, they revised their estimates of intelligence downward toward the "average." Interestingly, there don't seem to have been any parallel expectations about strength under pressure.

The Experimental Variables

Dependability, fairmindedness, and honesty are all image dimensions that were directly tied to the substance of the spot commercial. Anderson (1968) also found them to be very strongly related to overall liking/disliking—our last dependent variable, and therefore, the four factors are considered here together as a group (honesty showed the second highest relationship among the traits on the 555 word list, dependability was number eight, and understanding and openmindedness—the closest listed adjectives to fairminded—were numbers three and nine respectively). The pre- and posttreatment changes for these variables are presented in Figure 4.

Again, the changes are very substantial, all in the direction advocated by the political spot message, and highly significant statistically. By contrast, none of the fluff treatments produced statistically significant results, and the percentage changes are generally very small, both in absolute terms, and relative to the treatment conditions.

Dependability was referred to very explicitly in the spot in terms of Landers' high attendance record and there was a correspondingly large posttreatment increase in judgments of him on this trait—an average increase of 28 percent, compared to only 1.9 percent in the fluff condition. Compared to the other image items, presented in Figure 4, attendance rate is a relatively concrete, objectively verifiable dimension. Thus, it is not surprising that a directly related factor such as the dependability measure would show the biggest average percentage gain among them.

In a similar (though more indirect) manner, advocacy of legislation dealing with truth in advertising, campaign reform, and integrity would be expected to relate to perceptions of fairmindedness and honesty. The changes that took place in respondent evaluations of Landers after being exposed to the political spot are consistent with such an expectation. The mean judgment of Lander's fairmindedness increased over 12 percent and the average evaluation of his honesty went up 21.4 percent. Both these percentage increases are statistically significant ($p < .05$).

We are not certain just why fairmindedness showed a smaller percentage increase than honesty, but the postexperimental discussions gave some indication that in the minds of our subjects, it is entirely

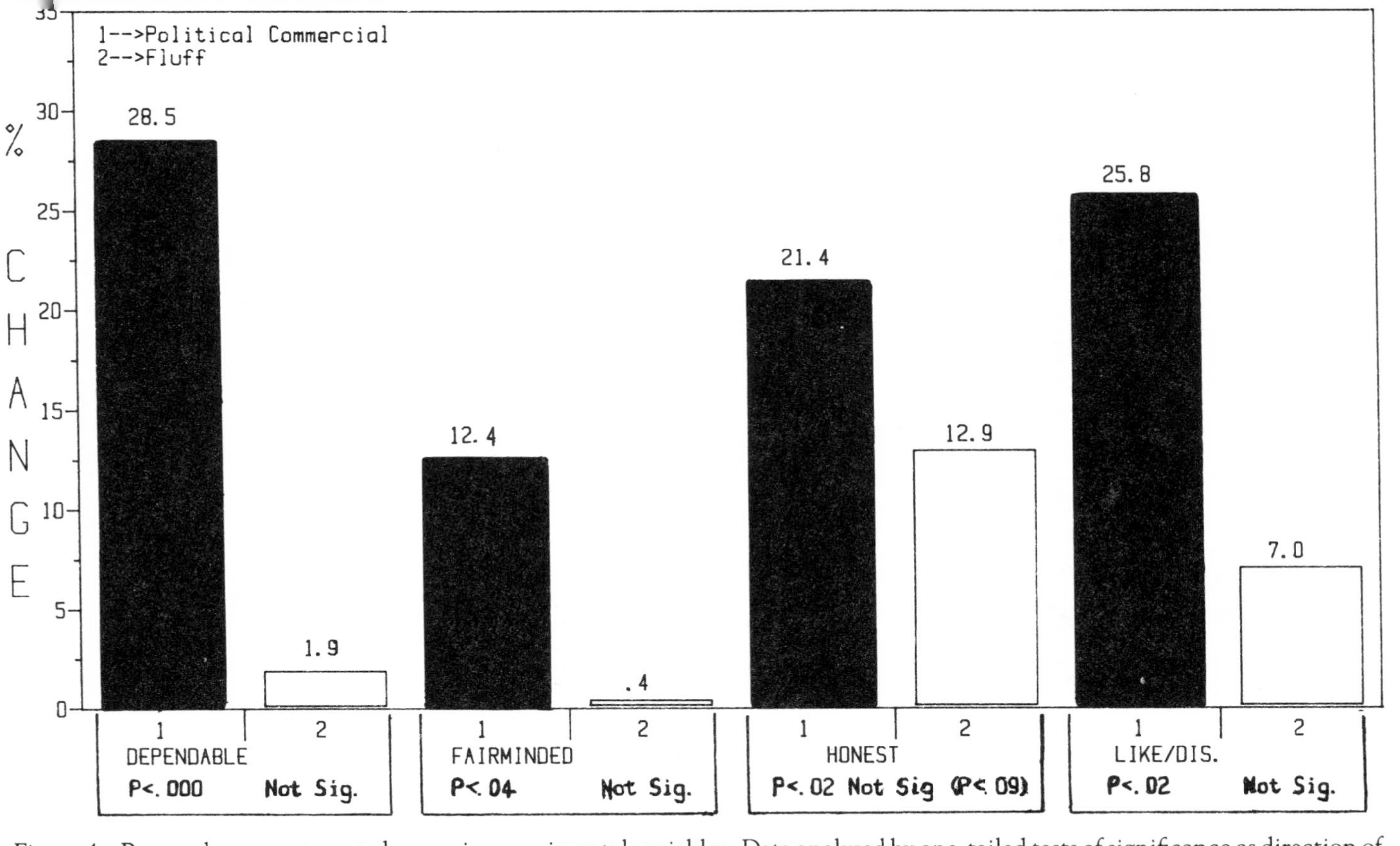

Figure 4. Pre- and posttreatment changes in experimental variables. Data analyzed by one-tailed tests of significance as direction of change was anticipated. $N = 109$.

possible for a person to be honest and truthful without necessarily being fair (i.e., he/she could still take advantage of others in an honest, but hard-bargaining way). We are similarly uncertain as to why perceptions of the honesty of Alan Scott, the fluff person, also showed a noticeable average increase (though the lesser magnitude and comparatively large standard deviation rendered it nonsignificant statistically). In the absence of any plausible explanation, we are inclined to view this as a chance variation without substantive meaning.

Figure four also indicates that following exposure to the political commercial, there was a substantial 26 percent increase in the average degree of overall liking expressed for Landers. A parallel increase took place in the average liking evaluation for Scott, but again, it was a relatively small and statistically nonsignificant one. The increase in liking for Landers is, of course, exactly what one would expect on the basis of common sense, to say nothing of Anderson's (1968) work on the relationship of the three preceding dimensions to overall "likeableness" ratings of the words. These results clearly suggest that if one can change specific aspects of a candidate's image, overall liking and disliking will probably follow suit.

A Comparison to the "Average Person"

The data presented so far have demonstrated substantial changes in respondent images of the individuals presented in the spot commercial, changes which are all highly significant statistically. Yet, to this point, we have only considered the amount of change in percentage terms. One might well ask change to what? For example, where does the candidate stand with respect to perceptions of the "average person"?

That data is presented in graph form in Figure 5. Based on this graph, we can see that following subject exposure to the experimental conditions, the average composite evaluation of the physical attractiveness of the two stimulus individuals and remained very close to the "average person" for both the fluff and the spot commercial treatments. Further, the fluff condition continued to yield very average evaluations across all the rest of the experimental variables except the general like/dislike dimension, where the typical rating fell to 70 percent of the mean subject evaluation of the average person.

In marked contrast to perceptions of physical attractiveness, when the same two individuals were presented as a Congressman in the spot commercials, they were subsequently judged to be 50% more intelligent

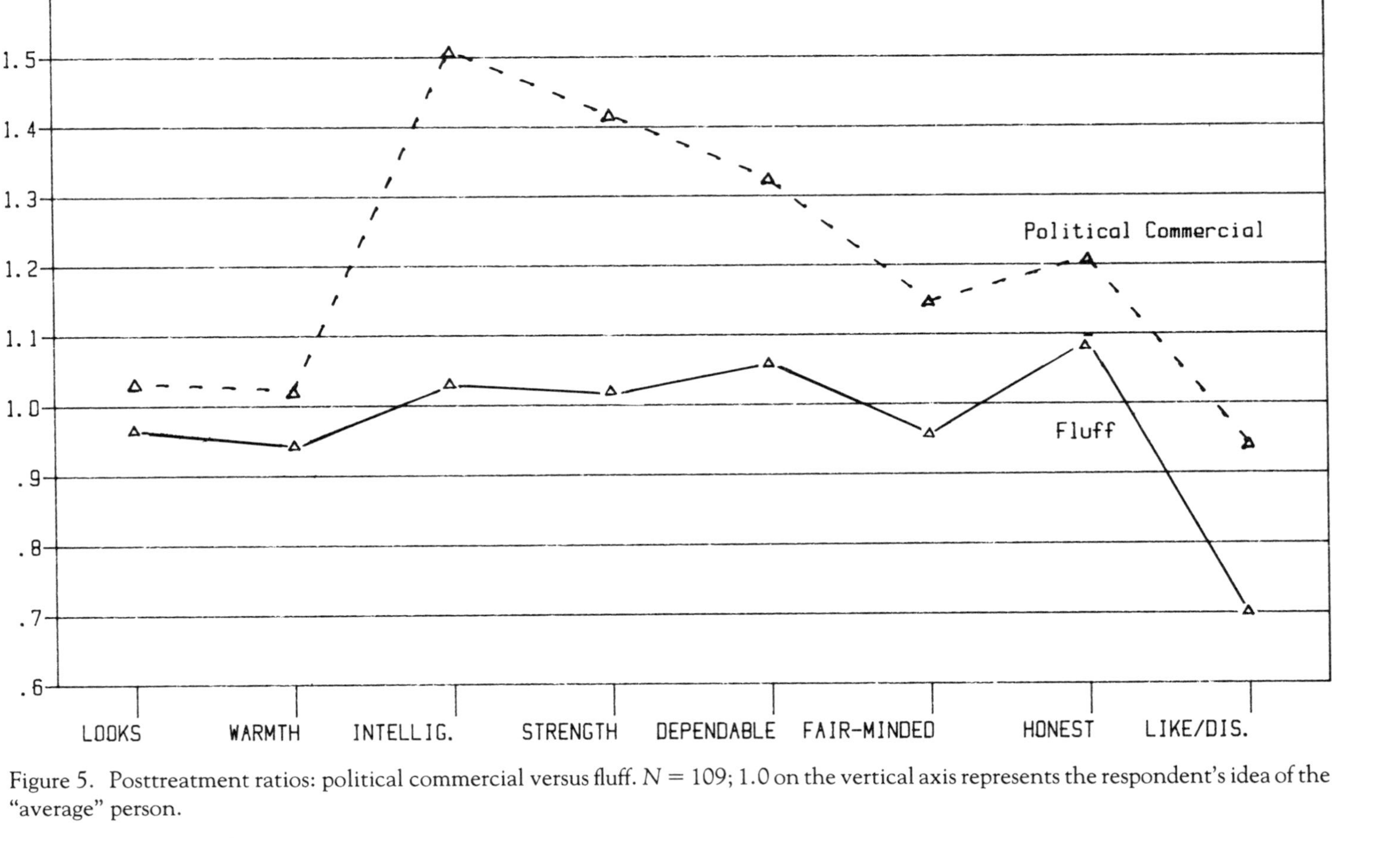

Figure 5. Posttreatment ratios: political commercial versus fluff. $N = 109$; 1.0 on the vertical axis represents the respondent's idea of the "average" person.

than the average person, slightly over 40% stronger under pressure, about 32% more dependable, about 15% more fairminded, and slightly over 29% more honest! They were also liked substantially more overall, though still at a level only approximately equal (94%) to the average person (the lower absolute values of the global like/dislike ratings for both stimulus persons are primarily artifacts of a variation in the scaling procedure for that variable).

CONCLUSIONS

The data presented in this report provide the first direct, ratio-scaled evidence that paid political spot commercials *can* make a significant impact on voter images of political candidates—in this case a fictitious U.S. Representative. One particularly striking aspect of these results is that many of the large, positive changes the commercial produced in respondent evaluations of the image of the Congressman—particularly honesty, dependability, and fairmindedness—run in a direction quite at odds with what the polls indicate about the prevailing contemporary American stereotypes of politicians.

To cite but one example involving the same level of political office, Gallup (July, 1981) asked a national probability sample to rate the honesty and ethical standards of congressmen on a scale running from very high to very low. Seventy-nine percent of the respondents rated them average or below, while only 2% rated them very high, and 10% chose the very low category. Earlier data from 1976 and 1977 shows almost identical patterns. Contrast these figures to the evaluations of our experimental subjects who generated a mean rating of the honesty of the fictitious congressman over 20% more honest than the average person. Clearly, it does pay to advertise!

There are, however, some qualifications that should be made. Patterson (1980) has argued that television makes most of its impact on candidate image very early in the campaign, particularly in the primaries when the voters have little prior information about the candidate. He goes on to suggest that once a candidate's image has been developed, new information is unlikely to generate any appreciable change. DeFleur and Ball-Rokeach (1975), and Strouse (1975) have all made similar points.

Jacobson (1975) has presented evidence which is in essential agreement with the research just cited and in light of his results has concluded that the impact of television campaigning on electoral outcomes varies a good deal, depending upon the office and type of election. He further concluded that such impact will be greater for offices other than the presidency—as well as in primary elections—to acquire the nomination to a given office.

We would agree that to a significant degree, the results presented in this report represent a kind of optimal impact situation. The candidate presented in the study was entirely unknown to the subjects prior to the experimental showing and there were no competing messages. There were, therefore, no preexisting images or impressions to overcome and no countervailing information to contend with. There was also no partisan identification assigned to the Congressman in the portion of the data presented in this report. Therefore, there was no such cue to stimulate party loyalties in a manner that might impact on or in some way mediate the image formation process.

At the same time, it is also true that this study has the very considerable advantage of having isolated the effect of one particular message while either excluding or holding other possible sources of influence relatively constant—much as a physicist would try to do when determining something like the rate of acceleration of a falling body. The measuring technique employed has also made it possible to speak meaningfully about the exact percentage magnitude of the changes produced by the experimental manipulations. Almost all of the prior research in this area has been limited by relatively crude measuring instruments and/or a host of uncontrolled factors acting and interacting in unknown ways, thereby obscuring and probably significantly distorting the results. That we should obtain changes as large as those that occurred in this study following a single exposure to a brief thirty-eight second message from an openly biased source strikes us as quite remarkable.

Any statement we might make that goes beyond asserting that televised political spot ads can significantly alter voter images of political candidates is admittedly speculation on our part. Having offered up that caveat, we would like to conclude by noting our agreement with the notion (and no small amount of evidence in the persuasion literature in psychology) that paid political ads are apt to be most effective early on in the game when the candidate is little known, in primaries where the convenient cue of party identification is absent, in lower level races where the candidates are not heavily covered by the media and hence are likely to have little other information to go on, or as Nimmo (1970), Schwartz (1973), and Napolitan (1972) have all indicated in one way or another, when the candidate is able to exploit (i.e.

develop desired associations with) strongly held preexisting viewpoints of the voters.

We don't agree with either Jacobson (1975) or Patterson and McClure (1976) that presidential races are necessarily any different from other levels of political office in the extent to which candidate image is manipulable by paid political advertising. There is no solid evidence to support that claim. Rather, it seems to us a reasonable assumption that the only relevant difference lies in the fact that presidential candidates have often had significant prior exposure in the media and therefore, are more apt to evoke some preexisting image in the minds of the public before the campaign has begun.

When that preexisting image is poorly developed or absent, the effect of the media on image formation is likely to be every bit as great as for any other office—in fact, probably greater due to the massive media expenditures involved in a modern presidential campaign. The Carter and Hart phenomenon of recent presidential contests would certainly be in accord with such a view.

Once created, candidate images are likely to act as an inertia factor, lessening the impact of subsequent propaganda efforts. Thus, if the candidate is able to bring about the establishment of a positive image early in the game, it might be expected to function as a sort of buffer to the onslaughts of the opposition. Conversely, an early image could become an albatross for the candidate if the inertia it creates helps to preserve something negative (one is reminded of the Muskie crying episode in 1972).[2]

• 9 •

Candidate Image Formation

The Role of Information Processing

Gina Garramone

THE PURPOSE of much television political advertising is to create a favorable candidate image in the eyes of the voters. The manner in which political commercials influence candidate image, however, is not clear. The transactional model of mass communication effects holds that effects can be best understood by combining knowledge of message characteristics with an understanding of orientations of the audience members to those messages (McLeod & Becker, 1981). The present research fits such a transactional model, exploring the roles of both message characteristics (i.e., commercial type) and audience orientations (i.e., motivation) in candidate image formation. In addition, the contingent role of audience information processing is investigated.

This research employs a schema approach to information processing. Schemata are defined as cognitive representations of generic concepts. They include the attributes that constitute the concept and relationship among the attributes (Rumelhart & Ortony, 1977). For example, a schema for politicians might include the knowledge that they are elected; they are usually male; they are middle-aged or older; they have opinions on defense spending, etc. Schemata guide information processing by determining what information is acquired, how it is processed, and how it is utilized (Wyer, Srull, Gordon, & Hartwick, 1982).

A schema approach is chosen for two reasons. First, schema theories have been tested repeatedly and substantiated experimentally for nonpolitical information (Cantor, 1981; Schank & Abelson, 1977), and are now being successfully applied to political thinking (Lau, 1984; Fiske & Kinder, 1981; Graber, 1984). Second, individuals have at their disposal a large number of concepts, or schemata, with which they can process information. They use a subset of these schemata when processing information regarding a particular object or event. Two factors which influence schema choice are attributes of the stimulus (Cantor & Mischel, 1977; Taylor & Fiske, 1978; Graber, 1984) and audience goals (Cohen & Ebbesen, 1979; Graber, 1984). If message characteristics such as commercial type are conceptualized as attributes of the stimulus, and if audience orientations such as motivations are conceptualized as audience goals, then commercial type and audience motivation may determine what schemata are used in information processing. The nature of the information processing, in turn, may influence candidate image formation.

The present research, therefore, will investigate the interrelationships of audience motivation, commercial type, and information processing, and their effects on candidate image formation.

Determinants of Candidate Image

Candidate image is defined as the sum of the perceived personal and professional characteristics of the candidate. Earlier research exploring the main effects of commercial type (e.g., issue versus image) and audience motivation on candidate image identified a significant impact of commercial type, but conflicting results for audience motivation. Kaid and Sanders (1978) found that the candidate image resulting from "image" political commercials is less positive than that resulting from "issue" commercials. Although there is no consensus in the literature on a definition of issue versus image commercials, the labels will be used here to distinguish commercials which fall at opposite ends of a continuum in terms of the amount or prominence of several attributes. For example, issue commercials tend to have more or give greater prominence to information regarding the candidate's policy stands than do image commercials. Image commercials, on the other hand, tend to have more or give greater prominence to information regarding the candidate's personal qualities. The less positive effect of image commercials uncovered by Kaid and Sanders may derive from viewer's distrust of candidates who attempt to procure votes without announcing their policy stands. Based on the Kaid and Sanders findings, the following prediction is made:

> H_1: Exposure to image commercials will result in a less positive candidate image than will exposure to issue commercials.

Evidence from research on the influence of audience motivation on image formation is equivocal. While Warr and Knapper (1968) found that the perceiver's motive influenced impressions formed, two more recent studies (Cohen and Ebbesen, 1979; Garramone, 1983) have found no effect of motivation on valence of the image or impression formed. Because of the contradictory findings regarding the effect of motivation on image formation, no hypotheses are offered.

The effect of commercial type on candidate image may depend on the audience's motivation for attending to the commercial. The closer the match between what the individual seeks and what she/he is provided, the more positive should be the resulting reaction. Therefore, candidate image should be most favorable when audience motivation and commercial type match.

Two motivations for attending to political content in the media are to learn the candidates' personal qualities (i.e., image-motivated) and to learn the candidates' issue stands (i.e., issue-motivated; Garramone, 1983; 1984). The matching commercial types would be image commercials and issue commercials, respectively. If candidate image is most favorable when audience motivation and commercial type match, then

> H_{2a}: For image-motivated individuals, exposure to image commercials will result in a more positive candidate image than will exposure to issue commercials.
> H_{2b}: For issue-motivated individuals, exposure to issue commercials will result in a more positive candidate image than will exposure to image commercials.

Determinants of Information Processing Behavior

Although commercial type and audience motivation may have direct effects on candidate image, they may also have indirect effects via information processing behavior.

Audience Motivations.

Motives influence the schemata chosen for information processing. The motivation to learn the personal qualities of a candidate, for example, may elicit a schema very different from that elicited by a motivation to learn a candidate's issue stands. The former task involves impression formation, and should elicit a schema useful for making personality judgments—for example, a schema of abstract personality traits. The latter task, on the other hand, should elicit a schema useful for the rote learning (i.e., recall) of more specific, more objective information.

The differences between such schemata have implications for information processing. For example, individuals with an impression formation motive tend to encode information in larger "units" and recall less detail than individuals with a recall motive (Cohen & Ebbesen, 1979). This implies that individuals processing information for image formation purposes may be particularly likely to encode information in a more general, less detailed form.

A reinterpretation of Zajonc's (1960) cognitive tuning research provides additional support for this hypothesis. Zajonc found that the cognitive structures of individuals expecting to merely receive information describing another person contained less specific information and more general concepts than did the cognitive structures of individuals expecting to transmit this person information to another. If we interpret Zajonc's anticipated receiver-only condition to correspond to Cohen and Ebbesen's impression-formation condition, and the anticipated receiver-transmitter condition to correspond to Cohen and Ebbesen's recall condition, Zajonc's findings support the notion that individuals with an impression-formation motivation tend to encode information in the form of general concepts (e.g., "intelligent," "liberal"), rather than more specific concepts (e.g., "graduated at the top of his class," "voted against a ceiling on foodstamps"). Cohen and Ebbesen and Zajonc attribute their findings to the nature of the schemata activated by the individual's information processing goals.

These two lines of research suggest that:

> H_3: Individuals attending to political commercials to learn the candidate's personal qualities (i.e., image-motivated) will use more general concepts in information processing than will individuals attending to learn the candidate's issue stands (i.e., issue-motivated).

Impression formation is an inferential task in which the individual making the judgment frequently goes beyond the information available.

A personality trait schema, with its interrelationships among abstract trait concepts, may foster the drawing of inferences. For example, the information that a candidate is friendly may lead to the inference that he is also trustworthy. This suggests that image-motivated individuals may be more likely to make inferences in their information processing.

> H_4: Image-motivated individuals will display more inference information processing of political commercials than will issue-motivated individuals.

If schemata direct people to attend to only information that is particularly relevant to their goals (Wyer & Carlston, 1979), then image-motivated idividuals should attend to information most useful for image formation. This might include information explicitly denoting the candidate's personal qualities (e.g., a voice-over saying the candidate "cares"), or information from which image inferences may easily be drawn (e.g., candidate pictured with his family). Such "image" information, therefore, should receive greater attention and greater encoding by the image-motivated than by the issue-motivated individual.

> H_5: Image-motivated individuals will display more image information processing of political commercials than will issue-motivated individuals.

If people attend to and encode only the selected aspects of information that are particularly relevant to their goals, and if information channels are perceived to differ in the amount of such information they contain, then perhaps individuals will differentially attend to channels based on their motivations. The candidate's facial expressions, body postures, and motions are all video-contained information relevant to image judgments. Experimental (Garramone, 1983) and survey (Garramone, 1984) research indicates that an image motivation in attending to political commercials results in greater attention to the video content than does an issue motivation.

> H_6: Image-motivated individuals will display more visual information processing of political commercials than will issue-motivated individuals.

Commercial Type

Attributes of the stimulus information also influence schema choice. For example, content in the first part of a message may activate schemata which are used in subsequent processing. Thus if the concept "conservative" is stressed in the first part of a political message, the likelihood of later information being encoded in terms of this concept is increased. Also, drawing attention to different characteristics of a message may influence processing. For example, messages presented via a multichannel medium such as television may accentuate one channel over another, increasing the likelihood that information in the accentuated channel is encoded.

Issue and image commercials differ in the amount of several attributes they possess, or in the prominence given those attributes. These differences may influence the nature of the information processing elicited by each type of commercial. For example, issue commercials generally feature the candidate on camera, explaining his policies either to the camera (i.e., talking head) or to constituents represented in the commercial. Image commercials, on the other hand, tend to tell the viewer about the candidate's personality qualities (e.g., a voice-over or testimonial) or allow the candidate to demonstrate these qualities by his actions (e.g., kissing babies, working late into the night, spending time with his family). The prominence of information about the candidate's personal qualities in image commercials should result in greater attention to and encoding of such information.

> H_7: Exposure to political image commercials will result in more image information processing than will exposure to political issue commercials.

In addition to emphasizing image content, image commercials emphasize the visual content. In issue commercials, production techniques tend to be simple and actions featured of little dramatic interest, facilitating the viewer's attention to the candidate's words. Image commercials tend to use more complex production techniques (e.g., montage) and often feature settings or behaviors of dramatic interest inherently (e.g., candidate's small children playing in the foreground) or because of their uniqueness to the particular political commercial (e.g., candidate sitting on the front porch with a coffee mug). The prominence of visual information in such commercials should increase the salience and encoding of such visual information. As noted by Rossiter and Percy (1980), visual commercial content is especially capable of stimulating visual imagery.

> H_8: Exposure to political image commercials will result in more visual information processing than will exposure to issue commercials.

While information in issue commercials may be very specific and explicit (e.g., "As mayor, I intend to make jobs for San Diegans top priority."), the information in image commercials tends to be both more general (e.g., "He's the right man for a tough job.") and more subtle (e.g., picturing the candidate with his family may be a subtle way of saying that he's a dedicated family man). Image commercials, therefore, should result in greater processing with general concepts than should issue commercials. Graber's (1984) research on news processing supports this prediction: when news stories included clear generalizations, people tended to process the information in abstract terms.

> H_9: Exposure to political image commercials will result in more use of general concepts in information processing than will exposure to issue commercials.

While the general and subtle nature of the information presented in image commercials should foster the drawing of inferences, the prominence of the visual content may also do so. According to Borgida and Nisbett (1977), visually encoded information "remains in thought longer and triggers more inferences because of its greater dramatic interest and salience" (p. 269).

> H_{10}: Exposure to political image commercials will result in more inference information processing than will exposure to issue commercials.

Although no hypotheses are offered concerning the relationship between information processing and candidate image formation, the intervening role of processing hypothesized and the relationships already predicted suggest the nature of the processing/candidate image relationship. If exposure to political image commercials results in more image information processing, yet also in a less favorable candidate image than exposure to issue commercials, then image information processing should be negatively related to candidate image.

Method

To investigate the impact of audience motivation and commercial type on information processing and candidate image formation, an experiment was conducted in which both motivation and commercial type were manipulated.

Subjects and Design

Subjects in the experiment included 120 undergraduate students at Michigan State University who participated in partial fulfillment of an introductory consumer behavior course requirement. Subjects were randomly assigned to small, exposure groups of eight to ten persons.

A 2 × 2 factorial design was used, with thirty students assigned to each of the four conditions. In each condition, subjects were told that they would be watching two commercials for a political candidate. For the issue-motivation condition, subjects were instructed to watch the political commercials "to try to learn where the candidate stands on issues." For the image-motivation condition, subjects were instructed to watch the commercials "to learn the candidate's personal qualities." In the issue-commercial condition, subjects watched two issue commercials, and in the image-commercial condition, subjects watched two image commercials.

Stimuli

Videotape recordings of four political commercials for Roger Hedgecock, a San Diego mayoral candidate, were used in the experiment.[1] Both of the issue commercials portrayed the candidate explaining, in detail, his issue stands to constituents who had been affected by his policies. The first image commercial used a montage format, showing the candidate engaged in various activities (e.g., at meetings, parades, jogging) and featuring such voice-over comments as "not too busy to listen to the people" and "Roger Hedgecock cares." The second image commercial featured the candidate and his family thanking campaign volunteers for their efforts. The candidate and his wife were sitting on the front porch of their home, while their young children played in the foreground.

Dependent Variables

Information processing. Following exposure to the commercials, subjects were asked to "write down everything you recall from the commercials." Subjects' responses were coded with the sentence serving as the unit of analysis. Most subjects wrote their recall responses in the form of sentences. For those subjects listing phrases instead of sentences (e.g., "wife and kids"), the phrase served as the unit of analysis. All sentences were evaluated by two independent coders. For all categories, the intercoder reliability was above 90 percent.

The sentences were coded in terms of the four information processing variables. The use of general concepts in information processing was indicated by the word-to-sentence ratio because general concepts tended to be represented with fewer words than did more specific concepts (e.g., "family man" versus "pictured on the front porch with his wife and two little boys"). Inference processing was measured by the proportion of sentences making inferential (as opposed to factual) comments about the candidate. Examples of inferential comments are "Hedgecock seems to be a very warm person," and "Hedgecock appears to be a middle-class person." Image processing was indicated by the proportion of sentences referring to commerical content of an "image" (as opposed to issue) nature. Examples of image comments include "Shown sitting on front porch with his wife and kids," "Shown jogging," and "Says that Hedgecock cares." Finally, visual processing was measured by the proportion of sentences which referred to content presented only in the video portion of the commercial.

Candidate image. A candidate image rating was ascertained by asking subjects to rate the candidate on a seven-point scale for ten personality traits (competent, superficial, effective, opportunistic, qualified, intelligent, open-minded, arrogant, sympathetic, trustworthy). The ten ratings were summed to form an image index.

Analysis

The data are analyzed in three ways. First, the directional hypotheses are tested using one-tailed t-tests. Second, zero-order correlations are computed to assess the relationship between the information process variables and candidate image. And third, hierarchical regression analysis is used to determine the roles of the interaction of motivation and commercial type, and the information processing variables, in predicting candidate image.

Results

The results are described in the following order: (1) the influence of motivation and commercial type on candidate image; (2) the influence of motivation and commercial type on the information processing variables; (3) the relationship between information processing and candidate image; and (4) the interrelationships of all predictor variables in influencing candidate image.

Motivation and commercial type have neither main effects nor interaction effects on candidate image (Table 22). However, the difference in mean candidate image scores by commercial type is in the predicted direction.

The prediction that image-motivated individuals would use more general concepts in information processing (Hypothesis 3) is supported ($t(120) = 3.38$), $p < .001$). Hypothesis 4 failed to be supported as no difference emerged between image-motivated and issue-motivated individuals in their degree of inference information processing. Hypotheses 5 and 6 also failed to receive support, as the differences between image-and issue-motivated individuals, while in the predicted direction, did not reach significance.

The effects of commercial type on information processing are much stronger—Hypotheses 7 through 10 are confirmed. Exposure to image commercials results in more image processing ($t(120) = 11.85$, $p < .001$), more visual processing ($t(120) = 4.44$, $p < .001$), more use of general concepts ($t(120) = 3.79$, $p < .001$) and more inference processing ($t(120) = 1.70$, $p < .05$).

Only one interaction between motivation and commercial type on information processing emerged. While issue-motivated individuals display the same degree of visual processing regardless of the type of commercial to which they are exposed, image-motivated individuals display more visual processing when exposed to image commercials than when exposed to issue commercials ($F(1,116) = 8.75$, $p < .01$).

Zero-order correlations between the information processing variables and candidate image reveal only two significant relationships. Use of general concepts is negatively related to candidate image ($r = -.20$, $p < .05$) and inference processing is positively related to candidate image ($r = .19$, $p < .05$).

The lack of main effects of motivation and commercial type on candidate image, and the weak and mixed relationships between processing and candidate image, imply that the role of information processing may not be mediating, but rather contingent (McLeod & Reeves, 1980). That is, the effects of motivation and commercial type may not operate through information processing behavior, but rather may be contingent upon information processing behavior. To explore this possibility, hierarchical regressions were computed in which motivation, commercial type, and their interaction were entered as the first step, the processing

Table 22

Mean Scores of Candidate Image and Information Processing Variables by Motivation and Commercial Type[a]

	Motivation			Commercial type		
	Issue	Image	*t*	Issue	Image	*t*
Candidate Image	46.15	44.60	1.52	45.93	44.82	1.10
Processing						
General concepts	.09	.11	3.38[b]	.08	.11	3.79[b]
Inference	.17	.17	.00	.15	.20	1.70[b]
Visual	.28	.32	1.32	.22	.37	4.44[b]
Image	.52	.56	1.14	.34	.75	11.85[b]

[a] $N = 120$

[b] $P < .05$

variable was added as the second step, the two-way interactions of the processing variable with both motivation and commercial type were added as the third step, and the three-way interaction between the processing variable, motivation, and commercial type was added as the fourth step.

Significant interactions emerged for inference processing, image processing, and visual processing. Inference processing explains an additional 5 percent of the variance in candidate image, beyond that explained by motivation and commercial type (standardized regression coefficient $B = .22$, $p < .05$). Inference processing also interacts with commercial type in predicting candidate image (incremental $R^2 = .03$, $p < .05$). For individuals displaying a low degree of inference processing, issue and image commercials are equally effective. For individuals displaying a high degree of inference processing, however, issue commercials result in a more positive candidate image than do image commercials.

Similar relationships emerged for image processing. Image processing explains an additional 7 percent of the variance in candidate image, beyond that explained by motivation and commercial type ($B = .38$, $p < .01$). Image processing also interacts with commercial type in predicting candidate image (incremental $R^2 = .03$, $p < .05$). For individuals displaying a low degree of image processing, issue and image commercials are equally effective. For individuals displaying a high degree of image processing, issue commercials result in a more positive candidate image than do image commercials.

While no main effects of visual processing, nor two-way interactions, emerged, a three-way interaction between processing, motivation, and commercial type emerged. The amount of visual processing has less impact on candidate image when motivation and commercial type match (e.g., issue motivation and issue commercial) than when motivation and commercial do not match (incremental $R^2 = .05$, $p < .01$). When they do not match, the more visual processing, the more positive the candidate image.

Discussion

The purpose of the present research was to investigate the interrelationships of audience motivation, political commercial type, and information processing, and their effects on candidate image formation. Direct effects of motivation and commercial type, as well as indirect effects via information processing, were proposed.

The failure to find the hypothesized direct effects of audience motivation and commercial type suggested the need to investigate the information processing variables as contingent variables, specifying the conditions under which motivation and commercial type effects might occur. The analyses revealed that the presence and nature of commercial type effects depend on information processing behavior. For example, exposure to issue commercials results in a more positive candidate image than does exposure to image commercials, but only when the individual enagaes in a high degree of inference, or a high degree of image, information processing.

Both inference and image processing might be conceptualized as impression formation "styles," indicative of the encoding of impression formation-relevant information from a commercial. Perhaps when an individual is not processing with an impression formation style, issue and image commercials result in similar candidate images because the individual is not extracting impression formation-relevant information from either type of commercial. But when an individual is extracting such information from the commercials, issue commercials result in a more positive candidate image because they provide a bonus—issue information which might be integrated with the impression formation information in forming an overall candidate image.

The prevalence of impression formation schemata in political information processing (Lau, 1984; Graber, 1984) suggests that individuals may frequently process political commercials with impression formation "styles." If this is true, and if such individuals respond more favorably to issue than to image commercials, then the implications for campaign media planners are clear.

Several directions for future research may be suggested. First, the effects of motivations in addition to image formation and issue knowledge should be explored. For example, the effects of a motive to use acquired information in interpersonal political discussions might be compared to the effects of a motive to use acquired information for personal decision-making. Second, additional information-processing variables should be explored. For example, the occurrence of self references in information processing, sometimes used to indicate involvement, may vary by motivation or message characteristics. Finally, additional criterion variables should be assessed. While certain information processing variables may be relevant to candidate image formation, others may be important for the development of vote intention.

• 10 •

Hidden Myths in Televised Political Advertising

An Illustration

Dan Nimmo and Arthur J. Felsberg

What began as a trickle in the 1950s, especially the droplets of the "Eisenhower Answers the Nation" televised spots in 1952, has in the mid-1980s become a deluge (Kelley, 1956). Whether measured by the number of candidates employing television advertising, the national and/or subnational levels of campaigning, the spread of televised political merchandising to other nations, the quantity and quality of ads, the dollars spent; or the professional competence involved in production, there is no question that paid political advertising via television now constitutes the mainstream of modern electoral politics. Aware of the growing importance of electronic politics, either in direct competition with or as a supplement to organizational politics (Napolitan, 1972), scholars turned their attention to the flood of televised political advertising that poured forth over the last three decades. It was but a short time until papers read at professional conferences, articles in journals, and books detailed the not-so-clear-cut micro- and macropolitical effects of televised ads, their manifest content, allegedly distinct issue and image dimensions, the techniques of their production, the motives of their producers, rising production costs, their contributions and dangers to political systems, and their historical development (Kaid, 1981; Diamond & Bates, 1984).

The general tendency in the growing literature of studies of televised political advertising is to examine such ads within the context of the specific campaigns within which those ads appear. This has been quite natural in light of scholarly concern primarily with the direct political effects of advertising campaigns, be those effects on voting behavior, campaign costs, raising and/or lowering the likelihood of rational political discussion, or whatever. Relatively less attention has been directed at examining specific televised political advertising as representative of commercial advertising in general, especially in the way that such advertising reflects transcendent human aspirations and anxieties. In short, with such notable exceptions as the work of Combs (1979), little of the research concerning the role of televised political advertising has concerned itself with how specific ad campaigns both represent and promote enduring political myths. It is the purpose of this study to suggest one method for exploring the hidden myths of political advertising and to illustrate that method through a comparison of competing ads in a single campaign.

Leymore's "Spade to Dig With"

Several researchers have undertaken studies of the underlying structure of commercial advertising in efforts to tease out "ritual-like displays" that make transcendent appeals to audiences. Erving Goffman's (1979) investigation of gender display in advertising is but a leading example. By close examination of advertising via still pictures, Goffman illustrated how such relationships as function ranking, subordination, and withdrawals between the sexes are ritualized through the "picture frames" of commercial advertising. Employing the techniques of psycholinguistics, Michael Geis (1982) has illustrated how advertisers use language to make indirect claims for commercial products, thus exploiting the limited perceptual frames of audiences.

Although these inquiries raise interesting possibilities for examining the picture and perceptual frames of political advertising, studies of the content of televised political fare continue to concentrate upon manifest content, reflecting such specifics as candidate images, styles, issues, visual presentations of self, etc. To be sure, there have been efforts to explore such latent content in political ads as "idio-logical attributes" (Buss & Hofstetter, 1976) and structures of "benefit-seeking" and "benefit-promising" behavior (Rank, 1984), but the concern has focused upon the verbal components of spot ads to the exclusion of visual dimensions.

Recently Arthur Asa Berger (1981, 1982) has urged researchers interested in studying the content of televised programming to explore the utility of semiotic techniques in their analyses. Berger bases his analytical techniques, as do many other semantic analysts, upon the 1916 work of the Swiss linguist, Ferdinand de Saussure (1966). Saussure was interested in the study of signs, holding that a science that investigates the life of signs within a society was possible. That science, semiology, would study the relationships, components, and meanings of signs. Key in his framework was the view that the relation between the "signifier" component of a sign (i.e., the sound or other way of denoting a concept) and the "signified" (the concept evoked) is arbitrary. Put differently, nothing has meaning in itself; rather, meaning is created through the relationships of signs to one another. For instance, what one means when one speaks takes on any meaning at all only within the context of a more transcendent language, a social institution in which acts of speaking are related.

Berger offers examples of the signifier-signified distinction from the technology of TV. It is commonplace to find in textbooks on television production (e.g., Wurtzel, 1983) discussions on how to frame camera shots. Thus a high camera angle (signifier) looks down on a subject, yielding an appearance of small size and stature, hence, a sense of loneliness, lack of power, and loss of dominance in the subject televised, and one of power from the viewer's perspective (i.e., alternatives of what is signified). As a signifier the low camera angle looking up signifies power and dominance in the subject and powerlessness and subordination in the viewer.

Saussure's signifier-signified distinction for the coupling that is a sign is now sufficiently commonplace as to be taken for granted (for instance, how many TV production texts cite Saussure?) It is clearly implicit in Goffman's frame analysis of gender advertising. However, where it has been applied most systematically in the study of televised product and brand advertising, largely without recognition by students of political communication, is in the work of Varda Langholz Leymore. In her 1975 work, *Hidden Myth: Structure and Symbolism in Advertising,*

Leymore sets out a carefully devised method by which the "deep structure" of televised commercial advertising may be revealed.

With an avowed debt to Saussure, structural anthropologists Claude Lévi-Strauss and Edmund Leach, and to other structuralist thinkers, Leymore constructs what she labels "a spade to dig with." Leymore's construction consists of a technical discussion that need not be repeated here. (Interested readers should consult her neglected work.) Let it suffice to say, in oversimplifed terms, that Leymore regards advertising as a "process of transformation." That transformation consists of converting signs (the manifest message of ads) into "real life action," which is in the case of commercial advertising the exchange of money for goods. What Leymore constructs is an analytical spade to "reveal something about the message advertising conveys to the consumer" (p. 18). What that "something" is consists of "decoding," by following structuralist procedures, the "structure of a system" from the "apparent characteristics of the system." Using Saussure's terms, signifiers through transformation processes generate signified meanings. The task is to take a series of advertisements, examine the signifiers, explore generative processes, and define what is signified.

To accomplish the decoding of ads (i.e., to transform manifest into latent content), requires certain conditions be met. One of those is of such potential importance to political advertising that it should be singled out for comment. Namely, it is not sufficient, for instance, to analyze a single ad for a product or brand in isolation, either from other ads for that product or brand or in isolation from competing products or brands. All ads in the same product field must be included in the analysis. In this fashion what Leymore calls "Exhaustive Common Denominators" (EDCs) can be derived (i.e., hidden themes that run through all ads and define the whole system of advertising messages). Heeding this advice in the study of political advertising means collecting all ads of a particular form of expression in an electoral campaign.

Leymore distinguishes between "immobile expression" or "static" advertising in the form of print, and "mobile expression" "dynamic" ads on film and/or TV. In the former category, for instance, she analyzes ads for the competing products of butter and oleomargarine. On the surface the former is associated in ads with nature—basic goodness, soil and land, green pastures, the countryside, and cows and milk. Margarine ads remove the product from nature; the modern scientific nature of the product makes it healthful. But, notes Leymore, these surface themes appear in different settings. Butter is for a child's breakfast before school, a father eating a slice of bread and butter while reading the newspaper and being watched by a child, an elderly couple enjoying a bun, and young people at a barbecue. The transformation is from surface identification of butter with nature to concordance for the young, contentment for the old, love for children, care for fathers, etc. By contrast, margarine represents protest against concord, discontent with the way things are rather than contentment, etc. Through a continuous reduction of signifiers Leymore reaches an Exhaustive Common Denominator for butter-margarine advertising: butter is to margarine as peace is to war.

In similar fashion Leymore decodes ads in other product fields, including those for baby foods and competing products and for English and non-English cheeses and reveals ECDs (life versus death in the former, endogenous versus exogenous in the latter). But it is her analysis of mobility and expression in TV advertising between competing brands that is most closely related to the concerns of students of televised political advertising. Political candidates most frequently offer themselves as differing brands (with or without party affiliations being attached) of the same product (such as prospective governor, congressman, mayor, or other officeholder). To be sure, they may on occasion attempt to appear as competing products—a candidate of "new politics" such as George McGovern in 1972, or of "new ideas" such as Gary Hart in 1984 positioned at distance from the "old" ways—markedly distinct from all other products available. Nevertheless, the bulk of political advertising is between competing brands. In her example, Leymore contrasts ads for competing brands of washing powders. On the surface, one brand emphasizes its capacities for brightness, the other for whiteness. What is key, however, is the kind of world assumed to exist by each brand's ads. The brand emphasizing whiteness accepts the world as it is—peaceful, harmonious, a working-class haven. In that world it is sufficient and desirable merely to improve on the status quo. This the brand will do with its new improved formula. Good will thus get better. Its competitor, however, evokes a world that is hard, bullying, and ugly. The housewife's chores are never finished, for even if one's wash appears white there are always more dirty clothes in the hamper, irremovable spots, underarm stains. What is required is a tough, fast, hardworking powder, "a bright new powder for a bright new world." In sum, the ECD is for a powder that will improve a good world versus a powder that will conquer evil.

These, then, are the main features of Leymore's spade to dig with. Are they of any utility in uncovering the EDCs, the "hidden myths" of televised political advertising?

Digging Deeply into Televised Political Ads: The Illustration

The possibilities of using Leymore's spade to explore the hidden myths underlying televised political advertising can be demonstrated by focusing upon a single statewide gubernatorial contest. The electoral campaign took place in a southeastern state during 1978. Both candidates, hereafter designated as simply the Democrat and the Republican, won their party's nomination by capturing a plurality of votes in respective party primaries. Both had sought the office of governor four years earlier. The Democrat had done well in his party's primary in 1974 but had lost to the candidate who eventually was elected governor. The Republican had won his party's primary in 1974 but had lost the governorship in the general election. Both Democrat and Republican had sought elective office for the first time in 1974; the gubernatorial contest in 1978 thus was the second electoral outing for each.

The Democrat was a prominent banker within the state. Although known widely in business and corporate circles, until 1974 his political experience and name recognition was generally confined to the eastern part of the state. This was the area of his rural upbringing and of his first financial success as a petroleum dealer and farmer and then as a banker. The Republican was a lawyer, also from the eastern part of the state. However, he had been politically active for several years and had served as an administrative assistant to the senior U.S. Senator from the state.

Leymore argues that to probe the deep structure of advertising successfully it is best to have a total sample of all ads used in the product or brand campaign. In keeping with that recommendation this analysis employs all televised ads aired on behalf of both candidates during the 1978 general election contest. Such ads constitute a total sample of n = 63. Forty-two of those ads were aired on behalf of the Democrat, of which thirty-nine were televised spots, one a five minute documentary, and two half-hour documentaries. Twenty-one televised ads appeared for the Republican, one of which was a five minute documentary and the remainder brief spots. The documentaries produced for each candidate in fact consisted of material aired repeatedly in spot commercials. The spots themselves, in the case of each candidate, were separately produced and aired ads, but in many instances the variation in verbal and/or visual content from spot to spot was slight.

In employing Leymore's spade a first step is to examine the apparent characteristics of the advertising system as displayed in concrete verbal and visual materials. In this instance the most apparent characteristics of the candidates' ads are overall thematic consistencies. Repeated throughout ads for the Democrat is a rags-to-riches motif. The most typical of all ads aired for the Democrat, for example, begins with a televised long shot of a sunrise over a mountain with a pan to a rural valley and a country lane. There the Democrat appears attired in work clothes. In that setting—and with variations between ads—rural people testify to the Democrat's humble origins, hard work, and yeomanlike character. That setting is then juxtaposed with the Democrat as a campaigner, attired in business suit and tie and shaking hands at various gatherings, visual testimony to his success at transcending rural origins yet never sacrificing agrarian values.

Leymore writes, "Two brands can fight each other either by each maintaining that certain attributes are all its own and none characterizes the other; or they may both pursue the same line of reasoning, each striving to surpass the other" (1975, pp. 68–69). Burger King stresses the virtues of flame broiled hamburgers, Wendy's the custom ordered hamburger. In this respect neither purports to have attributes of the other. Coca Cola and Pepsi Cola, however, strive to surpass one another in better taste. The political campaign in question, on the surface, was one of candidates trying to outdo one another in their claims to be of humble origin and possessed with common, solid values. Hence, the Republican's ads also portrayed him in work clothes (a red plaid shirt became the symbol of his "walking" campaign across the state) and talking with "just plain folk." Unlike the Democrat, however, the Republican in his ads did not claim to have transcended his roots—although in fact he was a successful corporate attorney, concert pianist, and graduate of one of the nation's leading law schools.

It is possible to dig deeper and explore what underlies these most apparent thematic characteristics by first taking note of the most concrete of concepts repeated throughout each candidate's commercials. These are listed in Tables 23 and 24. Each concept or phrase appears repeatedly in each candidate's commercials. Although precise quantification is possible (and was performed), semiotic analysis does not employ standard content analytic techniques. What is key is identification of the concrete signifiers repeated in messages and not the number of times they appear.

On inspection it is noteworthy that characteristic signifiers appearing in one candidate's ads very infrequently characterize those of the opponent. Despite the seeming surface effort to surpass one another in appearing as populist candidates it is also apparent that there are differences in visions of what such appeals constitute. By examining each set of signifiers in detail can a researcher obtain differing Exhaustive Common Denominators for each candidate's advertising campaign or are they, like competing brands of beer, the same product with different packaging and brand labels?

It is at this point that decoding in search for a transformation process enters the analysis. Taken at face value the listing of concrete signifiers suggests no deeper, more abstract structure of myths. Yet taking such concrete signifiers and returning to a viewing of the political ads and close analysis of their transcripts raises possibilities. The surface theme, supported by the signifiers, suggests that each candidate has a different vision of the world—or at least of the state wherein the election takes place—and of how to cope with that world.

The Democrat as Self-Made Man

Consider first the Democrat. The rags-to-riches motif apparent in his advertising speaks to something more than merely the candidate himself. The candidate springs not only from a "humble background" and "humble beginnings" but from a world that is underdeveloped. There is no nostalgic recollection in the Democrat's ads about a bucolic paradise. This is not Rousseau's state of nature but instead one much closer to that of Hobbes. "I did grow up here in a very rural area," says the Democrat, "and grew up here in a house where we didn't have running water or electricity or indoor plumbing until I was a sophomore or junior in high school." Through a narrator another ad proclaims that the Democrat was "born in the poorest county" in the state, a county that "had not been introduced to luxuries." And, filmed while speaking before a group of women, the Democrat's wife describes her husband as a "plain old farm boy a lot more years of his life than he's been what most people consider a big business man." She reminds her audience that where the Democrat was born, "Dodson's Creek" was without "what a whole lot of people considered the necessities of life," indeed "one of the last places to get electricity."

At first blush what we have here is the "Log Cabin Campaign" common to America since the election of 1840 (Gerster & Cords, 1977). But a log cabin campaign and the mythology that accompanies it contains two elements not apparent in the Democrat's advertising. For one, in a log cabin campaign the candidate exploits his humble origins,

Table 23
Signifiers in the Democratic Gubernatorial Campaign

Signifiers and Signified*	
work hard (W)	development (P)
work his way up (W)	move forward (P)
work at friendship, communication (W)	move from shack to glass tower (P)
work given opportunity (W)	a leader, not a politician (P)
work for state, for people (W)	success (H)
workhands (W)	family man (H)
workclothes (W)	reach full potential (H)
stay with it, get things done (W)	a happy community (H)
motivate employees (W)	eliminate crime (H)
educate to find, keep jobs (W)	no more poor, unsafe roads, bridges (H)
second chances don't come easy (W)	better highways (H)
earned respect (W)	no high utility bills (H)
goin' to do things (W)	"someone to work, someone to care" (H)
went to work with thirsty determination (W)	"time to get government to work for us" (H)
hard earned dollars (W)	

pulled himself up by bootstraps (W)
state government is a big job (W)
work must be rewarded (W)
can't afford a day off (W)
hard work's the name of the game (W)
work with sun, sun-to-sun, all day long (W)
workin' two shifts (W)
make state a better place to live, work (W)
"I've always worked"
new day, ideas, direction, business, jobs,
  direction, plants, leadership, markets (P)
efficiency (P)
implement solutions (P)
change (P)
make a better place (P)
overcome humble beginnings (P)

---

*W = work signified, P = progress signified, H = happiness signified

TABLE 24
SIGNIFIERS IN THE REPUBLICAN GUBERNATORIAL CAMPAIGN

SIGNIFIERS AND SIGNIFIED*	
wheel-and-deal (D)	people the only special interest (F)
paroles and pardons (D)	with the people (F)
state income tax (D)	face-to-face (F)
poor education (D)	talking to working men and women (F)
conflicts of interest	walking the state (F)
throwin' money around (D)	returning to "X" (F)
spreading money (D)	down-to-earth (F)
patronage (D)	the touch of the people in his heart (F)
Lear jet (D)	a common man (F)
the incumbent governor (D)	pride in the state (P)
a clean-break (D)	embarrassed by current administration (P)
time for clean government (D)	integrity (P)
cold and snow (D)	the right man comes along (P)
cut all my ties (D)	make us proud again (P)
sold every share of stock (D)	

*D = dirt, cleansing of dirt signified; F = fold signified, P = pride signified

noting he is a common man who has been able to rise above them, yet would trade all of his success for the peace and tranquility of an earlier life. Second, log cabin campaigns do not identify all of society as people living in log cabins with the problems attendant thereto.

For the Democrat there is no hint that he ever wishes to return to his rustic background. What, in fact, he claims to be able to do is to lead all of his state's citizens out of precisely the kinds of conditions in which he was born and which he transcended. Close analysis of the Democrat's ads indicates a state which is in a condition of underdevelopment comparable to that which Dodson's Creek suffered from when the candidate was born. Consider the following litany of conditions and problems in the state: poor education in public schools (the state ranked 48th in the nation); a government remote from its people; government "solely in the hands of career politicians"; serious unemployment; absence of industry; rising crime rates; "roads and bridges poor and even unsafe for travel"; inefficient management of tax dollars; "inflation has blown utility bills sky high"; undeveloped natural resources "unparalleled in this nation"; eight hundred thousand people who are "old, or blind, or unable to support themselves"; three hundred thousand "in prisons, orphans, mentally or physically retarded"; "teenagers slaves to drugs or alcohol"; and eight hundred people, state employees, fired in one week."

The state, then, is itself a log cabin of humble origins, under- and undeveloped: "So what we need to do to reach our full potential is to bring all our folks together," urges the Democrat. And how is that to be accomplished? In much the same way that the Democrat "pulled himself up by his bootstraps." It takes work, something the Democrat has done "all his life." Here are samples of the work ethic in the Democrat's ads:

NARRATOR: [He] knows what it is to work hard, to start from the bottom, to work your way up.
NARRATOR: [He] will work closely with educators to improve education.
NARRATOR: You'd choose a leader who's successful, who works with people.
ENDORSING POL: [He] is not a man who inherited great wealth; he is a man who worked for it.
FRIEND: He and I was raised up together, worked together all our lives, until our service time. He used to work in the fields you see around here.
FATHER: I don't think there's any way in the world that you can put a man down and out if he's strictly honest and works hard!
THE DEMOCRAT: I've gotten up early all my life, before milkin' time, workin' hard. And I know what it's like to work for more. I think people respect persons who have worked hard. My dad used to say to me: "How have you boys done so well?" I said, "You try workin" two shifts.
WIFE: [He] believes a man who isn't willing to work given the opportunity isn't worth much, and I will tell you that he's one of the hardest working people I've ever known.
NARRATOR: [He] has worked hard all his life.
WIFE: He'll be one of the hardest working governors you ever had.
CAMPAIGN SONG: [He'll] make government work for us. Isn't it time for we the people to get government to work for us?
CAMPAIGN SLOGAN: Someone to work, someone to care.

Humble beginnings, then, must be surmounted, be they the humble origins of the candidate or of the state. Only through work can the state of nature where life is nasty, short, brutish, and cruel be transcended. Again, the Democrat: "We don't have to do things the way we've done 'em in the past just because they've been done that way." But, since "second chances don't come easy," according to the Democrat, if the state fails to work, and to allow him to work for it, it does so at its own peril. Filmed outside his boyhood home, the same house without electricity which he lived in for the first fifteen years of his life, the Democrat spoke of the things that must be done to make progress possible through inexpensive electricity. He ended with a telling phrase, one that said clearly how he actually felt about his underdeveloped humble origins: "And you know? We got to, or we'll be back here where I started."

Jacques Ellul (1958) once wrote that three major myths guide contemporary life—the myths of Work, Progress, and Happiness. Work is redeeming. Progress is inevitable through work. And, thereby, happiness is assured. These three myths provide what is signified in the Democrat's televised political advertising. (It is for this reason that the concepts listed in Table 23 for the Democrat are classified in the categories depicted.) Put simply, the state of nature reflected in the humble origins of an impoverished and undeveloped people is evil. What the Democrat's televised ads portray is a drama of redemption from evil. Thus the Democrat, playing the role of heroic exemplar as The Self-Made Man in American mythology (Cawelti, 1965), is saying that the citizens of his state—just as he once did—dwell in evil squalor. But he redeemed himself, as he continues to do, redeemed his origins and himself through the purifying punishment of work. So too can "We the people have a government to work for us." It is this myth of redemption of evil through Work, Progress, and Happiness as grasped by a Self-Made Man that is the Exhaustive Common Denominator.

The Republican as Mr. Clean

In describing advertising campaigns involving two competing brands Leymour makes clear that, unlike product campaigns, "the game becomes not one between pairs of oppository discrete values, or between absolutes, but one in which the comparative and the superlative dominate the scene" (1975, p. 69). Surface comparisons of the televised advertising campaigns of the Democratic and Republican candidates in the 1978 gubernatorial election in question certainly bear this out. As noted previously, an analysis of the apparent characteristics of competing ads suggests efforts on the part of each candidate to outdo the other in making populist appeals. But, as Leymore also demonstrates in her study of competing brands of washing powders, surface appearances of differences in comparative and superlative claims may mask what are actually two distinct visions of the way the world is and what must be done to cope with it. Such is the case in examining the televised political advertising of the Republican candidate in 1978.

The Republican campaign was carefully crafted and relied upon the expertise of a leading national campaign consulting firm headed by Douglas Bailey and John Deardourff. (The Democratic candidate employed a regional firm headed by consultant DeLoss Walker as well as the services of a local advertising agency.) The Bailey-Deardourff duo, as noted by Devlin (1982), typically prefers to rely upon a limited number of ads to express a clearcut series of themes. Such was the case of their advertising in the 1978 campaign.

Four years previously, the Republican had been defeated in his effort to win the gubernatorial election. In that campaign he had presented himself as politically experienced and a successful lawyer. His Democratic opponent in that election had opted for a more populist campaign. Noting this the Republican in 1978 took a strikingly different tack than in 1974. For one thing he emphasized that his campaign was designed to be close to, not remote from, voters. Speaking in his single documentary the Republican stresses this theme ("Honey" is the name of his wife): "Honey and I talk a lot about the fact that, in the last campaign, I don't think I gave the people a chance to get to know me, and I don't think I made a good enough effort to get to know them like I should 'a."

The campaign device, or gimmick, to symbolize such closeness to the people was one that had proved useful in earlier statewide campaigns in Illinois, Missouri, and Florida—namely, the walk across the state. Dressed in walking boots, work trousers, red flannel plaid shirt, and windbreaker, the Republican walked the state. That walk was prominently featured in his televised advertising (not to mention TV news of the campaign). Note the following exchange in one televised ad between the candidate and a national TV celebrity endorsing the Republican:

CELEBRITY: You say that you're gonna walk the length of the state. How you gonna do that? You gonna stop sometime; you can't go on all night.

CANDIDATE (chuckling): Well, it's a long way, about 1500 miles, but every day I, uh, I go back to my X.

CELEBRITY: You what?

CANDIDATE: My X. See, I've got a red crayon which I carry with me.

CELEBRITY: Uh, huh.

CANDIDATE: And each day when we stop I put an X down, just like this (makes an X), and then I'll go spend the night with a family somewhere.

The walk, the X, the commonplace attire, and the "getting to know you" approach—these are the apparent characteristics of the Republican campaign. Using Leymore's recommended spade what does one find by digging deeper beneath this surface? Turn first to the signifiers portrayed in Table 24 for the Republican. Note that they have been placed into three categories, labeled for analytic purposes as Dirt, Folk, and Pride. These three concepts provide the transformers that link the concrete signifiers to the hidden myth that is signified.

If the Democrat's televised ads envisioned a world (or state) of impoverished, undeveloped harshness, the Republican's ads portrayed a different world. Its defining characteristic was dirt. The world had become a dirty, filthy, grimy place. But what kind of dirt existed? First, the incumbent Democratic governor was being accused of using his pardoning power far too freely. A Republican commercial stressed this form of dirt. The Republican is at a construction site speaking with a worker in a hardhat:

WORKER: Is there nothing that anybody can do about the pardons?

THE REPUBLICAN: There's one thing that people can do, that's the petition drive. At every polling place across the state, somebody's standing there with a petition that says to the Governor, "Please don't do this, it would be wrong!"

And later another exchange:

WORKER: Well, how 'bout the paroles.

THE REPUBLICAN: If there's any one issue that I've heard about when I was walkin' across the state it was that.

Pardons and paroles are dirty. So is "wheeling and dealing" (be it by the incumbent governor or the opposing candidate): "We've had enough wheeling and dealing to last a lifetime; we don't need any more." There is also a griminess to patronage. The Republican sits casually in a family's living room located in a home where he will presumably spend the night before going back to his X:

WOMAN: You will have a patronage committee? Is that a must?

THE REPUBLICAN: Uh, no. I want people to come down and ask me to do things for their county. I don't want 'em to come in and say, "Now I want that interchange in my own backyard," or "I want a surplus car for my uncle," or "a prison for my brother-in-law." That's the kind of patronage I want thrown out of this state.

There is a strong suggestion that taxation policies might add to the state's grubbiness. For under the dirt of a proposed state income tax lies a filth spot that the Republican's ads suggest will not go away. Asked by a construction worker if he favors a state income tax, the Republican candidate said, "I'm not for it. Everybody always says, 'well, the income tax is a tax on rich people.' That's not true. It's a tax on working people." The construction worker responds, "Yeah, that's right!"

Income tax or not, extravagance at taxpayers' expense also signifies a dirty world. The state's governor at the time had at his disposal a Lear jet:

MAN: When you become governor, what are you gonna do with the Lear jet?

THE REPUBLICAN: I don't need it. Most people I've talked to would rather have a governor who's walked across the bad roads and bridges than one who's flown over 'em on his way to Jamaica with a soybean expert in his back seat (chuckles).

There is also dirt in the form of special interests. Note these statements made in people-on-the-street spot ads:

MAN (speaking of the Democrat): [He] may have more interests, special interests, that could interfere with his actin' on our behalf as governor.

WOMAN: "I don't think that a bank person should be representative of the public. I think there's a conflict of interest."

MAN: "It's going to be very difficult for him to make decisions that may conflict between the banker's interests and the best interests of the people."

But the root of the dirt, and ultimately of the form of evil that constitutes the Republican's advertised vision of the current state of the state, is money. In a series of people-on-the-street spots money equals dirt. For instance, a man says "Why would a person that ordinarily has enough money—uh, to be comfortable—be wantin' to spend millions of dollars for a job that pays so much less? It just doesn't add up." Or again, speaking of the Republican, a man says, "He's not a man who's, uh, spreadin' money" (i.e., dirt). Finally, there is this spot devoted to people on the street speaking of the Democrat:

MAN: I think he gets $55,000 as governor, and he can't live on that, and his brother's gonna give him like some $100,000 to live on.

SECOND MAN: The way I understood it was that he didn't think he could live on the governor's $50,000 (sic) a year.

THIRD MAN: He can't live on $50,000? He can't be helping the people.

WOMAN: I don't think he can truly represent the common people, the people who have to get by on a lot less than $50,000 a year.

The woman's utterance introduces a second transforming theme, one that tells the story of how a dirty world is going to be cleansed. Simply put, the Republican becomes the cleansing, thus redeeming, agent of the popular folk will. Three ideas comprise this story. First, the Republican must possess the qualities of a cleansing agent. Second, he must be the people's agent. Third, once the cleansing is accomplished, the world must be a whiter, brighter place.

The scrubbed and polished image of the Republican comes through in many of his televised ads. Typical is the one filmed as the Republican announced his candidacy on the front porch of his parents' home in a town in the eastern part of the state. Dressed in his walking clothes he remarks: "I've cut all my ties to my law firm. I've sold every share of stock that I had, which wasn't much to begin with. The only special interest that I've got left is the people." Does he regard himself as a cleansing agent? He does. Here are examples from spot ads spoken by the Republican or by those speaking on his behalf:

THE REPUBLICAN: You deserve better. But that will take a vote for change. A clean break, a decisive break, a complete break from the politics of the last four years.

MAN (who supported a losing Democrat in that party's primary but now will vote for the Republican): I figured we'd have good clean government with him, and in my opinion we'll have good clean government with [the Republican].

INDEPENDENT STATE LEGISLATOR: In my judgment, if we truly want a clean break from the past, then we need to consider [the Republican].

Even the circumstances surrounding the Republican's candidacy suggest cleanliness. The narrator of one of the spot ads suggests that cold is cleansing, that the candidate made his announcement of a "different kind of campaign" when "it was 8 degrees below zero." And from "those steps in the January snow, he and the people have been getting to know each other." Viewed in this perspective the walk across the state is a cleansing act. Indeed, one is reminded of a televised campaign for a commercial cleansing liquid, Mr. Clean, in viewing the Republican's commercials. Although professing that "I'm not a miracle worker," the Republican has a mysterious quality about him similar to the fictional Mr. Clean. For one thing, just as Mr. Clean popped up out of the blue in housewives' kitchens to alleviate their chores, so too does the Republican. He pops up "with a family somewhere" to spend the night, in "sixty-three different public schools," "down in zinc mines," "in houses," and "about every country store" where "there's more good advice than you get anywhere." The words of the Republican's campaign song are suggestive of the Mr. Clean miracle working formula:

> Wouldn't it be great?
> If the right man was there, with care and understanding,
> Walkin' arm-in-arm and hand-in-hand,
> Talkin' face-to-face, to get to know us better.
> Wouldn't it be great, if the right man was there?
> Wouldn't it be great, if [the Republican's] there?

So the Republican is clean and has cleansing properties. Is he also the people's agent? Clearly so. The televised ads are unfailing in their theme of populist redemption. A man-on-the-street claims the Republican is "real close to the people." Another notes the candidate is "not spending a lot of money but putting a lot of shoe leather to his campaign." A woman says, "I think that he is down-to-earth; he's just down-to-earth. I think he's just a down-to-earth person." In the same spot a man also says "He's a down-to-earth man." And, the ad closes with the woman again, "He's right down-to-earth in all steps (chuckles)." And, a woman-on-the-street remarks: "Well, what I say about him, he's a common man, and I think he has the feel of the people, the touch and the feel of the people in his heart. And he's not a rich man; and I think a rich man has the tendency to, uh, spend money more easily than, uh, people that are poor and have the touch of the people in the heart."

Not to be ignored in assessing the degree to which televised ads depicted the Republican as a cleansing, redeeming agent for the populace is, of course, the visual material. Frequently depicted as walking down a street of a small town, followed by townspeople, the ads are remininiscent of techniques employed in films about Jesus Christ passing through villages followed by worshippers and of techniques in Leni Riefenstahl's classic *Triumph of the Will* as she captures Adolf Hitler walking up a hillside thronged with admirers.

In commercial advertising housewives take pride when once-dirty cabinet tops sparkle, grimey floors begin to gleem, and ring-around-the-collar vanishes. And pride is the reward for selecting the Republican to clean up a dirty state government. In a fashion similar to the "He made us proud again" commercials devised by Bailey-Deardourff for the 1976 Republican presidential campaign, the Republican emphasizes pride as the payoff for cleanliness. Pictured strolling through a town square the

Republican says, "The people want a governor that they can be proud of, and if you'll give me some help, I'll give you a government you can be proud of (applause)." A narrator closes another commercial with "for a governor and a government you can be proud of." In education, teachers will be made proud since, "We've got to back up teachers who keep classrooms so people can learn something in them," notes Mr. Clean after popping into a classroom.

To paraphrase yet another commercial advertising campaign, dirt can't hide from statewide pride. And thus we have the hidden countermyth to the Democrat's redemption from impoverishment and humble beginnings via work. For the Republican the Exhaustive Common Denominator is redemption from dirty politics via a cleansing agent with the touch of the people in the heart. Thus the hidden campaign of 1978 pitted the Self-Made Man against Mr. Clean. In the end Mr. clean carried the day and won the election.

CONCLUSION

Berger (1981, p. 105) has correctly noted a key criticism that can be made of the type of semiotic/structuralist analysis undertaken here and by Leymore in her work on commercial advertising. It relates to the types of deep structures which are allegedly elicited from texts, films, or other materials. The criticism is that such structures are not really there. There are no hidden systems of sign relationships to be discovered, rather researchers invent such systems and impose them upon the materials. As Berger says, this is the "hocus-pocus" versus the "God's truth" controversy.

Berger sides with the semioticians and argues that the structures are there. Leymore takes the same position and argues that "all advertising is reducible to a system of EDCs, which could be split in turn into a system of symbols, designed to mobilize a system of values" (1975, p. 140). Whether hidden meanings actually exist in televised political advertising, however, may not be the crucial issue. One doubts that one could answer such a question with ease in any event. It is unlikely, for instance, that one could find professional political consultants agreeing that they indeed had such deep structures in mind when they produced their spots, documentaries, and minidocumentaries. This in itself would demonstrate little, for there is no reason to believe that consultants adapting to such taken-for-granted narratives as those of purification through work or through cleanliness would even be aware of such adjustments.

What is perhaps more to the point is whether or not viewers who are the target of televised political advertising consciously or unconsciously perceive the unifying but hidden myths that inform such efforts at political persuasion. It has not been the purpose here to respond to, let alone answer, that question. For researchers to do so requires a two-pronged attack. First, it will be necessary to take the content of televised political advertising far more seriously than heretofore has been the case. There is much to be learned about the image, issue, stylistic, and technical content of ads by examining manifest messages. But that is not the whole of advertising, neither from the standpoint of the "whole" of a single ad or the "wholes" that are the objects of structural analysis (Leymour, 1975, p. 19). Researchers must also turn their attention to latent content.

Second, conventional studies of persuasion effects on audiences will not help a great deal in detecting whether or not viewers perceive and respond to the hidden myths of televised political advertising. Probing for shifts in attitudes, values, and behavior may not be the critical line of investigation available. Rather what researchers might want to know is whether the overall impact of televised political advertising is to reinforce and enhance an entire sociopolitical structure that undergirds a political regime and/or system. This is a question certainly implicit in Edelman's seminal study of political symbolism (1964), but a question as yet not well addressed by students of political advertising. Is it possible, in short, that videopolitics contain not only hidden myths but hidden not overtly, readily measurable effects as well? Perhaps diversifying approaches to both the content and effects of televised political ads may suggest ways of addressing that question.

• 11 •

Uses and Perceptions of Political Television

An Application of Q-Technique

Michael W. Mansfield and Katherine Hale

The question of how people form perceptions of candidates through political advertising is one that has only recently been addressed from the perspective of motivation for viewing. The uses and gratifications paradigm, based on the concept that audience members are active, goal-directed consumers of media, has been concerned with various aspects of political communication, one of which is relationship of viewing motivations to political effects of the media (McLeod & Becker, 1981). While we do not view the process by which images are formed as an effect of viewing motivation, one might question whether persons who view political advertisements for certain reasons might differ from persons viewing for other reasons in the way they attend to the ads and in the information they then take into account when they construct images of the candidate.

Nimmo and Savage (1976) argue that voter images of candidates are neither stimulus-determined nor perceiver-determined but are a function of transactions between the "characteristics people project on the candidates and the qualities he tries to project to them" (p. 89). The images voters construct, then, are brought together as their own subjective knowledge comes into contact with the candidate's message. The uses and gratifications approach represents a perspective which concerns itself with the receiver's/perceiver's role in message selection. The particular dimension of that approach which studies the relationship of viewing motivation to message effect may address an important aspect of the transaction between candidate and voters. What motivates an individual to participate in that part of the exchange which exposes him to the candidate's message, and how does that motivation relate to his image construction?

From the uses and gratifications perspective, several studies have addressed the relationship of motives and effects in the broad context of political mass communication. McLeod, Becker, and Byrnes (1974) found that "information seekers" were less likely to pick up a newspaper's agenda than were "scanners," those reading with a low motivation level. Blumler and McQuail (1969) reported both magnification and diminishment of effects of exposure to British political party broadcasts as a result of strength of motivation. Several studies have focused on distinctions between gratifications sought and gratifications obtained, with attention to patterns of media use as they relate to viewing motivations and expectations of gratifications (Wenner, 1982; Palmgreen, Wenner, & Rayburn, 1980; Levy & Windahl, 1984).

In the specific area of political advertising, Atkin and Heald (1976) found that respondents who were seeking information recalled more information about the political advertising message than did respondents who were not actively seeking that information. Atkin, Bowen, Nayman, and Sheinkopf (1973) report that persons who attended to political ads to gain information tended to learn more about each candidate than did persons who watched because they could not avoid watching.

A recent study by Garramone (1983) uses an experimental design to address motivations and effects in the context of a televised political commercial. Specifically, Garramone attempted to measure "how media channel and audience motivation for attending to a political advertisement govern the process and effects of the ad." Subjects were told to attend to the advertisement either 1) to "learn where the candidates stand on issues" or 2) to "form an impression of the candidate's personality." Subjects told to watch for issue information learned more issue information and were more confident of that information than were subjects in the "personality" group. Subjects told to watch for "image" reasons (to form a personality impression) paid more attention to the video portion of the ad and were more confident of that information. Garramone uses "image" in the narrow sense here to refer to the nonissue information an advertisement attempts to portray about the candidate, perhaps roughly parallel to what Nimmo and Savage call "stylistic role." The evidence from the study seems to be that if "image- versus issue-motivated viewing of political ads" takes place, differences in attention and processing of information occur. However, as Garromone points out, those motivations were overtly manipulated in her study, and the natural occurrence of such dichotomized motivations has not been determined.

Rather than the researcher determining the subject's motivation for watching political commercials, this study is designed to replace the investigator's meaning, as imposed in the Garramone study, with the subject's meaning or motivation for viewing television, including political television such as political commercials, political conventions, news accounts of political figures and events. Our interest in this approach is predicated on the belief that what motivates an audience to attend to a political advertisement and the subsequent assigning of meaning to that advertisement is behavior that Brown (1980, p. 4) labels as subjective and operant. It is subjective "since each person's viewpoint, on political or on other matters, is simply that—his viewpoint." And, "it is operant because it exists naturally within a particular setting."

Once the individuals participating in this study had operated with a sample of statements in order to provide a model of their viewpoint vis-à-vis their motivations, they were exposed to a series of political advertisments and asked to model their viewpoint concerning what they saw. These two operantly subjective models could then be compared in order to learn more about how motivations influence one's perception of that to which they are exposed in political ads.

METHOD

To study political advertising as operant subjectivity is to examine the subjective viewpoint of varied audience members on varied matters under varying circumstances—but always from the point of view of each audience member rather than the point of view imposed upon that audience member by an outside observer. The process of analysis is not subjective; in fact there must be a means of objectively examining people's subjective opinions without intruding upon the personal nature of each opinion. Stephenson (1953) has provided a methodology and technique for accomplishing this task, one which Brown (1980) extends to the intensive study of political subjectivity. Q-methodology and Q-technique permit a person to express through a series of modeling operations, or behaviors, the very interaction of images in his or her own mind which constitutes that individual's personal viewpoint. Through the convergence of viewpoints audiences are created; when individuals converge on single viewpoints—or express consensus on certain matters—there is a general, universal audience.

Q-methodology is increasingly applied to the study of political communication. Bormann and his colleagues have applied Q-method to the analysis of a wide range of communication including the formulation and effectiveness of political speeches, the dramatic persona of political leaders, the salient rhetorical features in political cartoons, and a fantasy theme analysis of the 1980 U.S. presidential campaign (Bormann, Kroll, Watters, & MacFarland, 1984; Cragan & Shields, 1981). Nimmo and Savage (1976) employed Q-techniques to study candidate images in the 1972 U.S. presidential campaign and Nimmo, Mansfield & Curry (1978) examined effects of the 1976 presidential debates with Q-techniques.

Using Q-methodology a small, purposive sample of people, called a P-sample, rank orders a series of statements (or other items) under specific conditions. The rank ordering procedure is a sorting process (the Q-sort) whereby a respondent arranges the statements (the Q-sample) from those he/she most agrees with or finds most descriptive to those least agreeable, descriptive, etc. The resulting arrangement of items is a forced-sort variety, i.e., respondents place a specified number of statements in each of a specified number of categories along a continuum. In the sorting process the respondent is weighing each item with each other item. A person's overall rank-ordering, or sort, thus constitutes the product of his subjective musings. Comparing and contrasting respondents' sorts permits the grouping together of people who have subjectively appraised images in similar ways. Each grouping thus constitutes a separate audience created through operant subjectivity. For a detailed explanation of Q-methodology and Q-technique, see Brown (1980).

As noted above, in recent years the uses and gratifications approach to the study of media has become one of the dominant theoretical frameworks for inquiry into audience orientations. Assuming that the audience is goal-directed in its media use, researchers in that paradigm typically measure audience motivations by asking subjects to respond to something like the following: "Here are reasons other people have given for watching television. As I read each reason, please tell me how much that reason applies to you. If the reason very definitely applies, give it a 5; if it does not apply at all, give it a 1; if it applies somewhere in between give it a 2, 3, or 4, depending on how much it applies." The list of "gratification sought" items was then read to the respondent in random order. Some variation can be found in the number of "reasons for viewing" to which subjects were asked to respond. Some of the variance was the result of the researchers' decision concerning the number of gratification categories for which statements were generated.

The first phase of this study seeks to have subjects express their viewpoints regarding their own motivations for television viewing. In designing the structure for the Q-sample, we have used gratifications categories that seem to recur in the literature and which researchers seem to agree to some extent constitute the base from which statements of reason for media use are to be generated. These categories become levels of Main Effect A, "Gratifications."

In addition, use of political media fare, as well as general media use is a major focus of uses and gratifications research. For this reason, and because "political" programs (by our definition this includes such fare as news, documentaries of a political nature, coverage of political conventions, political advertising) constitute a significant amount of television programming, we included "viewing focus" as Main Effect B. These categories and foci can be represented formally as "effects" in a balanced block factorial design, for this study, as in Table 25.

Main Effect A is represented at three levels while Main Effect B is

TABLE 25
DESIGN OF MOTIVATION FOR TELEVISION VIEWING Q-SAMPLE

Effects	Levels		No.*	D.F.
A Gratifications	(a) surveillance/ vote guidance	(b) reinforcement	5	4
	(c) entertainment	(d) anticipated communication		
	(e) parasocial interaction			
B Viewing focus	(f) general	(g) political	2	1

*(Number of combinations: 5 × 2 = 10)

represented at two levels. This design, then, represents a gratifications approach in a formal manner.

There are 10 combinations of these levels of Table 25, one effect at a time, namely:

aa	bb	cc	dd	ee
fg	fg	fg	fg	fg

The basis now exists for composing a structured sample to fit the design, for any number of replications. We compiled a set of statements most representative of the various operationalizations of the use categories in uses and gratifications literature. While not exhaustive the list is definitive and constitutes the Q-sample for this study. The fifty statements replicate the 10 factorial combinations 5 times.

Given a structured sample of this kind, it is possible to conduct an experiment upon viewers of television in general and political television in particular. They can be induced to "think" about why they watch television under various conditions of experiment or instruction and to represent the outcome by a Q-sort in the Q-technique fashion. Thus we asked a group of individuals to array the fifty statements from those they think most representative of their reasons for viewing television to those least representative.

The P-sample of n = 42 was composed of undergraduate students from the University of Oklahoma who were enrolled in introductory communication classes in the summer of 1984. Each of the 42 subjects sorted the 50 items in the Q-sample along an 11 point continuum. In this process each subject selected the three statements "most characteristic" of why he/she watches television and placed them in a pile by themselves; then the three items considered "least characteristic" were placed in a separate pile; then the next three items perceived "most characteristic" were placed in a separate pile, the next three items "least characteristic" for another pile, etc. The result is a format for which a score is given to each of the fifty items of the Q-sample, on the basis of a forced quasi-normal frequency distribution. For our study we used the following distribution:

Value	+5	+4	+3	+2	+1	0	−1	−2	−3	−4	−5
Frequency	3	3	4	5	6	8	6	5	4	3	3

To examine the relationship between the respondents' expressed viewing motivations and the perceptions formed from actual exposure to political advertisements, we first constructed an eight minute videotape containing the majority of ads used for Pete Wilson in his successful 1982 California campaign for the United States Senate. Before selecting the ads to be edited together for the videotape, we content analyzed all the available ads. Because studies of political advertising have noted information about the candidate's image and his stand on issues as two major areas of content in political ads (Joslyn, 1980; Shyles, 1984; Hofstetter & Zukin, 1979), these were our major categories for content analysis of the Wilson ads.

Two separate panels of judges were asked to view each of the thirty second ads and classify them as either image- or issue-oriented, placing any ads that contained both image and issue in a third or "mixed" category. The panel used "image," as it is frequently employed in political communication research, to refer to the character attributes of candidates. Most research in political advertising pertinent to the "image" of candidates has focused on reference to the candidates' leadership, honesty, responsiveness, strength, etc. (Joslyn, 1980; Shyles, 1984). It should be noted that the use of the term "image" as character attributes of candidates is in contrast to the broader concept of an image as it refers to the individual's perception of the candidate, based on his subjective knowledge of the candidate—including his character attributes and his stand on issues—and the messages transmitted by the candidate (Nimmo, 1974; Nimmo & Savage, 1976). The second category utilized the concept of "issue" as referred to in most studies of political advertising as specific policy (Kaid & Sanders, 1978). This includes topics of citizen concern such as taxes, pollution, crime, etc. Following the content analysis, we selected approximately the same number of issue and image ads to include in the videotape and also included some from the mixed category.

As part of the editing process, we deleted from each ad anything which would identify Wilson's political party or the state of California on the assumption that some knowledge of party identification, geographic region, etc. could be expected to result in predispositions affecting our respondents' interpretation of the political ads to which we exposed them.

In generating a population of statements from which to select the Q-sample, we used two primary sources of descriptive characterizations of Pete Wilson's issue positions and character attributes. First were newspaper accounts of the California Senatorial campaign between Jerry Brown and Pete Wilson and of Wilson's earlier campaign for the Republican nomination. The newspapers examined included: *Los Angeles Times, San Diego Tribune, New York Times, Wall Street Journal, Washington Post,* and *Christian Science Monitor.* The second source was a set of written responses to Pete Wilson rendered by a panel of judges who viewed the tape of political ads. After viewing the ads the panel members wrote statements that were characteristic of candidate Wilson as they perceived him. It was from these sources that the population of statements was created.

In selecting a representative sample of statements from this population, we employed a balanced block factorial design to encourage even distribution of types or categories of statements. Because television ads contain information about the candidate's image and his stand on issues, a conclusion supported by audiences' self reports of the helpfulness of political ads in becoming better acquainted with candidates and their issue positions (Atkin et al., 1973), issue and image comprise Main Effect A. Another major distinction that emerged as we examined the population of statements was what we have termed "involvement"—whether the focus of statement is the candidate himself (whether character attribute or issue stand) or is directed outward, focusing on the candidate as he deals with society. Finally, statements about the candidate could be positive or negative, giving us our third Main Effect. The resulting balanced block factorial design appears in Table 26. Main Effects A, B, and C are all three represented at two levels. The sorting format thus appeared as follows:

Value	+5	+4	+3	+2	+1	0	−1	−2	−3	−4	−5
Frequency	3	4	5	6	6	8	6	6	5	4	3

Fifty-six items representing seven replications of the eight factorial combinations constituted the Q-sample for this phase of our analysis.

Table 26
Design of Candidate Evaluation Q-Sample

Effects		Levels		No.*	D.F.
A	Orientation	(a) Image	(b) Issue	2	1
B	Involvement	(c) Self	(d) Society	2	1
C	Valence	(f) Positive	(g) Negative	2	1

*(Number of combinations: $2 \times 2 \times 2 = 8$)

After viewing the eight minute videotape our original forty-two respondents who completed the first sort were now asked to rank order the fifty-six items of the second sort from "most characteristic" to "least characteristic" of Pete Wilson as they perceived him.

Results

Each person's sort constitutes the product of the subjective interaction that occurred as the individual considered each statement and compared each item with all other ones in the rank-ordering. In Q-methodology the rank-orderings for each person are correlated with all other subjects' sorts, with the resulting correlation matrix subjected to factor analysis to reveal what sets of people have rank-ordered statements in approximately the same fashion. This we did with the forty-two sorts fashioned by subjects prior to viewing the videotape and separately with the forty-two sorts obtained from respondents after they had viewed the videotape of Pete Wilson.

Television Viewing Motivations

We consider first, in uses and gratifications terms, viewing motivations of television. The first question is how many distinct ways did the forty-two subjects comprising our P-sample rank-order the fifty statements on viewing motivations contained in the Q-sample. Potentially there could have been forty-two distinctively different patterns, one for each subject responding to and transacting subjectively with the fifty reasons for why people watch television. Instead there were two. Twenty-five subjects displayed one pattern of beliefs, while seventeen held another.

To understand the different beliefs that distinquish the two sets of subjects it is important to examine the typical rank-orderings of each factor array. In this case, the respondents express two different explanations for their motivation for viewing television. The statements the twenty-five subjects comprising Factor 1 identified as most characteristic of why they watch television are:

23. Because it passes the time away, particularly when I'm bored. (+5)
45. Because I find certain TV programs, characters, and subjects inspirational. (+5)

21. Because it relaxes me. (+5)
44. TV serves as "company" in some situations. (+4)
7. To keep up with the main issues of the day. (+4)
10. To get a brief account of a variety of things. (+4)

At the other extreme are the statements found least characteristic of these subjects reasons for attending to television:

39. To help me persuade others to vote for my candidate. (−5)
27. To enjoy the excitement of an election race. (−5)
20. I like to see the politicians I support star on television. (−5)
47. To see and listen to attractive and pleasant political candidates. (−4)
49. The desire to experience political situations. (−4)
18. To remind me of my party's strong points. (−4)

By employing the categorical tags assigned to these statements by uses and gratifications researchers, we can conclude that these subjects watch television mainly for general entertainment and general parasocial interaction. They do seek some information about the main issues of the day and try briefly to keep abreast of a variety of things. They do not watch television for political reinforcement or political parasocial interaction. Neither do they watch TV coverage of political subject matter because it is entertaining or for anticipated communication.

The second pattern of viewing motivations is quite different from the first. The subjects loading on Factor 2 watch television in order to gain information. All six of the most characteristic statements are surveillance statements. The first four are general surveillance statements while the next two are political surveillance. The statements selected as most characteristic of their motivation for watching television are:

8. To keep up with what is going on in the country. (+5)
7. To keep up with the main issues of the day. (+5)
6. To find out the positions of important people concerning different national problems. (+5)
10. To get a brief account of a variety of things. (+4)
1. To keep up with what is going on in politics. (+4)
18. To see how the candidates stand on issues. (+4)

It is interesting to note that two of the surveillance statements specifically refer to issues. These subjects look to TV to keep up with the main issues of the day and to determine candidates' stands on issues. Keeping up with the positions of important people concerning national problems is possibly another statement that describes the issue interest of these respondents, since national problems are most often national issues. The statements least characteristic of why those loading on Factor 2 view television are:

25. Because it's a habit, just something to do. (−5)
31. To have something to do when friends come over. (−5)
12. Because I agree with what the commentators are saying. (−5)
47. To see and listen to attractive and pleasant political candidates. (−4)
22. Because it is exciting. (−4)
34. To help me understand and deal with relationships with my family and friends. (−4)

Subjects on this factor view TV fairly singlemindedly. They don't watch just to have something to do, or for general excitement, or to aid them in their general interaction with friends. Instead, they want information.

Differences in the two motivation factors become clearer upon examination of some of the discriminating statements. Listed below are statements and factor scores for those items on which the Z-scores for Factors 1 and 2 differ by + 1.0. These statements, while not necessarily most or least characteristic of either factor, are important indicators because they show contrast between the two factors.

23.	Because it passes the time away, particularly when I'm bored.	+5	−3
31.	To have something to do when friends come over.	+3	−5
25.	Because it's habit, just something to do.	+2	−5
22.	Because it is exciting.	+3	−4
24.	Because it provides a temporary escape from reality.	+3	−2
44.	TV serves as "company" in some situations.	+4	−1
3.	To see how the candidates stand on issues.	0	+4
1.	To keep up with what is going on in politics.	0	+4
6.	To find out the positions of important people concerning different national problems.	+1	+5
27.	To enjoy the excitement of an election race.	−5	0
4.	To judge what political leaders are like.	−1	+3
40.	To provide me with the background necessary to express my views to government officials.	−3	+1

38.	To use what I learn in political discussions.	−2	+1
36.	To support my own political viewpoints to other people.	−2	+1
46.	To compare my own ideas to what the politicians on TV say.	0	+3
49.	The desire to experience political situations.	−4	0

These statements illustrate that primary differences between the two Factors are use of television for entertainment and for general communication and social interaction, and in use of television for political motivations. Respondents on Factor 1, when compared to Factor 2, use television for entertainment and for general communication and social interaction, but not for political motivations. Respondents on Factor 2 use television more to gain information—particularly political information—and reject the entertainment and general communication and social interaction motivations. And while use of that information is not highly important to respondents on Factor 2 in political communication, it is more important to them than to respondents on Factor 1.

To complete our understanding of the two perceptions presented above it is helpful to examine those statements with which both factors agree or disagree.

Listed below are those consensus statements and factor scores for which one or both of the factors ranked in the "most" or "least" categories.

7.	To keep up with the main issues of the day.	+4	+5
10.	To get a brief account of a variety of things.	+4	+4
21.	Because it relaxes me.	+5	+3
47.	To see and listen to attractive and pleasant political candidates.	−4	−4
39.	To help me persuade others to vote for my candidate.	−5	−3
12.	Because I agree with what the commentators are saying.	−2	−5
20.	I like to see the politicians I support star on television.	−5	−2

In spite of the major differences between the two factors, there are some things they agree on. Both factors agree that they view to some extent to keep up with general issues and happenings of the day and for relaxation. Both Factors reject use of television for several reinforcement statements. A list of all fifty statements with factor scores can be found in Appendix 1.

As noted in Table 25 it was possible for our respondents to identify up to five different categorical reasons for why they watch television. Factor 1 combined categories into an "entertainment/social/nonpolitical" grouping, while surveillance/vote guidance was the primary motivation for Factor 2. Given these motivations or uses of television we were interested in what perceptions the subjects formed from exposure to a series of political advertisements and what, if any, was the relationship between their expressed motivations and perceptions formed.

CANDIDATE PERCEPTIONS

The results of the factor analysis of the forty-two sorts obtained after the subjects had viewed the videotape of Pete Wilson's political advertisements were two distinctive images of the candidate. The first profile is that of a candidate who is a concerned, caring man with personal appeal. He knows what he stands for, which is stronger criminal laws and penalties and a tough position on nuclear arms. Of the seven statements most characteristic of the candidate, as perceived by the twenty-eight subjects comprising this factor, four are issue statements showing an involvement with society; three are image. The "most" statements in rank order are:

45. He is concerned for the common/working man. (+5)
5. He knows what he stands for and communicates that message well. (+5)
43. He is for stronger criminal laws and penalties. (+5)
16. He really cares about people. (+4)
44. He wishes to create jobs for deserving youth. (+4)
6. He exhibits warmth and personal appeal on television. (+4)
46. He is tough on nuclear arms; he wants to stop the arms race. (+4)

The respondents reject the claim that he does not understand the key isues in America today and that his supposed concern is a sham leading him to show little concern for victims except to get votes. They disagree with the image statements that portray the candidate as a physically awkward, uncomfortable campaigner, ill at ease with people, and boosting his image by using those less fortunate. Statements least characteristic of the candidate are as follows:

37. His supposed concern is a sham. (−5)
54. He shows little concern for victims except to get votes. (−5)
8. His physical awkwardness hinders his candidacy. (−5)
9. He seems very uncomfortable as a campaigner. (−4)
12. He uses those less fortunate as a cheap image booster. (−4)
23. He doesn't seem to be at ease with people. (−4)
41. He doesn't understand the key issues in America today. (−4)

In contrast to the issue and image concerns expressed in the array of statements for Factor 1, the fourteen subjects loading on Factor 2 have chosen image statements for six of seven of the most characteristic statements. Also, five of the seven most characteristic items are negative in valence. The profile of the candidate for this factor is that of a know-it-all man-for-all-seasons who is trying to get elected by playing the role of Mr. Nice Guy, when all the time he is really manipulating issues for personal gain, and taking credit for things it took many people to accomplish. In spite of this they admit he is a man with the positive assets of personal magnetism and physical attractiveness who projects a warmth and personal appeal on television. The items most characteristic of the candidate as perceived by the subjects loading on this factor are:

11. He presents himself as a man with all the right answers. (+5)
28. He tries to project an image of being all things to all men. (+5)
13. He is trying to be elected by playing Mr. Nice Guy. (+5)
39. He manipulates issues for personal political gain. (+4)
1. His personal magnetism and physical attractiveness are positive assets. (+4)
6. He exhibits warmth and personal appeal on television. (+4)
14. He takes credit for accomplishments that many people contributed to. (+4)

This factor's preoccupation with statements of image was confirmed when they chose five of seven image items as least characteristic of the candidate. In other words, they focused on image even when they were selecting statements least like the candidate as they perceived him through his television ads. They reject the characterization of Wilson as an uncomfortable campaigner, ill at ease with people, whose awkwardness hinders his candidacy. Statements least characteristic of the candidate are:

9. He seems very uncomfortable as a campaigner. (−5)
23. He doesn't seem to be at ease with people. (−5)

8. His physical awkwardness hinders his candidacy. (−5)
22. He doesn't have the communication skills necessary to get people to work together for common goals. (−4)
29. He appeals to reason rather than people's emotions and prejudices. (−4)
47. He would save as many tax dollars as possible without cutting social problems. (−4)
19. He is less of a bureaucrat than most politicians. (−4)

Items on which the two factors differ help illustrate the unique point of view expressed by these two perceptions of the candidate. (Criteria for inclusion are the same as for discriminating statements in the motivation sort.) Statements include:

47.	He would save as many tax dollars as possible without cutting social problems.	+2	−4
20.	He is "everyman's" candidate; "he'll work for the good of all people."	+3	−3
5.	He knows what he stands for and communicates that message well.	+5	−1
16.	He really cares about people.	+4	−1
32.	He believes in a simple back-to-basics approach to government.	+2	−3
29.	He appeals to reason rather than people's emotions and prejudices.	0	−4
39.	He manipulates issues for personal gain.	−3	+4
12.	He uses those less fortunate as a cheap image booster.	−4	+3
14.	He takes credit for accomplishments that many people contributed to.	−2	+4
13.	He is trying to be elected by playing Mr. Nice Guy.	0	+5
26.	He is too much show and too little substance.	−3	+2
54.	He shows little concern for victims except to get votes.	−5	0

The discriminating statements highlight the positive-negative polarization that emerged when our subjects viewed the ads of the candidate and gave us their impression of what they saw.

Although there are those differences discussed above, there are some statements which both factors agree with or agree to disagree with. (Criteria for inclusion are the same as for consensus statements in the motivation sort.) These statements are:

43.	He is for stronger criminal laws and penalties.	+5	+3
6.	He exhibits warmth and personal appeal on television.	+4	+4
1.	His personal magnetism and physical attractiveness are positive assets.	+3	+4
45.	He is concerned for the common/working man.	+5	+2
44.	He is tough on nuclear arms; he wants to stop the arms race.	+4	+3
9.	He seems very uncomfortable as a campaigner.	−4	−5
8.	His physical awkwardness hinders his candidacy.	−4	−5
23.	He doesn't seem to be at ease with people.	−4	−5
22.	He doesn't have the communication skills necessary to get people to work together for common goals.	−3	−4

These consensus items demonstrate that all subjects universally believe candidate Wilson takes a stand on the issues and makes a good appearance on television. However, it should be noted that although they share these views, they do so for different reasons. Factor 1 admires the candidate's ability to express warmth, appeal, and take a stand on the issues while Factor 2 believes he exhibits these qualities in order to manipulate the public, a practice they do not admire. The statements comprising the Q-sort with the respective factor scores for the Wilson sort are presented in Appendix 2.

In an effort to assess whether or not the differing motivations of our subjects could be associated with the different perceptions of the candidate we crosstabulated respondents loading on the television viewing factors with these same respondents loading on the Wilson factors. The results are shown in Table 27.

Little difference was found for the two viewing motivation factors in the way they responded to the Wilson ads. Of subjects who watched television from the entertainment/social/general orientation, 68 percent loaded on Factor 1 for the Wilson sort, and 32 percent on Factor 2. For subjects who watched television primarily from a surveillance perspective, 71 percent loaded on Factor 1 of the Wilson sort, 29 percent on Factor 2.

Discussion

Some years ago communications scholars suggested a typology of media-person interactions that was intended to distinguish certain common

Table 27

Cross-Tabulation of Motivation for Viewing Factors with Candidate Evaluation Factors

	WILSON	
Television Viewing	Factor 1 (Positive Issue/Image Mix)	Factor 2 (Negative Image)
Factor 1 (Entertainment/Social/Nonpolitical)	68%	32%
Factor 2 (Surveillance)	71%	29%

constellations of disposition and response. The intention was to provide a framework "for the systematic ordering of gratification data and to provide a basis for classifying viewer concerns according to their meaning rather than their frequency of occurrence or salience to audience members" (McQuail, Blumler, & Brown, 1972 p. 161). The result has been several taxonomic schemas predicated on the central assumption of an active audience and on the postulation that the decision to enter into communication is motivated by goals and uses that are self-defined (Lin, 1977). This concept of an active audience has been criticized.

A major and often cited criticism is Elliot's contention that the uses and gratifications approach is overly "mentalistic" since it makes assumptions about individual mental processes that cannot be observed (Elliot, 1974). It is precisely the observation of these mental processes that led Stephenson to introduce Q—its methodology, method, and Q-sort technique—as an approach that has come to rest on the self as central to all else, since it is the total individual who entertains the subjective viewpoint, it must be the total individual that is the center of investigation (Stephenson, 1953). It is through intensive analysis of the subjective appraisals of a small sample of persons that one can properly address the questions posed concerning audience activity in the communication process.

In this study we have asked whether, given a certain body of assumptions about what politics is like as an activity, the formulations of uses and gratifications research assist us in analyzing communication peculiar to politics, that is, political communication. Two typologies of audience activity were constructed, not by the researchers, but by the subject who, when given an opportunity to model their impressions of their own TV viewing motivations, constructed two broad approaches to viewing behavior.

The first typology supports a conclusion that the gratifications people seek from television are not independent motives for some people. Although Palmgreen, Wenner, and Rayburn (1980) conclude that the seeking of entertainment and the seeking of parasocial interaction are independent motives for watching TV news we found them not to be independent motives for watching television in general. In fact the respondents comprising Factor 1 of our motivating Q-sort were motivated by entertainment, parasocial interaction, and general surveillance supporting earlier beliefs that in many people there coexists several important kinds of expectation and outlook (McQuail, Blumler, & Brown, 1972). Utilization of Q-methodology to test the independence of motives such as those discussed above in political television viewing would be of interest given the divergent findings of our study and those of Palmgreen et al.

The second typology is that of a person who more singlemindedly seeks information (surveillance) from television. Although both general and political information are sought, the main thrust is towards having information about events in the wider context of public affairs than towards stimuli for reflecting upon a set of more immediate experienced personal and non-political pleasure/social motivations.

The implication of these findings is that when subjects are allowed, by Q-technique, to synthesize their own value preferences regarding television viewing, the impressions that result reflect a total picture rather than an artificial compartmentalization of motivations. Q-methodology contributes to the study of viewing motivations because it "preserves the functional relationship among the parts which have status only within the context of the whole" (Brown, 1980, p. 173). Thus, it is possible to determine if there is one independent motivation for viewing television, as in the case of Factor 2, or multiple interdependent motives as illustrated in Factor 1.

In addition, the fact that respondents loading on Factor 1 were concerned only with general statements and not political ones, while subjects making up Factor 2 link the seeking of information for both general and political (surveillance/vote guidance) purposes supports the linking of surveillance and vote guidance by earlier uses and gratifications researchers (Katz, Blumler, & Gurevitch, 1973).

When we asked these same respondents who had told us why they watched television to attend to a series of political ads for a political candidate we were impressed by two results. First, one group of subjects perceived the candidate in a mix of both issue and image characteristics. A second group of individuals perceived the candidate in image terms emphasizing negative image aspects. In other words, there was no clear cut dichotomy between issue and image aspects as perceived by the respondents and projected by the candidate.

Secondly, results of previous studies (Garramone, 1983) would lead us to expect that the subjects viewing from different "motivational sets" would be likely to evaluate the candidate differently, and in correspondence with the motivational sets. Specifically, one would expect image-motivated subjects to respond to the candidate in the political ads video in terms of his image characteristics, and the issue motivated subjects to respond more to the candidate in terms of his "issue" stances.

Analysis of the surveillance Factor 2 depicts a profile of an information seeker who is interested in the main issues of the day (7), candidate stands on issues (3), national problems (6), and what's going on in politics (1) and the country (8). In other words these subjects are seeking issue information and might be expected to perceive the candidate from an issue perspective. The entertainment/social/general Factor 1 profile which blatantly rejects political reasons for watching TV in favor of passing the time away (23), relaxing (21), for company (44), and because it is inspirational (45) might be expected to be less issue- and more image-oriented in their perception of political candidate ads.

The majority of respondents from both factors formed a perception of the candidate based on a mix of both the issue and image aspects projected by the candidate in his ads. The remaining subjects from both sets of motivations constructed a negative perception of the candidate, primarily characterized by image statements. Hence, there is no evidence that the differing motivations of our respondents led to differing perceptions. There is, however, evidence that our subjects were involved in a perceptual activity of interpreting or creating meaning for what they saw in the candidate's ads. The result was no neat image versus issue dichotomy but rather an active process in which image and issue were mixed for one set of perceivers and the image perception of the other group of subjects specifically defined in negative terms. While we are not persuaded by this study that the uses and gratifications paradigm is particularly useful to the study of political advertising, we are convinced that Q-methodology offers insights into both political advertising and into uses and gratifications research. The potential it offers for tapping total viewpoints on viewing motivations and perceptions of candidates addresses the need to employ methods of operant subjectivity and intensive analysis and to discover shared and unique points of view from the standpoint of audiences rather than the observers. This speaks directly not only to the concerns of politics but to those concerned with understanding the communication process.

Appendix 1. Item Description and Factor Scores for Factors 1 and 2 of the Motivation Q-Sort

Item Description	Factor 1	Factor 2
1. To keep up with what is going on in politics.	0	+4
2. To help me make up my mind how to vote in an election.	−1	+1

3. To see how the candidates stand on issues.	0	+4
4. To judge what political leaders are like.	−1	+3
5. To keep up with the way government is doing its job.	+1	+3
6. To find out the position of important people concerning different national problems.	+1	+5
7. To keep up with the main issues of the day.	+4	+5
8. To keep up with what is going on in the country.	+3	+5
9. I want information I can trust.	+1	0
10. To get a brief account of a variety of things.	+4	+4
11. To get facts that support my views.	0	+2
12. Because I agree with what the commentators are saying.	−2	−5
13. Because it exemplifies values and behaviors that I either do believe or would like to.	0	−2
14. To feel that others think as I do.	−1	−3
15. To confirm which issues I think are important.	+1	+2
16. To remind me of my candidate's strong points.	−2	0
17. To see editorials and commentary about the elections which agree with my positions.	−1	0
18. To remind me of my party's strong points.	−4	−1
19. To get information to support the superiority of my candidate over others.	−2	−1
20. I like to see the politicians I support star on television.	−5	−2
21. Because it relaxes me.	+5	+3
22. Because it is exciting.	+3	−4
23. Because it passes the time away, particularly when I'm bored.	+5	−3
24. Because it provides a temporary escape from reality.	+3	−2
25. Because it's a habit, just something to do.	+2	−5
26. To judge which candidates are likely to win an election.	0	+2
27. To enjoy the excitement of an election race.	−5	0
28. To enjoy the drama of politics, such as elections, conventions, etc.	−3	0
29. Because it's often entertaining to see how politicians present themselves to the public.	0	+1
30. To enjoy the activities of powerful political figures.	−3	−1
31. To have something to do when friends come over.	+3	−5

32. To be with other members of the family or friends who are watching.	+2	−1
33. To give me something to talk about with other people.	+2	0
34. To help me understand and deal with relationships with my family and friends.	0	−4
35. To get an idea of how others act in social situations.	+1	−2
36. To support my own political viewpoints to other people.	−2	+1
37. So I can pass political information on to other people.	−3	0
38. To use what I learn in political discussions.	−1	+2
39. To help me persuade others to vote for my candidate.	−5	−3
40. To provide me with the background necessary to express my views to government officials.	−3	+1
41. Because sometimes it's like sharing experiences with others.	+2	−3
42. I want to see TV anchors and reporters who make the news somewhat human.	+1	−2
43. Because TV makes news seem closer and more real than other sources.	+2	+1
44. TV serves as "company" in some situations.	+4	−1
45. Because I find certain TV programs, characters, and subjects inspirational.	+5	+1
46. To compare my own ideas to what the politicians on TV say.	0	+3
47. To see and listen to attractive and pleasant political candidates.	−4	−4
48. To participate in a political world of significance, intensity, and larger-than-life-size people.	−2	−1
49. The desire to experience political situations.	−4	0
50. It's a way I can experience political situations that I can't attend in person.	−1	+2

Appendix 2. Item Description and Factor Scores for Factors 1 and 2 of the Candidate Evaluation

Item Description	Factor 1	Factor 2
1. His personal magnetism and physical attractiveness are positive assets.	+3	+4

2. He is the kind of man who will keep his promise.	+2	−3
3. His perseverance, firmness clearly projects a "take charge" image.	+3	−1
4. He is very "smooth" and has the "style" necessary for a senator.	+1	+3
5. He knows what he stands for and communicates that message well.	+5	−1
6. He exhibits warmth and personal appeal on television.	+4	+4
7. He is an honest sincere man.	+2	−2
8. His physical awkwardness hinders his candidacy.	−5	−5
9. He seems very uncomfortable as a campaigner.	−4	−5
10. This candidate isn't forceful enough to do us any real good in the U.S. Senate.	−2	0
11. He presents himself as a man with all the right answers.	+1	+5
12. He uses those less fortunate as a cheap image booster.	−4	+3
13. He is trying to be elected by playing Mr. Nice Guy.	0	+5
14. He takes credit for accomplishments that many people contributed to.	−2	+4
15. He is not self-oriented but is interested in service to others.	+2	−2
16. He really cares about people.	+4	−1
17. He is the kind of man you would like to have for a neighbor.	+3	0
18. He is able to get things done and this means charming and motivating people.	+1	0
19. He is less of a bureaucrat than most politicians.	0	−4
20. He is "everyman's candidate," he'll work for the good of all the people.	+3	−3
21. He learns from and is responsive to his constituents.	+1	0
22. He doesn't have the communication skills necessary to get people to work together for common goals.	−3	−4
23. He doesn't seem to be at ease with people.	−4	−5
24. He is no statesman, he is just another politician.	−2	+2
25. He is not responsive to the concerns of all groups.	−1	+1
26. He is too much show and too little substance.	−3	+2

27. He is insincere in his attention to minority groups.	−3	−2
28. He tries to project an image of being all things to all men.	+1	+5
29. He appeals to reason rather than people's emotions and prejudices.	0	−4
30. He is a middle-of-the-roader.	−2	−1
31. He is a good administrator.	+1	−1
32. He believes in a simple back-to-basics approach to government.	+2	−3
33. He can unite people in support of his policies.	0	−2
34. He is concerned with the public as a whole, not a collection of minority and majority groups.	+2	−3
35. He has the determination to stop government intervention in the private business sector.	0	−3
36. He is vague on the issues.	−2	+1
37. His supposed concern is a sham.	−5	−1
38. He places great emphasis on issues that he can personally do nothing about.	−1	+1
39. He manipulates issues for personal political gain.	−3	+4
40. He is extremely liberal.	−1	+1
41. He doesn't understand the key issues in America today.	−4	−2
42. His stand on issues offers nothing new or innovative.	−1	+2
43. He is for stronger criminal laws and penalties.	+5	+3
44. He wishes to create jobs for deserving youth.	+4	+3
45. He is concerned for the common/working man.	+5	+2
46. He is tough on nuclear arms; he wants to stop the arms race.	+4	+2
47. He would save as many tax dollars as possible without cutting social programs.	+2	−4
48. He is determined to provide for the future of our elderly citizens.	+3	+2
49. Preservation of the environment is one of his strongest concerns.	0	0
50. He doesn't seem to have a grasp of what the people really need.	−3	−2
51. Just because he did a good job as mayor he thinks he can represent the state in the U.S. Senate.	0	+3
52. He is naive in his belief that the programs of one area can work everywhere.	−1	+1

53. He would waste government money on social programs.	−1	+1
54. He shows little concern for victims except to get votes.	−5	0
55. He is too interested in domestic issues and doesn't pay enough attention to foreign affairs.	0	+1
56. He is too involved in trying to right social wrongs and would waste all our money on social programs.	−1	0

• 12 •

The Contagion from the Right

The Americanization of British Political Advertising

Karen S. Johnson and Camille Elebash

The relationships between political parties and the mass media have been virtually ignored in comparative politics literature. The general lack of systematic inquiry into this area is puzzling in that early comparativists recognized that a significant relationship existed between political parties and the mass media (Seymour-Ure, 1974, pp. 156–60). Ostrogorski, as early as 1902, suggested that British political parties found their newspapers to be "their most valuable auxiliaries" (p. 409). Similarly, Michels in 1915 wrote: "The press constitutes a potent instrument for the conquest, the preservation, and the consolidation of power on the part of the leaders" (p. 130). It was not until 1967 that a comparativist, Leon D. Epstein, suggested that "counter-organizational tendencies," namely the growth of modern technology and the professionalization of media skills, would "tend to substitute for large-scale membership organizations" (p. 233), i.e., political parties. However, Epstein's counter-organizational tendency thesis has been overlooked by comparativists in their enthusiasm for his critique of Duverger's *Political Parties* (1954) (see Johnson, 1981, pp. 122–23).

In order to develop a framework for analysis of British political advertising, it is first necessary to review Epstein's ground breaking work, *Political Parties in Western Democracies* (1967). Epstein defined a political party as "any group, however loosely organized, seeking to elect governmental office-holders under a given label" (Epstein, 1967, p. 9). Epstein viewed parties as responses to their environment. He wrote that "parties develop along with their circumstances in such a way as subsequently to affect in turn at least some of these arrangements" (1967, p. 19). Epstein attempted to study parties "in terms of their different functions in different societies at different times" (1967, p. 14).

Thus as changes in the society occur, the organizational style of parties and the functions parties perform will change also. As technological advances are made, and educational levels increase, and a home-centered middle-class life becomes the norm, the society will be profoundly changed. Modern technology and media professionalism will begin to substitute for large-scale membership parties. The result will be business-oriented middle-class parties (Epstein, 1967, pp. 233–57).

Epstein believed that the growth of modern technology and media professionalism would radically change the parties' electoral functions. First of all, the mass media would take over the functions of educating the people about an election and of getting out the vote. Modern polling techniques, advertising methods, and public relations strategies would dominate the arena of the electoral campaign. Secondly, paid professionals would replace volunteer workers, because the new campaign would require competent professional skills. And thirdly, large financial contributions would replace small donations or dues, for the new campaign would require huge outlays of money. This would open the door for the influence of large, wealthy groups, for the new campaigns would require the sponsoring of parties by huge contributors willing to spend a great deal for their interests (Epstein, 1967, pp. 234–60).

Epstein maintained that these changes and their resulting consequences were observable in an advanced stage in the United States and to a lesser degree in Europe (1967, p. 233). Moreover, he argues that there is evidence that this "Madison Avenue" campaign style is spreading from America to Europe. Epstein labels this phenomemon the "contagion from the right" (1967, pp. 257–60), and suggests there is an observable trend away from large socially integrated parties in societies with highly developed communications technology (1967, pp. 354–55).

This study examines one particular European nation, Great Britain, for possible evidence supporting the contagion from the right thesis. The study traces the evolution of political advertising in Great Britain, and presents a detailed quantitative and qualitative content analysis of the use of political advertising by the Conservative, Labour, and Social Democrat/Liberal Alliance parties during the 1983 general election.

Background

The British Political System

In order to examine British political advertising, it is first necessary to consider the nature of the British electoral system.

The 650-member House of Commons is the governing body of Great Britain. Each member of Parliament (M.P.) represents a single-member district; however, an M.P. does not have to live in the district from which he or she is elected. After the election, the leader of the majority party in the House of Commons becomes prime minister. The prime minister in turn selects the Cabinet. The Cabinet serves as the "central directing force within the machinery of government" (Punnett, 1971, p. 191).

The prime minister can ask the Crown to dissolve the Parliament at any time, so many Parliaments do not sit the full five years. Often the prime minister takes advantage of a period of "comparative government popularity" (Punnet, 1971, p. 32) by calling for the dissolution of Parliament. In other circumstances, the ruling party is in such grave political trouble that the prime minister is forced to ask for dissolution, as in 1924 (Punnet, 1971, p. 32–38). The process of dissolution often places the opposition party or parties at a disadvantage, for it allows little time for efficient planning and implementing of a political campaign. Dissolution must "come seventeen days before polling day, excluding Sundays and bank-holidays" (Punnett, 1971, p. 35). Thus, the entire electoral campaign is conducted within a three week period (about twenty-one days).

Traditionally, British elections were viewed as class conflicts (Abrams 1961; Punnett, 1971). The Conservatives were supported by the middle- and lower-middle class voters, Labour was supported by the skilled and unskilled working class, and the Liberals attracted votes from the middle and working classes (Abrams, 1961; Punnett, 1971, pp. 70–71). Thus, traditionally, the British electorate was divided into two classes, middle class and working class. However, the social composition of the British electorate has changed. Richard Rose writes that "five-sixths of the contemporary electorate no longer conforms to the traditional bowler hat vs. cloth cap model of British politics. Most voters today are literally and metaphorically hatless. The British electorate is now divided into three, not two, classes" (1983). The electorate is composed of three roughly equal groups: the middle class, 38 percent of the electorate; skilled manual workers, 32 percent; and the unskilled workers and people living solely on state pensions, 30 percent (Rose, 1983). The old class and partisan "loyalties which persuaded electors to vote the same way election after election are decreasing" (McKie, 1983).

From the early 1970s, researchers noticed changes in British electoral patterns. There has been a marked increase in electoral volatility (Blumler, 1975, p. 155). Approximately one-third of the electorate changes its vote from election to election (McKie, 1983). And, there has been a growing disillusionment with the Conservative and Labour parties (Ranney, 1975, p. 60). Rebel M.P.s have been elected as independent even after their constituency party organizations deserted them. These factors have led David Butler to conclude that "British voters are different today from those once solid creatures of habit that we learnt to know and trust in the 1950s. They, or many of them, have lost their traditional roots in class and parental loyalties and have started to switch from day to day under the stimulus of events" (1983).

The British Mass Media System

In order to understand the functioning of political advertising in Great Britain, it is first necessary to consider the mass media system.

Although regional newspapers and local newspapers are available in Great Britian, for the most part both the broadcast media and the print media are London-based and London-oriented (Punnett, 1971, p. 9). More newspapers are sold in Great Britain than in any other comparable western country (Punnett, 1971, p. 9). In 1971, the *News of the World* had the largest circulation of any newspaper in the world, and the *Daily Mirror* had the largest circulation of any daily newspaper in the world (Punnett, 1971, p. 9). When the national newspapers were no longer owned by political parties, a shift in journalistic behavior was observable. Journalists have changed from the party/parliamentary model of quoting party line, a passive acceptance of the status quo, to an independent/journalistic model of actively attacking and debating party lines (see Smith, 1979, pp. 20–21). No longer do parties define the agenda of a political campaign. Rather it is the newspaper and the broadcast media that define the political agenda (Seymour-Ure, 1977, p. 245). Recently, the media have adopted an antigovernment ethic—"a general assumption that government is wrong until proved right, inept unless demonstrably efficient. . . ." (Seymour-Ure, 1977, p. 246). Johnson (1979) found a preponderance of negative discussion in *The Daily Telegraph's* coverage of party leaders in the 1974 and 1979 general elections.

In Great Britain, there are two national television networks: the British Broadcasting Corporation (BBC) and the Independent Broadcasting Authority (IBA). In the beginning, broadcasters feared the potential power of the new medium, television. This led the broadcasters to ban all political news, and it was not until 1959 that the BBC presented the first fully reported general election (Seymour-Ure, 1974, p. 207). In 1974, both the BBC and the IBA increased their election coverage. It seemed that political broadcast journalism had come of age (Smith, 1976, pp. 202–3). Newscasts and documentaries are carefully controlled by the BBC and the IBA in order to provide fair and balanced coverage.

The BBC depends on a licensing fee placed on individual television sets for its revenue. Only the Parliament may raise the fee; therefore, the BBC is dependent on the government's goodwill for fee hikes (Smith, 1979, pp. 5–6). The IBA, earlier known as the Independent Television Authority (ITA), is a federal system. There is an ever-growing body of statutory law supervising the IBA.

Although the IBA does not allow programming to be sponsored, it does allow advertisers to buy broadcast time at break within programs and between programs (see Smith, 1979, pp. 7–8). Political advertising is not allowed either on the BBC or the IBA. However, there are a number of political party broadcast times allocated to parties on the basis of their showing in the last general election (see Smith, 1979, pp. 16–17). Ministers may request time during the course of a year to rally the public to political concern of general acceptance. Parties with opposing views are not allowed equal time. However, if the prime minister requests time to address a controversial issue, opposition parties are allowed equal time to respond (Smith, 1979, pp. 16–17).

However, during the election time period, free party election broadcasts (PEBs) are allowed to the parties by the broadcasters according to the time of day, length, and number. The parties and their advertising agencies control the content. In 1983, 5 ten minute PEBs were allotted to the Labour and Conservative parties, and four were allotted to the Alliance.

Obviously, this system favors those already in power (Parliamentary majority) and significant contenders for power (leading opposition parties). Parties of the extreme right such as the National Front and the parties of the extreme left such as the British Communist Party are excluded from the broadcasting system (see Smith, 1979, pp. 18–19).

According to Philip Circus, legal adviser to the Institute of Practitioners of Advertising, each candidate for Parliament is limited in the amount of money that can be spent for campaigning during the election period. By law, only 2,700 pounds (approximately $4,000 in 1983), plus 2.3d (3.4 cents) per voter, the average total being around 4,000 pounds ($6,000) per constituency (personal communication, 22 August 1983). For this reason, party leaders do not appear in any of their own national party election advertising, for the money would have to come out of their own local constituency budget. Although the opposition can put forth negative ideas about them. There is no limit to what can be spent by the parties for national political advertising (Punnett, 1971, p. 55). Party leaders may appear in the free PEBs.

HISTORY OF BRITISH POLITICAL ADVERTISING

Professional political advertising is a relatively new phenomenon in British politics. While records show that both the Conservative party and the Labour party consulted professional communicators in the early 1950s, the consultants served because of their own political affiliations on a voluntary basis (Johnson, 1981, p. 150).

It was not until 1959 that the Conservatives became the first party in Great Britain to pay for the advice of an agency, Colman, Prentis and Varley (Perry, 1983) . The party/agency relationship was an unusual one: the account executive was himself a Conservative candidate for Parliament (Butler & Rose, 1960, p. 17). The Conservatives were able to raise large sums of money, spending nearly one-half million pounds on advertising. Press and poster ads were designed to appeal to women and the prosperous section of the working class. Appeals were based on emotions rather than rational arguments (Butler & Rose, 1960, p. 18).

The Conservatives' acceptance of professional advertising occurred more readily than the Labour party's late

On the other hand, the Labour party believed that amateurism equaled sincerity in politics (Kingsley, 1983, and they did not question the ethics of using it for political purposes (Butler & Rose, 1960, p. 19).

On the other hand, the Labour party believed that amateurism equaled sincerity in politics (Kingsley, 1983, p. 1056). In addition, the Labour party distrusted advertising as a capitalist business practice (Kingsley, 1983, p. 1056). For many Labourites, advertising that projected a "slick American style" would be detrimental to the British political system (Kingsley, 1983, p. 1056).

Between 1959 and 1964, a notable change of attitude towards public relations and advertising occurred within the Labour party. The Conservatives' success in 1959 brought about the gradual realization on the part of party leaders that market research and press advertising was essential in a modern day campaign (Rose, 1965, p. 369). However, although the leaders grudgingly accepted these new communication techniques, they weren't overly enthusiastic about the prospects. In 1959, Labour Leader Aneurin Bevan complained that advertising was "taking the poetry out of politics" (Perry, 1983). A Labour M.P. maintained that political public relations were "alien to our British democracy" (*House of Common Debates,* 1960, July 1), and asked the House of Commons, "Do we want British politics to become a battle between two Madison Avenue advertising agencies?" (*House of Common Debates,* 1960, July 1).

During the 1964 campaign, Colman, Prentis and Varley continued as the Conservative advertising agency. But the party and the agency did not enjoy a productive working relationship. The party was in turmoil, and the agency found it difficult to design a campaign around a political organization in chaos. Agency partner Arthur Varley remarked: "We can't plug the leader just now, we don't even know who he is going to be. . . . We haven't any specific activity to advertise. So we're just advertising activity in general. Mind you, it's tricky trying to advertise a product if you don't really know what the product is." (Butler & King, 1965, p. 92). The Conservatives lost the election. In 1969, the Conservative party began to pursue strategic marketing strategies. The party hired Davidson, Pearce, Berry, and Tuck, Inc., to begin "target marketing" (Nimmo, 1970, p. 194). Barry Day, a media adviser and speech writer to Conservative prime minister Edward Heath (1970–1974), points out that it was "the first conscious effort to use established techniques of communications marketing on the British political scene. . . . The Programme was controlled by a tightly knit little group of professional communicators. . . . It was up to the party to decide on policy and content, and it was up to the specialists to communicate it as effectively as possible" (Day, 1982, p. 3).

In 1966, although the new Labour prime minister Harold Wilson was ideologically opposed to "slick" promotions, he began to urge the

Labour party to consider using more professional techniques in their political communications. Wilson complained that the Labour party was "a penny farthing machine in a jet propulsion era" (Wilson, 1966). But the Labour party was slow to respond, and elections came and went with very little change in campaigning techniques. In 1977, Labour prime minister James Callaghan sought the services of communcations professionals, but once again, it was on a volunteer basis. A "kitchen cabinet" of communications advisers was formed. Tim Delaney, creative director of Leagus Delaney Advertising; Edward Booth-Clibborn, chairman of Designers and Art Directors Association of London; and Trevor Eke, managing director of Playtex, Ltd., were among the influential professionals (Delaney, 1982, p. 28). However, the new kitchen cabinet found that it was not easy to change the communications direction of the Labour party. A member of the professional advising group, Edward Booth-Clibborn, points out that there were two factions within the Labour party, one at Number 10 Downing Street (the prime minister's residence), and the other at Transport House (trade union headquarters where the party at this time had a central office). Booth-Clibborn remarked that at Transport House, "they didn't understand nor even wanted to understand people like me" (E. Booth-Clibborn, personal communication, 4 October 1983).

In 1979, the Conservative party hired Saatchi and Saatchi, Garland-Compton (*Time,* 1979). The agency's Madison Avenue techniques quickly angered the more traditional Labour party. Labour Deputy Leader Denis Healey stood up in Parliament and accused the Tories of packaging the Conservative party as a baked bean. According to Andrew Rutherford, a representative of Saatchi and Saatchi, Garland-Compton, this impassioned speech made the Conservatives' use of the agency a campaign issue (A. Rutherford, personal communication, 3 September 1983). Labour Leader James Callaghan said in the 1979 campaign, "I don't intend to end this campaign packaged like cornflakes. I shall continue to be myself" (*Time,* 1979). A *Time* magazine reporter responded to this statement, "Margaret Thatcher, apparently, would rather be prime minister" (*Time,* 1979).

And that reporter might have been right. According to Michael Brunson, an Independent Television News representative, Thatcher as early as 1977 had set out to change herself and her image. With the help of American businessman David Reece, Margaret Thatcher began a program to remake herself. She took voice and diction lessons; she changed her hair and clothing styles; she lost weight, and she had her teeth capped (Brunson, personal communication, 6 September 1983). A new Margaret was born.

Thus, although the Conservative party had used media consultants off and on since the 1950s, the Labour party still refused to do so. However, the Labour party still ran an expensive campaign. The party bought newspaper advertising, paid pollsters, published party manifestos, and traveled about giving speeches. But, it was an internal party affair.

The 1983 General Election

The 1983 general election offered the British voter a genuine three-party election. In 1981 a group of Labour party members, unhappy with Labour's shift to the left, broke away to form the Social Democrat party (SDP). A year later they joined the well-established Liberal party to form the SDP/Liberal Alliance. Former Labour member Roy Jenkins became titular party leader.

The 1983 election marked the first time that both the Conservative and Labour parties had employed the services of advertising agencies: Saatchi and Saatchi again for the conservatives and Wright and Partners for the Labour party. In late 1981, the Gang of Four who left the Labour party to form the Social Democratic party hired Gold, Greenlees, and Trott advertising agency. The agency's main goal was to solve the new party's visibility problem. After the SDP/Liberal Alliance was formed and dissolution was called, the new Alliance ran out of money and Gold, Greenlees and Trott simply "vanished," according to Justin Cartwright, a Liberal consultant (J. Cartwright, personal communication, 13 October 1983).

In 1983, Saatchi and Saatchi did not enjoy as much freedom in their advertising strategies as they had in 1979. In 1981, the Conservatives hired a permanent Director of Marketing, Chris Lawson. Lawson shifted the Conservative's focus from "selling the party" to "marketing the party." This total marketing concept included the first direct mail campaign in a British political campaign and an ongoing research project called "Fast Feedback" (C. Lawson, personal communication, 17 October 1983). During the preelection months, the Conservatives were conducting focus groups on political words and phraseology. Their goal was to make the 1983 campaign one which all Britains could understand. The Conservatives developed their own highly sophisticated computer system. Using the computer, the Conservatives were able for the first time to run their own research and rapidly feed the information to the prime minister and her ministers. The party leaders were told the sort of things they should be talking about each day in speeches that would be covered by the news media. On any given day during the election period, all Tory spokesmen concentrated on the same subject, one that research had revealed to be on the people's minds (C. Lawson, personal communication, 17 October 1983).

The Labour party's first experience with an advertising agency was not a very healthy one. The 1983 internal party campaign committee (30–40 members) would not allow the ad agency Wright and Partners to attend meetings. And according to agency head Johnny Wright, the agency was not privy to party research information (J. Wright, personal communication, 10 October 1983). According to Labour deputy press officer, Jim Parish, the party itself was in turmoil, and to make matters worse, the ad agency and the party's own press department did not communicate with each other. An intolerable client/agency relationship developed (J. Parish, personal communication, 14 September 1983).

Because the new SDP/Liberal Alliance ran out of money, they had to turn to internal party members to provide them with political communications leadership. There was no money for print ads, but the job of producing the free party election broadcasts fell to Justin Cartwright, a professional partisan of the Liberal party who heads a television and film production company (J. Cartwright, personal communication, 13 October 1983). In order to counteract the Liberal influence, the SDP brought in an American, Charles Guggenheim, as a consultant. A total budget of 80,000 pounds (approximately $120,000) was given to them to produce the allotted four free party election broadcasts (J. Cartwright, personal communication, 13 October 1983). Interestingly enough the lack of paid political advertising did not appear to hurt the new party. During the election period, only the SDP/Liberal Alliance rose in the esteem of the public (+9 percent), while the image of the Conservatives lost ground (−15 percent), and Labour's image plummeted (−38 percent) (Worcester, 1983, p. 16). This finding stands in opposition to the mere exposure literature (Zajonc, 1968), and it seems to support the adages "familiarity breeds contempt" and "absence makes the heart grow fonder" (see Zajonc, 1968, p. 1).

METHODOLOGY

This study is based on a quantitative content analysis and a thematic analysis of British political advertising during the 1983 general election, May 20 through June 9.

The definition of "British political advertising" is in many ways a matter of debate. British psephologist David Butler recommends that researchers take "a broad view" of political advertising (D. Butler, personal communication, 8 September 1983). Political advertising, then, would include the dichotomy of paid advertisements in print and the hoardings and the unpaid-for party election broadcasts (PEBs). It is true that the paid aspect of political advertising is very important in that it gives the source the right to control the form and content of the message (Kaid, 1981, p. 250). However, given the tenet that the source controls the content of the message as at least part of the definition, then in Britain where the parties and/or their agencies produce all the PEBs, then the PEBs must be considered at least quasi-commercials. For this reason both print ads (newspapers, magazines, posters, bus-sides) and PEBs were studied.

Research Questions

This study answers a variety of questions such as the mode of the ad, the partisanship of the ad, the issue content of the ad, the party leader image portrayed in the ad, and demographic groups used in the ad (see Joslyn, 1980).

Sampling

The universe of print ads and PEBs used during the 1983 general election was obtained. For the Conservatives, six print ads and five PEBs were coded. For the Labour party, twenty-one print ads and five PEBs were coded. And for the Social Democratic party/Liberal Alliance, zero print ads and four PEBs were coded.

However, the authors were not able to obtain information pertaining to the placement of the print ads or as to the number of times each was used. The Conservative party kept very casual records of where their print ads were placed; their methods were deemed unreliable by the authors. The Labour party kept no records at all. Therefore, no weighting of the ads could be done.

The observation unit for the coding process was an ad unit. Each ad unit within an advertisement was coded. For example, several parties may be discussed. Each discussion of a particular party would be coded as a separate ad unit. The following number of ad units were coded: Conservatives, 19; Labour, 73; and, the Social Democrat party/Liberal Alliance, 12. All in all, 69 print ad units and 35 PEB ad units were examined.

Quantitative Content Analysis and Thematic Analysis Methods

The content analysis literature suggests two approaches to the study of media content: the hard approach and the soft approach (Frank, 1973, pp. 23–25). The hard approach may be viewed as simply counting "discrete and concrete quantifiable bits of data" (Frank, 1973, p. 23). The soft approach allows the coder(s) "to evaluate the entire Gestalt package" of the political ad (Frank, 1973, p. 23).

The hard and soft approaches have both strengths and weaknesses. The hard approach reduces possible subjective coding error, but it results in a loss of information. The soft form, a more wholistic approach, introduces a great deal of potential subjective error; however, it is quite possible that more of the coded information wil be retained in its natural content (see Frank, 1973, pp. 24–25). According to Frank (1973), the optimal technique is "the construction of a research design which utilizes both the hard and soft approaches to content analysis" (p. 25).

This study combines both the hard and soft approaches to content analysis. The study employs the soft approach in the thematic analysis technique adopted by Herbert Gans (1979) in his exploration of the mass media, *Deciding What's News.* This method is designed to discover any possible significant factors found in the ad units that were untouched by the quantitative content analysis (the hard approach). This analysis asks the questions, "What is the theme or 'spine' of this ad unit?" And, "How are these themes built upon each other?" This method is primarily qualitative.

The coding categories used in the quantitative content analysis were developed from an earlier content analysis of the news coverage of the 1974 and 1979 general elections in Great Britain made by one of the authors (Johnson, 1979, pp. 17–18; 69–83). In addition, the earlier work of Bowers (1972), Joslyn (1980), and Shyles (1983b) was very useful in gaining insight into content analyzing political advertising.

Six coding categories were used: the source of the ad unit, the party discussed, the party leader discussed, the mode of the ad, the partisanship of the ad, and, the substance of the ad.

1. *Source of the ad unit.* The originator of the ad unit and the medium of the ad unit were coded.

2. *The party discussed.* Ad units were coded according to the party under discussion.

3. *The party leader discussed.* Ad units were coded according to the party leader under discussion. In many instances, a party leader was not

mentioned. Remarks that personified a political party were not coded under this category.

4. *The mode of the ad unit.* Ad units were coded according to whether the remarks were in negative, positive, or normative form.

5. *The partisanship of the ad unit.* Ad units were coded according to whether they were nonpartisan, overtly partisan, or marginally partisan (see Joslyn, 1980, p. 93).

> *Nonpartisan* ads were ads in which no mention of partisanship was made or implied, either through the audio or visual portions of the ad. Ads of *overt partisanship* were ads in which the partisan identification . . . was clearly transmitted, either through visual or audio presentation of the party name. Ads of *marginal partisanship* were ads in which the party identification . . . was implied but not unambiguously presented (such as by criticizing the other party or by showing the candidate with a prominent member of the candidate's party). (Joslyn, 1980, p. 93)

6. *Substance of the ad unit.* One hundred forty-nine different themes were used to code the substance of the ad units. Of these, ninety-eight dealt with issues discussed in the campaign, and forty-four dealt with qualities associated with the party leaders. For purposes of analysis, issues were clustered into five categories: economic problems, general governmental problems and philosophy of government, foreign policy, social problems, and campaign techniques and problems. Qualities were clustered into eight categories: personal attributes, personal style, philosophy of the party leader, general professional capacities associated with the Prime minister, organizational changes supported by the party leader, perceived working relationships with other branches of government, the perceived role of public opinion in the political process, and the coping capacities of the party leader.

Data Gathering

Each ad unit was analyzed and coded on the basis of the themes expressed in the ad unit. However, a theme was coded only once for each story unit.

Two coders were used. The average intercoder reliability score was 92 percent, and the average intracoder reliability score for each coder was 97 percent and 98 percent respectively. Trouble spots were identified early into the coding, and special care was given in considering these themes. Thus, many problems of coding reliability were avoided.

Data Analysis[1]

The data was compiled through the use of simple rankings and percentages.

RESULTS

In 1983, the Conservative party set new landmarks in British political history. The party's increase in seats and in votes was the largest won by any party since 1935; the advance in the House of Commons from 339 of a total of 635 seats in 1979 to 397 seats of a total of 650 seats in 1983 was the largest ever by an incumbent government. (The increase in number of seats was caused by redistricting.) Margaret Thatcher became only the second conservative prime minister ever to be reelected after serving a full term; in 1900, Lord Salisbury was the first to do so (Havilland, 1983, pp. 23–27). The Labour setback was even more striking statistically than the Conservative win; the party lost more than one-quarter of its 1979 vote. Labour polled only 27.6 percent of the vote, while the new SDP/Liberal Alliance polled 25.4 percent of the vote (Butler & Waller, 1983, pp. 253–58).

Mode

Out of the 104 ad units examined, 50 positive ad units and 54 negative ad units were identified. Clearly, British political parties make use of both positive ads supporting their own cause and negative, direct reference, political attacks against their opponents (see Surlin & Gordon, 1977, pp. 89–98). Research indicates that these negative direct reference political ads can have substantial influence on voters' attitudes and beliefs (Patterson & McClure, 1973), particularly for those of lower socioeconomic status (SES) (Surlin & Gordon, 1977).

Of the 45 units discussing the Conservative party, 7 were found to be positive, and 38 were found to be negative. Of the 53 ad units discussing the Labour party, 39 were found to be positive, and 14 were found to be negative. And of the six ad units discussing the SDP/Liberal Alliance, four were found to be positive, and two were found to be negative. Thus, for the most part, the Labour Party and the SDP/Liberal Alliance ignored each other and concentrated instead on attacking the Conservatives.

The Conservatives on the other hand virtually ignored the SDP/Liberal Alliance and concentrated on the more established Labour party.

The Conservatives produced the greatest percentage of negative ad units with 63 percent of their total number of ad units devoted to attacking their opponents (overwhelmingly defined as the Labourites). Forty-seven percent of Labour's ad units were found to be negative. And 33 percent of the SDP/Liberal Alliance's ad units were found to be negative.

The Conservatives' predominantly negative political advertising became quite a controversial subject during the campaign. A newspaper ad comparing the Labour party manifesto and the Communist party manifesto pointed out eleven identical points in the two documents. Adding still more controversy was a newspaper and poster ad showing a man of Asian or West Indian descent. The headline read: "Labour says he's black, Conservatives say he's British." Labour Leader Michael Foot responded to these two particular ads when he said, "Saatchi and Saatchi are shameless in their peddling of falsehoods—ads that would be forbidden in the normal world of advertising" (Staff, 1983). The largest circulation minority newspaper in Britain, *The Caribbean Times*, refused to accept the racist ad, calling it "insulting, obnoxious, and immoral" (Cook, 1983).

Partisanship of Ad

As one might expect, the British political ads were for the most part overtly partisan. In fact, 92 percent of the 104 ad units coded demonstrated overt partisanship. The remaining 8 percent were ads of marginal partisanship (Joslyn, 1980, p. 93). All of this type were print ads.

Issue Content

Earlier research has criticized political advertising for distorting the political arena, primarily by emphasizing a candidate's personality over issue concerns (Kelley, 1960; McGinniss, 1969; Wykoff, 1968). However, more recent research in the United States has suggested "that more issue content is available from political advertisements than from network news coverage of political campaigns" (Shyles, 1983b, p. 333; Patterson & McClure, 1976; Devlin, 1973–74; 1977; Joslyn, 1980; Atkin, Bowen, Nayman & Sheinkopf, 1973).

For the 1983 election, the dominant form of content was issues. Seven hundred and twenty-five issue mentions were coded and 144 personal qualities were coded. The ratio of issues to personality attributes was 83 percent to 17 percent or 5 to 1.

However, this may be a bit misleading in that the issues found in the ads were treated very superficially. Party Leaders were against unemployment, but only rarely were solutions offered for the problem. Labour said they would increase government spending, and by doing so, the party would be "investing" in the British people. The Conservatives said they would decrease government spending, and by doing so, the party would be pursuing liberty, prosperity, security, and independence for the individual citizen. Detailed analysis of issue areas were not the norm. Similarly, Joslyn (1980) found in a content analysis of television ads in the U.S. that although the dominant type of content was issues that only one-fifth of the ads studied contained information on the actual issue positions of the candidate.

Economic problems and social problems were the dominant issues discussed by all three parties (see Table 28). Economic problems accounted for 32 percent of all issues mentioned, and social problems accounted for 28 percent of the issues mentioned. Unemployment, gov-

TABLE 28

1983: ISSUE CATEGORIES MENTIONED BY PRO-PARTY AND CON-PARTY SOURCES

	CONSERVATIVE MENTIONS	LABOUR MENTIONS	SDP/LIBERAL ALLIANCE MENTIONS
	Mentioned by Pro-Sources		
Economic Problems	35	88	11
General Govt. Problems	6	55	5
Foreign Policy	8	6	3
Social Problems	20	74	16
Campaign Techniques	9	27	9
Total	78	250	44
	Mentioned by Con-Sources		
Economic Problems	92	40	1
General Govt. Problems	39	11	6
Foreign Policy	15	12	0
Social Problems	59	27	5
Campaign Techniques	27	15	4
Total	232	105	16

ernment borrowing and spending, education, health care, housing, social security benefits, and fiscal policy were the most frequently mentioned concerns. Interestingly enough, the Falklands war was not mentioned in any ad. Apparently all three parties were scared to bring the topic up for fear that it would work against them.

The Conservatives targeted their issue discussion towards the new working class and the middle class. The Tory approach was to make the credibility of their opponents the number-one campaign issue (Kingsley, 1983, pp. 1056–59). The Conservatives were on the offensive, and they sought to remind the voters of the "Winter of Discontent," a time in 1979 when the unions virtually shut down the country through massive strikes. The Conservatives reminded the voters that it was the "union" party, i.e., the Labour party that had failed to control the powerful union bosses. And it was not until the Conservative party returned to power that the unions were controlled and order was restored to the country. This scenario is reinforced by an emphasis on the economic gains made by the Conservative party during 1979 through 1983.

The Labour party targeted their issue discussions towards an aging and shrinking minority of the old working class. For Labour, the dominant campaign issue was unemployment. Suddenly, it was a Labour party attacking the dole ques (social unemployment benefits). Labour accused the Conservatives of "paying people who want to work not to work." This attack placed the Labour party in a very precarious position in that the Labourites had long been supporters of unemployment benefits, and suddenly, they were attacking the very socialist benefits they had created. In addition, Labour pursued a strategy of pitting classes against each other. The party accused the Conservatives of believing "in Government by the few, for the few and against the interests of nearly all of us." Similarly, the Labourites depicted the Conservatives as living off the poor, working class, for the ads repeatedly referred to the Conservatives as "Tory vandals." In addition, the Labour party condemned Thatcher's working relationship with President Reagan and the United States. The party accused the U.S. repeatedly of getting "rich" off of Britain's citizens, referring to U.S. missile production and to U.S. oil companies in the North Sea area.

The SDP/Liberal Alliance tried to spread its issue appeal across all social groups. For the Alliance, the central campaign issue was the extremism and divisiveness of the other two parties (Kingsley, 1983, p. 1057). The new party said that the Labour party and the Conservative party were not the answer to Britain's troubles, for the clash between these two groups represented "the Neo-Marxists vs. the Victorians." And for the Alliance, the answers did not rest on either extreme. Rather, their leaders pointed to a middle-road, a road of compromise and negotiation. The Alliance talked of national unity, representative government, and coalition government.

Party Leader Images

Candidate images are composed of dimensions of understanding. Studies have shown that voters perceive candidates in terms of roles they appear to fill. These roles are the political role and the stylistic role (Nimmo & Savage, 1976; for similar categories ses Kjeldahl, Carmichael, & Mertz, 1971; Roberts, 1973). The political role of a candidate is composed of those acts which are germane to his position as a community leader. This involves his perceived qualifications—past, present, and future (Nimmo & Savage, 1976, p. 46). The stylistic role of a candidate refers to acts which are not directly political but involve personal qualities such as physical appearance, bearing, integrity, speech patterns, and personality projection (Nimmo & Savage, 1976, p. 46).

For this study, forty-four party leader images were clustered into eight categories: personal attributes, personal style, philosophy of the party leader, general professional capacities associated with the party leader, organizational changes supported by the leader, the perceived working relationship with other branches of government, the perceived role of public opinion in the political process, and the coping capacities of the party leader. These eight categories may be clustered again into two frameworks: the select personal image framework and the special issue image framework. The select personal image framework includes personal attributes, style, philosophy, general professional capacities, and coping capacities of the party leader. The special issue image framework refers to the organizational changes, working relationships, and public opinion's policy role that the party leader supports.

One hundred and forty-four party leader images were coded. Out of this, 135 select personal images (or 94%) and 9 special issue images (or 6%) were found. Personal attributes and personal style accounted for 41% and 27% respectively. Similarly, Graber (1976) found that "media audiences receive most information about general human qualities of candidates rather than about their professional qualifications" (p. 301). Johnson (1979) found that British news coverage of the 1974 and 1979 general election contained 96% select personal images and 4% special issue images (p. 39).

The Conservatives depicted Margaret Thatcher as a woman of principles. She was said to possess great leadership traits. Often, the camera caught her surrounded by men applauding her. Again and again, Thatcher was depicted as a strong leader that could control the unions at home and would be respected by world leaders.

The Labour party did not use their party leader Michael Foot as much as the Conservatives used Thatcher. Foot was depicted as a compassionate man who sympathized with the working people. And the party defended its record of leadership in the past. Foot was depicted as a man who would not let go of the "high" socialist ideals of the early Labour party movement.

The SDP/Liberal Alliance presented Jenkins as a man who would use restraint in dealing with battling factions. Jenkins was not a doctrinaire; he would be flexible. The Alliance under his leadership would steer a middle-of-the-road course. Jenkins would put the nation's interests over his party interests, and in this way, he would be able to unify the nation.

Conclusions

Past research has suggested that a candidate's image far outweighs the number of issues presented in political advertising (Kelley, 1960). However, this study revealed that in the 1983 election, advertising issue mentions outnumbered party leader images five to one. It must be remembered, however, that the party leaders do not usually appear in print ads, because the money would have to come from their own constituency advertising budgets. Traditionally, researchers have viewed "party image" as being much more important than "party leader image" in British elections (Punnett, 1971, p. 69; Crane, 1959).

However, these findings may be misleading on two counts. First, it may not be enough to simply count the number of issue mentions. There was little in-depth treatment of issues and potential solutions. The issues seemed little more than buzzwords and were couched in "personalistic encapsulations" (Pool, 1965, p. 177). Party leaders and party spokespersons claimed that the party and the leaders could handle the problem better than their opponents by virtue of who the leaders were, what party they belonged to, or what group(s) they were affiliated with. The political party as a unit was often personified in the political ads. The paucity of issue richness, i.e., specific detail was clearly seen by the lack of special issue images. Only 6 percent of the party leader images mentioned were concerned with special issue images.

Secondly, although the parties were personified and the issues were couched in "personalistic encapsulations," these potential party leader images were not coded as such because a specific party leader was not named or shown. In 65 percent of the ad units, a specific party leader was not mentioned.

It must be remembered in addition to these two factors that a British election focuses on "broadly the same issues and personalities at one end of the country and the other" (Seymour-Ure, 1974, p. 204). This creates a "nationalizing" tendency in the electoral process. Similarly, Punnett (1971) writes that "the effect of the mass media on elections has been to concentrate the electorate's attention on personalities, and the personalities of the party leaders in particular" (p. 204). Johnson (1979) found that *The Daily Telegraph* presented its readers with information concerning the personal characteristics of party leaders and the most general of leadership traits. Similarly, this study revealed that 68 percent of the party leader images mentioned in the political ads concerned personal attributes and general leadership style. The Political Editor of *The Sunday Times,* Hugo Young, called attention to the importance of the party leader in British politics when he wrote an article titled "A presidential landslide" (1983). And Kellner reported in the *New Statesman* that during the 1983 election, leader-oriented television coverage of all parties more than doubled that of the last election (1983).

In addition to the attention given party leaders, a personified party image, and personalistic encapsulized issues, there was a substantial amount of negativism in the political ads. A little over one-half of the ad units had direct reference negative attacks on opponents. Wamsley and Pride (1972) and Robinson (1976) have warned that an emphasis on the negative aspects of politics and governmental processes may be denigrative of the political system.

The accusation of "American-style" campaigning, gathering momentum in the 1979 British general election and recurring in 1983, has more than a few elements of truth; this is true despite the differences between the United States and British electoral systems.

The Conservatives have been accurately described by the press as the leader in the move toward U.S.-style promotion, but both the Labour party and the Social Democrat party/Liberal Alliance are moving with deliberate speed in the same direction.

In the 1983 election, "the Conservatives actually put on the best campaign and the Labour Party the worst in purely professional and technical ways; and, the Alliance put on the luckiest campaign" (D. Butler, personal communication, 8 September, 1983).

However reluctant the British might be to admit it, their tradition of "standing" for office rapidly appears to be giving way to "running" for office.

• 13 •

Political Advertising in Australia

A Dynamic Force Meets a Resilient Object

Helen O'Neil and Stephen Mills

Australia's most recent federal election, fought out in late 1984, showcased all the weapons at the disposal of the modern advertising agency: prime time TV buys for paid ads, snappy campaign jingles and slogans about family and nationalism, staged media events to grab the attention of the electronic news media, massive market research, and million dollar budgets.[1]

TV advertising has become entrenched in Australian politics over the last dozen years. For both major parties, competing for votes included competing for newer and better advertising techniques, as they regularly pour more than half their total campaign budgets into TV time buying, research, and production. If political ad campaigns are similar in style and content to the marketing of rival brands of soap, as critics so often say, then Madison Avenue could happily move out to Melbourne. Australian voters have long been awash with suds.

However, the 1984 Federal Election campaign was not a miniature replica of the American Presidential contest earlier that same year. To continue the analogy, there were clear local differences in the brands of "soap," and the ways they were marketed to Australian and American voters.

This article seeks to identify where and why local factors—institutional and attitudinal differences—have created an identifiable Australian advertising campaign. Our framework casts the growth of political advertising in Australia as a struggle between a dynamic technology and a resilient set of public institutions and beliefs. Unlike the Newtonian concept, this force is not irresistible nor is the object immovable. So the struggle has altered them both.

In the first part of this paper we outline the nature of this dynamic force with an outline history of Australian electoral advertising and a description of its key elements of style and tactics. This section concludes with a detailed description of the tactics employed by the main parties, the conservative-leaning Liberal party and left-leaning Australian Labor party (ALP) in the 1984 campaign. In the second section of the paper we outline the Australian institutions and attitudes which have acted to modify, and which have also been modified by, political advertising.

Advertising, a Dynamic Force

Early Years of Political Advertising

The earliest celluloid artifacts of Australian political advertising held in national archives date back to the 1920s. The campaign of the conservative Prime Minister Bruce produced film spots, apparently directed at audiences in silent movie theaters, linking Australian Labor party (ALP) officials with Communists and using unrestricted Asian immigration as a scare tactic (Byrnes, 1984). As a starting point in the story of Australian political advertising, these pretelevision efforts are evidence of an evergreen theme and tone in Australian electioneering.

Early television advertisements date back to the early 1960s, following naturally from the arrival of television in the mid 1950s. Since the political parties already employed advertising agencies for some pretelevision campaign work, it was natural for these agencies to apply to politics the expertise in the new medium they were developing for their commercial accounts.

But in these early years ads served strictly as adjuncts of campaign strategy rather than as integral or dominant elements. The ALP's ads were five minute minidocumentaries about party policy, featuring the party's deputy leader Gough Whitlam, who was much more telegenic than the old-style, crusty leader, Arthur Calwell. By 1966 the party's ad agency was coming under the influence of American-style candidate identification advertising. Mr. Bryce Courtenay, who designed the ads for the ALP's Hansen-Rubensohn-McCann-Erikson agency, says he was attracted by what he saw as "TV of promise rather than TV of accusation" (Byrnes, 1984, p. 20). This was an important move beyond the frequently vitriolic attacks which characterized much of Australia's electoral rhetoric, toward an emphasis on personalities instead.

The real breakthrough came in 1972 with Labor's successful "It's Time" campaign. Based on extensive electoral research, "It's Time" was targeted at the residents, especially the housewives, of marginal electorates in the new suburbs on city fringes. The campaign portrayed a vision of a new Australia emerging from the slumbers of a twenty-three year old Liberal Party administration. As the ads said, 1972 was "a time for moving, a time for everyone." In responding to the mood of the electorate this message of restlessness harmonized with the image of a progressive, youthful, on-the-move ALP promising change without hardship. "It's Time" became a self-fulfilling assertion; in the images which accompanied the swelling strains of the "It's Time" song—the young folk singer, the massed group of hot business stars—there was little room or need for politics or issues.

As well as the innovation of using almost purely visionary material, the ALP went further in 1972 by running these two minute ads before the election was even declared. Since Australian campaigns usually run only three or four weeks, this allowed advertising to stake out the campaign agenda ("It's Time") in advance.

Further, the ALP campaign closely complemented the unpaid media coverage of politics. What factual material there was in the ads centered on establishing the identity of Gough Whitlam, now party leader and soon to be prime minister. He was shown as a child, as a soldier, and as a lawyer, before finally being presented as the symbol of the climate of change and reform—the final shot of the "It's Time" ad was Whitlam's face above the slogan "It's Time."

Labor's win in 1972 gave political advertising credibility. The Liberal Party, now in opposition, began in earnest its research of the new methods. By 1975, when the Liberals returned to power under the leadership of Malcolm Fraser, both the parties were mounting national campaigns in which advertising, particularly on television, played an enormous role. Thus, this new technology is a phenomenon of only the past dozen years, its effectiveness roughly gauged by trial and error, with raw electoral success the sole criterion.

In 1975 the Liberals played back some of the ALP devices. A popular rock and soul singer recorded the Liberal theme song, which again featured a slogan—this time "Turn on the Lights." The visuals, such as the lights of a city skyline coming on at dusk, were emotive evocations of an Australia coming to life after the "dark" Labor years.

The slogan reflected another strong element of Australian political communication in advertising. Alongside the "positive" ads portraying the Liberals as responsible economic managers came a powerful campaign of "negative," attacking ads. While this was a natural response to the political situation—a bitter polarization of the community following the sacking of the Labor government in a constitutional crisis after a year of scandals—the negative campaign has almost become a hallmark of the Liberals' advertising. In 1975, these ads featured "The Three Dark Years" of Labor as a scrapbook with headlines, using news reportage to give credibility to the ads. The negative spot was developed further in the 1977 campaign when a voice sang "Memories" in the background to more scrapbook shots. There was even an echo of the format ad anti-Whitlam tone in the final phase of the 1983 campaign when the Liberals downplayed their positive slogan "We're not Waiting for the World" to run scare ads, unsuccessful this time, saying: "The Hawke Show—Don't Bother, it's a Whitlam Replay."

In the 1977 campaign, Australians witnessed another battle of the slogans: the Liberals came up with "Doing the Job"; Labor attacked high unemployment with "Get Australia Working." The pattern of ads and jingles was by now fairly well-established, although Gough Whitlam, now seen as a vote loser in his last campaign, was pushed to the background in the Labor spots. In some ads he was even replaced by animated figures.

Perhaps the most enduring image of the 1977 campaign was the Liberals' "Fistful of Dollars" ads. The image was of a fist clutching dollar bills—the amount the average family would receive from tax cuts and other promises made by the Liberals. It was a crisp visual short cut through detailed policy explanations, which kept attention on a specific issue, the sensitive "hip pocket nerve." It used TV's ability to project a sweeping vision to transmit a specific communication. Labor found the ads very difficult to counter through its chosen channel, the unpaid media where, their complexity was defeated by the simplicity of the TV image.

In 1980 Malcolm Fraser's Liberals were fighting again, as incumbents. Their campaign refined the issues-directed advertising and linked it with their negative campaign. They planned to campaign on the positives of Fraser's leadership and Australia's relative economic prosperity by, for example, interviewing travelers returning to Australia with "horror" stories of the price of milkshakes in Britain. However, these plans were abandoned when the polls unexpectedly began to show it would be a tight race. Instead, ads were prepared on "Labor's 20 percent inflation" and "Labor's so-called wealth tax." The pattern of specific negative messages is familiar. In 1980 the Liberals' ads were all put to air in the three weeks after the formal launch of the campaign, a time when the electorate's attention was presumed to be focused on the vote (Goot, 1983).

Labor did not respond to the wealth tax and inflation advertising through its own ads—and found once more that its spokesmen and women had enormous difficulty in getting their replies across in the unpaid media, which was preoccupied with reporting the horserace. Their difficulties were compounded by the Liberals' management of the news media, especially outlets owned by Rupert Murdoch's News Limited.

Labor did have some success, however, in co-opting the themes of nationalism and national development. This move was based on qualitative research findings that Australians were in a more patriotic, independent mood (Goot, 1983). The opposition's slogan was "Raise the Standard," and its jingle ran: "It's a golden wealthy country / Full of life and strength and might / And the standard should be rising." But in 1980 it seems the Liberals won the fight for image and managed to scare voters away from Labor: they were returned to Government.

In 1983 nationalism was the main visionary material in both the parties' advertising, although presented in sharply diverging ways and accompanied, once again, by a negative strategy towards the end of the campaign. This time Labor won.

Labor was able to build its visionary and policy advertising around the personality of its new leader Bob Hawke. Hawke was already a nationally known figure through his previous experience as leader of the Australian Council of Trade Unions, a largely favorable image as a strike-settler. As a strongly Australian figure he was easily cast as a symbol of the nationalism that Labor again wanted to project. And as an industrial peacemaker he was a potent symbol for the consensus style policies he proposed in the campaign. The Labor slogan "Bringing Australia Together" combined nationalism with self-styled consensus policies of "national reconciliation." He managed quickly to run the campaign on his own terms as if he, not the beleaguered Malcom Fraser, was the incumbent Prime Minister.

Labor's negative ads were typically focused on the issue of the economy. Australia's declining OECD (Organization for Economic Cooperation and Development) performance, for example, was dealt with vividly by a man representing Australia riding an escalator. Because he is walking backwards, he is overtaken by everyone else.

The Liberal advertising strategy, growing out of its "We're not waiting for the World" slogan drew heavily on Australian success symbols, particularly athletes including a Commonwealth Games gold medalist. But in an election campaign where the prime minister was making few promises and even fewer handouts, there was little material to build argument-style ads on.

But in the last days of the campaign the Liberals were again buying up broadcast time for a big offensive: a final attempt to reconstruct a prime ministerial image for Malcolm Fraser. In a series of two minute advertisements featuring the prime minister in his office, addressing the people of Australia as if on a nonpartisan matter, the Liberals tried to recapture the incumbent's role. These ads drew heavily on the formats developed for the free time broadcasts made on the ABC, giving the ads a seriousness not usually seen in spot advertising.

The 1984 Campaign

The ALP's National Secretary Bob McMullan blames Labor's unexpected difficulties in the 1984 campaign for the December 1 vote on the unusually long election period. Labor had devised a traditional campaign strategy for its advertising: a main theme of vision and argument, a very minor subplot of negative advertising, all grouped around the vote-winning personality of Prime Minister Bob Hawke. But by the time the votes came in, a seemingly impregnable lead in the polls had turned into a swing against the government. Labor, returned to power but with a reduced majority, began to regret its decision to set a campaign of eight weeks—twice the usual length—without modifying its campaign strategy. Its ad blueprint, along with its overall strategy, simply did not sustain itself over the length of the campaign; the electorate and the media became bored with the government message and paid attention instead to their opponents' themes of nuclear disarmament and the tax burden.

Meanwhile, the Liberal Party had begun running its election advertising two months before the election was even announced, adding a new phase to its campaign. Later it showed a greater flexibility than the Labor Party: as in 1980 and 1983 it produced new ads during the campaign to respond to issues arising from unpaid media or Labor advertising.

In 1983, Labor had relied heavily on public trust in Hawke's consensus message: "Bringing Australia Together." So for 1984, it was no surprise that Hawke should again play a central, indeed, solo role in the Party's 1984 advertising.

According to Mr. McMullan, Labor's strategy aimed to establish three basic arguments: (1) The government had significantly improved the nation's economic performance after the disasters of the last Liberal years; (2) The economic recovery still needed the careful handling Labor had proved it was capable of; and (3) The leadership of Bob Hawke was superior to the Liberal alternative. (Bob McMullan, personal communication, 1984). These points, which McMullan said were of equal importance, were encapsulated in the campaign slogan "Putting Australia First." It was an upbeat, visionary and positive strategy—partly, McMullan says, because the Opposition was trailing in the polls so badly at the time that no tactical purpose would be served by direct attacks.

The Labor Party aired two main sixty second commercials. The first, of which there were five slightly different versions, argued that the Australian economy under Labor was back on its feet. By "putting Australia first"—i.e. by voting Labor—Australians could achieve even greater feats. Most of the ad showed Australian men and women at work and leisure, including scenes from the National Economic Summit Hawke chaired at the start of his first term and, almost inevitably, the victory scenes from the American's Cup yacht race. For sixteen seconds, Hawke spoke to the camera about his record of achievement. The ad was backed by a jingle with the lyrics: "When Aussies work together, we're invincible, unstoppable, incredible . . ."

The second ad aimed to demonstrate that, though Hawke had made few promises when first elected, he had since delivered on those he had made. This ad reconstructed the policy speech Hawke had given in the 1983 campaign from the Sydney Opera House stage. Retaped by Hawke for this ad, the sixteen month old speech was punctuated by freeze frames and voice-overs of Hawke today explaining how he had implemented each earlier promise.

The only departure from this positive strategy was the "Mastermind" ad, which Labor officials described as "the most devastating piece of negative political advertising ever made in Australia" (Simper, 1984).

Based on a popular quiz show of that name, it featured a "contestant," who is asked "Prior to 1983, the Liberals held government for seven years. What was their greatest achievement?" The contestant answers, "Pass." "Which Liberal Party leader would make as good a Prime Minister as Bob Hawke?" "Pass." "Well, what is (National Party leader) Mr. Sinclair best known for?" By this time, the contestant looks confused as he again answers, "Pass." At the end of the sixty second ad, a voice says: "If you can't name one single contribution the Liberals have made, can you think of a single reason for voting for them?"

Anticipating Labor's incumbency strategy, the Liberals began advertising early. They also knew they were well behind in the polls; their own research showed voters believed the opposition leader Andrew Peacock had been overshadowed by Hawke and had yet to identify his own issues. The Liberals decided on a $500,000 "pre-campaign campaign"—an ID phase—in which Peacock hit Labor policies on taxation, superannuation, pensioners' assets test, and health costs. Liberal officials claim they succeeded in setting the agenda for the whole campaign with this series; according to the ALP, Peacock's popularity actually dropped during these early ads (Ramsay, 1984).

Certainly, the Liberals returned to these same issues in their thirty second ads during the general election. These featured an innovative "slice of life" technique, in which a "typical" family was shown reacting to the various impositions the Labor government had made on it. In one ad, an elderly woman is shown receiving a government letter which asks her to itemize her possessions; she phones her son in confusion. In another, a woman in hospital discusses her worries about health costs with her husband. In a third, a boss presents a retiring employee with a bonus check but warns him, "They've taxed 31 percent of the best years of your life." At the end of each "slice" Peacock appears and explains how life under his government would be better.

The Federal Director of the Liberal party, Tony Eggleton, describes the ads as "positive negatives"—attacking their opponents but outlining specific remedies for the problems they highlight. Eggleton described the 1984 campaign as probably the most disciplined the Liberals had ever run: they managed to present the five or six key issues they wanted to and tied them together under the ideologically apt slogan "Stand Up For Your Family" (Eggleton, personal communication, 1984).

Another ad in the series was a purer positive in the same "slice" method and with the same family emphasis: a family was shown discussing how they would benefit from the Liberals' tax rebate policies. This series of five ads in all ran for the last three weeks of the campaign. The only addition to the Liberals' repertoire of commercials went to air in the final week, before the start of the "blackout" (see Section Two) and following the televised debate between the two leaders which many commentators agreed Peacock had won. Reacting to the success of Labor's "Mastermind" ad, the Liberals developed a fifteen second parody. The contestant is asked to name someone who would make a better prime minister than Bob Hawke. His confident answer: "I watched the debate and there's no doubt about it. The best man to be pm would be Andrew Peacock." The quizmaster says: "Correct" and the ad fades on applause for the contestant.

The 1984 election campaign, representing as it does the state of the art in Australian political advertising, also encapsulated many traditional elements of the genre. Such elements, which we have emphasized here, include a substantial issue content in the ads and a frequent recourse to attack-style advertising.

It is not possible to draw generalizations about the relative reliance which the parties place on each kind of advertising; techniques have largely been shared. But one difference between the parties does recur: it appears the Liberals have been more flexible in planning their ad campaigns. They repeatedly seem to have been able to produce new ads late in a campaign when needed. The Labor party, on the other hand, seems to lock its advertising tactics into a wider campaign strategy. Indeed, the ALP's Bob McMullan said he believed advertising was only a "tool" of the overall campaign. While the Labor party remains reluctant or unable to adapt its tactics to respond rapidly to the Liberals, they may receive more surprises like the one they received in 1984.

Meeting a Resilient Object

Three principal features of Australian political life have influenced the kind of advertising parties have used to win votes. Chief among them is the parliamentary system of government and, closely related to that, the dominant role of the party structures. Secondly, there is a widespread ambivalence or cynicism about advertising. Thirdly, there is a long tradition in Australia of parliamentary and judicial rule-making in the electoral arena, as in society at large. This section will be principally taken up with a discussion of the third point. It is necessary, first, however, to describe—we hope without turning this article into a political science textbook—the way the first two have influenced the Australian ad campaign.

Parliament and Parties

The growth of TV, of political advertising, and of independent media consultants has been credited in the U.S. with helping to weaken the party structure and foster a new generation of candidate-entrepreneurs who win office by going outside their party's structure. (Diamond & Bates, 1984; Robert Squier, personal communication, 1984). In Australia this has not happened. To the extent that advertising has "taken over" electioneering, it has done so only through party channels. Within the parliamentary system of government, parties survive and flourish. They play the major, even the only, role in candidate selection, policy development, and campaigning. They can enforce—this is particulary true for the ALP—discipline in parliamentary voting and can penalize rebels by withdrawing preselection.

The vast majority of elected representatives owe their place to party politics. Since the Second World War the House of Representatives has been made up almost entirely of members of the ALP, the Liberal party or their rural coalition partners, the National party. The Senate has usually contained a number of small party representatives or independents but is also dominated by the major parties. In the context of election campaigns it is the parties which employ advertising agencies for campaigns and which dictate overall electoral strategies to them.

This overwhelming party strength has wrought several changes in election advertising. As the first section made clear, Australian advertisements can be strong on issue content. Election campaigns are traditionally started with a formal launch of the party's policy platform, which usually includes detailed manifestoes on such matters as tax cuts and economic growth. These platforms tend to provide a real indication of what the party would actually endeavor to do if elected. Party leaders have usually had "hands-on" experience in formulating and defending their platform through party and parliamentary forums.

The fact that opposition party leaders are typically well known as alternative prime ministers before the start of the campaign—rather than being nominated during the campaign—means that there is less need for identification spots. This is reinforced by the ruthlessly short election campaign periods, usually only four weeks long, which simply reduce the time available to stage multiphase advertising. Campaign budgets and long-term strategic planning have been constrained by the frequency with which prime ministers have exercised their right to call elections before the full three year parliamentary term has expired.[2]

The rarity of true ID campaigns—the ALP's in 1972 and Liberals' in 1984—underlines the regularity with which advertising has been presented in a three-phase strategy of positive ("explain") negative ("attack") and visionary ("feel good") advertisements. It should be noted, however, that recent campaigns have seen the start of an ebb in these trends. Both parties, and particularly the ALP, have placed growing emphasis on the personality of the leaders themselves. This is especially true in the case of the current prime minister, Bob Hawke, the stamp of whose forceful character and personal commitment to consensus-style government is on every party advertisement.

Public Ambivalence

Political advertisers have also been constrained by a prevailing public ambivalence, even cynicism, about their role in the electoral process. This attitude takes several forms: dismay about what is perceived as an ugly Americanism; fear about the costs of advertising; and doubts about the morality of advertising. Advertising columnist R. R. Walker observed, for example, "Does political advertising really work? . . . Given the increasing presidential style of our elections, maybe some ceiling on exposure and expenditure should be set before the American-style media madness engulfs us all" (*The Age,* 1984b). Similarly, an editorialist in *The Age* commented with relief, "In Australia we have not, fortunately, arrived at the position which applies in America where only millionares or their protégés can afford to win nomination and election as President" (*The Age,* 1984a).

Within the parties themselves, similar strains of ambivalence can be found. The Liberal party recently completed a survey which expressed doubts about the effectiveness of its "blitzkreig" advertising performance over recent campaigns (Grattan, 1984). In the Labor party, repugnance at the size of the party's advertising budget is allied to a long-standing fear of being outspent by the traditionally wealthier Liberal party. After the "wealth tax" ad, one senior ALP figure said what the party needed was "a couple of vicious and utterly cynical ad men to do to the Liberals what they do to us" (Goot, 1983). For the left of the ALP, mistrust of the power of advertising springs in part from its mistrust of the power of mass media overall. For many years, one plank of the ALP's platform was the establishment of a party-owned newspaper to sidestep the perceived pro-Liberal bias of the newspaper chains.

Perhaps this is changing since the 1984 campaign was the first under which parties received public funding for their campaigning. Both parties reported that some individual and institutional donors had shied off because of the disclosure provisions. And though neither party has at the time of writing released details of its spending, it seems 1984 was not the most expensive campaign on record.

On the basis of their 1983 votes, the ALP expected to receive $A 3.7 million and the Liberals $A 2.3 million for the 1984 campaign. In 1983, by comparison, the traditionally bigger-spending Liberals spent about $A 4 million—more than they had budgeted for due to a very expensive final week when Malcolm Fraser, staring defeat in the face, ordered up a massive last-gasp advertising effort. The ALP spent about half that amount (Hughes, 1983).

According to Eggleton, over 60 percent of his 1984 total campaign budget was devoted to TV advertising with further spending for radio and newspaper ads. It is possible that the new funding rules, with their elaborate disclosure provisions to monitor how the parties dispose of taxpayers funds, will reduce some of the public's and the ALP's ambivalence about TV advertising.[3]

Regulation and Political Advertising

The history of Australian legislation on political advertising is a journey influenced by two powerful but conflicting ideals, which have swayed the legislators' path as television has steadily become more powerful. One of these ideals is electoral freedom: the principle that candidates and political parties should be entitled to the maximum freedom in presenting their campaign claim with only the voter as judge and regulator of the contest. The other ideal is electoral fairness: the belief that rules created by parliament are necessary to protect and enhance the contest by limiting the potential for unfair advantage gained by abuse of power and money. If the first implies a free market of political philosophies and policies, the second implies a mixed market, subject to selective government intervention.

This section gives four illustrations of the state of play in the conflict between these ideals. It is clear from them that many Australians accept a degree of parliamentary and judicial regulation of political advertising—

in pursuit of the goal of electoral fairness—which would be unacceptable and probably unachievable in a First Amendment society such as the United States. In each case, Parliament acted after the event to correct a specific perceived abuse. In the process, the regulations may have curtailed the privileges of media or political organizations. But by and large they have been defended, and largely accepted, as valid exercises of government action to defend, not to encroach on, the public interest. However, it is also clear that the ad hoc and reactive way in which these regulations have been formulated has raised practical and philosophical problems which may lead—and in the first illustration, have already led—to a retraction of "fairness" regulation in favor of the ideal of electoral freedom.

Political Advertising In The Courts

In late 1980, the then prime minister, Malcolm Fraser, sent the nation to the polls. It was a gamble for Fraser, who hoped he could win a new mandate to cope with expected tough economic times ahead, and who calculated he could beat the then opposition leader, Bill Hayden. But almost immediately after the election campaign began, public opinion polls showed Hayden and the Labor party leading the government by an astounding sixteen points.

The unexpected surge to Labor put the carefully planned Liberal party advertising campaign in disarray (Rawlinson, 1983). The Liberals had planned two major commercials exploiting Labor's expected vulnerability on its spending proposals and a series of cheap, flexible ten second spots highlighting the prime minister to build on the contrasts between the two leaders. As these failed to reverse Labor's dominance in the polls, the Liberals turned in some desperation during the final week of the campaign to a new ad strategy.

A new, controversial set of spots was broadcast and published. Known as the "wealth tax" ads, they were as tough and as negative as any ads in Australian electoral history. They may have helped reverse the Labor tide and win the elections for Malcolm Fraser, but they also sparked a bitter dispute about electoral honesty: a microcosm of the freedom versus fairness debate.

One of the wealth tax ads stated:

> Labor calls it the "wealth tax," but it would really attack the unwealthy.

> Labor's so-called "wealth tax" would hit hundreds of thousands of Australian families who own modest homes which have risen in value.
>
> Under Labor's 20 percent inflation, they would become a target for Labor's "wealth tax."
>
> Labor's new taxes!
>
> Where else would they get the money for all their promises?
>
> Lead on Liberal. (Goot, 1983, p. 190).

Labor's actual policy on tax reform was quite different, and far less inflammatory, as party officials said loudly at the time and ever since.

But the vivid advertisements—the fear-inspiring words superimposed on the warm and familiar images of the "threatened" suburban homes—had already gone to air in electorally sensitive "swing" suburban seats in Melbourne and Sydney. It is difficult to determine just how many votes in these seats were changed by the last-minute Liberal ads. But the Federal Director of the Liberal party, Tony Eggleton, said later, "That was the only campaign where I could say with any certainty that it (advertising) made a real difference. Labor's wealth tax probably moved us back from the edge in the last few days of that campaign and we only got that through a concentrated campaign of television advertising" (Byrnes, 1984, p. 22).

In the bitter postelection period, both Labor party and Democrat officials decided to appeal the outcome in a High Court case, by testing an obscure provision of the Commonwealth Electoral Act of 1918. The basis of their suit was Section 161(e) of the Act which made it an offense to publish material containing "any untrue or incorrect statement intended or likely to mislead ot improperly interfere with any elector in, or in relation to, the casting of his vote." The case posed fundamental questions about the nature of advertising, as well as powers of the Court. Could section 161(e), dating to the first decades of the nation's history, relate to political advertising? Could it relate to broadcast material? Should the Court attempt to decide how many votes had been affected? Could it overturn the election result on the basis of misleading ads?

In the event, the Court chose a much more narrow interpretation of Section 161(e). The judges said Parliament had intended only to prevent misinformation about the process of casting votes (such as how-to-vote directions which would render the vote invalid, or wrong information about the hours and places of polling). The Court said the section was not aimed at limiting the ways candidates could influence voters in choosing whom to support (In Re Commonwealth, 1981). The wider implications of the case remained latent.

A License To Lie?

Three years later, after Labor's Bob Hawke had replaced Malcolm Fraser as prime minister in the March 1983 Federal Elections, Parliament began a sweeping renovation of the Electoral Act. A Joint Select Committee (i.e., multipartisan and bicameral) on electoral reform was set up under the chairmanship of Labor M.P. Dr. Dick Klugman.[4]

Political advertising was not one of the specific terms of references of the Klugman Committee, which was preoccupied instead with the larger problems of creating Australia's first Federal system of public funding of elections. In the massive legislative revision this entailed, only one submission to the committee directly addressed Section 161(e)—and that urged the strengthening of the section to clear up the loophole left in the Evans case (Lindell, 1983).

The submission did warn that a "good deal of thought" would be necessary to resolve both the philosophical and practical problems of widening the scope of the section. But it seems neither the submission nor the committee gave excessive consideration to the implications of the suggestion. With the memory of the High Court decision still fresh, the Committee voted to make a new, tougher section.

Under its recommendation, it would be an offense during an election campaign to "print, publish or distribute, or cause to be printed, published or distributed, any electoral advertisement containing a statement (a) that is untrue; and (b) that is, or is likely to be, misleading or deceptive."[5]

Parliament accepted the recommendation, and so Australia became the only democracy to make an offense of deceptive election advertising. The new ban explicitly applied to "any" electoral advertisement, printed or broadcast. The penalties for breeches were one thousand dollars for individuals and five thousand dollars for bodies corporate. To enforce the ban, candidates or the Australian Electoral Commission could seek an injunction, including an interim injunction, to prevent any allegedly untrue advertising. The controversy that followed was a classic summary of the tensions inherent in the dual Australian commitment to electoral freedom and electoral fairness. To many, the ban prevented politicians from giving themselves a "license to lie" (Macklin, 1984). The new ban on dishonesty seemed to its supporters a sensible way of protecting the body politic from electronically airborne infectious diseases.

As the then Attorney-General, Senator Gareth Evans, said in a submission to the Klugman Committee urging the new ban be modified but retained: "Such is the power and reach of the mass media that a false statement in an advertisement may do irreparable damage to the electoral prospects of the candidate or party affected before any correction or denial can be issued" (Evans, 1984).

For defenders of the new law, the classic statement of the need for rules to create electoral fairness was contained in the words of Chief Justice of the High Court, Sir Isaac Isaacs: "The vote of every elector is a matter of concern to the Commonwealth, and all are interested in endeavoring to secure . . . that the voter shall not be led by misrepresentation or concealment of any material circumstance into forming and consequently registering a political judgement different from that which he would have formed and registered had he know the real circumstances" (Smith v. Oldham, 1912).

Supporters of the new section could point to their legislation which already prohibited false advertising: the Trade Practices Act 1974. If politicians were willing to regulate the product claims of other members of society, their argument ran, they should apply the same restraint to themselves.

If "caveat emptor" is insufficient protection, then so surely is "let the voter beware." But as the Klugman Committee found when it met again in early 1984 to consider amending its new amendment, there is a complex mixture of practical and philosophical objections.

It is clear, for instance, the Committee had underestimated the difficulties raised by the creating injunctive relief. As it now stood, injunctions could be sought by any publicity-seeking minor candidate, possibly disrupting the entire election campaign. But this posed the dilemma: if the law was to be enforceable, genuine complainants needed access to the courts during, and not after, the election campaign (Fleming, 1984).

The new ban also posed severe compliance problems. Some party officials were alarmed at the legal costs and delays they faced in ensuring their ads were not untrue. Media organizations, who were also caught in the wide ambit of the new section, were upset at the risks they now faced and the costs involved in ensuring they did not unwittingly run misleading advertisement.[6]

These problems of implementation were symptoms of the basic, philosophical problem. How would the courts, lawyers, party officials, editors, and so on decide just what was "true" in a political context? As one Labor backbench senator put it with only a little hyperbole, "This is (one) of the basic philosophical questions that hundreds of philosophers in universities for hundreds of years have tried to tackle" (Ray, 1984).

Essentially, the Klugman Committee found itself deciding the difference between opinions, predictions, and statements of fact. Many Labor M.P.s wanted to prevent a repetition of the wealth tax ads. But which of the following would be banned under the Act: "ALP policy is to introduce a wealth tax"? "Many people believe the ALP will introduce a wealth tax"? "The ALP intends to introduce a wealth tax"?

The then Attorney-General's submission was that the law be modified to apply only to statements of fact (such as "The ALP policy contains a commitment to a wealth tax" or "Mr. X has said his party will") and not to predictions, judgments, or arguments. The Attorney argued, "In my view, the general objective of fairness in elections provides the justification for a provision which imposes the obligation of accuracy—or at least an obligation to avoid untrue and misleading or deceptive statements—upon those engaged in political advertising" (Evans, 1984, p. 2).

In it conclusions, the Klugman Committee rejected that proposal. "In its present broad scope the section is unworkable and any amendments to it would be either ineffective, or would reduce its scope to such an extent that it would not prevent dishonest advertising." The Committee stated that as desirable as fair advertising might be, "it is not possible to achieve . . . by legislation."

As for the parallel with Trade Practices legislation, it asserted political advertising differs from other advertising in that it promotes "intangibles, ideas, policies, and images." Or as Professor Henry Mayer, Professor of Political Theory at the University of Sydney told the committee: "Political advertising by its very nature in a party system must knock the other side. But, unlike most other comparative advertising, it deals only to a limited extent with hard data. In politics, it is not possible to find out 'the truth' about what will work as a policy" (Mayer, 1984).

The Committee's conclusion was a classic summary of the case for unregulated electoral freedom rather than regulated fairness: "The safest course, which the committee recommends, is to repeal the section effectively leaving the decision as to whether political advertising is true or false to the electors and to the law of defamation."

Was this a victory for the free market place of political ideas—or simply a recognition that regulation, however desirable, was simply impossible in this case? Whether there is a parliamentary trend away from regulation can be tested in the future by its action on two bellwether examples of electoral regulation: the ban on dramatizations and the electoral "blackout."

Dramatization: Real-life Advertising?

John Henry Austral was a 'man-in-the-street' character in a series of radio broadcasts in the 1940s. The original purpose of this fictitious, eponymous, national character was to provide a new form of commentary about the then Labor government. But Mr. Austral has a second role, for contemporary observers of Australian political advertising, because he plays an important part in the continuing balancing act between electoral freedom and fairness.

Austral was the invention of advertising staff of the Liberal party, then recently formed and still in opposition. Wanting to communicate with voters in a novel way, the party hit upon sponsoring radio plays. Actors were hired to mimic the voices of Labor party leaders, while Austral was presented as an informed commentator in what became a series of dramatizations of current political events. Much of the series was devoted to alleging and dramatizing links between Labor and international communism.

The Austral series ran for eighteen months before the 1949 elections, to large nationwide audiences. When the votes were in, the Liberals had won and began an unbroken twenty-three years in office. It's impossible, again, to gauge the real impact of the Austral broadcasts on the voter of the time. But it is clear they broke new ground and posed early questions about the role of broadcasting in the electoral process.

The response to these questions was a typically Australian one: regulation. Amendments were passed to the Broadcasting and Television Act which outlawed "the dramatization of any political matter which is then current or was current at any time during the last 5 preceding years."

Despite the fluidity of its language—officials are not sure exactly what constitutes a "dramatization"—this section remains in force. Producers planning a television play about the "sacking" of the Whitlam Government in 1975—the most important event of recent Australian political history—had to wait until the early 1980s before going ahead.

The Klugman Committee heard evidence from the Liberal party that the ban on dramatizations should be repealed as an unwarranted interference with the public's right to information and views. But the

Labor party urged the retention of the ban to prevent dramatizations which were "politically unfair." In its report, the Committee noted that no one had suggested the compromise of restricting the ban to the election period so it would apply only to advertising. However, the Committee was prepared to go one step further and concluded, "there is no justification for retaining the ban on dramatization, even for political advertising." Parliament has yet to act on this recommendation.

The Election "Blackout": Becoming a Grayout?

One of the most characteristically Australian electoral institutions is the "blackout." Until 1983, electronic broadcasters were prevented from putting to air any election-related material—news or advertising—from the Wednesday midnight of the last week of the campaign to the close of polling on Saturday. The blackout did not apply to advertising or newsreporting by newspapers.

This blackout was intended to prevent any candidate from obtaining an unfair advantage by broadcasting an unanswerable smear or allegation in the final days of the campaign. As candidates came to rely more and more on TV for their campaigns the blackout meant the electioneering ground to a halt two full days before the vote. In 1983, the newly elected Labor government moved to change the blackout to a kind of grayout. TV and radio election news reports and commentaries were exempted from the ban, but advertising was not.

Both the blackout and the ban on dramatizations date from the early post-World War II days of electronic broadcasting, when both audiences and broadcasters were less sophisticated and less adept at the new technology. Perhaps the steps towards removing those bans reflect a growing confidence in the ability of the electorate and politicians to handle their electronic responsibilities without regulation. But perhaps, too, the apparent reluctance to go the whole way reflects a lingering and deepseated unease about the risks of unfairness in an electronic election.

Certainly, the extent and nature of parliamentary and judicial supervision of the public debate would surprise many Americans accustomed to the absolute freedom of speech and of the press granted by the First Amendment. There is no similar constitutional or statutory guarantee in Australia. In its place has risen a thicket of libel and defamation laws which has operated, at the margin, to restrict some criticisms and to protect some reputations (Pullan, 1984).

As political journalists, we do not believe this tradition of limited regulation has prevented the creation of a robust political debate and a robustly independent media. But it remains true that many Australians, probably most, accept that free and fair political contests are best achieved through, rather than despite, government intervention in the market place of political ideas.

Free Time

One of the reasons political advertisements succeed is that they are short, crisp messages which can go straight to the heart of the matter—and straight to the heart of the voter. Critics are disillusioned by this brevity and emotionalism. They see political spots as incapable of seriously presenting complex, political issues, emphasizing instead the politician's personality, which may be irrelevant to his/her ability to solve political problems. In their bid to ensure politics does not die from terminal trivialization, some critics have suggested that paid advertisements be abolished. In their place, they suggest borrowing the idea of free time rules.

Australia has for many years had just such a system of free time. Political parties are allocated blocks of free air time on the national broadcaster, the ABC, during election campaigns to communicate their policies. The amount of time they receive is determined by the number of votes they received at the previous election. In 1980, for instance, the Liberals and the ALP received 135 minutes of free time each and the Australian Democrats 30 minutes (Goot, 1983).

Leaders of the major parties also have their policy speeches broadcast live on the ABC and the commercial networks. This springs from Section 116(3) of the Broadcasting and Television Act which requires commercial broadcasters to "afford reasonable opportunities for the broadcasting . . . of election matters to all political parties."

The Klugman Committee is currently considering whether to expand or alter the free time provisions, though the system works smoothly enough. However, we suggest that free time advocates look closely at the Australian experience before attributing enormous virtues to it. For the lesson is that free time rules do not automatically lead to a more "serious" political debate nor are they immune from ordinary political pressures to simplify and emotionalize. Indeed, Australian free time broadcasts are at times indistinguishable from paid spots. The 1984 campaign provided the clearest illustration yet of this trend.

Both parties used large slabs of their paid TV time within their free time appearances. The Liberals, for example, taped talks by Andrew Peacock in which parts of the "slice" ads were incorporated. When he spoke about the assets test, the shot was cut away to the scene of the elderly woman receiving her letter about the assets test. The Labor party did much the same, with talks by Hawke interspersed with ad footage and jingles. As prime minister, Hawke, of course, had the advantages of incumbency, but for these spots party officials decided not to tape the talks from the prime ministerial offices in Parliament House as they looked "too ordinary." Instead, a prime ministerial "set" was constructed.

The overlap between ads and free time was enhanced this year because of a rule change which applied for the first time. Both major parties had separately petitioned the ABC to reduce the minimum time slot for the free time from five minutes to two. Officials of both parties sought the change because the shorter slots would attract larger audiences and could be aired more frequently.

There do remain, however, some cases where the free time allows parties to put out messages they lack the resources, time, or inclination to hit in paid TV. The last weeks of the 1984 campaign for instance saw a sudden surge of support for the newly formed Nuclear Disarmament party (NDP), largely in protest at government policies. Free time offered the government the opportunity to respond to the NDP without altering its overall advertising strategy.

This trend toward overlap between free and paid TV time can be strongly discerned in the fate of the telecast policy speech. The policy speech is one of the abiding institutions of the Australian election campaign. Since the dawn of time, almost, leaders have addressed an audience of party faithful to outline their principal promises and plans. The arrival of radio and TV may have enlarged the audience, but surprisingly few modifications were made to format until recently. As late as Malcolm Fraser's last campaign in 1983, the TV audience had to peer over the shoulders of the live crowd to hear the prime minister.

The Labor campaign in 1980 marked one departure from this format: when Bill Hayden delivered his speech one night and had it broadcast the following night to allow time to correct any delivery flaws and to maximize coverage.

But the 1983 speech by Hawke was so different it may have done away with the old policy speech forever. Delivered at the Sydney Opera House to a lunchtime crowd of selected party faithful, the speech was edited for telecast that night. During the rest of the campaign, excerpts of the speech reappeared as the party's paid ads. The whole strategy showed a tight coordination of the paid and unpaid messages to increase voter recognition of Hawke's personality and promises.

The format was repeated in 1984: a silver-gray prime minister on the silver-gray stage set at the Opera House (good colors for TV and handsomely offset Labor party logos since 1980). The sixty-five minute speech was cut down to thirty minutes for free broadcasts that night; subtitles were added to emphasize the key points; frequent cut away shots showed the applauding audience.

The Liberals copied the idea for 1984 and even elaborated on it. Instead of a single policy speech launch in the evening they developed a "launch day." Early morning radio appearances by Peacock were followed by a 9 a.m. media release of a "Future Directions" manifesto, a lunchtime rally in downtown Melbourne at which Peacock spoke and then, in the evening, the broadcast of a pretaped thirty minute Peacock chat to the viewers. Eggleton explained: "Instead of . . . forcing the TV viewer to feel an outsider (as in the old-style rallies) we paid them the courtesy of doing it specially for them."

Both parties have thus moved away from using their policy speech free time for a simple broadcast of an event. Instead, the event has been substantially adapted to make it better TV. At the same time, the free time messages have been brought under the umbrella of, and made to reassemble, the party's total paid media message.

Conclusion

Electoral advertising in Australia shares many of the characteristics of paid political TV in the U.S. At the same time, Australian political strategies have produced a genre of TV spots which is a distinct species, a product identifiably their own.

Diamond and Bates nominate four basic types of election advertising: spots at the beginning of the campaign which identify the candidate; spots which argue; spots which attack; and spots which at the end of a campaign conjure up the candidate's vision of the nation (Diamond & Bates, 1984). In Australian ads, we can discern elements of each of these types. But looking at our ads through the eyes of Diamond and Bates is like looking at an object through a kaleidoscope: all the pieces are there, but they have been rearranged into new combinations.

Specifically, we find Australian ads deal less with identification and more with arguing and attacking. Visionary ads do not occur as the quiet finale to a campaign but increasingly provide a theme for the entire strategy.

Much of this is to be expected in a parliamentary context. Rivals for the prime ministership rarely need to be introduced to an electorate already familiar with them as party leaders. Instead, the issue content of argumentation and attack advertising reflects the wider political debate between parties which formulate politics in frequent, sharp, and specific contrast. And with four week election campaigns, it should be no surprise that different functions of advertising are not run as separate phases of a strategy, as happens in the U.S., but are bound up in intense, multipurpose ad messages.

Grafting advertising onto a parliamentary system in this way has caused controversy and resentment, as the wealth tax ad showed. Beyond this, advertising in Australia has also proved its potential to leap outside the existing bounds of parliamentary politics-as-usual. The successful visionary campaigns have redefined, or recreated, politics on a new level. The "It's Time" vision, or the vision of national reconciliation articulated by Hawke in 1983, were not mere sugary confections at the end of a campaign dealing with other issues; they magnified and indeed they were the issues. When political commentators worry about Australian politics becoming more "presidential," they could draw more ammunition from this development.

This analysis supports our broad theme. There is a struggle between political advertising and Australian political institutions and attitudes. This struggle has produced regulation aimed at enhancing electoral fairness by restricting the freedom with which political advertisers can communicate with voters. However, the recent failed attempt to outlaw untrue advertisements may herald a move away from regulation. Where Parliament has sought to enhance fairness with free time rules, political advertisers have managed to say pretty much what they wanted to say regardless of regulation.

The recent regulation covering public funding of elections, and the related opening up of party campaign records, may in time reduce public cynicism about advertising. For the time being, however, the typical response to this continuing struggle has been either to scorn advertising strategies as a dangerous Americanism or to dismiss them as ugly accretions to a political system with which they are basically incompatible. Neither fear nor complacency are appropriate, we believe. Neither answers adequately the ultimate question in any proper assessment of advertising: does it work?

As in other countries, there is no definitive proof about the ability of advertising to swing votes. Even the one ad series considered by politicians and other insiders to have been most powerful—the wealth tax ad—was discounted in a recent study investigating links between voting behavior and advertising time buying.

Perhaps, however, the search for hard proof about the impact of advertising is a futile one. What is probably more important is the fact that they are believed to be necessary by most political strategists. Advertising has acquired perceived success among these operators, whether for agenda-setting or leading attacks. This belief in the need for advertising has locked both parties into an escalating competition. Neither side is prepared to risk doing without. At this metacampaign level, being seen to advertise is perhaps as important as the content of advertising. If this observation is true, advertising will continue to play a dominant role in Australian election campaigns.

Notes

References

Notes

4. Corporate Advocacy Advertising as Political Communication

1. The term "corporate advocacy" was selected because it has been applied previously to the phenomenon of corporate America's participation in the public market place of ideas (Heath, 1980; Crable & Vibbert, 1983). This paper does not attempt to draw a distiction between advocacy efforts by an individual "corporation," and advocacy efforts by an industry.

2. The newspaper advertisements examined in this study were placed by the industry during the time period from the accident itself to the national elections in November of 1980.

3. Several scholars have maintained that the ability to define a situation or event helps give one symbolic control (Gregg, 1971; Hall, 1982; p. 87; Bosmajian, 1974; Bachrach & Baratz, 1962; Bachrach & Baratz, 1963; Lukes, 1981).

4. The Committee for Energy Awareness was founded "immediately after" Three Mile Island (Burnham, 1979c, p. B11), "as part of the industry's new effort to combat bad publicity" ("Nuclear Industry versus Amory Lovins," 1980, p. 573). The C.E.A. was part of the Edison Electric Institute which is a trade association of utility companies. The C.E.A.'s main job was to "provide a focused industry response" to Three Mile Island, which "was acknowledged as a major setback to nuclear energy" (Burnham, 1979c, p. B11).

5. Other examples of ads using this same theme include ConEdison's full-page ad in the *New York Times* on 6 August 1979, which began with the headline, "OPEC has raised your electric bill again. Are you ready to fight back?" (p. A18); and the July 26 advertisement from "the stockholders of New York State's investor-owned electric utilities," which offered atomic power as "A Way to help Free New York State From OPEC" (p. A20). "America's Rural Electric Systems" placed two ads of this type. The first opened with the unhappy prospect, "If you like the gasoline shortages of the 70s, you'll love the electrical power shortages of the 80s and 90s" (1979, p. E19); and the second with the warning, "You can't stockpile kilowatts for lean years" (1979, p. E21). Also

included in this type of appeal would be the Edison Electric Institute's "Open letter to President Carter" printed in the *Washington Post* (1979, p. E8).

6. The Kemeny Commission did conclude that even in the event of a core meltdown, there was a high probability that the containment building "would have been able to prevent the escape of a large amount of radioactivity." However, the Commission went on to say that that conclusion "approach[ed] the limits of our engineering knowledge of the interactions of molten fuel, concrete, steel and water, and even the best available calculations have a degree of uncertainty associated with them. The Commission stated further that "these results . . . hold only insofar as our assumptions are valid. We cannot be absolutely certain of these results" (Lanouette, 1980, p. 26).

7. There were other industry advertisements that attempted to assert the industry's definitional hegemony over the safety issue. These included the ad placed by the Edison Electric Institute which proclaimed that "The safety of nuclear power plants is our top priority too" (1979, p. A32). In addition, there were industry ads that addressed directly the public's concern with radiation. These included an ad by the Committee for Energy Awareness which bore the heading "We get more radiation in our living rooms than from nuclear power plants" (1980, p. B7); and one by Commonwealth Edison entitled "Radiation and the Future of Kimberly Michelle Mayberry" (1980, p. 8).

5. THE TELEVISED POLITICAL SPOT ADVERTISEMENT: ITS STRUCTURE, CONTENT, AND ROLE ON THE POLITICAL SYSTEM

1. The eight image categories described by the Delphi Panel were as follows:

Altruism: including references to candidates'concern with the needs of others, moral purpose, selflessness, benevolence, generosity, or lack of same.

Competence: referring to candidates' abilities, skills, knowledge, efficiency, or lack of same.

Experience: including references to candidates' background, past record, accomplishments, roles, jobs, activities, or lack of same.

Honesty: including candidates' dignity, veracity, sincerity, uprightness, candor, frankness, or lack of same.

Leadership: including references to candidates' superintendance, chieftainship, stewardship, guidance, direction, forward-looking tendencies, readiness, or lack of same.

Personal characteristics: including references to candidates' individual personality traits, adaptableness, tenderness, humor, sagacity, constancy, faith, humanity, cheerfulness, or lack of same.

Strength: including reference to candidates' rigor, robustness, vitality, will, resoluteness, sustenance, firmness, resilience, or lack of same.

Other special qualities: including references to candidates' "charisma," "niceness," "newness," or lack of same.

The nine issue categories described by the Delphi Panel were as follows:

Carter's Record as President: including references to the blunders, failures, and errors of the incumbent, or lack of same.
Domestic: including references to national welfare, social programs, education, crime and violence, civil rights, industry and nongovernmental institutions, or lack of same.
Economy: including references to economic growth, recession, standard of living, business and finance, costs, prices, the work force, earning and buying potentials, or lack of same.
Energy: including references to alternative energy sources, the work of running machines, heating homes, the impact of the energy policy on ecology, or lack of same.
Federalism: including the status and value of governmental agencies, bureaucracy, and their contribution to the running of government, or lack of same.
Foreign Policy—Foreign Relations: including references to international relationships, agreements, resolutions, negotiations among nations, foreign trade, international troublespots, institutions, or lack of same.
Government Management: including references to financial programs of government, policies of taxation, budget, fiscal policy, the financial status of government, or lack of same.
National Security—Military Strength: including references to military aggression, international enemies, maintenance of safe margins of weapons, protection against threats to physical survival, maintenance of peace, avoidance of war, or lack of same.
National Well-being: including the vision of the American Dream and continuance and growth of the nation, or lack of same.

The operational definitions of variables comprising the construct of methods of presentation were as follows:

Voice of Announcer: This variable was defined as the time in seconds in each commercial devoted to speech by a professional narrator.
Voice of Candidate: as above, time devoted to speech by any current candidate.
Voice of Citizens: time devoted to speech by plain folks, voters.
Voice of Famous Persons: time in seconds devoted to speech by noncandidate public officials, actors, candidate family members, and other media personalities.

Music: time in seconds devoted to the presence of instrumental music (including drumming) or singing.

Crowd Sounds: time in seconds devoted to the presence of cheers, applause, chants, and whistles as part of the audio track.

Talking Candidate Visuals: time devoted to visuals of speech by candidate.

Talking Citizen Visuals: time devoted to visuals of speech by citizens.

Talking Famous Person: same as above, except coding was done for famous persons.

Neutral Camera Angle: time in seconds in each commercial devoted to live action visuals featuring objects shot with a camera that appeared to be level with the featured object's height.

Nonneutral Camera Angles: as above, but done for visuals featuring objects shot with a camera that appeared to be above or below the featured object's height.

Direct Orientation of Candidate to Camera: time in seconds devoted to visuals of talking of candidates who appeared to look directly at the viewer.

Indirect Orientation of Candidate to Camera: time devoted to visuals of candidates who appeared not to look directly at the viewer.

Live Action Exterior Locale: time devoted to live action, outdoor locations.

Live Action Interior Locale: time devoted to live action, indoor locations.

Candidate Formal Dress: time in seconds in each commercial devoted to live action of candidates wearing suits with the jacket on and the tie tied.

Candidate Informal Dress: time in seconds in each commercial devoted to live action of candidates not wearing suits with the jacket on and tie tied.

Visual Transitions: defined as the total number of times for each commercial that cuts, wipes, and dissolves occurred.

Visual Still Pictures—Candidates: time devoted to motionless visuals of any candidate.

Visual Still Pictures—Noncandidates: time devoted to motionless visuals not containing any candidate.

Live Action Nontalking Noncandidates: defined as the time in seconds in each commercial devoted to noncandidate, motion visuals that did not contain any talking persons.

Live Action Nontalking Candidates: defined as the time in seconds in each commercial devoted to motion visuals of any current candidate not engaged in speech.

2. The preceding material is taken from personal correspondence with Professor Murray Edelman, Department of Political Science, University of Wisconsin, 5 December 1983.

6. Political Advertising and the Meaning of Elections

1. For a more extensive discussion of these four approaches, see Joslyn (1984), Chapter 9.

2. Advertisements may contain a reference to more than one personal attribute; in fact, most of them do. As Table 19 indicates, every attribute mentioned was coded for each ad.

8. Political Commercials and Candidate Image: The Effect Can Be Substantial

1. The author wishes to take this opportunity to express his sincere appreciation to Ms. Shannon Thompson. Without her unflagging help and insightful comments, this research effort would quite literally have been impossible.

2. In some of his post-1976 work, Patterson has moderated his views in a direction that appears to be more compatible with the preceding interpretation. He has, for instance, noted (1980) that the early establishment of a favorable image might be important from the perspective that, once formed, it tends to carry over into later stages of the campaign.

9. Candidate Image Formation: The Role of Information Processing

1. The author would like to thank Professor Robert Meadow of the Annenberg School of Communication—University of Southern California for providing the stimulus political commercials.

12. The Contagion from the Right: The Americanization of British Political Advertising

1. The authors would like to thank Gary Copeland for his help in structuring a computer program.

13. Political Advertising in Australia: A Dynamic Force Meets a Resilient Object

1. The authors wish to thank the following people for their generous assistance in providing information for this article: Mr. Tony Eggleton, Federal

Director of the Liberal party of Australia; Dr. Colin Hughes, head of the Australian Electoral Commission; Mr. Bob McMullan, National Secretary of the Australian Labor party; Mr. Peter Willis, private secretary to then Attorney-General of the Commonwealth of Australia, Senator the Hon. Gareth Evans, QC; and Mrs. Alexandra Zubrzycki and Mr. Simon Balderstone of *The Age* newspaper, Melbourne.

The article was written during and immediately after the 1984 Federal election campaign. At the time of writing, the future course of Klugman Committee recommendations and of Government responses to them cannot be predicted.

2. Seven elections have been held in the last twelve years: 1972 (won by Gough Whitlam, ALP), 1974 (Whitlam), 1975 (Malcolm Fraser, Liberal Party), 1977 (Fraser), 1980 (Fraser), 1983 (Bob Hawke, ALP), 1984 (Hawke).

3. Under Section XX of the revised Commonwealth Electoral Act, broadcasters, publishers, and printers are, after election campaigns, now required to furnish the Australian Electoral Commission with details of who placed election advertising and how much they were charged. When tabulated, these figures will provide valuable new data about advertising practices.

In addition to the legislation itself, a useful source of explanatory information about the new public funding system is available in the two-volume Election Funding and Financial Disclosure Handbook published by the Australian Electoral Commission (Canberra, 1984). It outlines the entitlements and obligations of political parties (Vol. 1) and broadcasters (Vol. 2).

4. First Report of the Joint Select Committee on Electoral Reform, Chapter 11, "Political Advertising and Broadcasting of Political Matter" September 1983, Parliament of the Commonwealth of Australia.

The Committee's second report, dealing with the retraction of the amendment, was printed in August 1984.

5. Under the new numbering of the Act, the former S116(e) became S329.

6. This and subsequent material about the Committee's work is drawn from its Second Report.

References

ABC Television Network News (1980, July 13). 7:00 p.m. E.S.T.

Abrams, M. (1961). Social class and British politics. *Public Opinion Quarterly, 25*, 342–51.

Abramson, P. R. (1978). Generational replacement and partisan dealignment in Britain and the United States. *British Journal of Political Science, 8*, 505–9.

Adams, W. C. (1978). Visual analysis of newscasts: Issues in social science research. In W. C. Adams & F. Schreibman (Eds.), *Television network news: Issues in content research.* Washington DC: Television and Politics Study Program at George Washington University.

The Age. (1984a, May 8).

The Age. (1984b, December 5).

Agranoff, R. (Ed.). (1976). *The new style in election campaigns* (2nd ed.). Boston: Holbrook Press.

Alexander, H. (1966). *Financing the 1964 election.* New Jersey: Citizen's Research Foundation.

Alexander, H. (1971). *Financing the 1968 election.* Lexington: D. C. Heath.

Alexander, H. (1976). *Financing the 1972 election.* Lexington: D. C. Heath.

Anderson, C. M. (1972). In search of a visual rhetoric for instructional television. *Audio Visual Communication Review. 20*, 43–63.

Anderson, J. E. (1975). *Public policy-making.* New York: Praeger.

Anderson, J. E., Brady, D. W., & Bullock, C. (1978). *Public policy and politics in America.* North Scituate, MA: Duxbury Press.

Anderson, N. H. (1968). Likeableness ratings of 555 personality trait words. *Journal of Personality and Social Psychology, 9*, 272–79.

Anderson at crossroads in his campaign for White House. (1980, April 6). *New York Times*, 6.

Arcelus, F., & Meltzer, A. (1975). The effects of aggregate economic variables on Congressional elections. *American Political Science Review, 69*, 1232–39.

Asher, H. (1980). *Presidential elections and American politics,* Homewood, IL: The Dorsey Press.

Atkin, C. K., Bowen, L., Nayman, O. B., & Sheinkopf, K. G. (1973). Quality versus quantity in televised political ads. *Public Opinion Quarterly, 37,* 209–24.

Atkin, C. K., & Heald, G. (1976). Effects of political advertising. *Public Opinion Quarterly, 40,* 216–28.

Atomic power's future. (1979, April 9). *Time,* p. 20.

Atwood, L. E., & Sanders, K. R. (1976). Information sources and voting in a primary and general election. *Journal of Broadcasting, 20,* 291–302.

Bachrach, P., & Baratz, M. S. (1962). Two faces of power. *American Political Science Review, 56,* 947–52.

Bachrach, P., & Baratz, M. S. (1963). Decisions and nondecisions: An analytical framework. *American Political Science Review, 57,* 632–42.

Bailey, D. (1977). Statement at the Speech Communication Association Convention, Washington DC (audio transcript).

Baker, P. M. (1977). On the uses of psychophysical methods in the study of social status: A replication and some theoretical problems. *Social Forces, 55,* 898–920.

Barber, J. D., (Ed.). (1978). *Race for the presidency: The media and the nominating process.* Englewood Cliffs, NJ: Prentice-Hall.

Barthes, R. (1977). *Image, music, text.* New York: Hill and Wang.

Baskin, O. (1976, April). *The effects of televised political advertisements on candidate image.* Paper presented at the International Communication Association Convention, Portland, OR.

Battlin, T. C. (1964). Directing. In R. L. Hilliard (Ed.), *Understanding television.* New York: Hastings House.

Beck, P. A. (1979). The electoral cycle and patterns of American politics. *British Journal of Political Science, 9,* 129–56.

Beik, L. (1962). Immediate recall of TV commercial elements. *Journal of Advertising Research, 2,* 13–18.

Bennett, W. L. (1975). Political scenarios and the nature of politics. *Philosophy and Rhetoric, 8,* 23–43.

Berelson, B., Lazarsfeld, P., & McPhee, W. (1954). *Voting.* Chicago: University of Chicago Press.

Berger, A. A. (1981). Semiotics and TV. In R. P. Adler (Ed.), *Understanding television.* New York: Praeger.

Berger, A. A. (1982). *Media analysis techniques.* Beverly Hills, CA: Sage.

Berger, A. A. (1984). *Signs in contemporary culture.* New York: Longman.

Berlo, D. K., Lemert, J. B., & Mertz, R. J. (1969–70). Dimensions for evaluating the acceptability of message sources. *Public Opinion Quarterly, 33*, 563–76.

Bernstein, R. (1977). Divisive primaries do hurt: U.S. Senate races, 1956–1972. *American Political Science Review, 71*, 540–45.

Birdwhistell, R. L. (1970). *Kinesics and context.* Philadelphia: University of Pennsylvania Press.

Bishop, G. F., Meadow, R. G., & Jackson-Beeck, M., (Eds.) (1980). *The presidential debates.* New York: Praeger.

Bitzer, L. (1981). Political rhetoric. In D. D. Nimmo & K. R. Sanders (Eds.), *Handbook of political communication.* Beverly Hills: Sage.

Blankenship, J., Fine, M. G., & Davis, L. K. (1983). The 1980 Republican primary debates: The transformation of actor to scene. *Quarterly Journal of Speech, 69*, 25–36.

Blumler, J. G. & McQuail, D. *Television in politics.* Chicago: University of Chicago Press, 1969.

Blumler, J. (1975). Mass media roles and reactions in the February election. In H. Penniman (Ed.), *Britain at the polls.* Washington DC: American Enterprise Institute for Public Policy research.

Boorstin, D. (1972). *The image: Or what happened to the American dream.* New York: Atheneum.

Borgida, E., & Nisbett, R. E. (1977). The differential impact of abstract vs. concrete information on decisions. *Journal of Applied Social Psychology, 7*, 258–71.

Bormann, E. G., Kroll, B. S., Watters, K., & McFarland, D. (1984). Rhetorical visions of committed voters: Fantasy theme analysis of a large sample survey. *Critical Studies in Mass Communication, 1*, 287–310.

Bosmajian, H. A. (1974). *The language of oppression.* Washington DC: Public Affairs Press.

Boulding, K. E. (1961). *The image.* Ann Arbor: University of Michigan Press.

Bowers, T. (1972). Issue and personality information in newspaper political advertising. *Journalism Quarterly, 49*, 446–52.

Breglio, V. (1983, October 12). Statement at the University of Rhode Island (printed transcript).

Brown, S. R. (1980). *Political subjectivity: Applications of Q-methodology in political science.* New Haven: Yale University.

Brownstein, C. N. (1971). Communication strategies and the electoral decision making process: Some results from experimentation. *Experimental Study of Politics*, 37–50.

Bukro, C. (1979a, June 5). Nuclear power Vietnamized. *Chicago Tribune,* 6.

Bukro, C. (1979b, June 6). U.S. split on nuclear power use, pollster says. *Chicago Tribune,* 3.

Bullock, C. S., Anderson, J. E., & Brady, D. W. (1983). *Public policy in the eighties.* Monterey: Brooks/Cole Publishing.

Burgoon, J. (1980). Nonverbal communication research in the 1970s: An overview. In D. Nimmo (Ed.), *Communication Yearbook IV.* New Brunswick, NJ: Transaction Press.

Burgoon, M. (1974). *Approaching speech communication.* New York: Hall, Rinehart, and Winston.

Burnham, D. (1979a, March 30). Nuclear accident is laid to failure of several systems at plant. *New York Times,* A1.

Burnham, D. (1979b, September 23). Three Mile Island accident: A cloud over atomic power. *New York Times,* A1, A48.

Burnham, D. (1979c, December 26). Pronuclear groups seek citizen action. *New York Times,* A1, B11.

Burnham, D. (1980, March 16). Inactive reactors: One year's toll of Three Mile Island. *New York Times,* F1, F9.

Burnham, D. (1983, October 27). What you see is probably what you're going to get. *Providence Evening Bulletin,* A6.

Burnham, W. D. (1965). The changing shape of the American political universe. *American Political Science Review, 59,* 7–28.

Burns, K. L. & Beier, E. G. (1973). Significance of vocal and visual channels in the decoding of emotional meaning. *Journal of Communication, 23,* 118–30.

Buss, T. F., & Hofstetter, C. F. (1976). An analysis of the logic of televised campaign advertisements. *Communication Research, 3,* 367–92.

Butler, D. (1983, May 14). How TV could tip the balance? *The Times.*

Butler, D., & King, A. (Eds.)(1965). *The British general election of 1964.* London: MacMillan.

Butler, D., & Rose, R. (1960). *The British general election of 1959.* London: MacMillan.

Butler, D., & Waller, R. (1983). Labour and Alliance have mountains to scale. In the *Times* Staff (Eds.), *The Times Guide to the House of Commons* Bury St. Edmunds, Suffolk England: St. Edmunds Press.

Byrnes, P. (1984, November 10). Memories, scores and that nice warm feeling. *Sydney Morning Herald Magazine,* 18–22.

Campbell, A. (1966). Surge and decline: A study of electoral change. In A. Campbell, P. Converse, W. E. Miller, & D. E. Stokes (Eds.), *Elections and the political order.* New York: John Wiley.

Campbell, A., Converse, P., Miller, W. E., & Stokes, D. E. (1960). *The American voter.* New York: John Wiley.

Canberra (1984). *Election funding and financial disclosure handbook,* Vols. I & II. Sydney: Australian Electoral Commission.

Cantor, N. (1981). A cognitive-social approach to personality. In N. Cantor & J. F. Kihlstrom (Eds.), *Personality, cognition, and social interaction.* Hillsdale, NJ: Lawrence Earlbaum Associates.

Cantor, N., & Mischel, W. (1977). Traits as prototypes: Effects on recognition memory. *Journal of Personality and Social Psychology, 35,* 38–48.

Carpenter, F. B. (1867). *Six Months at the White House with Abraham Lincoln.* New York: Hurd and Houghton.

Cawelti, J. G. (1965). *Apostles of the self-made man.* Chicago: University of Chicago Press.

Chafee, S. H. (1980). Time of decision and media use during the Ford-Carter campaign. *Public Opinion Quarterly, 44,* 53–69.

Chagall, D. (1981). *The new kingmakers.* New York: Harcourt, Brace, Jovanovich.

Chambers, W. N. (1963). *Political parties in a new nation.* New York: Oxford.

A choice not an echo. (1979, April 23). *Time,* 42.

Clines, F. X. (1980, April 11). About politics: Three Mile Island and the 1980 campaign. *New York Times,* D14.

Clymer, A. (1979, April 12). Nuclear plant toll. *New York Times,* A23.

Cohen, C. E., & Ebbesen E. B. (1979). Observational goals and schema activation: A theoretical framework for behavioral perception. *Journal of Experimental Social Psychology,* 1979, *15,* 305–29.

Coleman, R., & Rainwater, L. (1978). *Social Standing.* New York: Basic Books.

Collins, H. (1979). *Threads of history.* Washington, DC: Smithsonian.

Columbian Centinel (1800, October 11).

Combs, J. E. (1979). Political advertising as a popular mythmaking form. *Journal of American Culture, 2,* 331–40.

Comstock, G., Chaffee, S., Katzman, N., McCombs, M., & Roberts, D. (1978) *Television and human behavior.* New York: Columbia University Press.

Consigny, S. (1974). Rhetoric and its situations. *Philosophy and rhetoric, 7,* 175–86.

Converse, P. E., Miller, W. E., Rusk, J. G., & Wolfe, A. C. (1969, December). Continuity and change in American politics: parties and issues in the 1968 Election. *American Political Science Review, 63,* 1083–1105.

Cook, S. (1983, May 24). Tory ad rejected by West-Indian newspaper. *The Daily Telegraph.*

Cook, T. D., & Campbell, D. T. (1979). *Quasi-experimentation: Design and analysis issues for field settings.* Evanston, IL: Northwestern University Press.

Cousins, N. (1979, September 29). Q & A that raises more Q's than A's. *Saturday Review,* 10.

Cover, A. (1977). One good term deserves another: The advantage of incumbency in Congressional elections. *American Journal of Political Science, 3,* 523–41.

Cover, A., & Brumberg, B. (1982). Baby books and ballots: The impact of Congressional mail on constituent opinion. *American Political Science Review, 76,* 347–56.

Crable, R. E., & Vibbert, S. L. (1983). Mobil's epideictic advocacy: Observations of Prometheus-Bound. *Communication Monographs, 50,* 380–94.

Cragan, J. J., & Shields, D. C. (Eds.) (1981). *Applied communication research.* Prospect Heights, IL: Waveland.

Crane, P. (1959). What's in a party image? *Politics Quarterly,* 230–43.

The critical problem of nuclear power (1979, April 16). *Business Week,* 27–28.

Cronkite, G. (1984). Prception and meaning. In J. Bowers, & C. Arnold (Eds.), *Handbook of rhetorical and communication theory.* Boston: Allyn and Bacon.

Crotty, W. J., & Jacobson, G. C. (1980). *American parties in decline.* Boston: Little Brown.

Davidson, D. K. (1981). *Toward a theory of videostyle: Three hurdles to election.* Paper presented at the meeting of the Southwestern Social Science Association, Dallas TX.

Davidson, D. K. (1982). Candidate evaluation: Rational instrument or affective response? Doctoral dissertation completed at Florida State University.

Davidson, D. K., & Kaid, L. L. (1984). *Candidate and producer perspectives on videostyle: A multi-case study of U.S. Senate races.* Paper presented at the meeting of the American Political Science Association, Washington, DC.

Day, B. (1982). The politics of communications, or the communications of politics. In R. Worcester & D. Harrop (Eds.), *Political communications.* London: G. Allen and Unwin.

DeFleur, M. L., & Ball-Rokeach, S. J. (1975). *Theories of mass communication.* New York.

De Jouvenel, B. (1963). *The pure theory of politics.* New Haven: Yale University Press.

Delaney, T. (1982). Labour's advertising campaign. In R. Worcester & D. Harrop (Eds.), *Political communications.* London: G. Allen and Unwin.

Denton, R. E., Jr. (1982). *The symbolic dimensions of the American presidency.* Prospect Heights, IL: Waveland Press.

Devlin, L. P. (1973–74). Contrasts in Presidential campaign commercials of 1972. *Journal of Broadcasting, 18,* 17–26.

Devlin, L. P. (1977). Contrasts in Presidential campaign commercials of 1976. *Central States Speech Journal, 28,* 238–49.

Devlin, L. P. (1981). Reagan's and Carter's ad men review the 1980 television campaigns. *Communication Quarterly, 30,* 3–12.

Devlin, L. P. (1982). Contrasts in Presidential campaign commercials of 1980. *Political Communication Review, 7,* 1–38

DeVries, W., & Tarrance, V. L. (1972). *The ticket-splitter.* Grand Rapids, MI: William B. Eerdmans.

Diamond, E., & Bates, S. (1984). *The Spot.* Cambridge, MA: MIT Press.

Donohue, T. E. (1973–74). Impact of viewer predispositions on political TV commercials. *Journal of Broadcasting, 18,* 3–16.

Douglas, J. (1972, March). The verbal image: student perceptions of political figures. *Speech Monographs, 39,* No. 1, 10.

Dryer, E. C. (1971–72). Media use and electoral choices: Some political consequences of information exposure, *Public Opinion Quarterly, 35,* 544–53.

Duverger, M. (1954). *Political parties.* (Barbara North and Robert North, Trans.). London: Methuen.

Dybvig, H. E. (1970). An analysis of political communication through television produced by the Robert Goodman Agency, Inc. Unpublished Doctoral dissertation completed at Southern Illinois University.

Edelman, M. (1964). *The symbolic uses of politics.* Urbana IL: University of Illinois Press.

Ehrenhalt, A. (1983). *Politics in America.* Washington, DC: Congressional Quarterly Press.

Eisenhower, D. D. (1963). *Mandate for change.* Garden City: Doubleday.

Eisenstein, S. M. (1948). *The film sense.* London: Faber and Faber.

Ekman, G. (1962). Measurement of moral judgment: A comparison of scaling methods. *Perceptual and Motor Skills, 15,* 3–9.

Elliott, P. (1974). Uses and gratifications research: A critique and sociological alternative. In J. Blumler and E. Katz (Eds.), *The uses of mass communication.* Beverly Hills, CA: Sage.

Ellsworth, John W. (1965). Rationality and campaigning: A content analysis of the 1960 Presidential campaign debates. *Western Political Quarterly, 18,* 794–802.

Ellul, J. (1958). *Modern myths.* Diogenes, 23, 23–40.

Emerson, D. H. (1982). The decline of political parties, communications revolution in politics. *Proceedings of the Academy of Political Science, 34.*

Epstein, L. (1967). *Political parties in western democracies.* New York: Frederick Praeger Publishers.

Erikson, R. (1971). The advantage of incumbency in Congressional elections. *Polity,* 3, 395–405.

Erickson, R. (1976). Is there such a thing as a safe seat? *Polity,* 8, 623–32.

Evans, G., (Hon. Q. C.)(1984, June 14). Submission to the second report of the Joint Select Committee on Electoral Reform, Parliament of the Commonwealth of Australia.

Farrell, T. B., & Goodnight, G. T. (1981). Accidental rhetoric: The root metaphors of Three Mile Island. *Communication Monographs,* 48, 271–300.

Federal Communication Commission. (1969). Survey of political broadcasting primary and general election campaigns of 1968.

Fenno, R. F., Jr. (1978). *Homestyle: House members in their districts.* Boston: Little, Brown, and Co.

Field, J. O., & Anderson, R. E. (1969). Ideology in the public's conceptualization of the 1964 presidential election. *Public Opinion Quarterly,* 33, 380–98.

Fiske, J., & Hartley, J. (1978). *Reading television.* London: Methuen & Co.

Fiske, S. T., & Kinder, D. R. (1981). Involvement, expertise, and schema use: Evidence from political cognition. In N. Cantor & J. F. Kihlstrom (Eds.), *Personality, cognition, and social interaction.* Hillsdale, NJ: Lawrence Earlbaum Associates.

Flanigan, W. H. & Zingale, N. H. (1975). *Political behavior of the American electorate.* Boston: Allyn and Bacon.

Fleming, M. (1984, May 3). Minutes to Dr. R. Klugman, Joint Select Committee on Electoral Reform, Commonwealth of Australia.

Fleming, M. C. (1977). The picture in your mind. *Audio Visual Communication Review,* 25, 43–62.

Frank, R. S. (1973). *Message dimensions of television news.* Lexington, MA: D. C. Heath.

Frank, R. S. (1977). Nonverbal and paralinguistic analysis of political behavior: The first McGovern-Humphrey debate. In M. G. Hermann (Ed.), *A psychological examination of political leaders.* New York: Free Press.

Freeman, D. (1980). *A constructivist approach to political candidate perceptions.* Paper presented at the Epistemology and Methodology Division of the Eastern Communication Association.

Friedman, H. S., Mertz, T. I., & DiMatteo, M. R. (1980). Perceived bias in the facial expressions of television news broadcasters. *Journal of Communication, 30,* 103–11.

Gans, H. (1979). *Deciding what's news.* New York: Vintage Books.

Gantz, W. (1981). The influence of researcher methods on television and newspaper news credibility evaluations. *Journal of Broadcasting, 25,* 155–69.

Garramone, G. (1983). Issue versus image orientation and effects of political advertising. *Communication Research, 10,* 59–76.

Garramone, G. M. (1984). Audience motivation effects: More evidence. *Communication Research, 11,* 79–96.

Gartner, T. C. E. (1979, May 18). Official's view of U.S. nuclear option. *San Francisco Chronicle,* 32.

Geis, M. L. (1982). *The language of television advertising.* New York: Academic Press.

Gerster, P., & Cords, N. (1977). *Myth in American history.* New York: Glencoe.

Ginsberg, B. (1972). Critical elections and the substance of party conflict: 1844 to 1968. *Midwest Journal of Political Science, 16,* 603–25.

Goffman, E. (1959). *The presentation of self in everyday life.* New York: Doubleday.

Goffman, E. (1979). *Gender advertising.* New York: Harper & Row.

Goldenberg, E. N., & Traugott, M. W. (1979). *Resource allocations and broadcast expenditures in congressional campaigns.* Paper presented at the annual meeting of the American Political Science Association, Washington DC.

Goldenberg, E. N., & Traugott, M. W. (1980). *Campaign effects on outcomes in the 1978 congressional elections.* Paper presented at the National Science Foundation Conference on Congressional Elections, Houston, TX.

Goot, M. (1983). The media and the campaign. In H. Penniman (Ed.). *Australia at the polls, the national elections of 1980 and 1983.* Washington and Sydney: American Enterprise Institute and George Allen and Unwin.

Graber, D. A. (1976). *Verbal behavior and politics.* Chicago: University of Illinois Press.

Graber, D. A. (1981). Political languages. In D. Nimmo & K. R. Sanders (Eds.), *Handbook of political communication. Beverly Hills: Sage.*

Graber, D. (1984). *Processing the news: How people tame the information tide.* New York: Longman.

Graham, B., & Rowe, J. L. (1979, April 15). Problems plagued nuclear industry before Three Mile Island. *Washington Post,* A10.

Grattan, M. (1984, September 27). *The Age.*

Gregg, R. (1971). The ego function of the rhetoric of protest. *Philosophy and Rhetoric, 4,* 71–91.

Hall, S. (1982). The rediscovery of "ideology:" Return of the repressed in media studies. In M. Gurevitch, T. Bennett, & J. Woollacott (Eds.), *Culture, society and the media.* New York: Methuen.

Hamilton, C., & Ostendorf, L. (1963). *Lincoln in photographs: An album of every known pose.* Norman, OK: University of Oklahoma Press.

Harper's Weekly (1892, October 8), 971.

Harper's Weekly (1884, October 11), 669.

Harrell, J., & Linkugel, W. A. (1978). On rhetorical genre: An organizing perspective. *Philosophy and Rhetoric, 11,* 262–81.

Harrison, R. P. (1981). *The cartoon: Communication to the quick.* Beverly Hills: Sage.

Havilland, J. (1983). Conservative lead was never challenged. In the *Times* Staff (Eds.), *The Times guide to the House of Commons* Bury St. Edmunds, Suffolk England: St. Edmunds Press.

Heasman D. (1961–62). The prime minister and the cabinet. *Parliamentary Affairs, 15,* 461–84.

Heath, R. L. (1980). Corporate advocacy: An application of speech communication perspectives and skills–and more. *Communication Education, 29,* 370–77.

Hell no, we won't glow (1979, May 21). *Time,* 17–18.

Hertsgaard, M. (1980, March 8). There's life after T. M. I. *Nation,* 269–71.

Hibbing, J. R. & Brandes, S. L. (1983). State population and the electoral success of U.S. senators. *American Journal of Political Science, 27,* 808–19.

Hinkley, B. (1967). Interpreting house midterm elections. *American Political Science Review, 61,* 694–700.

Hinton, R. (1959–60). The prime minister as an elected monarch. *Parliamentary Affairs, 13,* 297–303.

Hofstetter, C. R. (1976). *Bias in the news.* Columbus: Ohio State University Press.

Hofstetter, C. R., & Buss, T. F. (1980). Politics and last-minute political television. *Western Political Quarterly, 33,* 24–37.

Hofstetter, C. R., & Judge, M. J. (1974). Content analysis of taped television stories: Coding manual. Ohio State University Polimetrics Laboratory Working Paper No. 2.

Hofstetter, C. R., & Zukin, C. (1979). TV network news and advertising in the Nixon and McGovern campaigns. *Journalism Quarterly, 56,* 106–15, 152.

Hofstetter, C. R., Zukin, C., & Buss, T. F. (1978). Political imagery and information in an age of television. *Journalism Quarterly, 55,* 562–69.

Hollander, M., & Wolfe, D. A. (1973). *Nonparametric statistical methods.* New York: John Wiley and Sons.

Holsti, O. R. (1969). *Content analysis for the social sciences and humanities.* Reading, MA: Addison Wesley Publishing.

Hone, P. (1969). *The diary of Philip Hone,* Allan Nevins (Ed.), New York: Kraus Reprint.

House of Commons Debates (1960). (Vol. 627, Col. 788). London: Her Majesty's stationary office.

Hughes, C. A. (1983). An election about perceptions. In H. Penniman (Ed.), *Australia at the polls, the national elections of 1980 and 1983.* Washington and Sydney: American Enterprise Institute and George Allen and Urwin.

Humke, R. G. (1975). Candidates, issues, and party in newspaper political advertisements. *Journalism Quarterly, 52,* 499–504.

Hunsaker, D. M. & Smith C. R. (1976). The nature of issues: A constructive approach to situational rhetoric. *Western Journal of Speech, 40,* 144–56.

Hyde, R. C. (1979). Three Mile Island: PR's Balaklava. *Public Relations Journal, 35,* 12–14.

The Illustrated London News. (1864, October 15).

In Re Commonwealth Electoral Act (1981). Evans v. Crichton-Brown. *Australian Law Review, 33,* 609.

Isenhour, J. P. (1975). The effects of context and order in film editing. *Audio Visual Communication Review, 23,* 69–80.

Iyengar, S., Peters, M. D., & Kinder, D. R. (1982). Experimental demonstrations of the "not so minimal" consequences of television news programs. *American Political Science Review, 76,* 848–58.

Jacobson, G. (1975). The impact of broadcast campaigning on electoral outcomes. *Journal of Politics, 37,* 769–95.

Jacobson, G. (1983). *The politics of congressional elections.* Boston: Little, Brown, and Company.

Jamieson, K. H. (1984). *Packaging the presidency: A history and criticism of presidential advertising.* New York: Oxford University Press.

Johnson, K. (1981). Political party and media evolutions in the United States and Great Britain: A comparative functional analysis. *Proceedings of the Fourth Annual Communications Research Symposium, 4.* University of Tennessee, Knoxville.

Johnson, K. (1979). *The daily telegraph as an image resource: A semantic content analysis.* Unpublished master's thesis, University of Tennessee, Knoxville.

Johnson, T. A. (1979, May 19). NAACP reaffirms its support of development of nuclear energy. *New York Times,* A8.

Jones, G. (1964–65). The prime minister's power. *Parliamentary Affairs, 18,* 167–85.

Joslyn, R. A. (1980). The content of political spot ads. *Journalism Quarterly, 57,* 92–98.

Joslyn, R. A. (1981). The impact of campaign spot advertising on voting defections. *Human Communication Research, 7,* 347–60.

Joslyn, R. A. (1984). *Mass media and elections.* Reading, MA: Addison-Wesley Publishing.

Kaid, L. L. (1975). *Political television commercials: An experimental study of type and length.* Paper presented at the International Communication Association Convention, Chicago, IL.

Kaid, L. L. (1976). Measures of political advertising. *Journal of Advertising Research, 16,* 49–53.

Kaid, L. L. (1981). Political advertising. In D. D. Nimmo & K. R. Sanders (Eds.), *Handbook of political communication.* Beverly Hills: Sage.

Kaid, L. L., & Sanders, K. R. (1978). Political television commercials: An experimental study of type and length. *Communication Research, 5,* 57–70.

Katz, E., Blumler, J. G., & Gurevitch, M. (1973). Uses and gratifications research. *Public Opinion Quarterly, 37,* 509–23.

Kavanagh, D. (1977). Party politics in question. In D. Kavanagh & Richard Rose (Eds.), *New Trends in British Politics.* London: Sage.

Keating J. P., & Latane, B. (1976). Politicians on TV: The image is the message. *Journal of Social Issue, 32,* 116–32.

Kelley, S., Jr. (1956). *Professional public relations and political power.* Baltimore: John Hopkins Press.

Kelley, S., Jr. (1960). *Political campaigning: Problems in creating an informed electorate.* Washington DC: The Brookings Institute.

Kellner, P. (1983, August 26) The last television election? *New Statesman,* 7–8.

Key, V. O., Jr. (1942). *Politics, parties, and pressure groups.* New York: Thomas Crowell.

Key, V. O., Jr. (1966). *The responsible electorate.* New York: Vintage Books.

Kinder, D. R. (1978). Political person perception: The asymmetrical influence of sentiment and choice on perceptions of presidential candidates. *Journal of Personality and Social Psychology, 36,* 859–71.

Kinder, D. R., Peters, M. D., Abelson, R. P., & Fiske, S. T. (1980). Presidential prototypes. *Political Behavior, 2,* 315–37.

Kingsley, D. (1983, July/August). Photography and the election. *Creative Camera,* 1056–59.

Kjeldahl, B., Carmichael, C., & Mertz, R. (1971). Factors in a presidential candidate image. *Speech Monographs, 38,* 129–33.

Kostroski, W. (1978). The effect of number of terms on the re-election of senators 1920–1970. *Journal of Politics, 40,* 488–97.

Kraus, S. (Ed.). (1962). *The great debates.* Indiana: Indiana University Press.

Kraus, S. (Ed.). (1968). *The great debates. Glouchester, MA: Peter Smith.*

Kraus, S. (Ed.). (1979). *The great debates,* Ford-Carter, 1976. Bloomington: Indiana University Press.

Kraus, S., & Davis, D. (1976). *The effects of mass communication on political behavior.* University Park, PA: Pennsylvania State University Press.

Krippendorff, K. (1980). *Content analysis: An introduction to its methodology.* Beverly Hills: Sage.

Krugman, M., & Hartley, E. L. (1970). Passive learning from television. *Public Opinion Quarterly, 34,* 184–94.

Lang, K., & Lang, G. (1968). *Politics and television.* Chicago: Quadrangle Books.

Lanouette, W. J. (1980, January). The Kemeny Commission report. *Bulletin of the Atomic Scientists,* 20–31.

Larkin, E. F. (1979). Consumer perceptions of the media and their advertising content. *Journal of Advertising, 8,* 5–7.

Lau, R. R. (1984). *Political schemas, candidate evaluations, and voting behavior.* Paper presented to the 19th Annual Carnegie Symposium on Cognition, Carnegie-Mellon University, Pittsburgh.

Lazarsfeld, P., Berelson, B., & Gaudet, H. (1944). *The people's choice.* New York: Columbia University Press.

Lee, J. M. (1917, 1923). *History of American journalism.* Boston and New York: Houghton Mifflin.

Lee, R. S. H. (1978). Credibility of newspaper and TV news. *Journalism Quarterly, 55,* 282–*

Leslie's Weekly (1904, October 23), 342.

Levy, M. R., & Windahl, S. (1984). Audience activity and gratifications: A conceptual clarification and exploration. *Communication Research, 11,* 51–78.

Leymour, V. L. (1975). *Hidden myth: Structure and symbolism in advertising.* New York: Basic Books.

Lin, N. (1977). Communications effects: Review and commentary. In B. Rubin, (Ed.), *Communication Yearbook I,* New Brunswick, NJ: Transaction Books.

Lindell, G. J. (1983, July 1). Submission to the first report of the Joint Select Committee on Electoral Reform, Parliament of the Commonwealth of Australia.

Lodge, M. (1981). *Magnitude scaling.* Beverly Hills: Sage.

Lodge, M., Cross, D., Tursky, B., Tanenhaus, J., & Reeder, R. (1976). The psychophysical scaling of political support in the "real world." *Political Methodology, 2,* 159–82.

Lodge, M., & Tursky, B. (1979). Comparisons between category and magnitude scaling of political opinion employing SRC/CPS items. *American Political Science Review, 73,* 50–66.

Lord, F. M. (1967). A paradox in the interpretation of group comparisons. *Psychological Bulletin, 68,* 304–5.

Lord, F. M. (1969). Statistical adjustments when comparing preexisting groups. *Psychological Bulletin, 72,* 336–37.

Lukes, S. (1981). *Power: A radical view.* London: MacMillan Press.

McBath, J. H., & Fisher, W. R. (1969). Persuasion in presidential campaign communication. *Quarterly Journal of Speech, 55,* 17–25.

McCain, T. A., Chilberg, J., & Wakshlag, J. (1977). The effect of camera angle on source credibility and attraction. *Journal of Broadcasting, 21,* 35–46.

McClure, R. D., & Patterson, T. E. (1974). Television news and political advertising: The impact on voter beliefs. *Communication Research, 1, 3–31.*

McClure, R. D., & Patterson, T. E. (1976). Print versus network news. *Journal of Communication, 26,* 23–28.

McCombs, M. E., & Shaw D. L. (1972). The agenda-setting function of the mass media. *Public Opinion Quarterly, 36,* 176–87.

McCombs, M. E. & Shaw D. L. (1977). The agenda-setting function of the press. In M. McCombs & D. Shaw (Eds.), *The emergence of American political issues.* St. Paul: West Publishing.

McCroskey, J. (1966). Scales for the measurement of ethos. *Speech Monographs. 33,* 65–72.

McGinniss, J. (1969). *The selling of the President 1968.* New York: Trident Press.

McGrath, J. E. & McGrath, M. F. (1962). Effects of partisanship on perception of political figures. *Public Opinion Quarterly, 26,* 235–48.

McGrory, M. (1979, April 14). A curious mandate. *San Francisco Chronicle,* 32.

McKie, D. (1983, June 3). Charting a dealignment decade. *The Guardian.*

Macklin, M. (1984). Dissenting Report. In Second report of the Joint Select Committee on Electoral Reform, Parliament of the Commonwealth of Australia.

McLeod, J. M., & Becker, L. B. (1981). The uses and gratifications approach. In D. D. Nimmo & K. R. Sanders (Eds.), *Handbook of political communication.* Beverly Hills, CA: Sage.

McLeod, J. M., & Becker, L. B. (1974). Testing the validity of gratification measures through political effects analysis. In J. G. Blumler & E. Katz (Eds.), *The uses of mass communication: Current perspectives on gratification research.* Beverly Hills: Sage.

McLeod, J. M., Becker, L. B., & Byrnes, J. E. (1974). Another look at the agenda-setting function of the press. *Communication Research, 1,* 131–66.

McLeod, J. M., Glynn, C. J., & McDonald, D. G. (1983). Issues and images: The influence of media reliance on voting decisions. *Communication Research, 10,* 37–59.

McLeod, J. M., & Reeves, B. (1980). On the nature of mass media effects. In S. B. Withey & R. P. Abeles (Eds.), *Television and social behavior: Beyond violence and children.* Hillsdale, NJ: Erlbaum.

MacNeil, R. (1968). *The people machine: The influence of television on American politics.* New York: Harper and Row.

McQuail, D., Blumler, J., & Brown, J. (1972). The television audience: A revised perspective. In D. McQuail (Ed.), *Sociology of mass communication.* Harmondsworth, England: Penguin.

McQuitty, L. L. (1957). Elementary linkage analysis for isolating orthogonal and oblique types and typal relevancies. *Educational and Psychological Measurement, 17.*

Mandall, L. M., & Shaw, D. (1973). Judging people in the news—unconsciously: Effect of camera angle and bodily activity. *Journal of Broadcasting, 17,* 553–62.

Markus, G. B. (1982). Political attitudes during an election year: A report on the 1980 NES panel study. *American Political Science Review, 76,* 538–60.

Mayer, H. (1984). Testimony before the Joint Select Committee on Electoral Reform, Parliament of the Commonwealth of Australia.

Mayhew, D. R. (1974). Congressional elections: The case of the vanishing marginals. *Polity, 6,* 295–317.

Meadow, R. G., & Sigelman, L. (1982). Some effects and noneffects of campaign commercials. *Political Behavior, 4,* 163–75.

Mendelsohn, H., & O'Keefe, G. J. (1976). *The people choose a president: Influences on voter decision making.* New York: Praeger.

Meyer, T. P., & Donohue, T. P. (1973). Perceptions and misperceptions of political advertising. *Journal of Business Communication, 10,* 29–40.

Michels, R. (1915). *Political parties: A sociological study of the oligarchical tendencies of modern democracy.* New York: Hearst's International Library.

Miller, M. (1973). *Plain speaking: An oral biography of Harry S. Truman.* New York: Berkley Publishing.

Miller, W. E., & Levitin, E. E. (1976). *Leadership and change: Presidential elections from 1952 to 1976.* Cambridge, MA: Winthrop Publishers.

Miller, A. H., & Mackuen, M. (1979). Learning about the candidates: The 1976 presidential debates. *Public Opinion Quarterly, 43,* 326–46.

Miller, A. H., Miller, W. E., Raine, A. S., & Brown, T. A. (1976, September). A majority party in disarray: Policy polarization in the 1972 election. *American Political Science Review, 70,* 753–78.

Minow, N. N., Burch, D., Corcoran, T. G., Heard, A., & Price, R. (1969). *Voter's time: Report of the Twentieth Century Fund Commission on Campaign Cost in the Electronic Era.* New York: Twentieth Century Fund.

Mitchell, R. C. (1980). Nuclear power and public opinion: Before and after Three Mile Island. *Current,* 34–37.

Moskowitz, H. R., & Chandler, J. (1979). Magnitude estimation scaling for child respondents: A psychological approach. *Viewpoints, 19,* 29–35.

Mott, F. L. (1962). *American journalism.* New York: MacMillan.

Mulder, R. (1979). The effects of televised political ads in the 1975 Chicago mayoral election. *Journalism Quarterly, 56,* 335–41.

Nadeau, R. (1958). Hermogenes on "stock issues" in deliberative speaking. *Speech Monographs, 25,* 59–66.

Nadel, M. V. (1976). *Corporations and political accountability.* Lexington, MA: D. C. Heath.

Napolitan, J. (1972). *The election game and how to win it.* New York: Doubleday.

Napolitan, J. (1976). Media costs and effects in political campaigns. *Annals of AAPSS, 427,* 114–24.

Newman, R. P. (1961). Analysis and issues: A study of doctrine. *Speech Monographs, 25,* 43–54.

New York Times (1980, February 24) 4, 2.

Nie, N. H., Verba, S., & Petrocik., J. R. (1976). *The changing American voter.* Cambridge, MA: Harvard University Press.

Nigro, F. A., & Nigro, L. G. (1977). *Modern public administration.* New York: Harper and Row.

Nimmo, D. (1970). *The political persuaders: The techniques of modern election campaigns.* Englewood Cliffs, NJ: Prentice-Hall.

Nimmo, D. (1974). *Popular images of politics.* Englewood Cliffs, NJ: Prentice-Hall.

Nimmo, D. (1976). Political image makers and the mass media. *Annals of the AAPSS, 427,* 33–44.

Nimmo, D. (1978). *Political communication and public opinion in America.* Santa Monica, CA: Goodyear Publishing.

Nimmo, D., & Combs, J. (1976). *Mediated political realities.* New York: Longman.

Nimmo, D., Mansfield, M., & Curry, J. (1978). Persistence in change and candidate images. In C. F. Bishop, R. G. Meadow, & M. Jackson-Beeck, (Eds.), *The presidential debates.* NY: Praeger.

Nimmo, D., & Savage, R. (1976). *Candidates and their images.* Santa Monica, CA: Goodyear Publishing.

Nuclear energy: Survival at stake. (1980, January). *Nation's Business,* 52–62.

Nuclear industry versus Amory Lovins. (1980, August 1). *Science,* 573.

The nuclear nightmare. (1979, April 19). *Time.* 8–19.

Nuclear power in 1980 (1980, January). *Bulletin of the Atomic Scientists,* 17–20.

Ogden, D. M. Jr., & Peterson, A. L. (1968). *Electing the President.* San Francisco: Chandler Publishing.

O'Keefe, M. T., & Sheinkopf, K. G. (1974). The voter decides: candidate image or campaign issue? *Journal of Broadcasting, 18,* 403–12.

O'Reilly, R. (1980). Summary—commercial allocation Campaign 80. Unpublished document provided by Managing Director of Campaign 80.

Orne, T. (1962). On the social psychology of the psychology experiment. *American Psychologist, 17,* 776–83.

Osgood, C. E., Suci, G. J., & Tannenbaum, P. H. (1971). *The measurement of meaning.* Urbana, IL: University of Illinois Press.

Ostendorf, L., & Holzer, H. (1976, Summer). The John Henry Brown miniature of Lincoln: A critical re-assessment. *Lincoln Herald.*

Ostrogorski. (1902). *Democracy and the organizations of political parties.* (Frederick Clarke, Trans.). London: Macmillan.

Owens, J., & Olson, E. (1980). Economic fluctuations and congressional elections. *American Journal of Political Science, 24,* 469–93.

Page, B. I. (1978). *Choices and echoes in presidential elections.* Chicago: University of Chicago Press.

Palda, K. S. (1973). Does advertising influence votes? An analysis of the 1966 and 1970 Quebec elections. *Canadian Journal of Political Science*, 6, 638–55.

Palmgreen, P., Wenner, L. A., & Rayburn, J. D. (1980). Relations between gratifications sought and obtained: A study of television news. *Communication Research*, 7, 161–92.

Parker, G. R. (1980). The advantages of incumbency in House elections. *American Politics Quarterly*, 8, 449–64.

Parker, G. R. (1981). Interpreting candidate awareness in U.S. congressional elections. *Legislative Studies Quarterly*, 6, 219–34.

Patterson, T. E. (1980). *The mass media election.* New York: Praeger.

Patterson, T. E. (1982). Television and election strategy. *Communications revolution in politics, proceedings of the Academy of Political Science*, 34.

Patterson, T. E. (1983). Money rather than TV ads judged "root cause" of election costliness. *Television/Radio Age*, 44, 130–32.

Patterson, T. E., & McClure, R. D. (1973). Political spot advertising on television: Spot commercials in the 1972 presidential election. *Maxwell Review*, 99, 57–69.

Patterson, T. E., & McClure, R. D. (1974). Political advertising: Voter reaction to televised political commercials. *Monograph of Citizen's Research Foundation.*

Patterson, T. E., & McClure, R. D. (1976). *The unseeing eye.* New York: Putnam.

Perry, J. (1983, May 25). Admen take over Britain's elections; U.S. gets the blame. *The Wall Street Journal*, 1.

Philport, J. C., & Balon, R. E. (1975). Candidate image in a broadcast debate. *Journal of Broadcasting*, 19, 184.

Pierce, J. C. (1970). Party indentification and the changing role of ideology in American politics. *Midwest Journal of Political Science*, 14, 25–42.

Pomper, G. M. (1975). *Voter's choice.* New York: Dodd, Mead.

Pomper, G. M. (1977). The decline of the party in American elections. *Political Science Quarterly*, 92, 21–41.

Pool, I. de S. (1965). *Candidates, issues and strategies.* Cambridge, MA: MIT Press.

Primeau, R. (1979). *The rhetoric of television.* New York: Longman.

Propaganda. (1979, August 17). *New York Times*, A24.

Pullan, R. (1984). *Guilty secrets—free speech in Australia.* Methuen, Australia.

Punnett, R. (1971). *British government and politics.* (2nd. ed.). New York: W. W. Norton.

Ramsay, A. (1984, December). *The National Times,* 12–18.

Rank, H. (1984). *The pep talk.* Park Forest, IL: The Counter-Propaganda Press.

Ranney, A. (1975). Selecting the candidate. In H. Penniman (Ed.), *Britain at the polls.* Washington, DC: American Enterprise Institute for Public Policy Research

Rawlinson, M. (1983). The Liberal Party. In H. Penniman (Ed.), *Australia at the Poll, the national elections of 1980 and 1983.* Washington and Sydney: American Enterprise Institute and George Allen and Unwin

Ray, R. (1984, October 16). *Senate Hansard,* 174.

Risks and rewards propel candidates toward Tuesday (1980, April 7). *New York Times, 4.*

Roberts, C. (1973). Voting intentions and attitude change in a congressional election. *Speech Monographs, 40,* 49–55.

Robinson, J. P. (1974). The press as king-maker: What surveys from the last five campaigns show. *Journalism Quarterly, 51,* 587–606.

Robinson, M. (1976). Public affairs television and the growth of political malaise: The case of "The Selling of the Pentagon." *American Political Science Review, 70,* 409–32.

Roper. (1969).

Roper Organization. (1983). *Trends in attitudes toward television and other media: A twenty-four year review.* New York: Television Information Office.

Rose, E. D., & Fuchs, D. (1968). Reagan vs. Brown: A TV image playback. *Journal of Broadcasting, 12,* 247–60.

Rose, R. (1965). Pre-election public relations and advertising (appendix 4). In D. Butler & A. King (Eds.), *The British general election of 1964* London: MacMillan.

Rose, R. (1983, May 26). 1983: Farewell to cloth cap politics. *The Telegraph.*

Rosenfeld, L., & Civikly, J. M. (1976). *With words unspoken.* New York: Holt, Rinehart, and Winston.

Rossiter, J. R., & Percy, L. (1980). Attitude change through visual imagery in advertising. *Journal of Advertising, 9,* 10–16.

Rothschild, M. L., & Ray, M. L. (1974). Involvement and political advertising effect: An exploratory experiment. *Communication Research,* 264–85.

Rubin, B. (1967). *Political television.* Belmont, CA: Wadsworth Publishing Co.

Rumelhart, D. E., & Ortony, A. (1977) The representation of knowledge in memory. In R. C. Anderson, R. J. Spiro, & W. E. Montague (Eds.), *Schooling and the acquisition of knowledge.* Hillsdale, NJ: Lawrence Earlbaum Associates.

Rutland, R. A. (1973). *The newsmongers: Journalism in the life of the nation 1690-1972.* New York: Dial Press.

Sabato, L. (1981). *The rise of political consultants.* New York: Basic Books.

Sadowski, R. P. (1972). Immediate recall of TV commercial elements revisited. *Journal of Broadcasting, 16,* 277–87.

Saint George, A., & Robinson-Weber, S. (1983). The mass media, political attitudes, and behavior. *Communication Research, 10,* 487–508.

Sandman, P. M., & Paden M. (1979, July/August). At Three Mile Island. *Columbia Journalism Review,* 43–50, 52, 54–58.

Saussure, F. (1966). *Course in general linguistics.* New York: McGraw-Hill.

Schank, R., & Abelson, R. P. (1977). *Scripts, plans, goals, and understanding: An inquiry into human knowledge structures.* Hillsdale, NJ: Lawrence Erlbaum Associates.

Schuyten, P. J. (1979, April 9). Scientists and society's fears. *New York Times,* A1, D9.

Schwartz, T. (1973). *The responsive chord.* Garden City, NY: Anchor Press/ Doubleday.

Seymour-Ure, C. (1974). *The political impact of the mass media.* Beverly Hills: Sage.

Seymour-Ure, C. (1977). Political communication and the mass media. In D. Kavanagh & R. Rose (Eds.), *New trends in British politics.* London: Sage.

Shabad, G., & Anderson, K. (1979). Candidate evaluations by men and women. *Public Opinion Quarterly, 18,* 35.

Shabercoff, P. (1979, May 7). Most unions' leaders still favor building atom plants to get jobs. *New York Times,* B13.

Shama, A. (1974). Political marketing: A study of the voter decision-making process and candidate marketing strategy. *American Marketing Association Combined Proceedings,* 381–85.

Shannon, J. *Money and politics.* New York: Random House.

Sharps, W. S. (1959). *Dictionary of cinematography.* London: Fountain Press.

Sheinkopf, K. G. (1972). The functions of political advertising for campaign organizations. *Journal of Marketing Research, 9,* 401–5.

Shinn, A., Jr. (1969). An application of psychophysical scaling techniques to the measurement of national power. *Journal of Politics, 31,* 932b2*51.

Shneidman, E. (1963). The language of politics. In L. Arons & M. A. May, (Eds.), *Television and human behavior.* New York: Appleton Century Crofts.

Shyles, L. (1983a). *Defining the "images" of presidential candidates from televised political spot advertisements.* Paper presented at the International Communication Association Convention, Dallas.

Shyles, L. (1983b). Defining the issues of a presidential election from televised political spot advertisements. *Journal of Broadcasting, 27,* 333–43.

Shyles, L. (1984a). Defining the "images" of presidential candidates from televised political spot advertisements. *Political Behavior, 6.*

Shyles, L. (1984b). The relationships of images, issues, and presentational methods in televised political spot advertisements for 1980's American presidential primaries. *Journal of Broadcasting, 28.*

Silber, I. (1971). *Songs America voted by.* Harrisburg, PA: Stackpole Books.

Simper, E. (1984, November 9). *The Australian.*

Smith, A. (1976). A maturing teleocracy: Observations on the television coverage of the British general elections of 1974. In L. Maisel (Ed.), *Changing campaign techniques: Elections and values in contemporary democracies. Sage electoral yearbook, Vol. 2.* London: Sage.

Smith, A. (1979). Britain: The mysteries of modus vivendi. In A. Smith (Ed.), *Television and political life: Studies in six European countries.* New York: St. Martins Press.

Smith v. Oldham (1912). 15 *Commonwealth Law Reports,* 361. Quoted in the second report of the Joint Select Committee on Electoral Reform, Parliament of the Commonwealth of Australia, 1984.

Sontag, S. (1977). *On photography.* New York: Delta.

Staff. (1983, May 23). 16,000 Tory pitch for black vote. *The Daily Telegraph.*

Starr, R. (1980, October). The Three Mile shadow, *Commentary,* 48–55.

Stephenson, W. (1953). The study of behavior: Q-Technique and its methodology. Chicago: University of Chicago.

Sterling, C. H., & Haight, R. R. (1978). *The mass media: Aspen Institute guide to communication industry trends.* New York: Praeger.

Stevens, S. S. (1975). *Psychophysics: Introduction to its perceptual, neural, and social prospects. New York: John Wiley.*

Stimson, J. A. (1975). Belief systems: Constraint, complexity, and the 1972 election. *American Journal of Political Science, 19,* 393–417.

Strouse, J. C. (1975). *The mass media, public opinion, and public policy analysis.* Columbus, OH: Charles E. Merrill Publishing, Co.

Surlin, S. H., & Gordon, T. F. (1976). Selective exposure and retention of political advertising. *Journal of Advertising Research, 5,* 32–44.

Surlin, S. H., & Gordon, T. F. (1977). How values affect attitudes toward direct reference political advertising. *Journalism Quarterly, 54,* 89–98.

Swanson, D. L. (1973). Political information, influence, and judgment in the 1972 presidential campaign. *Quarterly Journal of Speech, 59,* 130–42.

Taylor, M. (1979, June 7). Nuclear industry's plan to woo the public. *San Francisco Chronicle,* 1, 20.

Taylor, P., & Fedler, F. (1978a). Broadcasting's impact on selection of news stories by readers. *Journalism Quarterly, 55,* 301–5.

Taylor, P., & Fedler, F. (1978b). Broadcasting's impact on selection of newstising, *5,* 32–37.

Taylor, S. E., & Fiske, S. T. (1978). Salience, attention, and attribution: Top of the head phenomena. In L. Berkowitz, (Ed.), *Advances in experimental social psychology.* New York: Academic Press.

Teeter, R. (1979). *1978 congressional post-election survey.* Washington DC: National Republican Congressional Committee.

Television: Medium of choice and necessity. (1977, January 3). *Broadcasting,* 74.

Television advertising plays big role in most campaigns. (1980, January 20). *Chicago Tribune.*

Thimmesch, N. (1979, October 22). Nuclear industry starts shoving back at ax-grinders. *Chicago Tribune,* 2.

Thompson, W. N. (1972). Stasis in Aristotle's rhetoric. *Quarterly Journal of Speech, 58,* 134–41.

Tiemens, R. K. (1978). Television's portrayal of the 1976 Presidential debates: An analysis of visual content. *Communication Monographs, 45,* 362–70.

Time Magazine. (1979, April 23), p. 42.

Traugott, S. (1984). *Personal communication.*

Tryon, W. W. (1977). Psychophysical scaling and hierarchy construction. *Journal of Behavior Therapy, 8,* 53–56.

Tufte, E. R. (1975). Determinants of the outcomes of midterm congressional elections. *American Political Science Review, 69,* 812–26.

Utility execs to hit the road (1979, September 27). *Lafayette Journal and Courier,* A2.

Vogler, D. J. (1983). *The Politics of Congress.* 4th ed. Boston: Allyn and Bacon.

Wamsley, G., & Pride, R. (1972). Television network news: Re-thinking the iceberg problem. *The Western Political Quarterly, 25,* 434–50.

Wanat, J. (1974). Political broadcast advertising and primary election voting. *Journal of Broadcasting, 18,* 413–22.

Warr, P. B., & Knapper, C. (1968). *The perception of people and events.* London: John Wiley.

Warshaw, P. R. (1978). Application of selective attention theory to television advertising displays. *Journal of Applied Psychology, 63,* 366–72.

Washburn, W. (1972, October). Campaign banners. *American Heritage.*

Wattenberg, M. P. (1981). The decline of political partisanship in the United States: Negativity or neutrality. *American Political Science Review, 75,* 941–50.

Wattenberg, M. P. (1982). From parties to candidates: Examining the role of the media. *Public Opinion Quarterly, 46,* 216–27.

Wegener, B. (Ed.). (1982). *Social attitudes and psychophysical measurement.* Hillsdale, NJ: Lawrence Erlbaum Associates.

Wenner, L. A. (1982). Gratifications sought and obtained in program dependency: A study of network evening news programs and *60 Minutes. Communication Research, 9,* 539–60.

Westlye, M. C. (1983). Competitiveness of senate seats and voting behavior in senate elections. *American Journal of Political Science, 27,* 253–83.

Wheatley, J. J. (1968). Influence of commercial's length and position, *Journal of Marketing Research, 5,* 199–202.

White, G. A. (1978). *A study of access to television for political candidates.* Cambridge, MA: Institute of Politics, J.F.K. School of Government.

Wicker, T. (1979, April 24). Nuclear counterattack. *New York Times,* A19.

Wilson, C. E. (1978). Public perceptions of media accuracy. *Journalism Quarterly, 55, ro*73–76.*

Wilson, H. (1966). *Our penny farthing machine.* (Labour pamphlet; available from the Labour party, c/o Tim Delaney, 150 Walworth Rd. London SE17).

Woll, P. (1974). *Public policy.* Cambridge, MA: Winthrop Publishers.

Wood, S. C. (1982, November). *Eisenhower answers America: A critical history.* Paper delivered at the Convention of the Speech Communication Association, Louisville, KY.

Worcester, R. (1983). *MORI: British public opinion, general election 1983.* London: Market Opinion Research International.

Worth, S. (1981). *Studying visual communication.* Philadelphia: University of Philadelphia Press.

Wurtzel, A. (1983). *Television production.* New York: McGraw-Hill.

Wyckoff, G. (1968). *The image candidates.* New York: Macmillan.

Wyer, R. S., & Carlston, D. (1979). *Social cognition, inference, and attribution.* Hillsdale, NJ: Erlbaum.

Wyer, R. S., Srull, T. K., Gordon, S. E., & Hartwick J. (1982). Effects of processing objectives on the recall of prose material. *Journal of Personal and Social Psychology, 43,* 674–78.

Wyler, A., Masuca, M., & Holmes, T. (1971). Magnitude of life events and seriousness of illness. *Psychosomatic Medicine,* 115–22.

Young, H. (1983, May 11). A presidential landslide. *The Sunday Times.*

Zajonc, R. B. (1960). The process of cognitive tuning in communication. *Journal of Abnormal and Social Psychology, 61,* 159–67.

Zajonc, R. B. (1968). Attitudinal effects of mere exposure. *Journal of Personality and Social Psychology Monograph Supplement,* 9, 1–27.